A
MODEL IMPLEMENTATION
OF
STANDARD PASCAL

Prentice-Hall International
Series in Computer Science

C. A. R. Hoare, Series Editor

BACKHOUSE, R. C., *Program Construction and Verification*
BACKHOUSE, R. C., *Syntax of Programming Languages, Theory and Practice*
de BAKKER, J. W., *Mathematical Theory of Program Correctness*
BJORNER, D., and JONES, C.B., *Formal Specification and Software Development*
CLARK, K. L., and McCABE, F. G., *micro-PROLOG: Programming in Logic*
DROMEY, R. G., *How to Solve it by Computer*
DUNCAN, F., *Microprocessor Programming and Software Development*
ELDER, J., *Construction of Data Processing Software*
GOLDSCHLAGER, L., and LISTER, A., *Computer Science: A Modern Introduction*
HEHNER, E. C. R., *The Logic of Programming*
HENDERSON, P., *Functional Programming: Application and Implementation*
HOARE, C. A. R., *Communicating Sequential Processes*
HOARE, C. A. R., and SHEPHERDSON, J. C., (Eds.) *Mathematical Logic and Programming Languages*
INMOS LTD., *Occam Programming Manual*
JACKSON, M. A., *System Development*
JOHNSTON, H., *Learning to Program*
JONES, C. B., *Systematic Software Development Using VDM*
JOSEPH, M., PRASAD, V. R., and NATARAJAN, N., *A Multiprocessor Operating System*
LEW, A., *Computer Science: A Mathematical Introduction*
MacCALLUM, I., *Pascal for the Apple*
MacCALLUM, I., *UCSD Pascal for the IBM PC*
MARTIN, J. J., *Data Types and Data Structures*
POMBERGER, G., *Software Engineering and Modula-2*
REYNOLDS, J. C., *The Craft of Programming*
TENNENT, R. D., *Principles of Programming Languages*
WELSH, J., and ELDER, J., *Introduction to Pascal, 2nd Edition*
WELSH, J., ELDER, J., and BUSTARD, D., *Sequential Program Structures*
WELSH, J., and HAY, A., *A Model Implementation of Standard Pascal*
WELSH, J., and McKEAG, M., *Structured System Programming*

A
MODEL IMPLEMENTATION
OF
STANDARD PASCAL

Jim Welsh
University of Queensland, Australia

Atholl Hay
Edinburgh Regional Computer Centre, University of Edinburgh, Scotland

Prentice/Hall PHI International

ENGLEWOOD CLIFFS, NEW JERSEY   LONDON   MEXICO   NEW DELHI
RIO DE JANEIRO   SINGAPORE   SYDNEY   TOKYO   TORONTO   WELLINGTON

Library of Congress Cataloging-in-Publication Data

Welsh, Jim, 1943–
  A model implementation of standard Pascal.

  Bibliography: p.
  Includes index.
1. PASCAL (Computer program language)
I. Hay, Atholl.   II. Title.
QA76.73.P2W45   1986   005.13'3   85-28086

ISBN 0-13-586454-2

British Library Cataloguing in Publication Data

Welsh, Jim
  A model implementation of standard Pascal. —
  (Prentice-Hall International series in computing science)
  1. PASCAL (Computer program language)
  I. Title   II. Hay, Atholl
  005.13'3   QA76.73.P2

  ISBN 0-13-586454-2

© **1986 Prentice-Hall International (UK) Ltd**

PRENTICE-HALL INC., *Englewood Cliffs, New Jersey*
PRENTICE-HALL INTERNATIONAL (UK) LTD. *London*
PRENTICE-HALL OF AUSTRALIA PTY LTD, *Sydney*
PRENTICE-HALL CANADA INC., *Toronto*
PRENTICE-HALL HISPANOAMERICANA S.A., *Mexico*
PRENTICE-HALL OF INDIA PRIVATE LTD, *New Delhi*
PRENTICE-HALL OF JAPAN INC., *Tokyo*
PRENTICE-HALL OF SOUTHEAST ASIA PTE LTD, *Singapore*
EDITORA PRENTICE-HALL DO BRASIL LTDA, *Rio de Janeiro*
WHITEHALL BOOKS LTD, *Wellington, New Zealand*

Printed and bound in Great Britain for
Prentice-Hall International (UK) Ltd,
66 Wood Lane End, Hemel Hempstead, Hertfordshire, HP2 4RG
at the University Press, Cambridge.

1 2 3 4 5   90 89 88 87 86

ISBN 0-13-586454-2

CONTENTS

Part 2:   The P-Machine

Part 3:   The Postmortem Generator

FOREWORD

The major challenge which faces modern Computer Science is to match in computer software the amazing improvements in economy, quality and reliability which have been achieved by the designers of computer hardware. This will require improved standards of specification, improved efficiency and reliability in meeting those specifications, and improved methods of competitive marketing and distribution of software products. The major objective of the Prentice-Hall International Series in Computer Science is to contribute towards these improvements. Publication of this book will contribute in three ways:

Firstly it places in the public domain a complete implementation of the International Standard for the PASCAL programming language. The implementation itself also conforms precisely to the standard except at a few well-documented points where type recasting is needed for code generation purposes. It will thereby assist in rapid and widespread propagation of the standard, for the benefit of all who write programs in PASCAL.

Secondly, it is an example of a large program designed, documented, and laid out to be read as literature. The authors have exposed every detail of design and coding to the scrutiny of their professional colleagues. A study of this work, and a determination to achieve similar publication quality in programming, will lead to a general raising of professional standards.

Finally the open publication of computer programs is a very effective way of distributing a source license, unbundled from an object license, and at a price considerably lower than is currently charged. Licenses for machine-readable copies and for commercial exploitation must be negotiated separately.

This book makes no claim to perfection, and its readers are invited to make their own contribution to its aims. Reports of defects and suggestions for improvements should be sent to the authors and to:

The Editor,
Software Practice and Experience,
John Wiley and Sons Ltd.,
Boffins Lane,
Chichester,
West Sussex PO19 1UD,
U.K.

It is hoped that corrections and other relevant correspondence will be published rapidly in that medium, which should be consulted by intending implementors.

C. A. R. Hoare

Executable Standard Pascal
Model Implementation software
is available from the
British Standards Institute,
Maylands Avenue, Hemel Hempstead,
Hertfordshire HP2 4SQ, England.

(Telephone: 0442 3111)

PREFACE

This text presents a model implementation of the programming language Pascal, which conforms to the standard definition of the language. The implementation is itself written entirely in Pascal. As such, it may be of interest to implementors of Pascal or Pascal-like languages, to students of language implementation, and to those interested in Pascal as a language for medium-scale software development.

The language Pascal has been a major influence in the teaching and application of computer programming. The reason for this influence is that Pascal embodies a well-chosen range of program and data structuring concepts in a clear and simple notation. This combination of power and simplicity was unmatched by any alternative language at the time of Pascal's definition, and has remained so for most of the fifteen years since. While Pascal lacks one or two concepts now recognised as important to good program design, it remains the primary vehicle for teaching computer programming in most universities, the most practical language available for many programming applications, and the yardstick by which new language designs are judged.

A secondary but important factor in the initial success of Pascal was the ease with which compilers for the language were produced for many computers. This ease of implementation stemmed from the facts that Pascal was powerful enough to express its own compilers, that Pascal compilers were written in Pascal from the outset, and that successive compilers were derived from their predecessors by appropriate bootstrapping techniques. In this way a family of Pascal compilers for many different computers developed from the initial compiler produced at ETH Zurich, with corresponding benefits in their speed of implementation, cost of implementation, and reliability. To a significant degree, this proliferation of self-implementing compilers was as significant a milestone in compiler technology, as Pascal itself was in language design.

These merits of Pascal and its implementations have been widely recognised for some time, but renewed interest in the language and its implementation has been generated by the establishment, by the British Standards Institution (BSI) and the International Standards Organisation (ISO), of an international standard definition of Pascal. The strategy taken in this standardisation process was a very conservative one. Only two language features were added to the original language design, and in all other respects the standard sought to define precisely the established features of the language, eliminating minor ambiguities and omissions in its original definition. In this respect the standard took one major step, in that it defined for the first time the complete range of dynamic semantic errors that may occur during execution of Pascal programs. While detection of these errors by implementations is not mandatory, it is clearly a desirable option to be provided. Their definition represented a significant challenge to language implementors.

The implementation presented in this volume is a direct response to that challenge. Its purpose is to bring together in a demonstration system the range of techniques required for a complete implementation of ISO standard Pascal, including the detection of all dynamic semantic errors. As such it may serve as reference for those producing further implementations of Pascal, or adapting existing implementations to the requirements of the ISO standard.

The Model Implementation follows the tradition of most Pascal implementations, in that it is written entirely in Pascal itself. In this respect Pascal's most significant shortcoming is the lack of any module construct for the subdivision of large programs into units of manageable size. In developing the Model Implementation, a logical modular structure has been used, which is expressed informally in the program texts within the limits imposed by the syntax of Pascal. In this sense, the programs provide a case-study of the extent to which such structure can be expressed in standard Pascal.

The Model Implementation has been developed in close collaboration with those responsible for production of the Pascal Validation Suite, at the National Physical Laboratory (NPL) in England, and at the University of Tasmania, Australia. The Model Implementation and the Validation Suite are complementary in the sense that passing every test in the Validation Suite has been a minimal requirement for the Model Implementation throughout its development, and experience with the Model Implementation has helped to eliminate several inadequacies in the Suite and to suggest additional tests for inclusion in it.

Development of the Model Implementation was carried out in the Department of Computation at the University of Manchester Institute of Science and Technology (UMIST), with financial assistance from the UK Department of Industry. All rights to the Model Implementation as a software product belong to UMIST, though by agreement, machine-readable copies are distributed by BSI or its agents on UMIST's behalf. This publication in book form is also made with UMIST's permission. The camera-ready copy was produced using facilities in the Department of Computer Science at the University of Queensland, Australia.

The Model Implementation has been derived chiefly from Pascal implementations developed at the Queen's University of Belfast, which in turn were influenced by early Pascal implementations from ETH Zurich. As for many implementations, it would be impossible to attribute exact authorship of the various techniques used, and due acknowledgement is hereby made of all contributions and influences that may be detected. We must, however, thank by name Niklaus Wirth, for giving us Pascal in the first place, and Tony Hoare, who has encouraged the implementation efforts of one of us throughout the history of Pascal. Of fellow implementors, those deserving special mention are Urs Ammann and his colleagues at ETH Zurich, Jim Miner and his colleagues at the University of Minnesota, Arther Sale at the University of Tasmania, Bill Findlay and David Watt at the University of Glasgow, and the long-serving compiler-team members in Belfast, Colum Quinn, Kathleen McConnell and Dave Bustard, who may recognise many identifiers and code fragments in the Model Implementation as their own. Finally, we are grateful to Brian Wichmann and his colleagues Peter Wilkinson and Guy O'Neill at NPL, for their collaboration, support and patience in testing the Model Implementation against the Pascal Validation Suite.

Jim Welsh and Atholl Hay

INTRODUCTION

Parts 1, 2, and 3 of this text are the three programs which comprise the Model Implementation of Standard Pascal. Throughout the text the term "standard Pascal" is used to mean the programming language Pascal as defined by standard BS 6192 and ISO 7185, and the term "the Pascal standard" refers to these definitions.

These programs are:

1   a model compiler which enforces all mandatory requirments of the Pascal standard on each program input to it, and generates an equivalent "P-code" object program;
2   a P-machine which interprets a P-code program to simulate its executable effect, including detection of all errors defined by the Pascal Standard;
3   a post-mortem generator which examines the "corpse" of an executed P-code program to determine its cause of termination and to re-create the program's final state in source language terms;

The Model Compiler is a conventional one-pass Pascal compiler comprising a machine-independent program analyser cleanly interfaced to a target machine-dependent code generator. It accepts an ISO Standard Pascal source program and generates an equivalent P-code object program for interpretive execution on the P-machine. A high degree of run-time security is provided by generating error-checking code for each of the distinct errors defined in the Pascal Standard.

The P-machine program should be regarded as an operational definition rather than a production interpreter. Being written in Pascal, it relies on a host Pascal processor for all arithmetic functions and fixed and floating-point I/O. If these host functions are deviant, the Model Implementation may exhibit deviant behaviour also. Moreover, an implementation of files and program parameters cannot be given a general expression in Standard Pascal. Consequently, the P-machine as published here provides communication with the external environment only via the program parameters Input and Output, together with an interface for the implementation of file I/O in general.

The Postmortem Generator supplements each error report with a trace-back of all active blocks, together with a symbolic variable dump of each. It is called whenever the P-machine detects an error, but the means by which this is achieved is necessarily system-dependent.

CHAPTER 1

Compiler Overview

{

The overall function of the model compiler is summarised by its program heading which is as follows:

}

program ModelCompiler
(SourceFile, ListFile, ErrorFile, CodeFile,
NameFile, CodeMap, DataMap);

{

The input and output files listed as program parameters have the following nature and purpose:

SourceFile   is an input text file which contains the Pascal program to be compiled in the format prescribed by the Pascal standard.

ListFile   is an output text file to which a line numbered listing of the compiled program is output if requested, together with an indication of all errors detected during compilation, as described in Chapter 4.

ErrorFile   is an input text file of explanatory error messages used in listing generation, as described in Chapter 4.

CodeFile   is an output file which contains the P-code object program generated from the input source program. The nature of the P-code generated is described in Chapter 11 and the way in which CodeFile is written is described in Chapter 15.

NameFile   is an output file to which the spellings of all identifiers needed in the provision of source-related post-mortem diagnostics are written.

DataMap   is an output file which describes the nature and representation of the variable data created by each block of the P-code program in execution. Together with NameFile this information enables a source-related post-mortem dump of all variable values to be generated.

CodeMap   is an output file which relates the P-code object string to the block and line structure of the source program compiled. It enables any execution point in the object program to be related to the corresponding source.

These files, or rather the definition of their contents, represent the functional specification of the model compiler. The overall design by which the compiler meets this specification may

1

be summarised as follows.

Primarily the compiler is split into an *analyser*, which applies the rules of the Pascal Standard to the source program, and a *generator*, which produces an equivalent P-code program. The overriding design aim was that the analyser should be completely independent of the code to be generated, and that the generator for any given object code should require minimal knowledge of the internal working and data strutures of the analyser.

The analyser and generator communicate through a well-defined interface, with a secondary interface for the generation of supplementary information required for post-mortem diagnosis. In principle this interface is the starting point for implementing the generation of any form of object code, though in practice much of the existing generator logic may be useful for many implementations. Alternatively substitution of an empty generator, i.e. a set of interface procedures with null bodies, creates a *static checker* which will enforce all compiletimes rules on the program input without generating any object program.

The way in which this overall compiler structure has been expressed as a sequence of informal Pascal modules or "chapters" is outlined below. Further detail of design decisions within these modules is given in the chapter concerned.

To maintain a syntactically correct Pascal program all global data declarations must precede the procedures that use them. Thus Chapter 2 contains all such declarations required in the compiler itself. It should be read, however, in conjunction with the chapters that follow, which explain the nature and purpose of the data types and structures concerned.

Chapter 3 defines the range of compile-time options provided for within the model compiler, although this version does not implement any means of selecting options at compile-time as this depends on the compiler's environment and mode of operation.

Chapter 4 provides the procedures used to manipulate the input source file and output listing file by the analyser, and to a limited extent by the generator.

Chapter 5 summarises the code generation interface between the analyser and the generator, while Chapter 6 summarises the additional interface used by the analyser to generate the Datamap and Codemap files for post-mortem diagnosis.

Chapters 7-10 together form the source program analyser. Chapter 7 implements lexical analysis of the input source character stream. Chapter 8 summarises the syntax analysis strategy used and defines the utility procedures which enable its implementation. Chapter 9 summarises the data structures used for semantic analysis and defines the procedures and functions used in their manipulation. Chapter 10 provides the syntax/semantic analyser proper in the form of a recursive descent syntax analyser with imbedded semantic interludes.

Chapters 11-28 together form the object program generator, with Chapter 11 providing an overview of the generator structure involved.

}

{

CHAPTER 2

Global Definitions
and Declarations

Because of the rigid order of definitions and declarations imposed by Pascal, this chapter contains all of the global definitions and declarations on which the procedures in the subsequent chapters depend. In this chapter, only a brief indication of the overall nature of the constants, types and variables introduced is given, together with a reference to the chapter in which they are used. A more detailed explanation of the nature and purpose of each is given in the referenced chapter itself.

2.1 A Global Label!

The source-handler procedure ReadNextLine (chapter 4) uses the global label 13 to die gracefully on encountering an unexpected end of program file. Fatal error 421 is reported and control is transferred to the main program point at which the listing file is concluded in the usual way.

}

label 13;

{

2.2 Global Constants

}

const

{ Constants used by the option-handler, chapter 3 }

Level0 = 0;   { conform to ISO 7185, level 0 }
Level1 = 1;   { conform to ISO 7185, level 1 }

{ Constants used by the source handler, chapter 4 }

LineMax = 121;   { maximum source line }
StartCode = 0;   { analysis error code base }
MaxCode = 499;   { total error range: 0..499 }
AnalysisBase = StartCode;   { analysis errors: 1..300 }
PredictedBase = 300;   { runtime errors: 301..400 }
SystemBase = 400;   { system limit errors: 401..420 }
FatalBase = 420;   { fatal errors: 421..450 }
LinesPerText = 2;   { lines per error text }

3

{ Constant used by the diagnostics handler, chapter 6 }

NilSerial = 0;   { unallocated serial number }

{ Constants used by the lexical analyser, chapter 7 }

NoWords = 47;	{ upper bound of word symbol table }
AlfaSize = 12;	{ size of alfa header string }
ChunkLength = 4;	{ size of trailing alfa chunks }
DefaultSpelling = '????????????';	{ default alfa header }

{ Constants used in semantic analysis, chapter 9 }

DispLimit = 20;	{ upper bound of display }
GlobalLevel = 1;	{ scope level of program block }

{

The following constants describe the model P-machine for which code is generated. Their values are strictly dependent on the host Pascal environment in which the model implementation is to run. An implementor must

1.   Investigate how the host Pascal processor implements the packed-variable:-

HostWord : packed array[HostWordSize] of HostBit

If HostWord[0] is mapped onto the most significant bit position, then set the constant IndexedFromLeft to the value true. Otherwise, set it to false.

2.   Redefine the constants prefixed 'MC' for the host machine.

}

IndexedFromLeft = true;	{ for host Pascal compiler }
MCBitsPerWord = 32;	{ bits per memory-word }
MCWordSetBits = 31;	{ bits per set-word }
MCBitsPerByte = 8;	{ bits per memory-byte }
MCBytesPerWord = 4;	{ mcbitsperword div mcbitsperbyte }
MCMaxBitNum = 31;	{ mcbitsperword-1 }
MCMaxSetBit = 30;	{ mcwordsetbits-1 }
MCMaxByteNum = 3;	{ mcbytesperword-1 }
MCMaxint = 2147483647;	{ max mc-integer value }
MCMaxDigits = 10;	{ digits in mcmaxint }
MCMaxintDiv10 = 214748364;	{ mcmaxint div 10 }
MCMaxintMod10 = 7;	{ mcmaxint mod 10 }
MCRealSize = 2;	{ real size in words }
MCMaxByte = 255;	{ max mc-byte value }
MCUndefinedChar = 255;	{ 'undefined' character value }
MCMaxChar = 255;	{ max mc-char value }
MCMaxSet = 256;	{ maximum members per set }
MCMaxMemWord = 16383;	{ max memory-word address }

{
The following constants define the opcode values used in P-Machine instructions. The form
and effect of each instruction is defined in the P-Machine implementation itself.
}

{ GROUP 1 - inline constants }

ConstShort =   0;
ConstWord =   32;
ConstMultiple =   34;
ConstRefMultiple =   36;
ConstSet =   38;

{ GROUP 2 - memory access instructions. }

{ local block }	{ global block }	{ enclosing block }
LoadShort = 40; LoadLocal = 48; LoadRShort = 50; LoadRefLocal = 58; StoreShort = 60; StoreLocal = 68;	LoadGlobal = 70; LoadRefGlobal = 72; StoreGlobal = 74;	LoadEnclosing = 76; LoadRefEnclosing = 78; StoreEnclosing = 80;

{ intermediate block }	{ indirect access }	{ packed field access }
LoadIntermediate = 82; LoadRefIntermediate =84; StoreIntermediate =86;	LoadIndirect = 88; IndexShort = 89; Index = 96; IndexRef = 98; IndexCAP = 100; StoreIndirect = 101; AdjustPlus = 102; AdjustP1 = 104; AdjustMinus = 105; AdjustM1 = 107; AddAddress = 108;	LoadBit = 109; LoadPacked = 110; StoreBit = 111; StorePacked = 112; IndexPackedRef = 113; IndexPackdCAP = 114; IndexSubWord = 115; AdjustPackedRef = 116;

{ byte access }	{ multiple word access}	{ CAP access }
LoadByte = 117; StoreByte = 118; LoadByteRef = 119; IndexByteRef = 120;	LoadMultiple = 121; StoreMultiple = 123; StoreRepeated = 125; Move = 127;	SizeCAP = 129; MoveCAP = 130; DuplicateCAP = 131; ReleaseCAP = 132;

{ GROUP 3 - top of stack operations. }

{ logical operations }   { scalar operations }   { integer comparisons }

AndOperation = 133;   Increment = 135;   TestIEqual = 150;
NotOperation = 134;   Incl = 137;   TestIUnequal = 151;
                                Decrement = 138;   TestILess = 152;
                                Dec1 = 140;   TestILtOrEqual = 153;
                                AbsInteger = 141;
                                NegateInteger = 142;
                                SquareInteger = 143;
                                AddInteger = 144;
                                SubInteger = 145;
                                MultInteger = 146;
                                DivInteger = 147;
                                ModInteger = 148;
                                OddInteger = 149;

{   value checks }   { scalar range checks }   {   real operations }

CheckTopValue = 154;   CheckLimits = 156;   Float = 160;
CheckTopDefined = 155;   CheckLower = 157;   AbsReal = 161;
                                CheckUpper = 158;   NegateReal = 162;
                                CheckCAP = 159;   SquareReal = 163;
                                CheckForLower = 242;   AddReal = 164;
                                CheckForUpper = 243;   SubtractReal = 165;
                                                               MultiplyReal = 166;
                                                               DivideReal = 167;

{ transfer functions }   { real comparisons }   { pointer operations }

TruncateReal = 168;   TestREqual = 170;   LoadPointer = 174;
RoundReal = 169;   TestRUnequal = 171;   TestPEqual = 175;
                                TestRLess = 172;   TestPUnequal = 176;
                                TestRLtOrEqual = 173;   CheckPointer = 241;

{ string operations }   { set operations }   { set comparisons }

TestSEqual = 177;   LoadSet = 181;   TestSetEqual = 189;
TestSUnequal = 178;   StoreSet = 182;   TestSetUnequal = 190;
TestSLess = 179;   MakeSingletonSet = 183;   TestSubset = 191;
TestSLtOrEqual = 180;   MakeRangeSet = 184;   InSet = 192;
                                SetUnion = 185;   CheckSetLimits = 193;
                                SetIntersection = 186;   CheckSetUpper = 194;
                                SetDifference = 187;
                                SetExpand = 188;

{ GROUP 4 - jumps. }

{   simple jumps }   {   false jumps }   {   special jumps }

JumpForward = 195;   FJumpForward = 199;   FJumpConditional = 202;
JumpBack = 196;   FJumpBack = 200;   TJumpConditional = 203;
JumpVia = 197;   FJumpVia = 201;   CaseJump = 204;
JumpOut = 198;

{ GROUP 5 - block calls. }

{   block entry }   {   block exit }

MarkStack = 205;   EndProcedure = 211;
CallGlobal = 206;   EndFunction = 212;
CallLocal = 207;   EndMultiFunction = 213;
Callevel = 208;
CallOuter = 209;
CallForml = 210;

{ GROUP 6 - store management. }

New1 = 214;
Dispose1 = 216;
CheckNew1 = 218;
CheckDsp1 = 219;
CheckDsp2 = 220;

{ GROUP 7 - special operations. }

NoOperation = 221;   CheckWord = 228;
PresetWord = 222;   CheckRepeated = 229;
PresetRepeated = 223;   CheckVntField = 230;
LoadStack = 225;   TrapError = 231;
DuplicateStack = 226;   TrapIfTrue = 232;
PopStack = 227;   TrapIfFalse = 233;

Escape = 255;

{ GROUP 8 - class 2 (escaped) operations. }

{ input-output   }   { input-output }   { predefined operations}

CheckReadMode = 256;   PutFile = 266;   Pack = 276;
CheckWriteMode = 257;   WriteCharacter = 267;   Packc = 277;
RewriteFile = 258;   WriteBoolean = 268;   Unpack = 278;
ResetFile = 259;   WriteCString = 269;   Unpackc = 279;
EndOfLine = 260;   WriteInteger = 270;   Sine = 280;
EndOfFile = 261;   WriteFloatedReal = 271; Cosine = 281;
GetFile = 262;   WriteFixedReal = 272;   NaturalExp = 282;

ReadInteger = 263;   WriteLine = 273;   NaturalLog = 283;
ReadReal = 264;   PageFile = 274;   SquareRoot = 284;
ReadLine = 265;   CloseFile = 275;   ArcTangent = 285;
CheckBuffer = 287;

MapProgParam = 286;

MaxPcode = 287;

{ Constants used by the code-file emitter, chapter 15 }

MaxPcodeByte = 255;   { logical byte capacity - 1 }
DataWordLimit = 511;   { control data buffer upper bound }
CodeWordLimit = 575;   { code buffer upper bound }
CodeByteLimit = 2303;   { codewordlimit*mcbytesperword + mcbytesperword - 1 }

{ control data table header layout }

ParamsOffset = 0;   { |codebase-1| = parameter size }
LocalsOffset = 1;   { |codebase-2| = stack size }
LocksOffset = 2;   { |codebase-3| = lock stack size }
SerialOffset = 3;   { |codebase-4| = 0/pmd block serial }
HeaderSize = 4;   { control data header size }

{ stack frame layout }

FirstOffset = 0;   { first available frame offset }
FrameSize = 6;   { stack-frame header size }

{ Constants used by the object-program generator, chapters 12-28 }

FileSize = 5;   { file-variable size }
CAPBpSize = 3;   { conformant array bound pair block size }
DefaultBufferSize = 64;   { default file-buffer word size }
BufferVarOffset = 2;   { buffer-variable offset in text file variable }
MaxLevels = 9;   { max variant nesting level }
MaxCaseGap = 10;   { max discontinuity in case jump tables }
LockSize = 3;   { size of lock-stack entry }
FileLockOffset = 1;   { file lock word offset }
FileLockBit = 0;   { file lock bit posititon }
HeapLockOffset = -2;   { heap lock word offset }
HeapLockBit = MCMaxBitNum;   { heap lock bit position }

{

2.3 Global Types
}
type

{ Types applied globally }
HostWord = integer;
Scalar = 0..maxint;

DeclKind = (Predefined, Declared);

StdProcFuncs = (Getp, Putp, Resetp, Rewritep, Readp, Writep, Readlnp, Writelnp,
           Pagep, Newp, Disposep, Packp, Unpackp, Absf, Sqrf, Oddf, Succf, Predf,
           Ordf, Chrf, Truncf, Roundf, Sinf, Cosf, Expf, Lnf, Sqrtf, Arctanf, Eoff,
           Eolnf);

TypeForm = (Scalars, SubRanges, Pointers, Arrays, CAPSchema, Records, Sets, Files,
           VariantPart, Variant);

SetForms = (Unpacked, IsPacked, Constructed);

IdClass = (Domain, Types, Consts, Vars, Bound, Field, Proc, Func, Prog);

{ Types describing the model P-machine }

MCBit = 0..1;
MCByte = 0..MCMaxByte;
MCWord = HostWord { target=host };
MCScalar = 0..MCMaxint;
MCIntegerForm = HostWord { MC-integer-space: target=host };
MCRealForm = real { MC-real-space: target=host };
MCCharSet = 0..MCMaxChar;
MCBitRange = 0..MCBitsPerWord;
MCBitIndex = 0..MCMaxBitNum;
MCSetBits = 0..MCMaxSetBit;
MCBitArray = **packed array** [MCBitIndex] **of** MCBit;
MCByteIndex = 0..MCMaxByteNum;
MCByteArray = **packed array** [MCByteIndex] **of** MCByte;
MCWordSet = **set of** MCSetBits;

WordCast = (AsSet, AsBits, AsBytes, AsReal, AsValue, AsLabel);
MCWordForm = **packed record**
                case WordCast **of**
                  AsSet: (WSet: MCWordSet);
                  AsBits: (WBits: MCBitArray);
                  AsBytes: (WBytes: MCByteArray);
                  AsReal: (WReal: MCRealForm);
                  AsValue: (WValue: MCWord);
                  AsLabel: (Linked: Boolean; Address: MCScalar)
             end;

WordRange = 0..MCMaxMemWord;
DataRange = 0..DataWordLimit;
CodeRange = 0..CodeWordLimit;
CodeByteRange = 0..CodeByteLimit;

WordEntry = ˆListWord;
ListWord = **record** Word: MCWordForm; Next: WordEntry **end**;

{ Types used by the option-handler, chapter 3 }

OptionContext = (Locally, Globally);
OptionClass = (BoolClass, IntClass);
OptionType = (Listing, Checks, PMDump, Level, Margin, Other);
BoolOptions = Listing..PMDump;

```
IntOptions = Level..Margin;
SetOfOptions = set of OptionType;
```

{ Types used by the source-handler, chapter 4 }

```
LinePosition = 1..LineMax;
TextPosition = record LineNumber: Scalar; CharNumber: LinePosition end;

ErrorSpan = 0..MaxCode;
ErrorEntry = ^ErrorRec;
ErrorRec = record
              ErrorCode: ErrorSpan; ErrorPosition: TextPosition; Next: ErrorEntry
           end;
ErrorList = record First, Last: ErrorEntry end;

SourceLine = record
                Line: array [LinePosition] of char; FirstLine, BlankLine: Boolean;
                FirstRead, FirstNonBlank, LastNonBlank, LastSignificant: LinePosition;
                Position: TextPosition; ErrorsToReport, ErrorStarted: Boolean;
                ErrorsOnThisLine, EarlierErrors: ErrorList
             end;
CodeAddress = Scalar;
```

{ Types used by the object-program generator interface, chapter 5 }

```
ValueKind = (OrdValue, IntValue, BoolValue, CharValue, RealValue, SetValue,
             StringValue, PntrValue);
ObjectValue = record
                 WordSize: WordRange;
                 case Kind: ValueKind of
                   OrdValue, IntValue, BoolValue, CharValue: (Ival: MCIntegerForm);
                   RealValue: (Rval: MCRealForm);
                   SetValue: (Setval: WordEntry);
                   StringValue: (Length: MCScalar; Stringval: WordEntry);
                   PntrValue: (Pval: WordEntry)
              end;
ValueDetails = record
                  Value: ObjectValue;
                  case Kind: ValueKind of
                    OrdValue: (Ival: integer);
                    IntValue, BoolValue, CharValue, RealValue, SetValue, StringValue:
                       (Length: 0..LineMax; String: packed array [1..LineMax] of char);
                    PntrValue: ()
               end;
AddressLevel = 0..DispLimit;
RuntimeAddress = packed record BlockLevel: AddressLevel; WordOffset: WordRange end;
FieldLevel = Scalar;
FieldOffset = packed record
                 WordOffset: WordRange; Level: FieldLevel;
                 case PartWord: Boolean of
                   false: (WordSize: WordRange);
                   true: (BitSize: MCBitRange; BitOffset: MCBitIndex)
              end;
```

```
BlockLabel = packed record BlockLevel: AddressLevel; EntryOffset: MCByte end;
StatementLabel = BlockLabel;

RepKind = (ForScalar, ForSet, ForArray, ForARecord, ForVntRecord, ForFile, ForPnter,
            ForVariant, ForSelector, ForCAP, ForReal, ForString, ForOther);
MachineValue = packed record
                            Multiple: Scalar;
                            case Defined: Boolean of
                            false: ();
                            true: (Magnitude: MCIntegerForm)
                        end;
TypeRepresentation = packed record
                                WordSize: WordRange; BitSize: MCBitRange;
                                Kind: RepKind; CheckValue: MachineValue;
                                Min, Max: MCIntegerForm;
                                PresetCode, PostsetCode, CheckCode: BlockLabel;
                                Selector: FieldOffset
                            end;
JumpType = (IfFalse, IfTrue, IfFalseConditional, IfTrueConditional, Absolute);
FixUpEntry = ^FixUpRecord;
FixUpRecord = record
                    JumpKind: JumpType; JumpAddress: CodeByteRange;
                    Next: FixUpEntry
                end;
CodeLabel = record
                Linked: Boolean; LinkIndex: MCByte;
                case Expected: Boolean of
                    false: (Address: CodeByteRange);
                    true: (LastReference: FixUpEntry)
            end;
StackTop = (TopOfStack, NextToTop);

FileModes = (Inspection, Generation);
OutputKind = (IntKind, RealKind, CharKind, BoolKind, StringKind, DefaultKind);
InputKind = IntKind..CharKind;
FormatKind = (Default, Floating, Fixed);

{ Types used by the diagnostics handler, chapter 6 }

SerialRange = Scalar;

{ Types used by the lexical analyser, chapter 7 }

SymbolType = (Ident, IntConst, RealConst, CharConst, StringConst, NilSy, NotSy,
            MulOp, AddOp, RelOp, LeftParent, RightParent, LeftBracket,
            RightBracket, Comma, Semicolon, Period, Arrow, Colon, Becomes, Thru,
            LabelSy, ConstSy, TypeSy, VarSy, FuncSy, ProcSy, PackedSy, ArraySy,
            RecordSy, SetSy, FileSy, BeginSy, IfSy, CaseSy, RepeatSy, WhileSy,
            ForSy, WithSy, GotoSy, EndSy, ThenSy, ElseSy, UntilSy, OfSy, DoSy,
            ToSy, ProgramSy, OtherSy);
OpType = (Mul, Rdiv, AndOp, Idiv, Imod, Plus, Minus, OrOp, LtOp, LeOp, GeOp, GtOp,
            NeOp, EqOp, InOp, NotOp, SingleOp, RangeOp);
```

```
AlfaIndex = 1..AlfaSize;
AlfaHead = packed array [AlfaIndex] of char;
AlfaEntry = ^AlfaRecord;
AlfaRecord = record
                Chunk: packed array [1..ChunkLength] of char; NextChunk: AlfaEntry
             end;
Alfa = record Head: AlfaHead; Tail: AlfaEntry end;

SetOfSymbols = set of SymbolType;
```

{ Types used in static semantic analysis, chapters 9,10 }

```
TypEntry = ^TypeRecord;
IdEntry = ^IdRecord;
FormalEntry = ^FormalRecord;
LabelEntry = ^LabelRecord;
ScopeCopy = ^ScopeRecord;

ListEntry = ^ListRecord;
ListRecord = record Id: IdEntry; Next: ListEntry end;
IdList = record FirstEntry, LastEntry: ListEntry end;
IdSet = IdList;

TypeRecord = packed record
                Serial: SerialRange; Next: TypEntry;
                Representation: TypeRepresentation;
                case Form: TypeForm of
                  Scalars:
                    (case ScalarKind: DeclKind of
                       Predefined: ();
                       Declared: (FirstConst: IdEntry));
                  SubRanges: (RangeType: TypEntry; Min, Max: ObjectValue);
                  Pointers: (DomainType: TypEntry);
                  Sets: (FormOfSet: SetForms; BaseType: TypEntry);
                  Arrays:
                    (PackedArray, StringConstant: Boolean;
                     AelType, InxType: TypEntry);
                  CAPSchema:
                    (PackedSchema, ValueSchema, FirstIndex: Boolean;
                     CompType, InxSpec: TypEntry;
                     LowBdAddress, HighBdAddress: RuntimeAddress);
                  Records:
                    (FileFree, PackedRecord: Boolean; FieldScope: IdEntry;
                     FixedPart: IdEntry; VarPart: TypEntry);
                  Files: (PackedFile, TextFile: Boolean; FelType: TypEntry);
                  VariantPart:
                    (TagType: TypEntry; TagField, SelectorField: IdEntry;
                     FirstVariant: TypEntry);
                  Variant:
                    (VarFileFree, Distinct: Boolean; SubFixedPart: IdEntry;
                     NextVariant, SubVarPart: TypEntry;
                     VariantValue: ObjectValue)
             end;
```

```
SetOfIdClass = set of IdClass;
IdKind = (Actual, Formal);
KindOfVar = (ValueParam, VarParam, LocalVar);
ScopeNumber = integer;
IdRecord = packed record
                    Serial: SerialRange; Name: Alfa; LastUse: ScopeNumber;
                    LeftLink, RightLink: IdEntry; IdType: TypEntry;
                    case Klass: IdClass of
                      Domain, Types: ();
                      Consts: (Values: ObjectValue; SuccId: IdEntry);
                      Vars: (VarKind: KindOfVar; VarAddress: RuntimeAddress);
                      Field: (Offset: FieldOffset; Tag: Boolean; NextField: IdEntry);
                      Bound: (BdAddress: RuntimeAddress; NextBound: IdEntry);
                      Proc, Func:
                          (case PfDecKind: DeclKind of
                            Predefined: (PfIndex: StdProcFuncs);
                            Declared:
                                (Formals: FormalEntry;
                                case PfKind: IdKind of
                                  Actual:
                                      (CodeBody: BlockLabel; FormalScope: ScopeCopy;
                                      Assignable, Assigned: Boolean;
                                      case Forwrd: Boolean of
                                        false: (Result: RuntimeAddress);
                                        true: (Declaration: TextPosition));
                                  Formal: (FAddress: RuntimeAddress)));
                      Prog: (ProgBody: BlockLabel);
              end;
ParmKind = (BoundParm, ValueParm, VarParm, ProcParm, FuncParm);
FormalRecord = packed record
                    Next: FormalEntry; Section: Scalar; FormalType: TypEntry;
                    case Parm: ParmKind of
                      BoundParm, ValueParm, VarParm: ();
                      ProcParm, FuncParm: (ItsFormals: FormalEntry)
              end;
LabelDepth = 1..maxint;
LabelRecord = record
                    LabelValue: ObjectValue; NextLabel: LabelEntry;
                    LabelledCode: StatementLabel;
                    case Defined: Boolean of
                      false: (Declaration: TextPosition; MaxDepth: LabelDepth);
                      true:
                        (case Accessible: Boolean of
                          false: ();
                          true: (DefinedDepth: LabelDepth))
              end;
```

```
ProgPmEntry = ^ProgPmRecord;
ProgPmRecord = record
                    Name: Alfa; Declaration: TextPosition; ParamId: IdEntry;
                    NextParam: ProgPmEntry
                 end;

FrameEntry = ^FrameRecord;
ScopeKind = (ActualBlock, FormalBlock, RecordScope);
ScopeRecord = record
                    ScopeNo: ScopeNumber; Locals: IdEntry;
                    case Scope: ScopeKind of
                        ActualBlock, FormalBlock:
                            (Threatened: IdSet; TypeChain: TypEntry; LabelChain: LabelEntry;
                             SavedFrame: FrameEntry);
                        RecordScope: (RecordType: TypEntry; FieldsPacked: Boolean)
                 end;
DispRange = 0..DispLimit;
RefSecurity = (Secure, MayBeInsecure);

{ Types used by the storage allocator, chapter 13 }

Shapes = (Word, WordStructure, PartWrd, PartWrdStructure);
TypeCode = (None, Indirect, Inline);
TypeActions = (Presets, Postsets, ValueChecks);
ManualEntry = ^ManualItem;
ManualItem = record
                    ItsShape: Shapes; ItsRepresentation: TypeRepresentation;
                    ItsCode: TypeCode; ItsOffset: FieldOffset; Repeated: Scalar;
                    NextItem: ManualEntry
                 end;
ManualList = record FirstEntry, LastEntry: ManualEntry end;
FrameRecord = record
                    NextOffset, LockDepth, MaxDepth: WordRange;
                    PresetList, PostsetList: ManualList; CAPList: IdList; Next: FrameEntry
                 end;

{ Types used by the code-file emitter, chapter 15 }

Pcodes = 0..MaxPcode;
PcodeByte = 0..MaxPcodeByte;

BlockPtr = ^BlockRecord;
BlockRecord = record DataBase: DataRange; EntryLabel: BlockLabel; Next: BlockPtr end;

{ Types used by the object-program generator, chapters 16-26 }

StackEntry = ^StackNode;
Accesses = (Local, Enclosing, Intermediate, Global);
AccessOps = (LoadOp, StoreOp, LoadRefOp);

BpEntry = ^BpRecord;
RangeEntry = BpEntry;
```

```
BpRecord = record
                Size: WordRange; Lower, Upper: MCIntegerForm; Next: BpEntry;
                case CAPBounds: Boolean of
                    false: ();
                    true: (BpAddress: RuntimeAddress)
            end;
ActualKind = (IsValue, IsVar, IsBlock, IsBounds, IsRef);
ActualEntry = ^ActualRecord;
ActualRecord = record
                Next: ActualEntry;
                case Kind: ActualKind of
                    IsValue, IsRef, IsVar, IsBlock:
                        (ActualParam: StackEntry; FormalRep: TypeRepresentation);
                    IsBounds: (BpList: BpEntry)
                end;
IndexEntry = ^IndexRecord;
IndexRecord = record
                TheIndex: StackEntry; Factor: MCIntegerForm; Next: IndexEntry;
                case CAPIndex: Boolean of
                    false: (Lower, Upper: MCIntegerForm);
                    true: (BpAddress: RuntimeAddress)
                end;
RefClasses = (VarRef, TagRef, PnterRef, FileRef);
OperatorKind = (Unary, Binary, Standard, Condition, BlockCall, CAPLoad, RangeChk,
                ReadOp);
Unaries = (NegateOp, FloatOp);
OperandKind = (AnInteger, AReal, ABoolean, ASet, AString, APointer, AFile);
NodeKind = (Reference, BlockRef, Result, Address, AConstant, Operation);
KindOfRangeCheck = (SubrangeChecks, TransferChecks, MemberChecks);
Offsets = -MCMaxMemWord..+MCMaxMemWord;

AnOperator = (CheckSelector, SetSelector, CheckIfActive, CheckIfNew, CheckFile,
                SetALock);
AncillaryEntry = ^AncillaryRecord;
AncillaryRecord = record
                Next: AncillaryEntry;
                case WhichOp: AnOperator of
                    CheckSelector:
                        (SelectorField: FieldOffset; SelectorValue: MCIntegerForm);
                    SetSelector: (Selector: BlockLabel; TagValue: MCIntegerForm);
                    CheckIfActive: (SelectorLevel: FieldLevel);
                    SetALock: (LockWord: Offsets; LockBit: MCBitIndex);
                    CheckIfNew, CheckFile: ();
                end;
AncillaryList = record FirstEntry, LastEntry: AncillaryEntry end;

IOFileEntry = ^IOFileRecord;

StackNode = record
                NextNode: StackEntry; DataRep: TypeRepresentation;
                DataBytes: MCScalar; Vulnerable, MayHaveOverflowed: Boolean;
```

```
    RunError: Scalar; CheckList: AncillaryList;
  case Kind: NodeKind of
    Reference:
      (BaseAddress: RuntimeAddress; Adjustment: Offsets; Level: Scalar;
       Indirect: Boolean; AccessList: StackEntry; Class: RefClasses;
       case PartOfWord: Boolean of
         false:
           (case Indexed: Boolean of
             false: ();
             true: (Indices: IndexEntry));
         true:
           (BitSize: MCBitRange; BitOffset: MCBitRange;
            OnByteBoundary: Boolean;
            case IndexedPartWord: Boolean of
              false: ();
              true: (Index: IndexEntry)));
    BlockRef:
      (CallToBeGenerated: Boolean; First, Last: ActualEntry;
       OldDepth: Scalar;
       case BlockKind: IdKind of
         Actual: (BlockBase: BlockLabel);
         Formal: (FormalAddress: RuntimeAddress));
    Result: ();
    Address:
      (case Loaded: Boolean of
         false: (APartWord: Boolean; TempAddress: RuntimeAddress);
         true: ());
    AConstant: (TheConst: ObjectValue);
    Operation:
      (OpGroup: OperandKind;
       case OpForm: OperatorKind of
         Unary: (UnaryEntry: StackEntry; UnaryOp: Unaries);
         Binary: (LeftEntry, RightEntry: StackEntry; BinaryOp: OpType);
         Condition: (Jump: JumpType; OpList: StackEntry);
         BlockCall: (FnBlockEntry: StackEntry);
         RangeChk:
           (CheckKind: KindOfRangeCheck;
            RequiredRange, TransferRange: RangeEntry;
            EntryToCheck: StackEntry);
         ReadOp: (Mode: IntKind..RealKind);
         CAPLoad:
           (CAPEntry: StackEntry; CAPPacked: Boolean;
            BpAddress: RuntimeAddress);
         Standard:
           (StdOp: StdProcFuncs;
            case Boolean of
              false: (StdEntry: StackEntry);
              true: (IOEntry: IOFileEntry)));
  end;
```

{ Types used by the with-statement controller, chapter 20 }
WithEntry = ˆWithRecord;
WithRecord = **record**
     BaseNum: DispRange; Entry: StackEntry; OldDepth: Scalar;
     Next: WithEntry
    end;

{ Types used by the standard procedures generator, chapter 21 }
IOFileRecord = **record**
      FileType: TypEntry; FileEntry: StackEntry; Next: IOFileEntry
     end;
RequestEntry = ˆRequestRecord;
RequestRecord = **record**
     Next: RequestEntry; Request: TypeRepresentation;
     ReqLevel: FieldLevel; SelectorField: FieldOffset;
     SelectorValue: MCIntegerForm
    end;

{ Types used by the case and for-statement controllers, chapter 22 }
CaseLabelEntry = ˆCaseLabelRecord;
CaseLabelRecord = **record**
     LabelValue: MCIntegerForm; LimbAddress: CodeByteRange;
     NextLabel: CaseLabelEntry
    end;
CaseEntry = ˆCaseRecord;
CaseRecord = **record**
     Selector: StackEntry; CaseCode: CodeLabel;
     MinLabel, MaxLabel: CaseLabelEntry; Next: CaseEntry
    end;
ForEntry = ˆForRecord;
ForRecord = **record**
     Incrementing: Boolean; ControlVar, FinalEntry: StackEntry;
     StartOfLoop, EndOfLoop: CodeLabel; Next: ForEntry
    end;

{ Types used by the type-specific envelope generator, chapters 25-26 }
TypeSpecificAction = **record**
      Request: TypeActions; Representation: TypeRepresentation;
      Invoked: (WithValue, WithRefrnce); Multiple: Scalar
    end;
LocalEntry = ˆLocalRecord;
LocalRecord = **record** LKind: KindOfVar; LAddress: RuntimeAddress **end;**

{ Types used by the data-map and code-map emitters, chapter 27 }
DataName = Scalar;
MapIndex = Scalar;
DataObject = **packed record**
      ObjSerial: SerialRange;
      case ObjClass: IdClass **of**
       Domain: ();

```
Types:
  (ObjRepresentation: TypeRepresentation;
   case ObjForm: TypeForm of
     Scalars:
       (case ObjScalarKind: DeclKind of
          Declared: (ObjFirstConst: SerialRange);
          Predefined: (StdType: (IntStd, RealStd, CharStd)));
     SubRanges:
       (ObjRangeType: SerialRange;
        ObjMin, ObjMax: ObjectValue);
     Sets: (SetIsPacked: Boolean; ObjBaseType: SerialRange);
     Pointers: (ObjDomain: SerialRange);
     Arrays:
       (ArrayIsPacked: Boolean;
        ObjLowBound, ObjHighBound: ObjectValue;
        ObjAelType, ObjInxType: SerialRange);
     CAPSchema:
       (SchemaIsPacked: Boolean;
        ObjCompType, ObjInxSpec: SerialRange;
        ObjLowAddr, ObjHighAddr: WordRange);
     Records:
       (RecordIsPacked: Boolean;
        ObjFixedPart, ObjVarPart: SerialRange);
     Files:
       (FileIsPacked, FileIsText: Boolean;
        ObjFelType: SerialRange);
     VariantPart:
       (ObjTagField, ObjTagType, ObjFstVariant:
           SerialRange;
        ObjSelector: FieldOffset);
     Variant:
       (VariantIsDistinct: Boolean;
        ObjSubFixedPart, ObjSubVarPart, ObjNextVariant:
           SerialRange;
        ObjVariantValue: ObjectValue));
Consts:
  (ConstName: DataName; ConstValue: ObjectValue;
   NextConst: SerialRange);
Vars, Bound:
  (VarName: DataName; VarType: SerialRange;
   IsVarParam: Boolean; LocalAddress: WordRange;
   NextLocalVar: SerialRange);
Field:
  (FieldName: DataName; FieldType: SerialRange;
   ObjOffset: FieldOffset; NextField: SerialRange);
Prog, Proc, Func:
  (BlockName: DataName; BlockBody: MapIndex;
   FirstLocalVar: SerialRange)
end;
```

```
TokenKinds = (StartBody, FlowToken, EndBody);
MapToken = packed record
                    case Kind: TokenKinds of
                        StartBody: (BlockSerial: SerialRange; StartLine: Scalar);
                        FlowToken: (CodeOffset, FlowLine: Scalar);
                        EndBody: (JumpTableSize, CodeTableSize: Scalar)
                    end;
NameByte = 0..MCMaxChar;
{
```

2.3 Global Variables

```
}

var

{ Variables used by the option-handler, chapter 3 }

Requested, LocallyRequested: SetOfOptions;
OptionValue: array [IntOptions] of integer;

{ Variables used by the source handler, chapter 4 }

Ch: char;
Source: SourceLine;
ErrorCount: Scalar;
Reported: packed array [ErrorSpan] of Boolean;
SourceFile, ListFile, ErrorFile: text;

{ Variables provided for use with the object code generation interface, chapter 5 }

CodeIsToBeGenerated: Boolean;

EmptyRepresentation, RealRepresentation, BooleanRepresentation, CharRepresentation,
IntegerRepresentation, PointerRepresentation, DefaultRepresentation:
    TypeRepresentation;
UndefinedValue: MachineValue;
NilValue, EmptyValue, FalseValue, TrueValue, ZeroValue, ZeroReal, OneValue,
MaxintValue, MinLabValue, MaxLabValue, MinCharValue, MaxCharValue, LineFeed,
PageThrow, DefaultLayout, DefaultValue:
    ObjectValue;
DefaultAddress: RuntimeAddress;
DefaultOffset: FieldOffset;
DefaultLabel: BlockLabel;

{ Variable used by the diagnostics handler, chapter 6 }

NextSerial: SerialRange;

{ Variables used by the lexical analyser, chapter 7 }

Symbol: SymbolType;
Operator: OpType;
Constant: ValueDetails;
Spelling: Alfa;
```

StartOfSymbol: TextPosition;

SymbolStarters, Letters, Digits, LettersAndDigits, LowerCaseLetters: **set of** char;
PrecedingPeriod, TailToBeDisposed: Boolean;

{ Tables used by the lexical analyser, chapter 7 }

WordSymbol:
  array [1..NoWords] **of**
    record Spelling: AlfaHead; SymbolValue: SymbolType; OpValue: OpType **end**;
LastOfLength: **array** [0..AlfaSize] **of** 0..NoWords;

{ Variables used in syntax analysis, chapters 8,10 }

SymbolsSkipped, Recovering, ErrorReported: Boolean;
BlockBegSys, TypeBegSys, ConstBegSys, SimpTypeBegSys, TypeDels, StatBegSys,
FacBegSys, SelectSymbols, ParamBegSys, ConformantParamBegSys:
  SetOfSymbols;

{ Variables used by semantic analysis, chapters 9,10 }

IntType, RealType, BoolType, CharType, TextType, NilType, EmptyType, Unknown:
  TypEntry;
DummyVarId: IdEntry;

ScopeLevel, BlockLevel, LevelFound: DispRange;
Display: **array** [DispRange] **of** ScopeRecord;
NextScopeNo: ScopeNumber;
Depth: LabelDepth;
ControlVars: IdSet;

InputFile, OutputFile: IdEntry;

ExpType, VarType: TypEntry;
VntSelector: TypEntry;
PackedVar, SimpleVar, TagVar, NewRecVar: Boolean;

{ Variable used by the storage allocator, chapter 13 }

FrameLevel: AddressLevel;
ItemShapes: **array** [Boolean, Boolean] **of** Shapes;
PresetBuffer: **record** Shift, BitsFree: MCBitRange; Buffer: MCWordForm **end**;

{ Variables used by the code-file emitter, chapter 15 }

CodeFileSize: CodeAddress;
CodeFile: **file of** MCWord;
CodeCounter: CodeByteRange;
CodeBuffer: **packed array** [CodeByteRange] **of** MCByte;
DataCounter: DataRange;
DataStack: **array** [DataRange] **of** MCWordForm;
CurrentBlock: BlockPtr;
BlockIndex: MapIndex;

{ Variables used by the object program generator, chapters 16-26 }

SelectedFile: IOFileEntry;
HpRequests: **record** FirstReq, LastReq: RequestEntry; PointerEntry: StackEntry **end**;
ZeroEntry, DefaultWidth, TopStackEntry: StackEntry;

TopFrameEntry: FrameEntry;
TopWithEntry: WithEntry;
TopCaseEntry: CaseEntry;
TopForEntry: ForEntry;
BufferOffset: FieldOffset;
Overflow: **record** Occurred, Positive: Boolean **end**;
IntCodes, RealCodes, PtrCodes, SetCodes, StringCodes: **array** [OpType] **of** Pcodes;
AccessCodes: **array** [AccessOps, Accesses] **of** Pcodes;
ContextOfCheck: (IsSucc, IsPred, IsUnknown);
TransferCodes, CheckCodes: **array** [Boolean, Boolean] **of** Pcodes;
ProgPmCount: Scalar;

{ Variables used by the code-map and data-map emitters, chapter 27 }

LastFlowLine: Scalar;
CodeMapIndex: MapIndex;
CodeMap: **packed file of** MapToken;

DataMapIndex: SerialRange;
DataMap: **packed file of** DataObject;

NameFileIndex: SerialRange;
NameFile: **packed file of** NameByte;

{

CHAPTER 3

Option Handling

A number of features of the Model Compiler can be controlled as a set of options modelled by the type OptionType. The set of options for this implementation is relatively small, being concerned only with language level, source input margin setting, listing generation, runtime check generation and postmortem dump generation.

Values of the type OptionType are sub-classified into options which, by being essentially 'on' or 'off', are Boolean by nature, and options which by possessing an associated integer-value, are integer by nature. These two sub-groups are represented by subranges BoolOptionType and IntOptionType.

Boolean-valued options are held as the set variables Requested and LocallyRequested. The former represents global option values which must remain fixed throughout analysis, and the latter represents the current values of those options which may vary from one part of the program to another. The value associated with each integer option is stored in the array variable OptionValue. In this version of the Model Compiler, Boolean options are available to control generation of the listing output file, runtime checks and postmortem dumps, and two integer options are available to control source-line scanning and language conformance level.

Initial option values and the values of variables LocallyRequested and Requested are set by the procedure InitOptions. In general, facilities for overriding these default settings should be provided - either by accepting option specifications supplied by the user when the compiler is invoked, or by extracting them from special comments or ¨pragmas¨ embedded in the source program to be compiled. Since such facilities are either environment-dependent or outside the scope of the Pascal standard, no implementation is offered in this version of the Model Compiler.

}
procedure InitOptions;
```
  begin { initoptions }
    OptionValue[Level] := Level1; OptionValue[Margin] := LineMax;
    Requested := [Listing, Checks, PMDump];
    LocallyRequested := Requested - (Requested - [Listing])
  end { initoptions };
```

{

CHAPTER 4

Source Input
and
Listing Generation

Source input and listing generation are implemented by the following major procedures:-

NextCh   This procedure reads the next source character from the source file, copies it to the listing file, and leaves its value in the global variable Ch. A corresponding value representing the position of the character in the source text is left in the variable Source.Position. The analyser may copy and use this value in subsequent error reporting. Each end-of-line is transmitted as a blank character, but the function LineEnded returns true at this time, and false at all others.

Error   This procedure enables the analysis process to record error codes for incorporation in the output listing. Each error is reported using a numeric error code and a source text position obtained as explained above.

StartError   Some errors apply to a segment of source text, rather than a single point. The procedure StartError is used to indicate the start of such a segment. The segment is assumed to extend up to the next error point reported via Error.

Initialization of the listing generation variables is carried out by the procedure InitListing, which is called before the first call to NextCh. Finalisation is carried out by the procedure EndListing which is called after analysis is complete.

Actual input of source and output of listing is carried out on a line by line basis, as detailed below.

4.1 Error reporting

During analysis of each source line, error-code/position pairs are collected on two lists, one for errors referring to the current line, the other for those referring to lines already listed. All errors so collected are output to the listing when analysis of the line is complete, by the procedure ListErrors.

Errors referring to the line just listed are reported by using a numeric error code and marking the position in the line by an up-arrow marker. Errors that refer to an earlier line are reported using line and character numbers for the symbol(s) in error. A 'segment' of source text in error, as signalled by StartError, is indicated by a string of markers, beginning at the position signalled, and continuing until the position of the next error signalled.

23

```
}
procedure ClearErrorLists;
  begin
    with Source do
      begin
        ErrorsOnThisLine.First := nil; ErrorsOnThisLine.Last := nil;
        EarlierErrors.First := nil; EarlierErrors.Last := nil
      end
  end { clearerrorlists };
procedure Error(Code: ErrorSpan; Position: TextPosition);
  procedure AddTo(var List: ErrorList);
    var NewError: ErrorEntry;
    begin
      new(NewError);
      with NewError^ do
        begin ErrorCode := Code; ErrorPosition := Position; Next := nil end;
      with List do
        begin
          if First = nil then First := NewError else Last^.Next := NewError;
          Last := NewError
        end
    end { addto };
  begin { error }
    CodeIsToBeGenerated := false;
    if Position.LineNumber = Source.Position.LineNumber
    then AddTo(Source.ErrorsOnThisLine) else AddTo(Source.EarlierErrors);
    Source.ErrorsToReport := true
  end { error };
procedure StartError(Position: TextPosition);
  begin Error(StartCode, Position) end;
procedure ListErrors;
  var ThisError, NextError: ErrorEntry; NextPrintPosition: Scalar;
      LastArrowPosition: 0..LineMax; LastWasCode: Boolean;
  procedure StartErrorLine;
    begin
      writeln(ListFile); write(ListFile, ' *****   '); LastWasCode := false;
      NextPrintPosition := Source.FirstRead
    end { starterrorline };
  procedure PrintArrowAt(Position: LinePosition);
    begin
      if Position < NextPrintPosition then StartErrorLine;
      write(ListFile, '^': Position - NextPrintPosition + 1); LastWasCode := false;
      LastArrowPosition := Position; NextPrintPosition := Position + 1
    end { printarrowat };
```

```pascal
procedure PrintCode(Code: integer);
   var Width: 1..3;
   begin
      if Code < 10
      then Width := 1
      else if Code < 100 then Width := 2 else Width := 3;
      write(ListFile, Code: Width); LastWasCode := true;
      NextPrintPosition := NextPrintPosition + Width; Reported[Code] := true;
      ErrorCount := ErrorCount + 1
   end { printcode };
procedure PrintComma;
   begin
      write(ListFile, ', '); LastWasCode := false;
      NextPrintPosition := NextPrintPosition + 1
   end { printcomma };
begin { listerrors }
   with Source do
      begin
         writeln(ListFile);

         { report errors referring to the current line }

         StartErrorLine; LastArrowPosition := FirstNonBlank - 1;
         ThisError := ErrorsOnThisLine.First;
         while ThisError <> nil do
            begin
               with ThisError^ do
                  begin
                     if ErrorStarted
                     then while NextPrintPosition < ErrorPosition.CharNumber do
                             PrintArrowAt(NextPrintPosition);
                     if ErrorCode = StartCode
                     then begin
                             if ErrorPosition.CharNumber <> LastArrowPosition
                             then PrintArrowAt(ErrorPosition.CharNumber);
                             ErrorStarted := true
                          end
                     else begin
                             if ErrorPosition.CharNumber <> LastArrowPosition
                             then PrintArrowAt(ErrorPosition.CharNumber)
                             else if LastWasCode then PrintComma;
                             PrintCode(ErrorCode); ErrorStarted := false
                          end
                  end;
               NextError := ThisError^.Next; dispose(ThisError); ThisError := NextError
            end;
         if ErrorStarted
         then while LastArrowPosition < LastSignificant do
                 PrintArrowAt(NextPrintPosition);
```

```
        { report errors referring to an earlier line }
        ThisError := EarlierErrors.First;
        while ThisError <> nil do
           begin
             with ThisError^ do
                begin
                   StartErrorLine; write(ListFile, 'Error '); PrintCode(ErrorCode);
                   with ErrorPosition do
                      write
                        (ListFile, ' at character', CharNumber: 3, ' of line',
                            LineNumber: 6)
                end;
             NextError := ThisError^.Next; dispose(ThisError); ThisError := NextError
           end;
        writeln(ListFile); ErrorsToReport := ErrorStarted; ClearErrorLists
     end
  end { listerrors };
{
```

4.2 Source line input and listing

Source input and listing are driven by the succession of calls from the analyser to the procedure NextCh. For most Pascal processors the efficiency of this source character handling has a major impact on overall speed. The form of NextCh, and of the procedures that it calls, is chosen to maximise this speed within the limits of Pascal, and to facilitate further implementation-dependent optimisations if required.

Listing of the current source line and input of the next source line is triggered when the procedure NextCh has exhausted the current line buffer. The procedure ListThisLine lists the current line, with a preceding line number, if the list option has been requested. Otherwise the line is listed only if there are errors to report.

The procedure ReadNextLine refills the line buffer character by character and sets markers to the first and last significant characters. These markers enable leading and trailing blanks, and completely blank lines, to be screened from NextCh and the analyser that calls it. ReadNextLine is easily optimised in environments where whole line input is available, but even when character by character input is used, as here, the blank-screening logic gives faster processing in most environments.

```
}
procedure ListThisLine;
   var i: LinePosition;
   begin { listthisline }
     with Source do
        if (Listing in LocallyRequested) or ErrorsToReport
        then begin
                write(ListFile, Position.LineNumber: 6);
```

```
              if not BlankLine
              then begin
                      write(ListFile, '    ': 2 + FirstNonBlank - FirstRead);
                      for i := FirstNonBlank to LastNonBlank do write(ListFile, Line[i])
                   end;
              if ErrorsToReport then ListErrors;
              writeln(ListFile)
            end
  end { listthisline };
procedure ReadNextLine;
  var i: LinePosition;
  begin
    with Source do
      begin
        i := 1; FirstRead := i; BlankLine := true;
        if not FirstLine then readln(SourceFile);
        if eof(SourceFile)
        then begin
                StartOfSymbol.LineNumber := Position.LineNumber;
                Error(FatalBase + 1, StartOfSymbol); goto 13
             end;
        while not eoln(SourceFile) do
          begin
            Line[i] := SourceFile^;
            if Line[i] <> ' '
            then begin
                    if BlankLine
                    then begin FirstNonBlank := i; BlankLine := false end;
                    LastNonBlank := i
                 end;
            get(SourceFile); i := i + 1
          end;
        FirstLine := false
      end
  end { readnextline };
procedure FirstChOfNextLine;
  begin
    with Source, Position do
      begin
        ReadNextLine;
        while BlankLine or (FirstNonBlank >= FirstRead + OptionValue[Margin]) do
          begin ListThisLine; LineNumber := LineNumber + 1; ReadNextLine end;
        if LastNonBlank >= FirstRead + OptionValue[Margin]
        then LastSignificant := FirstRead + OptionValue[Margin] - 1
        else LastSignificant := LastNonBlank;
        CharNumber := FirstNonBlank; Ch := Line[CharNumber]
      end
  end { firstchofnextline };
```

```
procedure NextCh;
  begin
    with Source, Position do
      if CharNumber >= LastSignificant
      then if CharNumber = LastSignificant
           then begin CharNumber := CharNumber + 1; Ch := ' ' end
           else begin
                   ListThisLine; LineNumber := LineNumber + 1; FirstChOfNextLine
                end
      else begin CharNumber := CharNumber + 1; Ch := Line[CharNumber] end
  end { nextch };
function LineEnded: Boolean;
  begin with Source, Position do LineEnded := (CharNumber > LastSignificant) end;
{
```

4.3 Source initialisation and finalisation

Before analysis begins the procedure InitListing outputs an appropriate header to the listing file, initialises the source description variables, and inputs the first source line to make its first character available.

When analysis is complete the procedure EndListing lists the final line, if necessary. If errors have been reported during compilation it then retrieves and lists an explanatory message for each numeric error code actually used, from the text file ErrorFile. Finally the procedure prints a listing trailer showing the number of source lines compiled and number of errors reported.

}

```
procedure PrintBanner;
  begin
    writeln(ListFile, 'Model Pascal Compiler  version ....etc.');
    writeln(ListFile); writeln(ListFile)
  end { printbanner };
procedure InitListing;
  var Code: ErrorSpan;
  begin
    rewrite(ListFile);
    if Listing in LocallyRequested then PrintBanner;
    ErrorCount := 0;
    for Code := 1 to MaxCode do Reported[Code] := false;
    reset(SourceFile);
    with Source do
      begin
        Position.LineNumber := 1; ErrorStarted := false; ErrorsToReport := false;
        ClearErrorLists; FirstLine := true; FirstChOfNextLine
      end
  end { initlisting };
```

```pascal
procedure PrintErrorTexts;
  var Code, LastCode: ErrorSpan;
  procedure FindText;
    var i: integer;
    begin
      for i := 1 to (Code - LastCode - 1) * LinesPerText do readln(ErrorFile);
      LastCode := Code
    end { findtext };
  procedure PrintText;
    var Ch: char; i: 1..LinesPerText;
    begin
      for i := 1 to LinesPerText do
        begin
          if not eoln(ErrorFile)
          then begin
                 repeat
                   Ch := ErrorFile^; get(ErrorFile); write(ListFile, Ch)
                 until eoln(ErrorFile);
                 writeln(ListFile)
               end;
          readln(ErrorFile)
        end
    end { printtext };
  begin { printerrortexts }
    LastCode := 0;
    for Code := 1 to MaxCode do
      if Reported[Code] then begin FindText; PrintText end
  end { printerrortexts };
procedure EndListing;
  begin
    ListThisLine;
    if Listing in LocallyRequested then begin writeln(ListFile); writeln(ListFile) end;
    if ErrorCount > 0
    then begin
           reset(ErrorFile);
           if eof(ErrorFile)
           then writeln(ListFile, ' Error summary not available.')
           else PrintErrorTexts;
           writeln(ListFile); writeln(ListFile)
         end;
    write(ListFile, ' Compilation complete : ');
    if ErrorCount = 0
    then write(ListFile, '     No') else write(ListFile, ErrorCount: 7);
    writeln(ListFile, ' errors reported');
    writeln(ListFile, ' Source program        : ',
           Source.Position.LineNumber: 7, ' lines')
  end { endlisting };
```

{

CHAPTER 5

Object Program Generation

Object program generation is embedded within the syntactic-semantic analyser as a set of procedure calls. These calls and the types underlying their parameter lists, provide a generation interface which is independent of the precise object code to be generated. Between calls, the analyser stores and transmits data of these types but without any detailed knowledge of their internal nature.

Likewise, the generative procedures called may operate without any knowledge of the analyser's functioning or of the structures within which it stores the common data. In practice however it is unnecessarily cumbersome in a one pass system to segregate the analyser's data on types from those which determine and describe their representation in the object program. In these situations the interface allows the generative procedures to access the data-structures built by the analyser.

In this chapter the object-code-independent generation interface is described, and the generation procedures declared as forward procedures, so that calls to them within the analyser code in Chapters 9 and 10 can be made (and understood). The actual realisation of these procedures as generators for P-machine code is found in chapters 12 to 28.

In adopting any code generation interface, the analyser's behaviour following detection of errors must be determined. In the Model Compiler interface a global variable CodeIsTo-BeGenerated is provided, and initially set to true. Once an error is detected which endangers the validity of the sequence of calls made by the analyser on the generation interface, the analyser sets this variable to false. The code generator then ignores all interface calls thereafter.

5.1 Representation of Data Types

The representation and storage of data within the object program is described by the compiler as follows:

1. Each TypEntry carries a field Representation of type TypeRepresentation which describes how such data are to be represented in the object program.

2. Each IdEntry for a directly referenceable stored data item (variable, formal parameter or function result), carries a corresponding field of type RunTimeAddress which holds the necessary address co-ordinates for the run-time access of that data.

3.   Each IdEntry for a record field name carries a field Offset of type FieldOffset which specifies the field's run-time co-ordinates relative to those of the record as a whole.

Representations and field offsets are generated by the procedure SetRepresentationFor which determines the representation for a given type. For record types it also determines the field offset for each field identifier.

}

procedure SetRepresentationFor(TheType: TypEntry); forward;

{

Because any component array of a multi-dimensional array may be referenced individually, the representation of each dimension must be fully and separately specified. For structured types in general the representation of any component type must be set before that of the structured type. In the case of multidimensional array types, therefore, the representation of each dimension is set in turn, from the innermost to the outermost dimension.

Thus the type-definition

> multi = array [1..10, -100..100] of T;

gives rise to the calls:

SetRepresentationFor(TypEntry for array[-100..100] of T)
SetRepresentationFor(TypEntry for array[1..10] of array...)

For record types the linear lists of fields and variant structure entries located within the record type entry allow all field offsets and alternative variant representations to be determined by a single call to SetRepresentationFor.

For the proper implementation of files, and for the secure implementation of variables of other types, hidden procedures must be generated for initialising, finalising and intermediate inspection of these variables. In general this may be achieved by generating a module of internal or hidden procedures that perform type-specific presetting, postsetting and inspection, and recording their entry-points in the representation of the type entry. The generation of these internal procedures is assumed to be triggered by SetRepresentationFor to complete the representation of the type. Variables subsequently declared with the type may be initialised, finalised and checked by passing the variable address as a parameter to the appropriate internal procedure.

5.2 Variable Storage Allocation and Initialisation

5.2.1 Stack Frames and Variable Storage

Allocation of storage for variable data is handled by the following procedures:

}

procedure OpenStackFrame; forward;

procedure CloseStackFrame; forward;

procedure SaveStackFrame; forward;

procedure RestoreStackFrame; forward;

procedure SetAddressFor(VarId: IdEntry); forward;

{

Runtime storage for all variable data, other than dynamically allocated variables, is assumed to lie within a conventional runtime stack. This requires supporting compile-time analysis to compute the layout and total storage requirement for each stack frame. Procedure Open-StackFrame is used to initiate an image of the stack frame corresponding to the current block scope. Storage is then allocated within the stack frame as the parameters and variables of the block are declared. During analysis of the statement part of the block, additional storage may be required by the generated object code to hold saved operands, addresses and so on. When the block scope is closed, the analyser calls procedure CloseStackFrame to discard the record of the current stack frame.

To handle forward procedures and functions in a consistent manner, the analyser 'saves' and 'restores' the state of the current stack frame of every procedure and function between analysis of its heading and analysis of the corresponding block by calling procedures SaveStackFrame and RestoreStackFrame. For normal procedures and functions, these calls are adjacent, but for forward procedures and functions, analysis of other procedures and functions may intervene.

During analysis of declarations, variable, formal parameter and function result address coordinates are assigned within the current stack frame by calls to the procedure SetAddressFor.

The example below indicates the manner in which a stack-frame is created for a function block-scope. Note that the function result is assigned an address which is saved in the result field of the function identifier entry. Thus:

```
function F(A, B: integer): real;
    type T = 1..10;
    var  C: T;
    begin ...
```

results in the following sequence of interface calls:

```
OpenStackFrame
SetAddressFor(IdEntry for A)
SetAddressFor(IdEntry for B)
SaveStackFrame
RestoreStackFrame
SetAddressFor(IdEntry for F)
SetRepresentationFor(TypEntry for 1..10)
SetAddressFor(IdEntry for C)
```

The stack-frame is closed on completing analysis of the statement part of the block.

For convenience of analysis, storage allocation is also signalled for the parameter lists of formal procedures and functions, but the resulting stack frame is discarded as soon as the formal procedure or function heading has been processed.

5.2.2 Conformant Array Parameter Representation

The representation associated with (each dimension of) a conformant array schema is generated in a similar manner to that of a normal array type. However, for a conformant array schema each index-type-specification is represented by the allocation of a 'bound-pair block' of storage locations within the stack frame of the procedure or function concerned. During activation of the procedure or function, the values denoted by the pair of bound-identifiers contained by the index-type-specification, are held within implementation-defined locations of the bound-pair block. This block and the addresses of the bounds held within it are allocated by the procedure:

```
}
procedure SetBoundPairBlockFor(LowBound, HighBound: IdEntry); forward;
{
```

Conceptually, a bound-pair block associated with an outer dimension of a multi-dimensional conformant array schema is regarded as embracing the blocks associated with index-type-specifications of its component conformant-array-schema. In practice this is achieved by sequential allocation of bound-pair blocks from the outermost to the innermost dimension, so that the address of the outer bound-pair block gives implicit access to the immediately following inner blocks.

For example, the formal parameter declaration:

   A, B: array [M1..N1: integer; M2..N2: integer] of real

results in the following sequence of interface calls:

```
SetBoundPairBlockFor(IdEntry for M1, IdEntry for N1)
SetBoundPairBlockFor(IdEntry for M2, IdEntry for N2)
SetRepresentationFor(TypEntry for array [M2..N2: integer] of real)
SetRepresentationFor(TypEntry for array [M1..N1: integer] of ... )
SetAddressFor(IdEntry for A)
SetAddressFor(IdEntry for B)
```

The call to SetAddressFor for each conformant array parameter allocates storage for a descriptor or reference which, in conjunction with the corresponding bound pair blocks, enables access to the actual array. Allocation of the storage occupied by value conformant array parameters is discussed in Sections 5.2.2 and 5.11.

5.2.3 Initialisation and Finalisation of Variables

Variable initialisation and finalisation at block entry and exit are generated by procedures:

```
}
procedure InitializeVariables; forward;
procedure FinalizeVariables; forward;
{
```

In principle, each variable that is designated "undefined" at the start of a block must be initialised at block entry. In practice the analyser makes a single call to procedure InitialiseVariables to trigger the collective presetting of the local variables before code-generation for the statement part begins.

In general, the parameters of a procedure or function may be omitted from the initialisation process. However, the auxiliary variable associated with a value conformant array parameter may be created at this time using available heap storage, and initialised with the contents of the actual array. The auxiliary variable must then be mapped onto the formal parameter by overwriting the actual array reference. A complementary discussion on the auxiliary variable is contained in Section 5.11.

The procedure FinaliseVariables is called analagously immediately prior to leaving the block. In practice only file variables and value conformant array parameters need be processed: in the first case to close and terminate the file, and in the second case to discard the auxiliary variable.

5.3 Representation of Literal Values

The representation of literal values appearing in the analysed program must be determined by the code-generator. To enable this, the record type ValueDetails is provided. The analyser inserts the source representation of each literal into such a record, and then requests the code-generator to derive the corresponding object-value by calling the procedure Evaluate. This object-value is used thereafter to represent the literal across the interface.

}

procedure Evaluate(**var** SourceValue: ValueDetails); forward;

{

A number of semantic checks performed by the analyser require that the generator provides for comparison and negation of object-values. These are performed by the procedures:

}

procedure NegateValue(**var** Value: ObjectValue); forward;

function SameValue(Value1, Value2: ObjectValue): Boolean; forward;

function OrderedValues(Value1, Value2: ObjectValue): Boolean; forward;

{

The function:

}

function Range(Min, Max: ObjectValue): integer; forward;

{

is provided to enable the analyser to check the completeness of variant record parts, using the cardinality of the tag-type.

5.4 Block and Program Housekeeping

The object code generated for a Pascal program is assumed to be a set of code blocks, one for each source program block. Each code block is accumulated in a "code-space" which exists throughout the analysis of the corresponding source block, though in practice most implementations generate code for the current block only during analysis of the corresponding statement part.

To enable inter-block references (procedure and function calls), the analyser holds a variable CodeBody of generator-defined type BlockLabel within each procedure, function or program identifier entry. This variable is initialised by a call to the procedure FutureBlockLabel, and bound to the corresponding code block when the code space is opened.

The procedures OpenCodeSpace and CloseCodeSpace are responsible for maintaining the code space for a given code block and for filing its contents on the object program file.

}

procedure FutureBlockLabel(**var** L: BlockLabel); forward;

procedure OpenCodeSpace(**var** L: BlockLabel); forward;

procedure CloseCodeSpace; forward;

{

The program fragment:

```
        procedure Outer;
          procedure Inner;
             begin
                ...
             end;
          begin
          ...
          end ;
```

gives rise to the following series of interface calls:

```
    FutureBlockLabel(CodeBody for Outer)
    OpenCodeSpace(CodeBody for Outer)
    FutureBlockLabel(CodeBody for Inner)
    OpenCodeSpace(CodeBody for Inner)
    ...
    Code generation calls for Inner
    ...
    CloseCodeSpace
    ...
    Code generation calls for Outer
    ...
    Closecodespace
```

5.5 Operand Addressing

The code generation interface for variable access, expression evaluation, and assignment assumes a postfix code form (though the generating procedures called may transform this code thereafter). The generating calls represent operations on a hypothetical run-time stack of operand references and values.

Thus, variable access is realised by the following hypothetical operations:

}

procedure StackReference(Indirct: Boolean; Location: RuntimeAddress); forward,

procedure IndexedReference(PackedArray: Boolean; LowBound, HighBound: ObjectValue;
                                        Element: TypeRepresentation); forward;

procedure IndexedCAPReference(PackedSchema: Boolean;
                                            LowBoundAddress, HighBoundAddress:
                                            RuntimeAddress;
                                            BoundPairRepresentation, Component:
                                            TypeRepresentation); forward;

procedure VariantChecks(VarPart: TypEntry; FieldId: IdEntry); forward;

procedure FieldReference(Field: FieldOffset; TagField: Boolean); forward;

procedure PnterReference; forward;

procedure BufferReference(PackedFile, TextFile: Boolean;
                                        Element: TypeRepresentation); forward;

{

StackReference is the basic means of generating a reference to a variable, parameter or function result on the stack. Indirct is true for variable parameter references, false otherwise.

IndexedReference combines a reference to an array variable with the value of an index expression, to produce a reference to the element indexed. IndexedCAPReference does the same for conformant arrays, using the bound-pair whose addresses are supplied as additional parameters.

FieldReference converts a record variable reference to a reference to the field whose offset is specified. In the case of a variant field, however, the FieldReference operation is preceded by a call to VariantChecks which may generate a cascade of tag or selector checks to ensure that the variant containing the field is active.

PnterReference converts a pointer variable reference to a reference to the dynamic variable it points to, while BufferReference converts a file variable reference to a reference to the corresponding file buffer variable.

For example, given a variable declaration:

    var a: array [1..10, 1..20] of record b: ...; c: ... end;

a variable access of the form:

    a[i, j].c

would generate the following sequence of interface calls:

    StackReference(false, address for a)
    ...stack value of i....
    IndexedReference(false, objectvalue(1), objectvalue(10),
                                representation of array [1..20] of record...)
    ...stack value of j....
    IndexedReference(false, objectvalue(1), objectvalue(20),
                                representation of record...end)
    FieldReference(offset for c, false)

5.6 Operand Evaluation and Arithmetic

Primary operand values are placed on the stack either by converting a stacked reference, or by stacking an explicit literal value.

Thus variable values are placed on the stack by the following operations:

}

procedure DeReference(Representation: TypeRepresentation); forward;

procedure CAPDeReference(PackedSchema: Boolean;
                        LowBoundAddress, HighBoundAddress: RuntimeAddress;
                        BoundPairRepresentation, ComponentRepresentation:
                        TypeRepresentation); forward;

{

CAPDereference is used in the special case when the value of a conformant array parameter is to be assigned to another conformant array with the same schema.

Some variable values stacked in this way are subject to checking operations signalled by the following procedures:

}

procedure TailoredFactorCheck(Representation: TypeRepresentation); forward;

procedure UndefinedVariableCheck; forward;

{

TailoredFactorCheck is used to check that a dynamic record variable has not been 'tailored', i.e. created using the extended form of new. UndefinedVariableCheck is used to check that the variable value is not (wholly or partially) undefined.

Explicit literal values are stacked by the procedure:

}

procedure StackConstant(ConstValue: ObjectValue); forward;

{

Operand values on the stack may be modified or combined by a variety of operations to produce new operands. Integer arithmetic is effected by the following set of operations:

}

procedure IntegerFunction(WhichFunc: StdProcFuncs); forward;

procedure NegateAnInteger; forward;

procedure BinaryIntegerOperation(Operator: OpType); forward;

procedure OrdinalComparison(Operator: OpType); forward;

procedure RangeCheck(Min, Max: ObjectValue); forward;

{

IntegerFunction applies the standard functions, abs, sqr, add, succ, pred, ord, and chr, to the topmost operand on the stack (TOS). All ordinal types are assumed to use the same representation as integer. NegateInteger negates TOS, and BinaryIntegerOperation applies the operators +, -, *, div and mod to the two topmost operands (TOS-1) and (TOS).

Thus the integer expression -a+2*abs(b) would involve the following sequence of calls:

    StackReference(..., runtime address of a)
    Dereference(integer representation)
    NegateInteger
    StackConstant(objectvalue(2))
    StackReference(..., runtime address of b)
    Dereference(integer representation)
    IntegerFunction(absf)
    BinaryIntegerOperation(mul)
    BinaryIntegerOperation(plus)

OrdinalComparison applies the operators $=$, $<>$, $<$, $<=$, $>$ and $>=$ to (TOS-1) and (TOS) for all ordinal types.

In certain contexts, such as subrange variable assignment and parameter passing, an ordinal value on the stack is subject to an explicit range check signalled by the procedure RangeCheck. Note, however, that the range checks associated with array indexing, the function chr, and the implementation limits of integer arithmetic itself are implicit in the operations concerned and are not signalled explicitly.

Real arithmetic is implemented by a similar set of procedures, as follows:

}

procedure FloatInteger(StackPosition: StackTop); forward;

procedure RealFunction(WhichFunc: StdProcFuncs); forward;

procedure NegateAReal; forward;

procedure BinaryRealOperation(RealOperator: OpType); forward;

procedure RealComparison(Operator: OpType); forward;

{

The procedure FloatInteger signals the conversion of an integer value to the corresponding real value. Note, however, that it may apply either to the topmost or next-to-top operand, according to the parameter StackPosition.

Thus the real expression -1/x involves the following sequence of interface calls:

    StackConstant(objectvalue(1))
    StackReference(..., runtime address of x)
    Dereference(real representation)
    Floatinteger(NextToTop)
    BinaryRealOperation(rdiv)
    NegateReal

Boolean arithmetic is implemented by the following procedures:

}

procedure NegateABoolean; forward;

procedure BinaryBooleanOperation(Operator: OpType; FirstOperation: Boolean); forward;

procedure ExcludeConditions; forward;

{

The calls to BinaryBooleanOperation allow generation of either jump-out or full evaluation code. For each sequence of and's or or's compiled, an initial call to BinaryBooleanOperation, with First = true, is made between the first and second operands. Thus the expression:

(a = 0) or b or not c

involves the following interface call pattern:

```
...stack value of a...
StackConstant(objectvalue(0))
ScalarComparison(eqop)
BinaryBooleanOperation(true, orop)
...stack value of b...
BinaryBooleanOperation(false, orop)
...stack value of c...
NegateBoolean
BinaryBooleanOperation(false, orop)
```

In some contexts, however, such as Boolean assignments or Boolean comparisons, implementations which generate jumpout code for conditions must reduce a jumpout sequence to a simple Boolean value. The points to do so are signalled by an additional call to the procedure ExcludeConditions. Implementations which compute Boolean values throughout may ignore such calls.

Set arithmetic is provided by the following procedures:

}

procedure SingletonSet(SetRepresentation: TypeRepresentation); forward;

procedure RangeSet(SetRepresentation: TypeRepresentation); forward;

procedure BinarySetOperation(SetOperator: OpType); forward;

procedure SetComparison(SetOperator: OpType); forward;

procedure SetCheck(Min, Max: ObjectValue); forward;

{

Set constructors are implemented using the elementary SingletonSet and RangeSet operations, with calls to BinarySetOperation to combine the resultant components if necessary. Thus the constructor ['0', '2', '4'..'7'] involves the following sequence of interface calls:

```
StackConstant(objectvalue('0'))
SingletonSet(representation of set of char)     ....['0']
StackConstant(objectvalue('2'))
SingletonSet(representation of set of char)     ....['2']
BinarySetOperation(plus)                  ....['0', '2']
StackConstant(objectvalue('4'))
StackConstant(objectvalue('7'))
RangeSet(representation of set of char)     ....['4'..'7']
BinarySetOperation(plus)           ....['0', '2', '4'..'7']
```

A set value which is to be assigned to a set variable with a subrange base type is checked for assignment compatibility by the operation SetCheck.

The special comparisons required for pointer and string operands are implemented by the following additional procedures:

}
procedure PointerComparison(Operator: OpType); forward;
procedure StringComparison(Operator: OpType; Length: ObjectValue); forward;
{

5.7 Variable Assignment

An assignment is expressed as a single postfix operation which assumes the variable reference and expression value have already been stacked. Depending on whether the variable to be assigned is a tag field of a variant record this operation is expressed as a call to one of the following procedures:

}
procedure Assign(VarRep: TypeRepresentation); forward;
procedure AssignTag(SelectorRep: TypeRepresentation); forward;
{

In the case of Assign, the type representation parameter enables the generator to implement assignments to structured as well as simple variables. In the case of AssignTag, the parameter is assumed to contain information necessary to implement the checked selection and activation of the variant associated with the tag value.

5.8 With Statements

With statements are implemented by extending the reference interface described in 5.5 with the following procedures:

}
procedure OpenWith(WithBase: DispRange); forward;
procedure WithReference(WithBase: DispRange); forward;
procedure CloseWith; forward;
{

The operation OpenWith preserves the record variable reference currently on top of the stack, and associates it with the WithBase index supplied by the analyser. Subsequent WithReference operations which cite the same WithBase index recreate this record variable reference on the stack for use by a subsequent FieldReference operation. The operation CloseWith merely signals the point at which the record variable reference may be discarded.

Thus, given a declaration:

   var r: record a: integer; .... end

the statement:

with r do a := a + 1

involves the following sequence of interface calls:

```
StackReference(false, runtimeaddress of r)
OpenWith(n)
WithReference(n)
FieldReference(offset for a, false)
WithReference(n)
FieldReference(offset for a, false)
Dereference(integer representation)
StackConstant(objectvalue(1))
BinaryIntegerOperation(plus)
Assign(integer representation)
CloseWith
```

5.9 Standard Procedures

5.9.1 Standard input/output

All standard input/output operations are performed with respect to a file operand that is referenced explicitly or implicitly by the coresponding standard procedure parameter list. The procedures:

}

procedure SelectFile(FType: TypEntry); forward;

procedure DiscardFile; forward;

{

are used to preserve this reference and to discard it when analysis of the remaining i/o parameters is complete. SelectFile is provided with the TypEntry for the file operand, and assumes that (TOS) contains the file reference. To ensure this is so, the analyser inspects the standard procedure or function parameter list and automatically stacks a reference to the variables Input or Output if appropriate. Note, however, that in this case the StackReference-SelectFile sequence comes after the first variable or expression of a read or write statement has been stacked.

The procedures:

}

procedure FileOperation(Which: StdProcFuncs); forward;

procedure FileFunction(WhichFunc: StdProcFuncs); forward;

{

respectively implement the primitive operations get, put, reset, and rewrite, and the predicates eoln and eof. In the latter cases, FileFunction leaves the Boolean function result on the stack.

The procedures:

```
}
```
procedure ReadBuffer; forward;

procedure ReadNumeric(ReadMode: InputKind); forward;

procedure ReadLayout; forward;
```
{
```
are used to implement the standard procedures read and readln. The procedure Read-Numeric is used to read real or integer data from a text file. The procedure ReadBuffer is used for all other data and file types.

In the following examples the declarations:

> var   A: integer; B: real; C: char; F: text;

are assumed.

Thus:

> read(F, A);

generates the interface calls:

> StackReference(false, runtime address of F)
> SelectFile(TypEntry for text)
> StackReference(false, runtime address of A)
> ReadNumeric(IntKind)
> Assign(integer representation)
> DiscardFile

The procedure ReadNumeric receives a single parameter of type InputKind indicating whether the digit sequence on the text file is to be interpreted as a real or integer number. In either case, its effect is to stack the value read in addition to updating the buffer-variable accordingly.

The procedure ReadBuffer is used where no interpretive action is required. Thus:

> readln(C);

generates:

> StackReference(false, runtime address for C)
> StackReference(false, runtime address for Input)
> SelectFile(TypEntry for text)
> ReadBuffer
> Assign(char representation)
> ReadLayout
> DiscardFile

The standard procedures write, writeln, and page, are implemented by calls to:
```
}
```
procedure WriteBuffer; forward;

procedure WriteScalars(WriteMode: OutputKind; Format: FormatKind); forward;

procedure WriteString(ActualLength: ObjectValue; Format: FormatKind); forward;
procedure WriteLayout; forward;
{

where WriteScalars is chosen for integer, real, Boolean and formatted char values, Write-String for literal strings, and WriteBuffer for all other data types and file types. WriteLayout is called for both writeln and page, and uses the layout-character value on top of the stack to implement the appropriate formatting.

In the following example, the above declarations are assumed:

writeln('Answer = ', B: 12: 3);

generates:

StackConstant(objectvalue('Answer = '))
StackReference(for Output)
SelectFile(TypEntry for text)
WriteString(objectvalue(9), Default)
StackReference(false, runtime address of B)
DeReference(real representation)
StackConstant(objectvalue(12))
StackConstant(objectvalue(3))
WriteScalars(RealKind, Fixed)
StackConstant(objectvalue(LineFeed))
WriteLayout
DiscardFile

WriteString takes two parameters, the first being the character length of the string, and the second of type FormatKind, indicating formatting (if any) of the expression value.

5.9.2 Pack/Unpack.

The transfer procedures pack and unpack are implemented for both array and conformant array arguments by calls to:
}
procedure ArrayArrayOp(Which: StdProcFuncs;
                    UpLowBound, UpHighBound: ObjectValue;
                    UnpackedRep, PackedRep: TypeRepresentation;
                    PkLowBound, PkHighBound: ObjectValue); forward;
procedure ArrayCAPOp(Which: StdProcFuncs;
                    UpLowBound, UpHighBound: ObjectValue;
                    UnpackedRep, PackedRep: TypeRepresentation;
                    PkLowBoundAddress, PkHighBoundAddress:
                        RuntimeAddress); forward;
procedure CAPArrayOp(Which: StdProcFuncs;
                    UpLowBoundAddress, UpHighBoundAddress: RuntimeAddress;
                    BpRep, UnpackedRep, PackedRep: TypeRepresentation;
                    PkLowBound, PkHighBound: ObjectValue); forward;

procedure CAPCAPOp(Which: StdProcFuncs;
                          UpLowBoundAddress, UpHighBoundAddress: RuntimeAddress;
                          BpRep, UnpackedRep, PackedRep: TypeRepresentation;
                          PkLowBoundAddress, PkHighBoundAddress:
                          RuntimeAddress); forward;

{

The array bounds, or bound-pair-block addresses are supplied as parameters to indicate the number of array elements to be processed and to construct the appropriate range checks on the indexing expression. The first parameter indicates whether packing or unpacking is required.

In the following examples, the declarations:

  Type T = 1..10;

  procedure P(A: packed array [L1..U1: T] of char; B: array [L2..U2: T] of char);

  var C: packed array [T] of char; D: array [T] of char;

are assumed.

Then:

        pack(D, 1, C);

gives rise to the interface calls:

        StackReference(false, runtime address for D)
        StackConstant(objectvalue(1))
        StackReference(false, runtime address of C)
        ArrayArrayOp(packp, objectvalue(1), objectvalue(10),
                    char representation, char representation,
                    objectvalue(1), objectvalue(10))

and:

        Unpack(A, B, 1);

gives rise to the calls:

        StackReference(false, runtime address for A)
        StackReference(false, runtime address for B)
        StackConstant(objectvalue(1))
        CAPCAPOp(unpackp,
                    low bound address of B, high bound address of B,
                    CharRepresentation, CharRepresentation,
                    lowboundaddress of A, high bound address of A)

With the same context of stacked operands and index values, pack(B, 1, C) and unpack(C, 1, B) result in calls to CAPArrayOp since the unpacked-type in each case is a conformant array schema. Similarly, pack(D, 1, A) and unpack(A, D, 1) result in calls to ArrayCAPOp, since the unpacked-type in each case is an array-type.

5.9.3 New/Dispose

The dynamic storage procedures new and dispose are implemented by a sequence of calls to the procedures:

```
}
procedure HeapRequest(Requested: TypeRepresentation); forward;
procedure TailorRequest(SelectorRep, SelectedRep: TypeRepresentation); forward;
procedure HeapOperation(WhichPf: StdProcFuncs); forward;
{
```

made in a sequence of the form:

HeapRequest ... TailorRequest ... HeapOperation

where the TailorRequest calls are included only if case-constants are specified in the new or dispose parameter lists. The magnitude of the initial request is assumed to be embedded in the domain type representation which is passed as parameter to HeapRequest. The procedure TailorRequest takes two parameters: the first is the representation associated with the variant part containing the variant, and the second is the representation of the variant specified by the case-constant. It is assumed that in addition to storage requested, information can be extracted from these representations which allows the consistency checks between new and dispose to be applied. The appropriate allocation procedure is specified by the parameter to HeapOperation.

Assuming the definitions:

```
type   rec = record
                 f: integer;
                 case which: boolean of
                     false: ()
                     true: (sample: real)
             end;
   var   p: ^rec
```

then:

```
new(p, true);
```

gives rise to the sequence of calls:

```
StackReference(false, runtime address of p)
HeapRequest(representation for type rec)
TailorRequest(representation for variant part, representation for variant 'true')
HeapOperation(newp)
```

The sequence of request calls for dispose is identical but the first parameter is an expression and hence we have:

```
StackReference(false, runtime address of p)
DeReference(representation for ^p)
...
Calls as before
```

...
HeapOperation(disposep)

5.10 Control Statements

The code generated, whatever its form, is assumed to be for sequential execution. Each point that can be reached other than sequentially is represented at compile time by a record of type CodeLabel. These records are bound to points in the code by the procedures:

}

procedure NewCodeLabel(**var** L: CodeLabel); forward;

procedure FutureCodeLabel(**var** L: CodeLabel); forward;

procedure NextIsCodeLabel(**var** L: CodeLabel); forward;

{

NewCodeLabel is used for labels that are bound before they are referenced by any jump (i.e. backward jumps only). FutureCodeLabel and NextIsCodeLabel are used for labels that may be referenced before they are bound (i.e. forward jumps).

The jumps required by if, while and repeat statements are provided by the following operations:

}

procedure JumpOnFalse(**var** Destination: CodeLabel); forward;

procedure Jump(**var** Destination: CodeLabel); forward;

{

Thus the sequence of calls arising from a while statement:

> while c do s

would use two analyser-declared code labels (L1, L2, say) as follows:

> NewCodeLabel(L1)
> ... stack value of c ...
> FutureCodeLabel(L2)
> JumponFalse(L2)
> ... code for s ...
> Jump(L1)
> NextIsCodeLabel(L2)

The simple code label mechanism is not used for explicit statement labels declared and used in the Pascal program. Instead an analogous StatementLabel type is introduced to represent such labels, with the following operations available.

}

procedure FutureStatementLabel(**var** L: StatementLabel); forward;

procedure NextIsStatementLabel(**var** L: StatementLabel); forward;

procedure LabelJump(**var** Destination: StatementLabel; LabelLevel: DispRange); forward;

{

Implementations may or may not equivalence statement labels with code labels, depending on the nature of the object code to be generated.

Case statements require the following additional operations:

}

procedure OpenCase; forward;

procedure NextIsCase(CaseConst: ObjectValue); forward;

procedure CloseCase; forward;

{

Opencase is invoked immediately following evaluation of the case selector. Each label on a case limb is signalled by NextIsCase, and the final case limb is followed by a CloseCase operation. In addition a future code label is introduced to label the code after the entire case statement, and each case limb is followed by a jump to this label.

Thus a case statement of the form:

```
case x of
1: s1;
2, 4: s2;
   ...
end
```

involves an interface call sequence as follows:

```
...stack value of n...
FutureCodeLabel(aftercase)
OpenCase
NextIsCase(objectvalue(1))
...code for s1...
Jump(aftercase)
NextIsCase(objectvalue(2))
NextIsCase(objectvalue(4))
...code for s2...
Jump(aftercase)
   ...
Closecase
NextIsCodeLabel(aftercase)
```

For statements are handled by the following special operations:

}

procedure OpenFor(Increasing: Boolean; ControlMin, ControlMax: ObjectValue); forward;

procedure CloseFor; forward;

{

Assuming a declaration

```
var c: 1..10;
```

a statement of the form:

       for c := i to f do s

involves the following sequence of interface calls:

       StackReference(false, runtime address of c)
       ...stack value of i...
       ...stack value of f...
       Openfor(true, objectvalue(1), objectvalue(10))
       ...code for s...
       Closefor

5.11 Procedure and Function Calls

Procedure and function calls are implemented by calls to the interface procedures:

}

procedure StackActualBlock(**var** Body: BlockLabel); forward;

procedure StackFormalBlock(FAddress: RuntimeAddress); forward;

procedure CallBlock; forward;

procedure TakeResult(Representation: TypeRepresentation); forward;

{

made in a sequence:

   (StackActualBlock|StackFormalBlock)
   ... parameters ...
   CallBlock
   [TakeResult]

where the first call establishes the nature of the block called. For an actual block call, the parameter specifies the actual procedure or function entry point, but for a formal block call, the entry point is assumed to be embedded within the formal procedure or function parameter whose address is supplied by the parameter Faddress.

A function call transforms the stacked block reference into a result value whose representation is supplied to the generator by a call to procedure TakeResult.   Thus assuming:

   function G(I: integer): integer;

the call:

   G(X)

gives rise to the following interface calls:

   StackActualBlock(BlockLabel for G)

   ...

   parameters

   ...

   CallBlock
   TakeResult(integer representation)

Variable, value and procedural parameters are passed by calls to:
}
procedure OpenParameterList(ClassOfCall: IdClass); forward;
procedure PassBlock; forward;
procedure PassReference(RefStatus: RefSecurity); forward;
procedure PassValue(RepRequired: TypeRepresentation); forward;
procedure CloseParameterList; forward;
{
made in a sequence:

```
OpenParameterList
... PassReference|PassValue|PassBlock ...
CloseParameterList
```

OpenParameterList and CloseParameterList are called even for parameterless procedures or functions. PassReference takes a single parameter which indicates whether the actual variable parameter is potentially insecure. This enables the generation of runtime checks associated with the preservation of such 'extended' references.

Assuming the program fragments:

```
function F(I: integer): integer;

procedure G(function H(X: integer): integer);
   var Y, Z: integer;
   begin
      ...
      Z := H(Y);
      ...
   end;
```

A call to G passing the function F as actual parameter would result in:

```
StackActualBlock(BlockLabel for G)
OpenParameterList(proc)
StackActualBlock(BlockLabel for F)
PassBlock
CloseParameterList
CallBlock
```

and the call H(Y) inside the body of G results in the calls:

```
StackFormalBlock(runtime address of parameter H)
OpenParameterList(Func)
StackReference(false, runtime address for Y)
DeReference(integer representation)
Passvalue
CloseParameterList
CallBlock
```

TakeResult(IntegerRepresentation)

The conformant array parameter mechanism is implemented by calls to:

}

procedure StartBoundPairs; forward;

procedure PassArrayBoundPair(ActualLowBound, ActualHighBound, SchemaLowBound,
SchemaHighBound:
ObjectValue;
Element: TypeRepresentation;
ArrayPacked: Boolean); forward;

procedure PassCAPBoundPair(LowBoundAddress, HighBoundAddress: RuntimeAddress;
SchemaLowBound, SchemaHighBound: ObjectValue;
BoundPairRep: TypeRepresentation); forward;

{

made in a sequence:

StartBoundPairs ... PassArrayBoundPair|PassCAPBoundPair ...

StartBoundPairs is simply a trigger that informs the generator that series of array bounds is about to be passed. The bounds themselves are passed within the parameter lists of the procedures PassArrayBoundPairs and PassCAPBoundPairs. A reference to each actual array parameter is then passed, but for those passed by value, a call to procedure:

}

procedure MakeAuxiliary(RepRequired: TypeRepresentation); forward;

{

is inserted to allow a copy of the actual array to be made at the point of call. (For an alternative scheme of creating the copy, see Section 5.2.3)

Assuming the program fragment:

var a, b: array[1..10, -10..10] of integer;

procedure P(x, y: array [l1..u1: integer; l2..u2: integer] of integer);

a call P(a, b) generates the sequence:

StackActualBlock(entry BlockLabel for P)
OpenParameterList(proc)
StartBoundPairs
PassArrayBoundPair(.. array bounds 1 and 10 ..)
PassArrayBoundPair(.. array bounds -10 and 10 ..)
StackReference(false, runtime address of a)
DeReference(representation of array-type of a)
MakeAuxiliary(representation of array-type of a)
PassReference(secure)
StackReference(false, runtime address of b)
DeReference(representation of array-type of b)
MakeAuxiliary(representation of array-type of b)
PassReference(secure)

    CloseParameterList
    CallBlock

Prelude and postlude code supporting block entry and exit is generated by calls to:

}

procedure EnterProgram(ProgId: IdEntry; SourceLine: Scalar); forward;

procedure EnterPfBody(Pfid: IdEntry; SourceLine: Scalar); forward;

procedure LeaveProcedure; forward;

procedure LeaveFunction(Result: RuntimeAddress;
                              Representation: TypeRepresentation); forward;

procedure LeaveProgram; forward;

{

In the case of the block-entry procedures, unrestricted access is granted to the table entry for the block-identifier, to permit the generation of optimal entry-code sequences.

5.12 Program Parameters

The interface contains provision for the exchange of information between the object program and its environment by means of the calls:

}

procedure OpenProgParameterList; forward;

procedure AcceptProgParameter(ParamId: IdEntry); forward;

procedure ReturnProgParameter(ParamId: IdEntry); forward;

procedure CloseProgParameterList; forward;

{

In general, calls to AcceptProgParameter and ReturnProgParameter can be made for any type declared in the program, but in practice, they will most likely be used to construct a mapping between file parameters and the corresponding external physical files. This correspondence is sometimes established by using the file variable identifier spelling, and consequently the procedures are granted direct access to the identifier table entry for each program parameter.

Special processing is required for the variables Input and Output, whose appearance in the program parameter list also constitutes their point of declaration. For these variables, the analyser automatically makes calls to the i/o procedures to effect a reset for Input and a rewrite for Output.

Assuming the program fragments:

    program P(input, output, data);

      ...

    var data: file of integer;

      ...

    begin

the sequence of calls at entry to the program block is:

InitialiseVariables
OpenProgParameterList
AcceptProgParameter(IdEntry for input)
StackReference(false, runtime address for input)
SelectFile(TextType)
FileOperation(Resetp)
DiscardFile
AcceptProgParameter(IdEntry for output)
StackReference(false, runtime address for output)
SelectFile(TextType)
FileOperation(Rewritep)
DiscardFile
AcceptProgParameter(IdEntry for data)
CloseProgParameterList

with a corresponding sequence of calls prior to exit from the block.

5.13 Generator initialisation and finalisation

The procedure InitCodeGeneration is called before any other generation interface procedure
to initialise all variables and facilities made available by the generation interface. Similarly
the procedure EndCodeGeneration is called after all use of the interface is complete.
}
procedure InitCodeGeneration; forward;

procedure EndCodeGeneration; forward;

{

CHAPTER 6

Postmortem Diagnostics

In principle, the production of source-related diagnostics entails the construction of a "data map" containing a description of all types, enumeration constants, variables, parameters, and blocks declared in the program, together with a "code map" that allows a source-program line number to be deduced from an object program address.

The data map is constructed by procedure Filescope which systematically traverses the identifier and type sub-tables described in Chapter 9, making each entry available to the procedures FileId and FileType respectively. The linkages that exist between and within these tables may be preserved by recasting them in terms of unique serial numbers assigned to each data-item to be filed. Serial numbers are allocated in a monotonically increasing sequence by procedures ISerialise and TSerialise to each new identifier or type table entry.

The standard types are serialised and filed by procedure FileStdTypes during the initialisation phase of the compiler.

The code map is constructed by making the source program line number available to the code generator by means of a call to procedure Flowpoint immediately prior to analysis of each statement in a block.

The underlying mechanisms involved in creating the data map and the code map are described in Chapter 27.
}

```
procedure ISerialise(Id: IdEntry);
   begin
     if Id <> nil
     then begin Id^.Serial := NextSerial; NextSerial := NextSerial + 1 end
   end { iserialise };
procedure TSerialise(Typ: TypEntry);
   begin
     if Typ <> nil
     then begin Typ^.Serial := NextSerial; NextSerial := NextSerial + 1 end
   end { tserialise };
procedure FileAType(TheType: TypEntry); forward;
procedure FileId(Id, NextId: IdEntry); forward;
```

```
procedure FileScope(BlockId: IdEntry);
  var PreviousVar: IdEntry; ThisType: TypEntry;
  procedure FileLocalVars(Entry: IdEntry);
    begin
      if Entry <> nil
      then with Entry^ do
              begin
                FileLocalVars(RightLink);
                if Klass = Vars
                then begin FileId(Entry, PreviousVar); PreviousVar := Entry end;
                FileLocalVars(LeftLink)
              end
    end { filelocalvars };
  begin { filescope }
    with Display[BlockLevel] do
      begin { file types }
        ThisType := TypeChain;
        while ThisType <> nil do
          begin FileAType(ThisType); ThisType := ThisType^.Next end;

        { file local variables, including formal parameters }

        PreviousVar := nil; FileLocalVars(Locals);

        { file block }

        FileId(BlockId, PreviousVar)
      end
  end { filescope };
procedure FileStdTypes;
  { ... which have not yet been serialised }
  begin
    NextSerial := NilSerial + 1; TSerialise(IntType); FileAType(IntType);
    TSerialise(RealType); FileAType(RealType); TSerialise(CharType);
    FileAType(CharType);

    { serialise boolean constants }

    with BoolType^ do
      begin ISerialise(FirstConst); ISerialise(FirstConst^.SuccId) end;
    TSerialise(BoolType); FileAType(BoolType); TSerialise(TextType);
    FileAType(TextType)
  end { filestdtypes };
procedure FlowPoint(SourceLine: Scalar); forward;

procedure InitDiagnostics; forward;

procedure EndDiagnostics; forward;
```

{

CHAPTER 7

Lexical Analysis

Lexical analysis is carried out by the procedure NextSymbol. When called, NextSymbol scans the next language symbol in the source stream and returns a representation of it in the following global variables:

Symbol   in all cases Symbol represents the symbol scanned, as defined by the type SymbolType.

Operator   when Symbol = AddOp, MulOp or RelOp, Operator represents the particular operator scanned, as defined by the type OpType.

Spelling   when Symbol = Ident, the record variable Spelling holds the characters of the identifier scanned.

Constant   when Symbol = IntConst, RealConst, CharConst or StringConst, Constant holds a representation of the constant scanned.

StartofSymbol to facilitate error reporting the position of the initial character of the symbol scanned is left in the global variable StartofSymbol.

To initialise the lexical analysis process, and make the first symbol of the source program available, the procedure InitSymbol must be called before any call to NextSymbol.

7.1 Reserved word symbols

The lexical analyser distinguishes between identifiers and reserved word symbols by table look-up on the array WordSymbol. Entries in WordSymbol are sorted by word length, with an extra slot at the end of each sequence to allow fast look-up with guaranteed success. The procedure InitWords initialises the WordSymbol array and the auxiliary indexing array LastofLength.

}

```
procedure InitWords;
    const Irrelevant = NotOp;
    var LastEntered: 0..NoWords;
    procedure EnterWord(Name: AlfaHead; SValue: SymbolType; OValue: OpType);
        begin
            LastEntered := LastEntered + 1;
            with WordSymbol[LastEntered] do
                begin Spelling := Name; SymbolValue := SValue; OpValue := OValue end
        end { enterword };
```

55

```
begin { initwords }
  LastEntered := 0;
  LastOfLength[0] := LastEntered;
  EnterWord('               ', Ident, Irrelevant);
  LastOfLength[1] := LastEntered;
  EnterWord('IF             ', IfSy, Irrelevant);
  EnterWord('DO             ', DoSy, Irrelevant);
  EnterWord('OF             ', OfSy, Irrelevant);
  EnterWord('TO             ', ToSy, Plus);
  EnterWord('IN             ', RelOp, InOp);
  EnterWord('OR             ', AddOp, OrOp);
  EnterWord('               ', Ident, Irrelevant);
  LastOfLength[2] := LastEntered;
  EnterWord('END            ', EndSy, Irrelevant);
  EnterWord('FOR            ', ForSy, Irrelevant);
  EnterWord('VAR            ', VarSy, Irrelevant);
  EnterWord('DIV            ', MulOp, Idiv);
  EnterWord('MOD            ', MulOp, Imod);
  EnterWord('SET            ', SetSy, Irrelevant);
  EnterWord('AND            ', MulOp, AndOp);
  EnterWord('NOT            ', NotSy, Irrelevant);
  EnterWord('NIL            ', NilSy, Irrelevant);
  EnterWord('               ', Ident, Irrelevant);
  LastOfLength[3] := LastEntered;
  EnterWord('THEN           ', ThenSy, Irrelevant);
  EnterWord('ELSE           ', ElseSy, Irrelevant);
  EnterWord('WITH           ', WithSy, Irrelevant);
  EnterWord('GOTO           ', GotoSy, Irrelevant);
  EnterWord('CASE           ', CaseSy, Irrelevant);
  EnterWord('TYPE           ', TypeSy, Irrelevant);
  EnterWord('FILE           ', FileSy, Irrelevant);
  EnterWord('               ', Ident, Irrelevant);
  LastOfLength[4] := LastEntered;
  EnterWord('BEGIN          ', BeginSy, Irrelevant);
  EnterWord('UNTIL          ', UntilSy, Irrelevant);
  EnterWord('WHILE          ', WhileSy, Irrelevant);
  EnterWord('ARRAY          ', ArraySy, Irrelevant);
  EnterWord('CONST          ', ConstSy, Irrelevant);
  EnterWord('LABEL          ', LabelSy, Irrelevant);
  EnterWord('               ', Ident, Irrelevant);
  LastOfLength[5] := LastEntered;
  EnterWord('REPEAT         ', RepeatSy, Irrelevant);
  EnterWord('RECORD         ', RecordSy, Irrelevant);
  EnterWord('DOWNTO         ', ToSy, Minus);
  EnterWord('PACKED         ', PackedSy, Irrelevant);
  EnterWord('               ', Ident, Irrelevant);
  LastOfLength[6] := LastEntered;
  EnterWord('PROGRAM        ', ProgramSy, Irrelevant);
  EnterWord('               ', Ident, Irrelevant);
  LastOfLength[7] := LastEntered;
```

```
      EnterWord('FUNCTION      ', FuncSy, Irrelevant);
      EnterWord('            ', Ident, Irrelevant);
      LastOfLength[8] := LastEntered;
      EnterWord('PROCEDURE     ', ProcSy, Irrelevant);
      EnterWord('            ', Ident, Irrelevant);
      LastOfLength[9] := LastEntered;
      EnterWord('            ', Ident, Irrelevant);
      LastOfLength[10] := LastEntered;
      EnterWord('            ', Ident, Irrelevant);
      LastOfLength[11] := LastEntered;
      EnterWord('            ', Ident, Irrelevant);
      LastOfLength[12] := LastEntered
   end { initwords };
{
```

7.2 Representation of identifier spellings.

The analyser must accept identifiers of any length, treating all characters as significant. It does so by means of the type Alfa, holding up to twelve initial alphanumerics in the field Head of of each spelling, and appending the remainder in chained "chunks" of up to four characters each. All characters of an identifier are thus retained and regarded as significant.

The semantic analyser stores and compares the identifier spellings made available in this form. In principle identifier table searching requires functions of the form:

```
        function OrderedAlfa(a1, a2: alfa): Boolean;

        function SameAlfa(a1, a2: alfa): Boolean;
```

but because fast table searching is crucial the analyser is assumed to do direct comparisons of alfa heads, using < or >, and to call a function:

```
        function OrderedTails(a1, a2: alfa): Boolean;
```

only if the heads are identical. With this optimisation, the introduction of arbitrary length identifiers has no observable effect on compilation speed.

To enable recovery of heap storage used by identifier tails a procedure DisposeAlfa is provided, to be called for any alfa that is no longer required.

Identifier spellings that are not retained by the analyser must be disposed automatically. To this end the analyser is required to "copy" each spelling to be retained using the procedure CopySpelling. A spelling not copied in this way is disposed automatically by the next call to NextSymbol.

In some cases it is necessary for the analyser to reset the global variable Spelling, either to a spelling previously copied or to a synthetic spelling supplied as a string parameter. Procedures RestoreSpelling and MakeSpelling enable this to be done. The function AlfaLength is used to generate the NameFile for Postmortem generation.

}

```pascal
function OrderedTails(Tail1, Tail2: AlfaEntry): Boolean;
  begin
    if (Tail1 <> nil) and (Tail2 <> nil)
    then if Tail1^.Chunk < Tail2^.Chunk
        then OrderedTails := true
        else if Tail1^.Chunk > Tail2^.Chunk
            then OrderedTails := false
            else OrderedTails := OrderedTails(Tail1^.NextChunk, Tail2^.NextChunk)
    else OrderedTails := (Tail2 <> nil)
  end{ orderedtails };

function SameAlfa(Name1, Name2: Alfa): Boolean;
  var Equal: Boolean; Tail1, Tail2: AlfaEntry;
  begin
    Equal := false;
    if Name1.Head = Name2.Head
    then if (Name1.Tail <> nil) and (Name2.Tail <> nil)
        then begin
                Tail1 := Name1.Tail; Tail2 := Name2.Tail;
                while (Tail1^.Chunk = Tail2^.Chunk) and
                    (Tail1^.NextChunk <> nil) and
                    (Tail2^.NextChunk <> nil) do
                  begin Tail1 := Tail1^.NextChunk; Tail2 := Tail2^.NextChunk end;
                if (Tail1^.Chunk = Tail2^.Chunk) and (Tail1^.NextChunk = nil) and
                (Tail2^.NextChunk = nil)
                then Equal := true
            end
        else if (Name1.Tail = nil) and (Name2.Tail = nil) then Equal := true;
    SameAlfa := Equal
  end { samealfa };

function AlfaLength(Name: Alfa): Scalar;
  var Length: Scalar; Index: 1..AlfaSize; Trailer: AlfaEntry;
  procedure Count(c: char);
    begin
      if c <> ' ' then Length := Length + 1
    end { count };
  begin
    Length := 0;
    for Index := 1 to AlfaSize do Count(Name.Head[Index]);
    Trailer := Name.Tail;
    while Trailer <> nil do
      begin
        for Index := 1 to ChunkLength do Count(Trailer^.Chunk[Index]);
        Trailer := Trailer^.NextChunk
      end;
    AlfaLength := Length
  end { alfalength };
```

```
procedure DisposeAlfa(LongIdent: Alfa);
   var ThisEntry, NextEntry: AlfaEntry;
   begin
      NextEntry := LongIdent.Tail;
      while NextEntry <> nil do
         begin
            ThisEntry := NextEntry; NextEntry := ThisEntry^.NextChunk;
            dispose(ThisEntry)
         end
   end { disposealfa };
procedure DisposeSpelling;
   begin
      DisposeAlfa(Spelling); Spelling.Tail := nil; TailToBeDisposed := false
   end { disposespelling };
procedure CopySpelling(var Copy: Alfa);
   begin Copy := Spelling; TailToBeDisposed := false end;
procedure RestoreSpelling(Copy: Alfa);
   begin
      if TailToBeDisposed then DisposeSpelling;
      Spelling := Copy; TailToBeDisposed := (Spelling.Tail <> nil)
   end { restorespelling };
procedure MakeSpelling(Header: AlfaHead);
   begin
      if TailToBeDisposed then DisposeSpelling;
      Spelling.Head := Header; Spelling.Tail := nil
   end { makespelling };
{
```

7.3 The lexical analyser

The lexical analyser NextSymbol is a deterministic acceptor which determines its progress from the next available source character, with the following qualifications:

1.   The possibility of symbols ".." or ".)" immediately following an integer constant requires 2-character lookahead for their detection. In such cases the global flag PrecedingPeriod is set true to indicate to the subsequent call of NextSymbol that the period has already been scanned; at all other times PrecedingPeriod is false.

2.   Reserved word symbols are distinguished from identifiers of similar length by use of the WordSymbol array described in 7.1.

3.   The object value corresponding to an integer, real, character or string constant is obtained by collecting the source character sequence involved in a standard form and passing this to the generator procedure Evaluate.

```
}
```

```
procedure NextSymbol;
  label 9;
  var k: 0..AlfaSize; L: 1..NoWords; StillInteger, Negative: Boolean;
      LastWasQ, StringEnd: Boolean; LastEntry, NewEntry: AlfaEntry;
  function UpperCase(c: char): char;
    begin UpperCase := chr(ord(c) - ord('a') + ord('A')) end;
  procedure CopyChar(c: char);
    begin
      with Constant do
        begin Length := Length + 1; String[Length] := c end
    end { copychar };
  procedure DigitSequence;
    begin
      if Ch in Digits
      then repeat CopyChar(Ch); NextCh until not (Ch in Digits)
      else begin Error(1, Source.Position); CopyChar('0') end
    end { digitsequence };
  procedure SkipComment;
    begin
      NextCh;
      repeat
        while (Ch <> '*') and (Ch <> '}') do NextCh;
        if Ch = '*' then NextCh
      until (Ch = ')') or (Ch = '}');
      NextCh
    end { skipcomment };
  begin { nextsymbol }
    if TailToBeDisposed then DisposeSpelling;
    9:
      while Ch = ' ' do NextCh;
    StartOfSymbol := Source.Position;
    if Ch in SymbolStarters
    then case Ch of
            { analysis of special symbols other than word symbols }
            '+' :
              begin Symbol := AddOp; Operator := Plus; NextCh end;
            '-' :
              begin Symbol := AddOp; Operator := Minus; NextCh end;
            '*' :
              begin Symbol := MulOp; Operator := Mul; NextCh end;
            '/' :
              begin Symbol := MulOp; Operator := Rdiv; NextCh end;
            '=' :
              begin Symbol := RelOp; Operator := EqOp; NextCh end;
```

```
'<' :
  begin
    NextCh; Symbol := RelOp;
    if Ch = '='
    then begin Operator := LeOp; NextCh end
    else if Ch = '>'
         then begin Operator := NeOp; NextCh end
         else Operator := LtOp
  end;
'>' :
  begin
    NextCh; Symbol := RelOp;
    if Ch = '='
    then begin Operator := GeOp; NextCh end
    else Operator := GtOp
  end;
'(' :
  begin
    NextCh;
    if Ch = '.'
    then begin Symbol := LeftBracket; NextCh end
    else if Ch = '*'
         then begin SkipComment; goto 9 end
         else Symbol := LeftParent
  end;
')' :
  begin
    if PrecedingPeriod
    then begin Symbol := RightBracket; PrecedingPeriod := false end
    else Symbol := RightParent;
    NextCh
  end;
'[' :
  begin Symbol := LeftBracket; NextCh end;
']' :
  begin Symbol := RightBracket; NextCh end;
'.' :
  begin
    if PrecedingPeriod then PrecedingPeriod := false else NextCh;
    if Ch = '.'
    then begin Symbol := Thru; NextCh end
    else if Ch = ')'
         then begin Symbol := RightBracket; NextCh end
         else Symbol := Period
  end;
',' :
  begin Symbol := Comma; NextCh end;
':' :
  begin
    NextCh;
```

```
            if Ch = '='
            then begin Symbol := Becomes; NextCh end
            else Symbol := Colon
          end;
    ';' :
        begin Symbol := Semicolon; NextCh end;
    '@', '^' :
        begin Symbol := Arrow; NextCh end;
    '{' :
        begin SkipComment; goto 9 end;
    { analysis of word symbols and identifiers }
    'A', 'B', 'C', 'D', 'E', 'F', 'G', 'H', 'I', 'J', 'K', 'L', 'M', 'N', 'O',
    'P', 'Q', 'R', 'S', 'T', 'U', 'V', 'W', 'X', 'Y', 'Z', 'a', 'b', 'c', 'd',
    'e', 'f', 'g', 'h', 'i', 'j', 'k', 'l', 'm', 'n', 'o', 'p', 'q', 'r', 's',
    't', 'u', 'v', 'w', 'x', 'y', 'z' :
        begin
          k := 0; Spelling.Head := '               ';
          repeat
            k := k + 1;
            if Ch in LowerCaseLetters
            then Spelling.Head[k] := UpperCase(Ch) else Spelling.Head[k] := Ch;
            NextCh
          until (k = AlfaSize) or not (Ch in LettersAndDigits);
          if Ch in LettersAndDigits
          then begin
                  LastEntry := nil;
                  repeat
                    k := 0; new(NewEntry); NewEntry^.Chunk := '      ';
                    repeat
                      if Ch in LowerCaseLetters then Ch := UpperCase(Ch);
                      k := k + 1; NewEntry^.Chunk[k] := Ch; NextCh
                    until (k = ChunkLength) or not (Ch in LettersAndDigits);
                    if LastEntry = nil
                    then Spelling.Tail := NewEntry
                    else LastEntry^.NextChunk := NewEntry;
                    LastEntry := NewEntry
                  until not (Ch in LettersAndDigits);
                  LastEntry^.NextChunk := nil; TailToBeDisposed := true;
                  Symbol := Ident
              end
          else begin
                  Spelling.Tail := nil;
                  WordSymbol[LastOfLength[k]].Spelling := Spelling.Head;
                  L := LastOfLength[k - 1] + 1;
                  while WordSymbol[L].Spelling <> Spelling.Head do L := L + 1;
                  with WordSymbol[L] do
                    begin
                      Symbol := SymbolValue;
```

```
                    if Symbol in [MulOp, AddOp, RelOp, ToSy]
                    then Operator := OpValue
                end
            end
    end;
{ analysis of integer and real constants      }
'0', '1', '2', '3', '4', '5', '6', '7', '8', '9' :
    begin
        StillInteger := true; Constant.Length := 0;
        while Ch = '0' do NextCh;
        if Ch in ['1'..'9'] then DigitSequence else CopyChar('0');
        if Ch = '.'
        then begin
                NextCh;
                { if '.' is followed by a ')' or a second '.' then reset flag
                  and leave the '.' or ')' for the next call to nextsymbol }
                if (Ch = ')') or (Ch = '.')
                then PrecedingPeriod := true
                else begin
                        CopyChar('.'); StillInteger := false; DigitSequence
                    end
            end;
        if (Ch = 'e') or (Ch = 'E')
        then begin
                CopyChar('E'); StillInteger := false; NextCh;
                Negative := (Ch = '-');
                if Negative or (Ch = '+') then NextCh;
                if Negative then CopyChar('-') else CopyChar('+');
                DigitSequence
            end;
        if StillInteger
        then begin Symbol := IntConst; Constant.Kind := IntValue end
        else begin Symbol := RealConst; Constant.Kind := RealValue end;
        Evaluate(Constant);
        if (Ch in Letters) then Error(4, Source.Position)
    end;
{ analysis of a character string  }
' ' ' ' :
    begin
        LastWasQ := false; StringEnd := false; Constant.Length := 0; NextCh;
        repeat
            if LineEnded
            then begin Error(2, Source.Position); StringEnd := true end
            else if (Ch <> ' ' ' ') or LastWasQ
                then begin CopyChar(Ch); LastWasQ := false; NextCh end
                else begin
                        LastWasQ := true; NextCh; StringEnd := Ch <> ' ' ' '
                    end
```

```
                    until StringEnd;
                    with Constant do
                       if Length <= 1
                       then begin
                               if Length = 0 then Error(3, Source.Position);
                               Kind := CharValue; Symbol := CharConst
                            end
                       else begin Kind := StringValue; Symbol := StringConst end;
                       Evaluate(Constant)
                    end
             end
      else { deal with other (illegal) symbol }
          begin Symbol := OtherSy; NextCh end
   end { nextsymbol };
{
```

7.4 Lexical initialisation

The procedure InitSymbol, which is called before any other lexical utility, initialises the
reserved word table, the variables PrecedingPeriod and TailToBeDisposed, and the "constant" character sets used by NextSymbol and then calls NextSymbol to make the first symbol available to the syntax analyser.

}

```
procedure InitSymbol;
   begin
      InitWords; PrecedingPeriod := false; TailToBeDisposed := false;
      LowerCaseLetters :=
         ['a', 'b', 'c', 'd', 'e', 'f', 'g', 'h', 'i', 'j', 'k', 'l', 'm', 'n', 'o', 'p',
          'q', 'r', 's', 't', 'u', 'v', 'w', 'x', 'y', 'z'];
      Letters :=
         ['A', 'B', 'C', 'D', 'E', 'F', 'G', 'H', 'I', 'J', 'K', 'L', 'M', 'N', 'O', 'P',
          'Q', 'R', 'S', 'T', 'U', 'V', 'W', 'X', 'Y', 'Z']
         + LowerCaseLetters;
      Digits := ['0'..'9']; LettersAndDigits := Letters + Digits;
      SymbolStarters :=
         ['+', '-', '*', '/', '=', '<', '>', '(', ')', '[', ']', '.', ',', ':', ';', '^',
          '@']
         + Letters + Digits + [''''] + ['{'];
      NextSymbol
   end { initsymbol };
```

{

CHAPTER 8

Syntax Analysis
and
Syntax Error Recovery

8.1 Syntax analysis.

Syntax analysis is implemented as a set of recursive descent procedures based on syntax rules given in the ISO definition. The order, names, and nesting of the procedures is as follows:

Programme
  ProgramHeading
  Block
    LabelDeclarationPart
    Inconstant
    ConstDefinitionPart
    TypeDenoter
      OrdinalType
        EnumeratedType
        SubrangeType
      StructuredType
        ArrayType
        RecordType
          FieldList
        SetType
        FileType
      PointerType
    TypeDefinitionPart
    VarDeclarationPart
    PfDeclaration
      PfHeading
        FormalParameterList
    Selector
    Variable
    Call
    Expression
      SimpleExpression

        Term
          Factor
     BooleanExpression
     Statement
       Assignment
       GotoStatement
       CompoundStatement
       IfStatement
       CaseStatement
       WhileStatement
       RepeatStatement
       ForStatement
       WithStatement
     StatementSequence
     StatementPart

The procedure Selector implements the analysis of the syntax category variable (as does the procedure Variable which follows it) but assumes that the initial variable identifier has been checked and accepted before Selector is called.

The procedure Call is introduced to implement the analysis of the construct [actual-parameter-list] as it appears in function-designator and procedure-statement. It does so both for program-defined procedures and functions, and for the irregular parameter lists allowed for standard procedures and functions.

The syntax analysers are written on the assumption that the next syntactic goal can always be selected by inspection of (at most) the next incoming symbol (i.e. that the underlying grammar is LL(1)). This is not so at the following points in the syntax of Pascal:

1.   A statement beginning with an identifier may be either an assignment or a procedure call.

2.   A factor beginning with an identifier may be either a variable, a constant or a function call.

3.   A type beginning with an identifier may be either a named type already declared or a subrange whose lower bound is a constant identifier.

In all cases to resolve the choice on a purely syntactic basis would require a look ahead of a further symbol. However if parallel semantic analysis is used these choices can be resolved without further lookahead, by inspection of the current semantic attributes of the identifier involved. For this reason syntactic resolution of these choices is not attempted.

A similar problem arises with the actual parameter lists of the standard procedures and functions of Pascal which are analysed by special purpose syntax routines. These are again selected by a semantic rather than syntactic test.

The syntax of Pascal is also not LL(1) in variant records, where the syntax is effectively:

    "case" [identifier ":"] identifier "of" ...

In this case semantic resolution is not possible, and an ad-hoc lookahead technique is used.

8.2 Syntactic error recovery.

Recovery in the syntax analysis process following the discovery of a syntax error is incorporated into the syntax procedures on the following basis:

1. Each procedure when called is passed an actual parameter which is a set of symbols forming the (right) context of the string which it should scan. This context normally includes all symbols which may legitimately follow the string to be scanned, and such additional symbols as a superior (calling) procedure may wish to handle in the event of error recovery.

2. When entered the procedure may ensure that the current symbol is an acceptable starter for the string to be scanned, and if not scan forward until such a symbol is found (subject to 4. below).

3. When calling a subsidiary syntax procedure, the procedure passes on as context its own context plus those symbols if any which it may determine as right context for the substring to be scanned.

4. To recover from a syntax error the procedure may scan over (skip) any symbol provided it is not contained in the context passed to it.

5. On exit, the syntax procedure ensures that the current symbol is contained in the context passed to it, flagging a terminal error and skipping if this is not initially the case.

In practice this general recovery strategy may be omitted from those syntax procedures which are only used as an alternative or partial subpath of a superior procedure which inevitably enforces recovery.

8.3 Syntax utilities.

The following procedures enable the analysis and recovery strategies outlined above to be expressed neatly in the the analyser itself.

They also improve the quality of syntax error reporting by suppressing vague ¨unexpected symbol¨ messages whenever a more precise subsequent diagnosis is made available, using the global variables Recovering, SymbolsSkipped, and ErrorReported to do so.

Most syntax errors are reported using a code derived from the expected symbol, by the formula ord(expected symbol) + 10. Thus the codes used are interpreted as follows:

10. An identifier symbol was expected.
11. An integer-constant was expected.
...
57. A ¨program¨ symbol was expected.
58. Other symbols were expected.

In practice only a subset of these can be generated by the Pascal syntax analyser as some symbols are never mandatory.

The syntax analyser makes use of several ¨constant¨ sets of symbols during analysis. The variables used to hold these sets are initialised by the procedure InitSyntax, which must be called before syntax analysis is invoked.

```
}
function Missing(Symbol: SymbolType): integer;
   begin Missing := ord(Symbol) + 10 end;
procedure AcceptSymbol;
   begin
     if Recovering
     then begin
          if not ErrorReported
          then Error(Missing(OtherSy) + ord(SymbolsSkipped), StartOfSymbol);
          Recovering := false
        end;
     NextSymbol
   end { acceptsymbol };
procedure Accept(SymbolExpected: SymbolType);
   begin
     if Symbol = SymbolExpected
     then AcceptSymbol
     else begin
          Error(Missing(SymbolExpected), StartOfSymbol); ErrorReported := true
        end
   end { accept };
procedure AcceptEquals;
   begin
     if (Symbol = RelOp) and (Operator = EqOp)
     then AcceptSymbol else Error(60, StartOfSymbol)
   end { acceptequals };
procedure RecoverAt(RelevantSymbols: SetOfSymbols);
   begin
     if not Recovering
     then begin
          StartError(StartOfSymbol); Recovering := true; ErrorReported := false;
          SymbolsSkipped := not (Symbol in RelevantSymbols)
        end;
     while not (Symbol in RelevantSymbols) do NextSymbol
   end { recoverat };
procedure CheckContext(ContextExpected: SetOfSymbols);
   begin
     if not (Symbol in ContextExpected) then RecoverAt(ContextExpected)
   end { checkcontext };
procedure CheckNextOrContext(SymbolsExpected, DefaultContext: SetOfSymbols);
   begin
     if not (Symbol in SymbolsExpected)
     then RecoverAt(SymbolsExpected + DefaultContext)
   end { checknextorcontext };
```

```
procedure InitSyntax;
  begin
    BlockBegSys := [LabelSy, ConstSy, TypeSy, VarSy, ProcSy, FuncSy, BeginSy];
    ConstBegSys := [AddOp, IntConst, RealConst, CharConst, StringConst, Ident];
    SimpTypeBegSys := ConstBegSys + [LeftParent];
    TypeDels := [ArraySy, RecordSy, SetSy, FileSy];
    TypeBegSys := SimpTypeBegSys + TypeDels + [Arrow, PackedSy];
    StatBegSys := [BeginSy, GotoSy, IfSy, CaseSy, WhileSy, RepeatSy, ForSy, WithSy];
    FacBegSys :=
      [IntConst, RealConst, CharConst, StringConst, Ident, NilSy, LeftParent,
      LeftBracket, NotSy];
    SelectSymbols := [Arrow, Period, LeftBracket];
    ParamBegSys := [ProcSy, FuncSy, VarSy, Ident];
    case OptionValue[Level] of
      Level0 : ConformantParamBegSys := [];
      Level1 : ConformantParamBegSys := [PackedSy, ArraySy]
    end;
    Recovering := false
  end { initsyntax };
```

{

CHAPTER 9

Semantic Analysis
and
Semantic Error Recovery

Semantic analysis and semantic error recovery are implemented by enrichment of the syntax analyser with semantic interludes. These semantic interludes depend on the following globally-defined data structures and manipulative procedures.

9.1 Semantic error reporting.

Most semantic errors are reported relative to the current symbol in the program text. This is facilitated by the procedure SemanticError. Some errors however, are reported retrospectively, and relate to an earlier point in the program, e.g. a point of declaration. For these a direct call on the procedure Error is used.

}

procedure SemanticError(Code: Scalar);

  begin Error(Code, StartOfSymbol) **end**;

procedure SystemError(Code: Scalar);

  begin Error(Code + SystemBase, StartOfSymbol) **end**;

{

9.2 Identifier lists.

During the construction and analysis of identifier entries, it is sometimes necessary or convenient to hold and process sequential lists of these entries. The following procedures enable such lists to be manipulated, as records of type Idlist.

}

procedure StartList(**var** List: IdList);

  begin List.FirstEntry := **nil**; List.LastEntry := **nil end**;

procedure AppendId(**var** List: IdList; **var** Id: IdEntry);

  var NewEntry: ListEntry;

  begin

    new(NewEntry); NewEntry^.Id := Id; NewEntry^.Next := **nil**;

    if List.FirstEntry = **nil**

    then List.FirstEntry := NewEntry **else** List.LastEntry^.Next := NewEntry;

```
      List.LastEntry := NewEntry
   end { appendid };
procedure ForAll(List: IdList; procedure Action(Id: IdEntry));
   var ThisEntry: ListEntry;
   begin
      ThisEntry := List.FirstEntry;
      while ThisEntry <> nil do
         begin Action(ThisEntry^.Id); ThisEntry := ThisEntry^.Next end
   end { forall };
procedure DisposeList(List: IdList);
   var NextEntry, ThisEntry: ListEntry;
   begin
      NextEntry := List.FirstEntry;
      while NextEntry <> nil do
         begin
            ThisEntry := NextEntry; NextEntry := ThisEntry^.Next; dispose(ThisEntry)
         end
   end { disposelist };
{
```

In some contexts, however, a set rather than a list of identifiers is required. The following procedures allow such sets to be manipulated as records of the type Idset, using the same underlying representation as that for Idlist.

```
}
procedure StartSet(var S: IdSet);
   begin StartList(S) end;
function Includes(S: IdSet; Id: IdEntry): Boolean;
   var NextOnList: ListEntry;
   begin
      Includes := false; NextOnList := S.FirstEntry;
      while NextOnList <> nil do
         begin
            if NextOnList^.Id = Id then Includes := true;
            NextOnList := NextOnList^.Next
         end
   end { includes };
procedure Include(var S: IdSet; Id: IdEntry);
   begin if not Includes(S, Id) then AppendId(S, Id) end;
procedure Exclude(var S: IdSet; Id: IdEntry);
   var ThisEntry, PreviousEntry: ListEntry;
   begin
      PreviousEntry := nil; ThisEntry := S.FirstEntry;
```

```
      while ThisEntry <> nil do
        if ThisEntry^.Id = Id
        then begin
              if PreviousEntry = nil
              then S.FirstEntry := ThisEntry^.Next
              else PreviousEntry^.Next := ThisEntry^.Next;
              if ThisEntry = S.LastEntry then S.LastEntry := PreviousEntry;
              dispose(ThisEntry); ThisEntry := nil
          end
        else begin PreviousEntry := ThisEntry; ThisEntry := ThisEntry^.Next end
    end { exclude };
procedure DsposeSet(S: IdSet);
  begin DisposeList(S) end;
{
```

9.3 The semantic table and scope.

This holds an entry for each identifier, type or label which may appear in the program being compiled.

The table is organised as a stack of sub-tables, one for each identifier scope currently open, the nesting of these scopes being represented by the array Display as follows:

1. Each display entry points to the identifier, type and label sub-tables for that scope, and indicates whether the scope is one delimited by a block, or by a record type.

2. The global variables ScopeLevel and BlockLevel index the topmost scope and topmost block scope respectively within the display.

3. Display housekeeping is carried out by the procedures InitScope, OpenScope, SaveScope, RestoreScope and CloseScope.

The distinctive features of the Pascal rules of scope defined by the ISO standard are:

R1. The defining occurrence of an identifier must precede all corresponding applied occurrences in its scope, with one exception: a type-identifier may appear in a pointer-type definition before being defined in the same block. For example:

            pointer = ^sometype;
            ...
            sometype = domaintype;

     is legal.

R2. The defining occurrence of an identifier must not be preceded in its scope by an applied occurrence corresponding to a nonlocal definition of the same identifier. For example

            const n = 100;

            procedure P;
              type range = 1..n;
              var n: integer;
```
```

> begin ...

is illegal.

R3.   A distinction is made between the scope associated with a formal parameter list and the scope associated with the corresponding procedure or function block. Thus a type-identifier used in declaring a formal parameter may be redefined within the procedure or function block without violating rule R2. For example:

> function f(n: argument): result;
> var argument: integer;
> begin ...

is legal.

Apart from the pointer type problem which is discussed in section 9.4, rule R1 is enforced naturally by one-pass entry and search of the identifier sub-tables.

Rule R2 is enforced by a method due to Arthur Sale in which each new scope is assigned a monotonically increasing scope-number when opened. At each identifier occurrence the current scope-number is copied into a LastUse field in the identifier's table entry. A nonlocal identifier may be redefined in a new scope, only if the value of the LastUse field in the nonlocal entry is less than the new scope number.

Rule R3 is enforced by an extension of the LastUse mechanism which also accommodates the split scopes created by forward declarations. At the end of a formal parameter list the parameter scope is saved, to be restored at the start of the corresponding procedure or function block with a new scope-number. During restoration the LastUse field of each formal-parameter identifier entry is also updated to the new scope number. Non-local type-identifiers are unaffected by this process and may therefore be redefined in the block without violating R2.

In this implementation, the semantic-table has capacity for up to 19 nested scopes. When this is exceeded, an error is reported.
}
```
procedure InitScope;
  begin
    ScopeLevel := 0; BlockLevel := 0;
    with Display[0] do
      begin
        ScopeNo := 0; NextScopeNo := 1; Locals := nil; Scope := ActualBlock;
        StartSet(Threatened); TypeChain := nil; LabelChain := nil
      end
  end { initscope };
```

```
procedure OpenScope(Kind: ScopeKind);
  begin
    if ScopeLevel < DispLimit
    then begin
            ScopeLevel := ScopeLevel + 1;
            with Display[ScopeLevel] do
              begin
                ScopeNo := NextScopeNo; NextScopeNo := NextScopeNo + 1;
                Locals := nil; Scope := Kind;
                if Kind <> RecordScope
                then begin
                        StartSet(Threatened); TypeChain := nil; LabelChain := nil;
                        if Kind = ActualBlock then BlockLevel := ScopeLevel
                      end
                else begin FieldsPacked := false; RecordType := nil end
              end
          end
    else SystemError(1)
  end { openscope };
procedure SaveScope(var Scope: ScopeCopy);
  begin
    new(Scope); Scope^ := Display[ScopeLevel]; ScopeLevel := ScopeLevel - 1;
    BlockLevel := BlockLevel - 1
  end { savescope };
procedure RestoreScope(Scope: ScopeCopy);
  procedure UpdateIdUsage(Id: IdEntry);
    begin
      if Id <> nil
      then with Id^ do
              begin
                UpdateIdUsage(LeftLink); LastUse := NextScopeNo;
                UpdateIdUsage(RightLink)
              end
    end { updateidusage };
  begin {restorescope }
    ScopeLevel := ScopeLevel + 1; BlockLevel := BlockLevel + 1;
    Display[ScopeLevel] := Scope^; dispose(Scope);
    with Display[ScopeLevel] do
      begin ScopeNo := NextScopeNo; UpdateIdUsage(Locals) end;
    NextScopeNo := NextScopeNo + 1
  end { restorescope };
procedure CloseScope;
  begin
    if Display[ScopeLevel].Scope = ActualBlock then BlockLevel := BlockLevel - 1;
    ScopeLevel := ScopeLevel - 1
  end { closescope };
```

{

9.4 The identifier sub-tables.

The identifier sub-table for each scope contains an entry for each identifier declared in that scope. Each entry is a record of the variant record type IdRecord. The sub-table is held as a sorted binary tree, records being connected through their fields LeftLink and RightLink.

Insertion and lookup of identifiers within the sub-tables is provided by the two procedures NewId and SearchId. When necessary, a particular binary tree may be searched using the procedure SearchLocalId.

SearchLocalId involves no logic for error reporting or recovery, but recovery from errors involving duplicate, mis-used and undeclared identifiers is accommodated within NewId and SearchId as follows:

1. If NewId finds an entry for the identifier already in the current scope, an error is flagged but a second entry is still made (for possible selection by SearchId as below).

2. SearchId is passed a parameter specifying the acceptable classes of entry to be found. If the first entry encountered for the identifier is not of an acceptable class searching continues within the same scope for a possible duplicate entry. If no acceptable duplicate is found in the scope a misuse error is reported and a duplicate entry of acceptable class is created in the same scope.

3. If SearchId fails to find an entry in any scope for the identifier sought, an undeclared error is reported and an entry of acceptable class is created for the identifier, with otherwise default attributes, in the current block scope.

The forward binding of pointer domains required by scope rule R1 is complicated by the fact that pointer-type definitions can appear within nested record-scopes. For example:

    rec1 = record f: record n: ^d end; d: integer end;
    d = real;

is illegal since the identifier d is redefined as a field-identifier after an application as a domain-identifier in a nested record-scope. Correct handling of pointer domains is achieved by creating an immediate entry with the special class Domain for each identifier occurring as a domain type in the type definition part, if one does not already exist. This entry will subsequently be changed to class Types if a corresponding type definition is encountered, but in the meantime other usage errors will be detected by applying the Sale algorithm in the usual way. To support this strategy special procedures SearchDomain and BindDomain are provided within this identifier table handling section. SearchDomain determines if usage to date of an available type identifier implies immediate binding, and precludes further conflicting usage of the identifier (by adjusting LastUse for any entry within the current block). BindDomain carries out a previously delayed binding to a nonlocal type identifier when appropriate.

}

```
procedure CreateId(var Entry: IdEntry; ClassNeeded: IdClass);
   var NewEntry: IdEntry; CodeOfBody: BlockLabel; IdName: Alfa;
   begin
      { create new entry of appropriate class }
      case ClassNeeded of
         Domain : new(NewEntry, Domain);
         Types : new(NewEntry, Types);
         Consts : new(NewEntry, Consts);
         Vars : new(NewEntry, Vars);
         Field : new(NewEntry, Field);
         Bound : new(NewEntry, Bound);
         Proc : new(NewEntry, Proc);
         Func : new(NewEntry, Func)
      end;
      { set name, klass, and default attributes }
      with NewEntry^ do
         begin
            CopySpelling(IdName); Name := IdName; IdType := Unknown;
            LastUse := Display[ScopeLevel].ScopeNo; Klass := ClassNeeded;
            case Klass of
               Domain, Types : ;
               Consts :
                  begin Values := DefaultValue; SuccId := nil end;
               Vars :
                  begin VarKind := LocalVar; VarAddress := DefaultAddress end;
               Field :
                  begin Offset := DefaultOffset; Tag := false; NextField := nil end;
               Bound :
                  begin BdAddress := DefaultAddress; NextBound := nil end;
               Proc, Func :
                  begin
                     PfDecKind := Declared; PfKind := Actual; Formals := nil;
                     FutureBlockLabel(CodeOfBody); CodeBody := CodeOfBody;
                     Assignable := false; Assigned := false; Forwrd := false;
                     Result := DefaultAddress
                  end
            end
         end;
      Entry := NewEntry
   end { createid };
procedure EnterId(NewEntry: IdEntry; var Scope: IdEntry);
   var NewName: Alfa; ThisEntry, LastEntry: IdEntry; LeftTaken: Boolean;
   begin
      if Scope = nil
      then Scope := NewEntry
      else begin
            NewName := NewEntry^.Name; ThisEntry := Scope;
            repeat
               LastEntry := ThisEntry;
```

```
              if ThisEntry^.Name.Head < NewName.Head
              then begin ThisEntry := ThisEntry^.RightLink; LeftTaken := false end
              else if ThisEntry^.Name.Head > NewName.Head
                  then begin ThisEntry := ThisEntry^.LeftLink; LeftTaken := true end
                  else if OrderedTails(ThisEntry^.Name.Tail, NewName.Tail)
                      then begin
                              ThisEntry := ThisEntry^.RightLink; LeftTaken := false
                           end
                      else { duplicates go to the left }
                           begin
                              ThisEntry := ThisEntry^.LeftLink; LeftTaken := true
                           end
            until ThisEntry = nil;
            if LeftTaken
            then LastEntry^.LeftLink := NewEntry
            else LastEntry^.RightLink := NewEntry
          end;
      NewEntry^.LeftLink := nil; NewEntry^.RightLink := nil
  end { enterid };
procedure SearchLocalId(Scope: IdEntry; var Entry: IdEntry);
  label 1;
  var ThisEntry: IdEntry;
  begin
    ThisEntry := Scope;
    while ThisEntry <> nil do
      if Spelling.Head < ThisEntry^.Name.Head
      then ThisEntry := ThisEntry^.LeftLink
      else if Spelling.Head > ThisEntry^.Name.Head
          then ThisEntry := ThisEntry^.RightLink
          else if OrderedTails(Spelling.Tail, ThisEntry^.Name.Tail)
              then ThisEntry := ThisEntry^.LeftLink
              else if OrderedTails(ThisEntry^.Name.Tail, Spelling.Tail)
                  then ThisEntry := ThisEntry^.RightLink else goto 1;
    1: Entry := ThisEntry
  end { searchlocalid };
procedure SearchScopes(Inner, Outer: DispRange; var Entry: IdEntry);
  label 1;
  var Index: DispRange;
  begin
    for Index := Inner downto Outer do
      begin
        SearchLocalId(Display[Index].Locals, Entry);
        if Entry <> nil
        then begin LevelFound := Index; goto 1 end
      end;
    1:
  end { searchscopes };
```

```
procedure BindDomain(Domain: IdEntry);
    var TypeFound: Boolean; EntryFound: IdEntry; IdName: Alfa;
    begin
        RestoreSpelling(Domain^.Name); TypeFound := false;
        SearchScopes(BlockLevel - 1, 0, EntryFound);
        if EntryFound <> nil then TypeFound := EntryFound^.Klass = Types;
        with Domain^ do
            begin
                Klass := Types;
                if TypeFound then IdType := EntryFound^.IdType else SemanticError(101)
            end;
        CopySpelling(IdName); Domain^.Name := IdName
    end { binddomain };
procedure SearchDomain(var Entry: IdEntry);
    begin
        SearchScopes(ScopeLevel, 0, Entry);
        if Entry <> nil
        then begin
                if LevelFound < BlockLevel
                then begin
                        if Entry^.Klass = Types
                        then begin
                                if Entry^.LastUse < Display[BlockLevel].ScopeNo
                                then Entry := nil
                            end
                        else Entry := nil
                    end;
                if Entry <> nil then Entry^.LastUse := Display[ScopeLevel].ScopeNo
            end
    end { searchdomain };
procedure NewId(var Entry: IdEntry; ClassNeeded: IdClass);
    var NewEntry, LastEntry: IdEntry; DefiningLevel: DispRange;
    begin
        if (ClassNeeded = Field) or (Display[ScopeLevel].Scope = FormalBlock)
        then DefiningLevel := ScopeLevel else DefiningLevel := BlockLevel;
        SearchScopes(ScopeLevel, 0, LastEntry);
        if LastEntry <> nil
        then if (LevelFound <= DefiningLevel) and
                (LastEntry^.LastUse >= Display[DefiningLevel].ScopeNo)
            then SemanticError(102);
        CreateId(NewEntry, ClassNeeded);
        if ClassNeeded = Consts then NewEntry^.LastUse := Display[BlockLevel].ScopeNo;
        EnterId(NewEntry, Display[DefiningLevel].Locals); Entry := NewEntry
    end { newid };
procedure SearchId(AllowableClasses: SetOfIdClass; var Entry: IdEntry);
    var EntryFound: IdEntry; Suitable: Boolean;
```

```
    function MostLikelyOf(Classes: SetOfIdClass): IdClass;

      var LClass: IdClass;

      begin
         LClass := Types;
         while not (LClass in Classes) do LClass := succ(LClass);
         MostLikelyOf := LClass
      end { mostlikeyof };
   begin { searchid }
      SearchScopes(ScopeLevel, 0, EntryFound);
      if EntryFound = nil
      then begin
             SemanticError(101); CreateId(EntryFound, MostLikelyOf(AllowableClasses));
             EnterId(EntryFound, Display[BlockLevel].Locals); LevelFound := BlockLevel
           end
      else begin
             repeat
                Suitable := (EntryFound^.Klass in AllowableClasses);
                if not Suitable then SearchLocalId(EntryFound^.LeftLink, EntryFound)
             until Suitable or (EntryFound = nil);
             if Suitable
             then begin
                    if EntryFound^.Klass = Domain then BindDomain(EntryFound);
                    EntryFound^.LastUse := Display[ScopeLevel].ScopeNo
                  end
             else begin
                    SemanticError(103);
                    CreateId(EntryFound, MostLikelyOf(AllowableClasses));
                    EnterId(EntryFound, Display[LevelFound].Locals)
                  end
           end;
      Entry := EntryFound
   end { searchid };
{
```

9.5 The type sub-tables.

All types defined or declared within the program are represented by type entries whose form
is determined by the form of the type so represented (i.e. scalars, arrays, etc.). These entries
are constructed using a corresponding variant record type TypeRecord.

These type entries are accessed only via the identifier table entries for type identifiers, or via
the representation of the data objects (variables, constants, functions, expressions) whose
type they describe. Thus for example all identifier table entries have a common field IdType
which points to an underlying type entry (with an obvious interpretation for all classes of
identifier other than proc).

To enable storage control, the type entries associated with any scope are connected in a
linear chain through the pointer field next. New type entries for the current block scope are
created via the procedure NewType.

```
    }
procedure NewType(var Entry: TypEntry; FormNeeded: TypeForm);
    var NewEntry: TypEntry;
    procedure ChainAt(Level: DispRange);
       begin
         with Display[Level] do
            begin NewEntry^.Next := TypeChain; TypeChain := NewEntry end
       end { chainat };
    begin { newtype }
       case FormNeeded of
          Scalars : new(NewEntry, Scalars);
          SubRanges : new(NewEntry, SubRanges);
          Pointers : new(NewEntry, Pointers);
          Sets : new(NewEntry, Sets);
          Arrays : new(NewEntry, Arrays);
          CAPSchema : new(NewEntry, CAPSchema);
          Records : new(NewEntry, Records);
          Files : new(NewEntry, Files);
          VariantPart : new(NewEntry, VariantPart);
          Variant : new(NewEntry, Variant)
       end;
       with NewEntry^ do
          begin
            Form := FormNeeded; Representation := DefaultRepresentation;
            case FormNeeded of
               Scalars :
                  begin ScalarKind := Declared; FirstConst := nil end;
               SubRanges :
                  begin RangeType := Unknown; Min := ZeroValue; Max := OneValue end;
               Pointers :
                  DomainType := Unknown;
               Sets :
                  begin FormOfSet := Unpacked; BaseType := Unknown end;
               Arrays :
                  begin
                    AelType := Unknown; InxType := Unknown; PackedArray := false;
                    StringConstant := false
                  end;
               CAPSchema :
                  begin
                    PackedSchema := false; CompType := Unknown; InxSpec := Unknown;
                    LowBdAddress := DefaultAddress; HighBdAddress := DefaultAddress
                  end;
               Records :
                  begin
                    FileFree := true; PackedRecord := false; FieldScope := nil;
                    FixedPart := nil; VarPart := nil
                  end;
```

```
            Files :
              begin PackedFile := false; TextFile := false; FelType := Unknown end;
            VariantPart :
              begin
                TagType := Unknown; TagField := nil; SelectorField := nil;
                FirstVariant := nil
              end;
            Variant :
              begin
                VarFileFree := true; SubFixedPart := nil; NextVariant := nil;
                SubVarPart := nil; VariantValue := DefaultValue
              end
          end
        end;
      if FormNeeded = CAPSchema
      then ChainAt(BlockLevel - 1) else ChainAt(BlockLevel);
      TSerialise(NewEntry); Entry := NewEntry
    end { newtype };
{
```

9.6 The label sub-tables.

These are linear lists of entries, one for each label declared in that block scope, each entry being of the record type LabelRecord.

The validity of each label at its declaration, siting, and use (by a goto statement) is checked by the procedures NewLabel, DefineLabel and CheckLabel . To enforce the label accessibility rules, however, the analyser must also keep track of the depth of statement nesting by calling the procedures OpenLabelDepth and CloseLabelDepth. Through these the current depth of statement nesting is maintained as the variable Depth. When a new depth of nesting is "opened", Depth is merely incremented by 1. When that depth is closed however, the accessibility of all labels referenced or sited at that level must be reviewed. Specifically, an accessible label sited at that depth becomes inaccessible, and an unsited label referenced at that depth, may only be sited at a lesser depth thereafter. Finally, a transfer of control from an inner-block to an enclosing outer-block requires that the label site is at textual depth 1 of the outer block.

The label handling procedures report with the following error codes:
}

```
procedure SearchLabel(FirstLabel: LabelEntry; var Entry: LabelEntry);
  var Found: Boolean;
  begin
    Found := false; Entry := FirstLabel;
    while (Entry <> nil) and (not Found) do
      if SameValue(Entry^.LabelValue, Constant.Value)
      then Found := true else Entry := Entry^.NextLabel
  end { searchlabel };
```

```
procedure CreateLabel(var Entry: LabelEntry);
  begin
    with Display[BlockLevel] do
      begin
        new(Entry);
        with Entry^ do
          begin
            LabelValue := Constant.Value; NextLabel := LabelChain;
            FutureStatementLabel(LabelledCode); Defined := false;
            Declaration := StartOfSymbol; MaxDepth := maxint
          end;
        LabelChain := Entry
      end
  end { createlabel };
procedure NewLabel;
  var LocalLabel: LabelEntry;
  begin
    SearchLabel(Display[BlockLevel].LabelChain, LocalLabel);
    if LocalLabel <> nil then SemanticError(132) else CreateLabel(LocalLabel)
  end { newlabel };
procedure SearchAllLabels(var Entry: LabelEntry);
  label 1;
  var Level: DispRange; LabelFound: LabelEntry;
  begin
    Level := BlockLevel;
    repeat
      SearchLabel(Display[Level].LabelChain, LabelFound);
      if LabelFound <> nil
      then begin LevelFound := Level; goto 1 end;
      Level := Level - 1
    until Level = 0;
    { label not found: report an error and create a substitute }
    SemanticError(130); CreateLabel(LabelFound); LevelFound := BlockLevel;
    1: Entry := LabelFound
  end { searchalllabels };
procedure InitLabelDepth;
  begin Depth := 1 end;
procedure OpenLabelDepth;
  begin Depth := Depth + 1 end;
procedure DefineLabel;
  var Entry: LabelEntry;
  begin
    SearchAllLabels(Entry);
    if LevelFound <> BlockLevel
```

```
        then begin SemanticError(133); CreateLabel(Entry) end;
        with Entry^ do
          if Defined
          then SemanticError(134)
          else begin
                  if Depth > MaxDepth then SemanticError(135);
                  NextIsStatementLabel(LabelledCode); Defined := true; Accessible := true;
                  DefinedDepth := Depth
               end
    end { definelabel };
procedure CheckLabel(var Entry: LabelEntry);
  begin
    SearchAllLabels(Entry);
    with Entry^ do
      begin
        if LevelFound <> BlockLevel
        then MaxDepth := 1
        else if Defined
              then begin
                      if not Accessible then SemanticError(136)
                   end
              else if MaxDepth > Depth then MaxDepth := Depth
      end
    end { checklabel };
procedure CloseLabelDepth;
  var ThisLabel: LabelEntry;
  begin
    ThisLabel := Display[BlockLevel].LabelChain;
    while ThisLabel <> nil do
      begin
        with ThisLabel^ do
          if Defined
          then begin
                  if Accessible then Accessible := (DefinedDepth < Depth)
               end
          else if MaxDepth = Depth then MaxDepth := Depth - 1;
          ThisLabel := ThisLabel^.NextLabel
      end;
    Depth := Depth - 1
  end { closelabeldepth };
{
```

9.7 Storage recovery at scope closure.

On completing analysis of a block, a one-pass compiler can discard and subsequently re-use the storage occupied by all table entries created for that block. The procedure DisposeScope carries out this disposal process.

Certain semantic errors, such as unsatisfied label declarations or forward declarations are detected during storage disposal.

```
}
procedure DisposeScope;
  procedure DisposeFormals(NextFormal: FormalEntry);
    var ThisFormal: FormalEntry;
    begin
      while NextFormal <> nil do
        begin
          ThisFormal := NextFormal;
          with ThisFormal^ do
            begin
              if Parm in [ProcParm, FuncParm] then DisposeFormals(ItsFormals);
              NextFormal := Next
            end;
          dispose(ThisFormal)
        end
    end { disposeformals };
  procedure DisposeIds(Root: IdEntry);
    begin
      if Root <> nil
      then begin
            with Root^ do
              begin
                DisposeIds(LeftLink); DisposeIds(RightLink);
                if Name.Tail <> nil then DisposeAlfa(Name)
              end;
            case Root^.Klass of
              Types : dispose(Root, Types);
              Consts : dispose(Root, Consts);
              Vars : dispose(Root, Vars);
              Field : dispose(Root, Field);
              Bound : dispose(Root, Bound);
              Proc, Func :
                begin
                  with Root^ do
                    if PfKind = Actual
                    then begin
                          if Forwrd then Error(151, Declaration);
                          DisposeFormals(Formals)
                        end;
                  dispose(Root, Proc)
                end
            end
          end
    end { disposeids };
```

```
procedure DisposeTypes(FirstType: TypEntry);
  var ThisType, NextType: TypEntry;
  begin
    NextType := FirstType;
    while NextType <> nil do
      begin
        ThisType := NextType; NextType := ThisType^.Next;
        case ThisType^.Form of
          Scalars : dispose(ThisType, Scalars);
          SubRanges : dispose(ThisType, SubRanges);
          Pointers : dispose(ThisType, Pointers);
          Sets : dispose(ThisType, Sets);
          Arrays : dispose(ThisType, Arrays);
          CAPSchema : dispose(ThisType, CAPSchema);
          Records :
            begin
              with ThisType^ do DisposeIds(FieldScope);
              dispose(ThisType, Records)
            end;
          Files : dispose(ThisType, Files);
          VariantPart :
            begin
              with ThisType^ do
                if SelectorField <> TagField then dispose(SelectorField, Field);
              dispose(ThisType, VariantPart)
            end;
          Variant : dispose(ThisType, Variant)
        end
      end
  end { disposetypes };
procedure DisposeLabels(FirstLabel: LabelEntry);
  var NextLabel, ThisLabel: LabelEntry;
  begin
    NextLabel := FirstLabel;
    while NextLabel <> nil do
      begin
        ThisLabel := NextLabel;
        if not ThisLabel^.Defined then Error(131, ThisLabel^.Declaration);
        NextLabel := ThisLabel^.NextLabel; dispose(ThisLabel)
      end
  end { disposelabels };
begin { disposescope }
  with Display[ScopeLevel] do
    begin
      DsposeSet(Threatened); DisposeIds(Locals); DisposeTypes(TypeChain);
      DisposeLabels(LabelChain)
    end
end { disposescope };
```

{

9.8 Standard table entries.

Predefined identifiers and types supported by Pascal are held within the semantic table as a scope for a pseudo-block enclosing the main program (at display level 0). These entries are created by the procedure InitSemanticTables.

The type entries representing the standard types supported by the language (integer, real, boolean, char and text) are directly accessible via global pointer variables IntType, Real-Type, BooleanType, CharType, and TextType as well as via the identifier entries for "integer", "real", "boolean", "char", and "text".

}

```
procedure InitSemanticTables;
  procedure StdTypEntries;
    begin
      new(Unknown, Scalars, Declared);
      with Unknown^ do
        begin
          Representation := DefaultRepresentation; Form := Scalars;
          ScalarKind := Declared; FirstConst := nil
        end;
      new(IntType, Scalars, Predefined);
      with IntType^ do
        begin
          Representation := IntegerRepresentation; Form := Scalars;
          ScalarKind := Predefined
        end;
      new(RealType, Scalars, Predefined);
      with RealType^ do
        begin
          Representation := RealRepresentation; Form := Scalars;
          ScalarKind := Predefined
        end;
      new(CharType, Scalars, Predefined);
      with CharType^ do
        begin
          Representation := CharRepresentation; Form := Scalars;
          ScalarKind := Predefined
        end;
      new(BoolType, Scalars, Declared);
      with BoolType^ do
        begin
          Representation := BooleanRepresentation; Form := Scalars;
          ScalarKind := Declared
        end;
```

```
        new(NilType, Pointers);
        with NilType^ do
          begin
            Representation := PointerRepresentation; Form := Pointers;
            DomainType := Unknown
          end;
        new(EmptyType, Sets);
        with EmptyType^ do
          begin
            Form := Sets; FormOfSet := Constructed; BaseType := Unknown;
            Representation := EmptyRepresentation
          end;
        new(TextType, Files);
        with TextType^ do .
          begin
            Form := Files; PackedFile := false; TextFile := true; FelType := CharType
          end;
        SetRepresentationFor(TextType)
    end { stdtypentries };

  procedure StdIdEntries;

    var Entry, TrueEntry, FalseEntry: IdEntry;

    procedure EnterProcFunc(PfName: AlfaHead; PfClass: IdClass; Index: StdProcFuncs);

      var Entry: IdEntry;

      begin
        MakeSpelling(PfName); NewId(Entry, PfClass);
        with Entry^ do
          begin Klass := PfClass; PfDecKind := Predefined; PfIndex := Index end
      end { enterprocfunc };

    begin { stdidentries }
      { standard type identifiers }
      MakeSpelling('INTEGER      '); NewId(Entry, Types); Entry^.IdType := IntType;
      MakeSpelling('REAL         '); NewId(Entry, Types); Entry^.IdType := RealType;
      MakeSpelling('CHAR         '); NewId(Entry, Types); Entry^.IdType := CharType;
      MakeSpelling('BOOLEAN      '); NewId(Entry, Types); Entry^.IdType := BoolType;
      MakeSpelling('TEXT         '); NewId(Entry, Types); Entry^.IdType := TextType;

      { standard constant identifiers }
      MakeSpelling('MAXINT       '); NewId(Entry, Consts);
      with Entry^ do
        begin IdType := IntType; Values := MaxintValue end;
      MakeSpelling('TRUE         '); NewId(TrueEntry, Consts);
      with TrueEntry^ do
        begin IdType := BoolType; Values := TrueValue; SuccId := nil end;
      MakeSpelling('FALSE        '); NewId(FalseEntry, Consts);
      with FalseEntry^ do
        begin IdType := BoolType; Values := FalseValue; SuccId := TrueEntry end;
      BoolType^.FirstConst := FalseEntry;
```

```
    new(DummyVarId, Vars);
    with DummyVarId^ do
      begin
        Klass := Vars; IdType := Unknown; VarKind := LocalVar;
        VarAddress := DefaultAddress
      end;
```

{ standard procedure identifiers }

```
    EnterProcFunc('PUT          ', Proc, Putp);
    EnterProcFunc('GET          ', Proc, Getp);
    EnterProcFunc('RESET        ', Proc, Resetp);
    EnterProcFunc('REWRITE      ', Proc, Rewritep);
    EnterProcFunc('NEW          ', Proc, Newp);
    EnterProcFunc('DISPOSE      ', Proc, Disposep);
    EnterProcFunc('PACK         ', Proc, Packp);
    EnterProcFunc('UNPACK       ', Proc, Unpackp);
    EnterProcFunc('READ         ', Proc, Readp);
    EnterProcFunc('READLN       ', Proc, Readlnp);
    EnterProcFunc('WRITE        ', Proc, Writep);
    EnterProcFunc('WRITELN      ', Proc, Writelnp);
    EnterProcFunc('PAGE         ', Proc, Pagep);
```

{ standard function identifiers }

```
    EnterProcFunc('ABS          ', Func, Absf);
    EnterProcFunc('SQR          ', Func, Sqrf);
    EnterProcFunc('SIN          ', Func, Sinf);
    EnterProcFunc('COS          ', Func, Cosf);
    EnterProcFunc('EXP          ', Func, Expf);
    EnterProcFunc('LN           ', Func, Lnf);
    EnterProcFunc('SQRT         ', Func, Sqrtf);
    EnterProcFunc('ARCTAN       ', Func, Arctanf);
    EnterProcFunc('TRUNC        ', Func, Truncf);
    EnterProcFunc('ROUND        ', Func, Roundf);
    EnterProcFunc('ORD          ', Func, Ordf);
    EnterProcFunc('CHR          ', Func, Chrf);
    EnterProcFunc('SUCC         ', Func, Succf);
    EnterProcFunc('PRED         ', Func, Predf);
    EnterProcFunc('ODD          ', Func, Oddf);
    EnterProcFunc('EOF          ', Func, Eoff);
    EnterProcFunc('EOLN         ', Func, Eolnf);
  end { stdidentries };
begin { initsemantictables }
  InitScope; StdTypEntries; StdIdEntries; FileStdTypes
end { initsemantictables };
```

{

9.9 Type Analysis.

Much of the semantic analysis required by Pascal involves the examination and comparison of types as represented by the corresponding type entry records. The following procedures enable this analysis to be easily expressed within the analyser proper.

In all situations where the type of a data object is not determined, it is represented by a pointer value ¨unknown¨, which points to a suitable default type record. The type checking procedures take special action on encountering this value, so that normal type analysis can be expressed within the analyser without preliminary screening for indeterminate types at every point at which they might arise.

}

procedure StringType(**var** StringEntry: TypEntry);
  { This procedure generates a suitable type entry for the
   string currently described by the global variable Constant. }
  var IndexType, ArrayType: TypEntry; Length: ValueDetails;
  begin
    NewType(IndexType, SubRanges);
    with IndexType^ **do**
      begin
        RangeType := IntType; Length.Kind := OrdValue;
        Length.Ival := Constant.Length; Evaluate(Length); Min := OneValue;
        Max := Length.Value
      end;
    SetRepresentationFor(IndexType); NewType(ArrayType, Arrays);
    with ArrayType^ **do**
      begin
        AelType := CharType; InxType := IndexType; PackedArray := true;
        StringConstant := true
      end;
    SetRepresentationFor(ArrayType); StringEntry := ArrayType
  end { stringtype };

function String(TheType: TypEntry): Boolean;
  { This function decides if a type is a string type. }
  begin
    String := false;
    if TheType <> Unknown
    then with TheType^ **do**
        if Form = Arrays
        then if StringConstant
            then String := true
            else if PackedArray **and** (AelType = CharType) **and**
                (InxType <> Unknown)
                then if InxType^.Form = SubRanges
                    then if InxType^.RangeType = IntType

```
                              then String :=
                                    SameValue(InxType^.Min, OneValue) and
                                    OrderedValues(OneValue, InxType^.Max)
      end { string };
function Identical(Type1, Type2: TypEntry): Boolean;
      { This function decides if two types are identical. }
      begin
            Identical := (Type1 = Type2) or (Type1 = Unknown) or (Type2 = Unknown)
      end { identical };
function Compatible(Type1, Type2: TypEntry): Boolean;
      { This function decides if two types are compatible. }
      begin
            if Type1 = Type2
            then Compatible := true
            else if (Type1 = Unknown) or (Type2 = Unknown)
                  then Compatible := true
                  else if Type1^.Form = SubRanges
                        then Compatible := Compatible(Type1^.RangeType, Type2)
                        else if Type2^.Form = SubRanges
                              then Compatible := Compatible(Type1, Type2^.RangeType)
                              else if String(Type1) and String(Type2)
                                    then Compatible :=
                                          SameValue(Type1^.InxType^.Max, Type2^.InxType^.Max)
                                    else if (Type1^.Form = Sets) and (Type2^.Form = Sets)
                                          then Compatible :=
                                                Compatible(Type1^.BaseType, Type2^.BaseType) and
                                                ((Type1^.FormOfSet = Constructed) or
                                                (Type2^.FormOfSet = Constructed) or
                                                (Type1^.FormOfSet = Type2^.FormOfSet))
                                          else if (Type1^.Form = Pointers) and
                                                (Type2^.Form = Pointers)
                                                then Compatible :=
                                                      (Type1 = NilType) or (Type2 = NilType)
                                                else Compatible := false
      end { compatible };
function Ordinal(TheType: TypEntry): Boolean;
      { This function decides if a type is an ordinal type. }
      begin
            Ordinal := (TheType^.Form <= SubRanges) and (TheType <> RealType)
      end { ordinal };
function EmbeddedFile(TheType: TypEntry): Boolean;
      { This function checks a type for an embedded component-file. }
      begin
            with TheType^ do
                  case Form of
                        Scalars, SubRanges, Pointers, Sets, VariantPart : EmbeddedFile := false;
                        Arrays : EmbeddedFile := EmbeddedFile(AelType);
```

```
        CAPSchema : EmbeddedFile := EmbeddedFile(CompType);
        Records : EmbeddedFile := not FileFree;
        Variant : EmbeddedFile := not VarFileFree;
        Files : EmbeddedFile := true
      end
  end { embeddedfile };

procedure EnsureOrdinal(var TheType: TypEntry);
  { This procedure checks that a type is ordinal, reports an error if it
    is not, and returns a suitable substitute type pointer in this case. }
  begin
    if not Ordinal(TheType)
    then begin SemanticError(110); TheType := Unknown end
  end { ensureordinal };

procedure EnsureFormIs(FormRequired: TypeForm; var TheType: TypEntry);
  { This procedure checks that a type has the specified form, reports
    an error if it has not, and returns a substitute type in this case. }
  begin
    if TheType^.Form <> FormRequired
    then begin
         if TheType <> Unknown then SemanticError(110 + ord(FormRequired));
         NewType(TheType, FormRequired)
         end
  end { ensureformis };

function TaggedVarPart(ThisVarPart: TypEntry; TagId: IdEntry): TypEntry;
  { This function returns the variant-part type-descriptor within a
    given variant-part that contains the tag-field denoted by TagId. }
  function TaggedSubPart(Variant: TypEntry): TypEntry;
    var SubPart: TypEntry;
    begin
      repeat
        SubPart := TaggedVarPart(Variant^.SubVarPart, TagId);
        Variant := Variant^.NextVariant
      until (SubPart <> nil) or (Variant = nil);
      TaggedSubPart := SubPart
    end { taggedsubpart };
  begin { taggedvarpart }
    if ThisVarPart = nil
    then TaggedVarPart := nil
    else with ThisVarPart^ do
           if TagField = TagId
           then TaggedVarPart := ThisVarPart
           else TaggedVarPart := TaggedSubPart(FirstVariant)
  end { taggedvarpart };
```

```
function VariantField(VarPart: TypEntry; FieldId: IdEntry): Boolean;
    { This function decides if FieldId denotes a field of the record
      variant-part described by VarPart, rather than the fixed part.
      (It relies on the order of field-id serialisation to do so.) }
    begin VariantField := FieldId^.Serial > VarPart^.Serial end;
procedure GetBounds(OrdinalType: TypEntry; var Lower, Upper: ObjectValue);
    { This procedure returns the bound values of an ordinal type }
    var LastId, NextId: IdEntry;
    begin
      with OrdinalType^ do
        if Form = SubRanges
        then begin Lower := Min; Upper := Max end
        else if OrdinalType = CharType
            then begin Lower := MinCharValue; Upper := MaxCharValue end
            else if OrdinalType = IntType
                then begin
                        Lower := MaxintValue; Upper := MaxintValue;
                        NegateValue(Lower)
                    end
                else begin
                        Lower := ZeroValue; NextId := FirstConst; LastId := nil;
                        while NextId <> nil do
                            begin LastId := NextId; NextId := NextId^.SuccId end;
                        if LastId <> nil
                        then Upper := LastId^.Values else Upper := OneValue
                    end
    end { getbounds };
{
```

9.10 Conformant array handling

The following procedures and functions support the detection and manipulation of conformant array parameters. The functions ElementOf, IndexOf, ... enable conformant array schemas and fixed array types to be handled by the same code, where this is appropriate. The procedure WithSchema enables a number of analytic actions to be applied to a given schema.
}

```
function Conformant(TheType: TypEntry): Boolean;
    begin
      if TheType = nil
      then Conformant := false else Conformant := (TheType^.Form = CAPSchema)
    end { conformant };
```

```
function ElementOf(Structure: TypEntry): TypEntry;
  begin
    with Structure^ do
      if Form = Arrays then ElementOf := AelType else ElementOf := CompType
  end { elementof };
function IndexOf(Structure: TypEntry): TypEntry;
  begin
    with Structure^ do
      if Form = Arrays then IndexOf := InxType else IndexOf := InxSpec
  end { indexof };
function PackingOf(Structure: TypEntry): Boolean;
  begin
    with Structure^ do
      if Form = Arrays
      then PackingOf := PackedArray else PackingOf := PackedSchema
  end { packingof };
function MultiLevel(Structure: TypEntry): Boolean;
  var Component: TypEntry;
  begin
    Component := ElementOf(Structure);
    MultiLevel := (Component^.Form = Structure^.Form)
  end { multilevel };
function LastLevelOf(Structure: TypEntry): TypEntry;
  begin
    while MultiLevel(Structure) do Structure := ElementOf(Structure);
    LastLevelOf := Structure
  end { lastlevelof };
procedure WithSchema(Schema: TypEntry;
                       procedure Action(Packing: Boolean;
                             LowBdAddr, HighBdAddr: RuntimeAddress;
                             PairRep, ElemRep: TypeRepresentation));
  var Element: TypEntry;
  begin
    Element := ElementOf(LastLevelOf(Schema));
    with Schema^ do
      Action
        (PackedSchema, LowBdAddress, HighBdAddress, Representation,
           Element^.Representation)
  end { withschema };
{
```

9.11 Formal Parameter List Congruence

The function Congruent decides if two formal parameter lists are congruent.
}
function Congruent(Formals1, Formals2: FormalEntry): Boolean;
  var StillCongruent: Boolean;
  function EquivalentCAPSchemas(Type1, Type2: TypEntry): Boolean;
    var Comp1, Comp2: TypEntry;
    begin
      if (Type1 = Unknown) **or** (Type2 = Unknown)
      then EquivalentCAPSchemas := true
      else if Conformant(Type1) **and** Conformant(Type2)
          then begin
              Comp1 := Type1^.CompType; Comp2 := Type2^.CompType;
              EquivalentCAPSchemas :=
                Identical(IndexOf(Type1), IndexOf(Type2)) **and**
                (PackingOf(Type1) = PackingOf(Type2)) **and**
                ((Comp1 = Comp2) **or** EquivalentCAPSchemas(Comp1, Comp2))
          end
          else EquivalentCAPSchemas := false
    end { equivalentcapschemas };
  begin { congruent }
    StillCongruent := true;
    while StillCongruent **and** (Formals1 <> **nil**) **and** (Formals2 <> **nil**) **do**
      begin
        if (Formals1^.Parm = Formals2^.Parm) **and**
        (Formals1^.Section = Formals2^.Section)
        then case Formals1^.Parm **of**
            ValueParm, VarParm :
              StillCongruent :=
                Identical(Formals1^.FormalType, Formals2^.FormalType) **or**
                EquivalentCAPSchemas
                  (Formals1^.FormalType, Formals2^.FormalType);
            ProcParm :
              StillCongruent :=
                Congruent(Formals1^.ItsFormals, Formals2^.ItsFormals);
            FuncParm :
              StillCongruent :=
                Congruent(Formals1^.ItsFormals, Formals2^.ItsFormals) **and**
                Identical(Formals1^.FormalType, Formals2^.FormalType);
            BoundParm :
          end
        else StillCongruent := false;
        Formals1 := Formals1^.Next; Formals2 := Formals2^.Next
      end;
    Congruent := StillCongruent **and** (Formals1 = **nil**) **and** (Formals2 = **nil**)
  end { congruent };

{

9.12 Range Checks and Assignment Compatibility

The procedure DomainCheck generates any code necessary to check that the value of the expression just evaluated lies in the interval defined by the given type.

The procedure CheckAssigment generates any code necessary to check that the value of the expression just evaluated (which is of type Type2) is assignment compatible with type Type1, and to adjust the representation of the value.

}

```
procedure DomainCheck(TheType: TypEntry);
  begin
    if TheType^.Form = SubRanges
    then RangeCheck(TheType^.Min, TheType^.Max)
    else if TheType^.Form = Sets
        then if TheType^.BaseType <> Unknown
            then if TheType^.BaseType^.Form = SubRanges
                then SetCheck(TheType^.BaseType^.Min, TheType^.BaseType^.Max)
  end { domaincheck };
procedure CheckAssignment(Type1, Type2: TypEntry);
  begin
    if Compatible(Type1, Type2)
    then begin
        if EmbeddedFile(Type1) or EmbeddedFile(Type2)
        then SemanticError(150) else DomainCheck(Type1)
      end
    else if (Type1 = RealType) and Compatible(Type2, IntType)
        then FloatInteger(TopOfStack) else SemanticError(152)
  end { checkassignment };
```

{

9.13 For-statement Control Variable Checking

Enforcement of Pascal's restrictions on the control variable of a for statement involves

(a) constructing for each block the set of all local variables whose type makes them poten-
     tial control variables but which are "threatened" by assigning references within pro-
     cedures or functions local to the block; this set is held as the field Threatened in the
     corresponding scope record;

(b) maintaining the global set ControlVars of all variables in use as control variables at
     any point;

(c) checking that each new control variable encountered is not already a member of either
     of these sets;

(d)   checking at each assigning reference that the variable is not currently a member of
       ControlVars.

Actions (a) and (d) are carried out by the following procedure, which is called for each
assigning reference. Actions (b) and (c) are carried out by the for-statement analyser itself,
in Chapter 10.

}

procedure Threaten(V: IdEntry);
  begin
    if (V^.VarKind = LocalVar) **and** Ordinal(V^.IdType)
    then if LevelFound = BlockLevel
        then begin
            if Includes(ControlVars, V)
            then begin SemanticError(153); Exclude(ControlVars, V) **end**
          end
        else Include(Display[LevelFound].Threatened, V)
    end { threaten };

{

CHAPTER 10

Program Analysis

Program analysis is implemented by a recursive-descent parser enriched with semantic interludes. It is carried out therefore by a procedure Programme whose logic is derived directly from the syntax and semantic rules of the ISO standard. The principal aspects of this analysis are explained in the comments introducing corresponding sections.

}

procedure Programme;

   var ProgId: IdEntry; ProgParams: **record** First, Last: ProgPmEntry **end**;
      EntryLabel: BlockLabel; Externals: IdList;

{

10.1 Program-heading analysis.

For consistency in block handling the program identifier is represented by an identry ProgId, which is not part of any scope created during program analysis.

Program parameters are optional, and unrestricted in number or type. Each parameter is appended as an item of the list ProgParams, and duplicate items are reported as errors. Subsequently, the list is used during variable-declaration analysis, to bind program parameters onto matching variable identifiers. Analysis of the ProgParams list is continued by procedure VerifyProgParams, when the variable declaration part has been completely processed. Parameters that remain unbound are reported as errors and a consolidated list Externals of the variables bound is created, for processing at program entry and exit.

}

   procedure MakeProgEntry;

     var IdName: Alfa; EntryLabel: BlockLabel;

     begin
       new(ProgId, Prog);
       with ProgId^ **do**
         begin
           CopySpelling(IdName); Name := IdName; Klass := Prog;
           FutureBlockLabel(EntryLabel); ProgBody := EntryLabel
         end;
       ISerialise(ProgId)
     end;

```
procedure InitParams;
  begin
    with ProgParams do
      begin First := nil; Last := nil end
  end { initparams };
procedure Append(ThisParam: ProgPmEntry);
  begin
    with ProgParams do
      begin
        if First = nil then First := ThisParam else Last^.NextParam := ThisParam;
        Last := ThisParam
      end
  end { append };
procedure SearchProgParams(Name: Alfa; var TheParam: ProgPmEntry);
  var Found: Boolean;
  begin
    TheParam := ProgParams.First; Found := false;
    while (TheParam <> nil) and not Found do
      if SameAlfa(TheParam^.Name, Name)
      then Found := true else TheParam := TheParam^.NextParam
  end { searchprogparams };
procedure NewProgParam;
  var ThisParam: ProgPmEntry; NewPmName: Alfa;
  begin
    CopySpelling(NewPmName); SearchProgParams(NewPmName, ThisParam);
    if ThisParam <> nil
    then SemanticError(230)
    else begin
          new(ThisParam);
          with ThisParam^ do
            begin
              Name := NewPmName; Declaration := StartOfSymbol;
              if Name.Head = 'INPUT        '
              then begin
                     Spelling := Name; NewId(InputFile, Vars); ISerialise(InputFile);
                     InputFile^.IdType := TextType; SetAddressFor(InputFile);
                     ParamId := InputFile
                   end
              else if Name.Head = 'OUTPUT        '
                   then begin
                          Spelling := Name; NewId(OutputFile, Vars);
                          ISerialise(OutputFile); OutputFile^.IdType := TextType;
                          SetAddressFor(OutputFile); ParamId := OutputFile
                        end
                   else ParamId := nil;
              NextParam := nil
            end;
```

```
                Append(ThisParam)
           end
     end { newprogparam };
procedure VerifyProgParams;

  var Entry: ProgPmEntry;

  begin
     Entry := ProgParams.First;
     while Entry <> nil do
        begin
           with Entry^ do
              if ParamId = nil
              then begin Error(231, Declaration); ParamId := DummyVarId end
              else AppendId(Externals, ParamId);
           Entry := Entry^.NextParam
        end;
  end { verifyprogparams };
procedure AcceptParameter(ParamId: IdEntry);

  begin
     AcceptProgParameter(ParamId);
     if ParamId = InputFile
     then begin
             StackReference(false, InputFile^.VarAddress); SelectFile(TextType);
             FileOperation(Resetp); DiscardFile
          end;
     if ParamId = OutputFile
     then begin
             StackReference(false, OutputFile^.VarAddress); SelectFile(TextType);
             FileOperation(Rewritep); DiscardFile
          end
  end { acceptparameter };
procedure ProgramHeading;

  begin
     Accept(ProgramSy);
     if Symbol <> Ident then MakeSpelling('PASCAL        ');
     MakeProgEntry; Accept(Ident); InputFile := nil; OutputFile := nil; InitParams;
     if Symbol = LeftParent
     then begin
             repeat
                AcceptSymbol;
                if Symbol = Ident then NewProgParam;
                Accept(Ident);
                CheckNextOrContext([Comma, RightParent], [Semicolon] + BlockBegSys)
             until Symbol <> Comma;
             Accept(RightParent)
          end
  end { programheading };
```

{

10.2 Block Analysis

Block analysis is carried out by procedure Block, which assumes that a (program, procedure or function) identifier entry has already been created for the block, and that a scope has already been opened.

Syntax error recovery at block level is nonstandard in that a block is judged complete only when an 'end' symbol followed by the specified BlockFollower symbol (';' or '.') is detected.

}

```
  procedure Block(BlockFollower: SymbolType; BlockIdEntry: IdEntry);
    type DListEntry = ^Domains;
         Domains =
           record
             Declaration: TextPosition;
             DomainId: IdEntry;
             PointerType: TypEntry;
             NextDomain: DListEntry
           end;
    var BlockContext: SetOfSymbols; DomainList: DListEntry; AllTypesDefined: Boolean;
        FinalPart: StatementLabel;
    procedure PresetBlock;
      begin
        with BlockIdEntry^ do
          begin
            InitializeVariables;
            if Klass = Prog
            then begin
                    OpenProgParameterList; ForAll(Externals, AcceptParameter);
                    CloseProgParameterList
                 end
          end
      end { presetblock };
    procedure PostSetBlock;
      begin
        NextIsStatementLabel(FinalPart);
        with BlockIdEntry^ do
          begin
            FinalizeVariables;
            if Klass = Prog
            then begin
                    OpenProgParameterList; ForAll(Externals, ReturnProgParameter);
                    CloseProgParameterList
                 end
          end
      end { postsetblock };
```

{

10.3 Label-declaration analysis.

Labels are distinguished by their apparent integral values which must belong to the closed interval 0..9999. Semantic processing for labels has already been described in chapter 9, paragraph 6.

}

```
    procedure LabelDeclarationPart;
      begin
        repeat
          AcceptSymbol;
          if Symbol = IntConst
          then begin
                 NewLabel;
                 with Constant do
                   if OrderedValues(Value, MinLabValue) or
                      OrderedValues(MaxLabValue, Value)
                   then SemanticError(137)
               end;
          Accept(IntConst); CheckContext([Comma, Semicolon] + BlockContext)
          until Symbol <> Comma;
          Accept(Semicolon); CheckContext(BlockContext)
      end { labeldeclarationpart };
```

{

10.4 Constant definition analysis.

Constant definition analysis involves two major procedures:

(i)   InConstant, which analyses constant denotations and extracts their type and value;

(ii)   ConstDefinitionPart, which analyses a sequence of constant definitions, creating IdEntries for each constant identifier so defined.

Correct identifier usage is enforced by delaying the creation of each constant identifier entry until its constant denotation has been analysed, leaving the last-use mechanism to reject constant identifiers whose definition makes use of a nonlocal definition of the same identifier.

}

```
    procedure InConstant(Context: SetOfSymbols; var ConsType: TypEntry;
                         var ConstValue: ObjectValue);
      var IdConst: IdEntry; Sign: (None, Positive, Negative);
      begin
        ConsType := Unknown; ConstValue := DefaultValue;
        CheckNextOrContext(ConstBegSys, Context);
        if Symbol in ConstBegSys
        then begin
               if Symbol = CharConst
```

```
         then begin
                ConsType := CharType; ConstValue := Constant.Value;
                AcceptSymbol
             end
         else if Symbol = StringConst
             then begin
                    StringType(ConsType); ConstValue := Constant.Value;
                    AcceptSymbol
                 end
             else begin
                    Sign := None;
                    if (Symbol = AddOp) and (Operator in [Plus, Minus])
                    then begin
                         if Operator = Plus
                         then Sign := Positive else Sign := Negative;
                         AcceptSymbol
                       end;
                    if Symbol = Ident
                    then begin
                           SearchId([Consts], IdConst);
                           with IdConst^ do
                             begin
                               ConsType := IdType; ConstValue := Values
                             end;
                           AcceptSymbol
                       end
                    else if Symbol = IntConst
                         then begin
                                ConsType := IntType;
                                ConstValue := Constant.Value; AcceptSymbol
                              end
                         else if Symbol = RealConst
                              then begin
                                     ConsType := RealType;
                                     ConstValue := Constant.Value;
                                     AcceptSymbol
                                   end
                              else SemanticError(121);
                    if (Sign <> None) and (ConsType <> Unknown)
                    then if (ConsType <> IntType) and
                            (ConsType <> RealType)
                         then SemanticError(120)
                         else if Sign = Negative then NegateValue(ConstValue)
                 end;
           CheckContext(Context)
       end
   end { inconstant };
```

```
procedure ConstDefinitionPart;
  var ConstName: Alfa; ConstId: IdEntry; ConsType: TypEntry;
    ConstValue: ObjectValue;
  begin
    AcceptSymbol; CheckNextOrContext([Ident], BlockContext);
    while Symbol = Ident do
      begin
        CopySpelling(ConstName); AcceptSymbol; AcceptEquals;
        InConstant([Semicolon] + BlockContext, ConsType, ConstValue);
        RestoreSpelling(ConstName); NewId(ConstId, Consts);
        ConstId^.IdType := ConsType; ConstId^.Values := ConstValue;
        Accept(Semicolon); CheckContext([Ident] + BlockContext)
      end
  end { constdefinitionpart };
{
```

10.5 Type definition analysis.

Type definition analysis involves two major procedures:

(i)   TypeDenoter, which analyses any type denotation, creates a new type record to describe it if necessary, and returns a TypEntry pointing to its description;

(ii)   TypeDefinitionPart, which analyses a sequence of type definitions, creating IdEntries for each type identifier so defined.

Correct identifier usage is again enforced by delaying the creation of the type identifier entry until its type denotation has been analysed, but correct handling of pointer domains also requires use of a domain list to remember unbound pointer types, interim domain IdEntries, the procedures BindDomain and SearchDomain from section 9.4, and a variable AllTypesDefined to distinguish between type definition and variable declaration contexts.
}

```
procedure TypeDenoter(Context: SetOfSymbols; var TypeFound: TypEntry);
  var IdFound: IdEntry;
  procedure OrdinalType(Context: SetOfSymbols; var OrdTypEntry: TypEntry);
    var NewTypEntry: TypEntry; FirstIdEntry: IdEntry;
    procedure EnumeratedType;
      var LastId: IdEntry; NextValue: ValueDetails;
      procedure NewConstId;
        var ThisId: IdEntry;
        begin
          if Symbol = Ident
          then begin
                 NewId(ThisId, Consts); ISerialise(ThisId);
                 with ThisId^ do
                   begin
```

```
                        IdType := NewTypEntry; Evaluate(NextValue);
                        Values := NextValue.Value;
                        NextValue.Ival := NextValue.Ival + 1; SuccId := nil
                    end;
                if LastId = nil
                then NewTypEntry^.FirstConst := ThisId
                else LastId^.SuccId := ThisId;
                LastId := ThisId
            end;
        Accept(Ident)
    end;

  begin { enumeratedtype }
    NewType(NewTypEntry, Scalars); LastId := nil;
    with NextValue do
      begin Kind := OrdValue; Ival := 0 end;
    repeat
      AcceptSymbol; NewConstId;
      CheckContext(Context + [Comma, RightParent])
    until Symbol <> Comma;
    SetRepresentationFor(NewTypEntry); Accept(RightParent)
  end { enumeratedtype };

procedure SubrangeType;

  var FirsType, SecondType: TypEntry; FirstValue, SecondValue: ObjectValue;
  begin
    InConstant(Context + [Thru], FirsType, FirstValue);
    EnsureOrdinal(FirsType); Accept(Thru);
    InConstant(Context, SecondType, SecondValue); EnsureOrdinal(SecondType);
    NewType(NewTypEntry, SubRanges);
    if (FirsType <> Unknown) and (SecondType <> Unknown)
    then with NewTypEntry^ do
            begin
              Min := FirstValue; Max := SecondValue;
              if not Compatible(FirsType, SecondType)
              then SemanticError(122)
              else if FirsType <> Unknown
                  then begin
                          RangeType := FirsType;
                          if SecondType <> Unknown
                          then if OrderedValues(Max, Min)
                                  then SemanticError(123)
                      end
                  else RangeType := SecondType
            end;
    SetRepresentationFor(NewTypEntry)
  end { subrangetype };

begin { ordinaltype }
  CheckNextOrContext(SimpTypeBegSys, Context);
  if Symbol in SimpTypeBegSys
```

```
        then begin
              if Symbol = LeftParent
              then EnumeratedType
              else if Symbol = Ident
                    then begin
                          SearchId([Domain, Types, Consts], FirstIdEntry);
                          with FirstIdEntry^ do
                          if Klass = Consts
                          then SubrangeType
                          else begin
                                AcceptSymbol; NewTypEntry := IdType;
                                EnsureOrdinal(NewTypEntry)
                          end
                    end
              else SubrangeType;
              OrdTypEntry := NewTypEntry; CheckContext(Context)
        end
      else OrdTypEntry := Unknown
  end { ordinaltype };
procedure StructuredType;
  var PackFlag: Boolean;
  procedure ArrayType;
    label 9;
    var ElementType, Dimension, LastDimension: TypEntry;
    procedure NewDimension;
      var IndexType: TypEntry;
    begin
      OrdinalType(Context + [Comma, RightBracket, OfSy], IndexType);
      NewType(Dimension, Arrays);
      with Dimension^ do
        begin
          PackedArray := PackFlag; InxType := IndexType;
          { Dimensions are temporarily back-chained thru field AelType }
          AelType := LastDimension
        end;
      LastDimension := Dimension
    end;
  begin { arraytype }
    AcceptSymbol; Accept(LeftBracket); LastDimension := nil;
    while true do
      begin
        NewDimension;
        if Symbol <> Comma then goto 9;
        AcceptSymbol
      end;
    9: Accept(RightBracket); Accept(OfSy);
```

```
            TypeDenoter(Context, ElementType);
            { now reverse chaining and set representation at each level }
         repeat
            LastDimension := Dimension^.AelType;
            Dimension^.AelType := ElementType; SetRepresentationFor(Dimension);
            ElementType := Dimension; Dimension := LastDimension
         until Dimension = nil;
            TypeFound := ElementType
      end { arraytype };
   procedure RecordType;
      var LVarPart: TypEntry; LFixedPart: IdEntry; LFiles: Boolean;
      procedure FieldList(Context: SetOfSymbols; var FixedPart: IdEntry;
                          var VarPart: TypEntry; var AnyFiles: Boolean);
         { Although called fieldlist, this procedure accepts constructs of the form
            [ field-list [ ";" ] ]
         which is the only context in which a field-list can occur. }
         label 9, 19;
         var LastField, TagField, TagTypeId, FirstSubField: IdEntry;
            FieldsOfOneType: IdList; FirstName, TypeName: Alfa;
            FieldType, TagType, ThisVariant, LastVariant, LastDistinctVariant,
            SubVariantPart:
               TypEntry;
            VariantFiles, MultipleLabels, StillDistinct: Boolean;
            TagMin, TagMax: ObjectValue; Selections: ValueDetails;
            LabelCount: integer;
         procedure NewFieldId;
            var ThisField: IdEntry;
            begin
               if Symbol = Ident
               then begin
                     NewId(ThisField, Field); ISerialise(ThisField);
                     AppendId(FieldsOfOneType, ThisField)
                  end;
               Accept(Ident)
            end { newfieldid };
         procedure FixFieldId(ThisField: IdEntry);
            begin
               ThisField^.IdType := FieldType;
               if LastField = nil
               then FixedPart := ThisField else LastField^.NextField := ThisField;
               LastField := ThisField
            end { fixfieldid };
```

```
procedure NewVariantLabel;

  var LabelType: TypEntry; LabelValue: ObjectValue;

  begin
    InConstant
      ([Comma, Colon, LeftParent] + Context, LabelType, LabelValue);
    if not Compatible(TagType, LabelType)
    then SemanticError(124)
    else if OrderedValues(LabelValue, TagMin) or
            OrderedValues(TagMax, LabelValue)
      then SemanticError(125)
      else begin
              ThisVariant := LastVariant;
              while ThisVariant <> nil do
                begin
                  if SameValue(ThisVariant^.VariantValue, LabelValue)
                  then SemanticError(126);
                  ThisVariant := ThisVariant^.NextVariant
                end
           end;
    NewType(ThisVariant, Variant);
    with ThisVariant^ do
      begin NextVariant := LastVariant; VariantValue := LabelValue end;
    LabelCount := LabelCount + 1; LastVariant := ThisVariant
  end { newvariantlabel };

procedure CheckCompleteness;

  var Min, Max: ObjectValue;

  begin
    if TagType <> Unknown
    then begin
            GetBounds(TagType, Min, Max);
            if Range(Min, Max) <> LabelCount then SemanticError(127)
         end
  end { checkcompleteness };

procedure FixSelector;

  var SelectorType: TypEntry; SelectorId: IdEntry;

  begin
    with VarPart^ do
      if (TagField = nil) or MultipleLabels
      then begin
              Evaluate(Selections); NewType(SelectorType, SubRanges);
              with SelectorType^ do
                begin Max := Selections.Value; RangeType := IntType end;
              SetRepresentationFor(SelectorType);
              MakeSpelling(DefaultSpelling); CreateId(SelectorId, Field);
              SelectorId^.IdType := SelectorType;
              SelectorField := SelectorId
           end
```

```
          else SelectorField := TagField
      end { fixselector };
begin { fieldlist }
  CheckContext(Context + [Ident, CaseSy]);
  { fixed part, if any }
  FixedPart := nil; LastField := nil; AnyFiles := false;
  while Symbol = Ident do
    begin
      StartList(FieldsOfOneType);
      while true do
        begin
          NewFieldId;
          CheckNextOrContext
            ([Comma, Colon], Context + [Semicolon, CaseSy]);
          if Symbol <> Comma then goto 9;
          AcceptSymbol
        end;
      9: Accept(Colon);
      TypeDenoter(Context + [CaseSy, Semicolon], FieldType);
      AnyFiles := AnyFiles or EmbeddedFile(FieldType);
      ForAll(FieldsOfOneType, FixFieldId); DisposeList(FieldsOfOneType);
      LastField^.NextField := nil;
      if Symbol = Semicolon
      then begin
             AcceptSymbol; CheckContext([Ident, CaseSy] + Context)
           end
      else if Symbol = CaseSy then Error(25, StartOfSymbol)
    end;
  { variant part, if any }
  if Symbol = CaseSy
  then begin
         NewType(VarPart, VariantPart); AcceptSymbol;
         CopySpelling(FirstName); Accept(Ident);
         if Symbol = OfSy
         then begin TagField := nil; TypeName := FirstName end
         else begin
                RestoreSpelling(FirstName); NewId(TagField, Field);
                TagField^.Tag := true; ISerialise(TagField); Accept(Colon);
                CopySpelling(TypeName); Accept(Ident)
              end;
         RestoreSpelling(TypeName);
         SearchId([Domain, Types], TagTypeId);
         TagType := TagTypeId^.IdType; EnsureOrdinal(TagType);
         GetBounds(TagType, TagMin, TagMax);
         VarPart^.TagType := TagType; VarPart^.TagField := TagField;
         if TagField <> nil then TagField^.IdType := TagType;
         Accept(OfSy); MultipleLabels := false; LabelCount := 0;
         Selections.Kind := OrdValue; Selections.Ival := -1;
         LastVariant := nil;
```

```
              repeat
                LastDistinctVariant := LastVariant;
                while true do
                  begin
                    NewVariantLabel;
                    if Symbol = Comma
                    then MultipleLabels := true else goto 19;
                    AcceptSymbol
                  end;
                19: Accept(Colon); Selections.Ival := Selections.Ival + 1;
                Accept(LeftParent);
                FieldList
                  (Context + [RightParent], FirstSubField, SubVariantPart,
                    VariantFiles);
                AnyFiles := AnyFiles or VariantFiles; StillDistinct := true;
                while ThisVariant <> LastDistinctVariant do
                  with ThisVariant^ do
                    begin
                      VarFileFree := not VariantFiles;
                      SubVarPart := SubVariantPart;
                      SubFixedPart := FirstSubField; Distinct := StillDistinct;
                      ThisVariant := NextVariant; StillDistinct := false
                    end;
                Accept(RightParent); CheckContext(Context + [Semicolon]);
                if Symbol = Semicolon then AcceptSymbol
              until Symbol in Context;
              CheckCompleteness; FixSelector;
              VarPart^.FirstVariant := LastVariant
            end
        else VarPart := nil
      end { fieldlist };

  begin { recordtype }
    AcceptSymbol; OpenScope(RecordScope);
    FieldList(Context + [EndSy], LFixedPart, LVarPart, LFiles);
    NewType(TypeFound, Records);
    with TypeFound^ do
      begin
        FileFree := not LFiles; PackedRecord := PackFlag;
        FieldScope := Display[ScopeLevel].Locals; FixedPart := LFixedPart;
        VarPart := LVarPart
      end;
    CloseScope; Accept(EndSy); SetRepresentationFor(TypeFound)
  end { recordtype };

procedure SetType;

  var ElementType: TypEntry;

  begin
    AcceptSymbol; Accept(OfSy); OrdinalType(Context, ElementType);
    NewType(TypeFound, Sets);
```

```
      with TypeFound^ do
        begin
          if PackFlag then FormOfSet := IsPacked else FormOfSet := Unpacked;
          BaseType := ElementType
        end;
      SetRepresentationFor(TypeFound)
    end { settype };
  procedure FileType;

    var ElementType: TypEntry;

    begin
      AcceptSymbol; Accept(OfSy); TypeDenoter(Context, ElementType);
      NewType(TypeFound, Files);
      with TypeFound^ do
        begin
          PackedFile := PackFlag;
          if EmbeddedFile(ElementType)
          then begin SemanticError(128); ElementType := Unknown end;
          FelType := ElementType
        end;
      SetRepresentationFor(TypeFound)
    end { filetype };

  begin { structuredtype }
    if Symbol = PackedSy
    then begin PackFlag := true; AcceptSymbol end
    else PackFlag := false;
    CheckNextOrContext(TypeDels, Context);
    if Symbol in TypeDels
    then case Symbol of
            ArraySy : ArrayType;
            RecordSy : RecordType;
            SetSy : SetType;
            FileSy : FileType
         end
    else TypeFound := Unknown
  end { structuredtype };

procedure PointerType;

  var DomainEntry: DListEntry; ItsDomain: IdEntry; DomainNeeded: Boolean;

  begin
    NewType(TypeFound, Pointers); AcceptSymbol;
    if Symbol = Ident
    then begin
            DomainNeeded := true;
            if AllTypesDefined
            then begin
                    SearchId([Types], ItsDomain);
                    TypeFound^.DomainType := ItsDomain^.IdType;
                    DomainNeeded := false
```

```
                    end
              else begin
                    SearchDomain(ItsDomain);
                    if ItsDomain <> nil
                    then begin
                            if ItsDomain^.Klass <> Domain
                            then begin
                                    if ItsDomain^.Klass = Types
                                    then TypeFound^.DomainType :=
                                            ItsDomain^.IdType
                                    else SemanticError(104);
                                    DomainNeeded := false
                                 end
                         end
                    else NewId(ItsDomain, Domain)
                 end;
              if DomainNeeded
              then begin
                    new(DomainEntry);
                    with DomainEntry^ do
                      begin
                        Declaration := StartOfSymbol; DomainId := ItsDomain;
                        PointerType := TypeFound; NextDomain := DomainList
                      end;
                    DomainList := DomainEntry
                 end
           end;
        Accept(Ident); SetRepresentationFor(TypeFound)
     end { pointertype };
begin { typedenoter }
   CheckNextOrContext(TypeBegSys, Context);
   if Symbol in TypeBegSys
   then begin
           if Symbol = Ident
           then begin
                   SearchId([Domain, Types, Consts], IdFound);
                   if IdFound^.Klass = Types
                   then begin TypeFound := IdFound^.IdType; AcceptSymbol end
                   else OrdinalType(Context, TypeFound)
                end
           else if Symbol in SimpTypeBegSys
                then OrdinalType(Context, TypeFound)
                else if Symbol = Arrow then PointerType else StructuredType;
           CheckContext(Context)
        end
   else TypeFound := Unknown
end { typedenoter };
```

```
procedure TypeDefinitionPart;
  var TypeName: Alfa; NewTypEntry: TypEntry; IdFound: IdEntry;
      ThisDomain: DListEntry; DomainFound: Boolean;
begin
  AcceptSymbol; AllTypesDefined := false; DomainList := nil;
  CheckNextOrContext([Ident], BlockContext);
  while Symbol = Ident do
    begin
      CopySpelling(TypeName); AcceptSymbol; AcceptEquals;
      TypeDenoter([Semicolon] + BlockContext, NewTypEntry);
      RestoreSpelling(TypeName); DomainFound := false;
      SearchLocalId(Display[BlockLevel].Locals, IdFound);
      if IdFound <> nil then DomainFound := IdFound^.Klass = Domain;
      if DomainFound
      then IdFound^.Klass := Types else NewId(IdFound, Types);
      IdFound^.IdType := NewTypEntry; Accept(Semicolon);
      CheckContext([Ident] + BlockContext)
    end;

  { bind remaining domain-identifiers and fixup pointer types }
  while DomainList <> nil do
    begin
      ThisDomain := DomainList;
      with ThisDomain^ do
        begin
          StartOfSymbol := Declaration;
          if DomainId^.Klass = Domain then BindDomain(DomainId);
          PointerType^.DomainType := DomainId^.IdType;
          DomainList := NextDomain
        end;
      dispose(ThisDomain)
    end
end { typedefinitionpart };
{
```

10.6 Variable declaration analysis.

Within each variable declaration, variables are accumulated on an IdList VarsOfOneType for fix-up after the type denoter has been analysed. Variables declared at the outermost global level are checked against the ProgParams list for possible binding, as explained in 10.1.

```
}
    procedure VarDeclarationPart;
      label 9;
      var VarsOfOneType: IdList; VarTypEntry: TypEntry;
      procedure NewVarId;
        var VarIdEntry: IdEntry;
        begin
          if Symbol = Ident
          then begin
                  NewId(VarIdEntry, Vars); ISerialise(VarIdEntry);
                  AppendId(VarsOfOneType, VarIdEntry)
               end;
          Accept(Ident)
        end;
      procedure FixVarId(VarId: IdEntry);
        var ParamFound: ProgPmEntry;
        begin
          VarId^.IdType := VarTypEntry; SetAddressFor(VarId);
          if BlockLevel = GlobalLevel
          then SearchProgParams(VarId^.Name, ParamFound) else ParamFound := nil;
          if ParamFound <> nil then ParamFound^.ParamId := VarId
        end { fixvarid };
      begin { vardeclarationpart }
        AcceptSymbol; AllTypesDefined := true;
        repeat
          StartList(VarsOfOneType);
          while true do
            begin
              NewVarId;
              CheckNextOrContext
                 (BlockContext + [Comma, Colon] + TypeDels, [Semicolon]);
              if Symbol <> Comma then goto 9;
              AcceptSymbol
            end;
          9: Accept(Colon);
          TypeDenoter([Semicolon] + TypeDels + BlockContext, VarTypEntry);
          ForAll(VarsOfOneType, FixVarId); DisposeList(VarsOfOneType);
          Accept(Semicolon); CheckContext([Ident] + TypeDels + BlockContext)
        until (Symbol <> Ident) and not (Symbol in TypeDels)
      end { vardeclarationpart };
```

{

10.7 Procedure and function declaration analysis.

Analysis of procedure and function declarations involves the treatment of formal parameter lists and forward block identification.

A representation of the formal parameters is built as the list FormalList, which has one element for each parameter identifier. Each element records the kind of the formal parameter, and associated attributes needed for actual parameter checking or congruence testing. A formal parameter section involving a conformant-array-parameter-schema gives rise to an additional element of kind BoundParm, which does not correspond directly to a formal parameter, but is used to prompt the passing of actual array-bound values to the bound-identifiers of the schema. The completed formal list is attached to the IdRecord representing the procedure or function identifier.

The formal parameter identifiers are also treated as local variables and are entered into the symbol table at the newly created top-most scope level. At the end of the procedure or function heading this scope is automatically saved, and restored at the start of the corresponding block. As explained in chapter 9 this allows type identifiers used in the formal parameter list to be redefined within the block.

This saving and restoring also accommodates the split scopes created by forward declarations. If however the program repeats the formal parameter list of a forward-declared procedure or function special logic is included to discard and re-analyse the parameter list for error recovery purposes.

}

```
        procedure PfDeclaration;
            var BlockId: IdEntry; BlockKind: (Local, Forwerd { any others });
            procedure PfHeading(Context: SetOfSymbols; HeadingKind: IdKind;
                                var Pfid: IdEntry);
                var PfClass: Proc..Func; TypeId: IdEntry; FormalList: FormalEntry;
                    FuncType: TypEntry; AlreadyDeclared: Boolean;
                procedure FormalParameterList(Context: SetOfSymbols);
                    label 9;
                    var PfParam: IdEntry; ParamsOfOneType: IdList; ParamType: TypEntry;
                        VarMode, Packing, FirstOne: Boolean; LastFormal: FormalEntry;
                        SectionNumber: Scalar;
                    procedure NewParamId;
                        var ThisParam: IdEntry;
                        begin
                            if Symbol = Ident
                            then begin
                                    NewId(ThisParam, Vars); ISerialise(ThisParam);
```

```
                     if VarMode
                     then ThisParam^.VarKind := VarParam
                     else ThisParam^.VarKind := ValueParam;
                     AppendId(ParamsOfOneType, ThisParam)
                 end;
        Accept(Ident)
    end { newparamid };
procedure AppendFormal(ParamSpec: ParmKind);

  var ThisFormal: FormalEntry;

  begin
    new(ThisFormal);
    with ThisFormal^ do
      begin
        Section := SectionNumber; Parm := ParamSpec;
        case Parm of
          BoundParm, ValueParm, VarParm : FormalType := ParamType;
          ProcParm, FuncParm :
              begin
                ItsFormals := PfParam^.Formals;
                if Parm = FuncParm then FormalType := PfParam^.IdType
              end
        end;
        Next := nil
      end;
    if LastFormal = nil
    then FormalList := ThisFormal else LastFormal^.Next := ThisFormal;
    LastFormal := ThisFormal
  end { addtoformallist };
procedure FixParamId(ParamId: IdEntry);

  begin
    ParamId^.IdType := ParamType; SetAddressFor(ParamId);
    if VarMode
    then AppendFormal(VarParm) else AppendFormal(ValueParm)
  end { fixparamid };
procedure ProcOrFuncSpec;

  begin
    SetAddressFor(PfParam);
    with PfParam^ do
      if Klass = Proc
      then AppendFormal(ProcParm) else AppendFormal(FuncParm)
  end { procorfuncspec };
procedure VarOrValueSpec;

  begin
    if Conformant(ParamType) then AppendFormal(BoundParm);
    ForAll(ParamsOfOneType, FixParamId)
  end { varorvaluespec };
```

```
procedure IdentOrSchema(Context: SetOfSymbols;
                            var TypeFound: TypEntry);
var TypeId: IdEntry; Starters: SetOfSymbols;
procedure ArraySchema(Context: SetOfSymbols;
                            var TypeFound: TypEntry);
   label 9;
   var Schema, LastSchema, ComponentType: TypEntry;
      WeakStarters: SetOfSymbols;
   procedure IndexSpec(Context: SetOfSymbols);
      var BoundsOfASchema: IdList; IndexType: TypEntry;
      procedure ArrayBound(Context: SetOfSymbols);
         var BoundId: IdEntry;
         begin
            CheckNextOrContext([Ident], Context);
            if Symbol = Ident
            then begin
                    NewId(BoundId, Bound); ISerialise(BoundId);
                    AppendId(BoundsOfASchema, BoundId); Accept(Ident);
                    CheckContext(Context)
                 end
         end;
      procedure NewBoundPairBlock;
         begin
            with BoundsOfASchema do
               begin
                  SetBoundPairBlockFor(FirstEntry^.Id, LastEntry^.Id);
                  FirstEntry^.Id^.IdType := IndexType;
                  LastEntry^.Id^.IdType := IndexType
               end
         end { newboundpairblock };
      begin { indexspec }
         StartList(BoundsOfASchema); ArrayBound([Thru] + Context);
         Accept(Thru); ArrayBound([Colon] + Context); Accept(Colon);
         CheckNextOrContext([Ident], Context);
         if Symbol = Ident
         then begin
                 SearchId([Types], TypeId); IndexType := TypeId^.IdType;
                 Accept(Ident)
              end
         else IndexType := Unknown;
         EnsureOrdinal(IndexType); NewBoundPairBlock;
         NewType(Schema, CAPSchema);
         with Schema^ do
            begin
               PackedSchema := Packing; ValueSchema := not VarMode;
               FirstIndex := FirstOne; FirstOne := false;
```

```
            InxSpec := IndexType; CompType := LastSchema;
            with BoundsOfASchema do
               begin
                  LowBdAddress := FirstEntry^.Id^.BdAddress;
                  HighBdAddress := LastEntry^.Id^.BdAddress
               end
         end;
      LastSchema := Schema; DisposeList(BoundsOfASchema);
      CheckContext(Context)
   end { indexspec };

begin { arrayschema }
   WeakStarters := [LeftBracket, Ident]; Schema := nil;
   LastSchema := nil; Accept(ArraySy);
   CheckNextOrContext(WeakStarters, Context);
   if Symbol in WeakStarters
   then begin
         Accept(LeftBracket);
         while true do
            begin
               IndexSpec([Semicolon, RightBracket, OfSy] + Context);
               if Symbol <> Semicolon then goto 9;
               if Packing then SemanticError(250);
               AcceptSymbol
            end;
         9: Accept(RightBracket); Accept(OfSy)
      end;
   CheckContext(Context); IdentOrSchema(Context, ComponentType);
   if Schema <> nil
   then repeat
         LastSchema := Schema^.CompType;
         Schema^.CompType := ComponentType;
         SetRepresentationFor(Schema); ComponentType := Schema;
         Schema := LastSchema
      until Schema = nil;
   TypeFound := ComponentType
end { arrayschema };

begin { identorschema }
   Starters := ConformantParamBegSys + [Ident];
   CheckNextOrContext(Starters, Context);
   if Symbol in Starters
   then begin
         if Symbol = Ident
         then begin
               SearchId([Types], TypeId);
               TypeFound := TypeId^.IdType; Accept(Ident)
            end
         else begin
               if Packing then SemanticError(250);
               if Symbol = PackedSy
```

```
                    then begin Packing := true; AcceptSymbol end;
                    ArraySchema(Starters + Context, TypeFound)
                end;
            CheckContext(Context)
        end
    else TypeFound := Unknown
    end { identorschema };
begin { formalparameterlist }
    Accept(LeftParent); LastFormal := nil; SectionNumber := 0;
    CheckNextOrContext(ParamBegSys, [RightParent] + Context);
    while Symbol in ParamBegSys do
        begin
        SectionNumber := SectionNumber + 1;
        case Symbol of
            ProcSy, FuncSy :
                begin
                PfHeading
                    ([Semicolon, RightParent] + Context, Formal, PfParam);

                { discard scope created for parameter list of this parameter }
                CloseStackFrame; DisposeScope; CloseScope; ProcOrFuncSpec
                end;
            VarSy, Ident :
                begin
                StartList(ParamsOfOneType);
                if Symbol = VarSy
                then begin VarMode := true; AcceptSymbol end
                else VarMode := false;
                while true do
                    begin
                    NewParamId;
                    CheckNextOrContext
                        ([Comma, Colon], [Semicolon, RightParent] + Context);
                    if Symbol <> Comma then goto 9;
                    AcceptSymbol
                    end;
                9: Accept(Colon); Packing := false; FirstOne := true;
                IdentOrSchema
                    (Context + [Semicolon, RightParent], ParamType);
                if ParamType <> Unknown
                then if not VarMode and EmbeddedFile(ParamType)
                    then SemanticError(145);
                VarOrValueSpec; DisposeList(ParamsOfOneType)
                end
            end;
        if Symbol = Semicolon
        then begin
                AcceptSymbol;
                CheckNextOrContext(ParamBegSys, [RightParent] + Context)
```

```
                    end
              end;
          Accept(RightParent); CheckContext(Context)
      end { formalparameterlist };
procedure DuplicateParameterScope;
    begin
        { dispose the original formal scope }
        RestoreScope(Pfid^.FormalScope); RestoreStackFrame; CloseStackFrame;
        DisposeScope; CloseScope;
        { now open a scope for the duplicate fplist }
        OpenScope(ActualBlock); OpenStackFrame
    end { duplicateparameterscope };
procedure SaveParameterScope;
    var Temporary: ScopeCopy;
    begin
        SaveStackFrame; SaveScope(Temporary); Pfid^.FormalScope := Temporary
    end { saveparameterscope };
begin { pfheading }
    if Symbol = ProcSy then PfClass := Proc else PfClass := Func;
    AcceptSymbol; AlreadyDeclared := false;
    if Symbol = Ident
    then begin
            SearchLocalId(Display[ScopeLevel].Locals, Pfid);
            if Pfid <> nil
            then with Pfid^ do
                    AlreadyDeclared :=
                        Forwrd and (PfClass = Klass) and (PfKind = Actual)
        end
    else MakeSpelling(DefaultSpelling);
    if not AlreadyDeclared
    then begin
            NewId(Pfid, PfClass);
            if HeadingKind = Actual
            then begin ISerialise(Pfid); OpenScope(ActualBlock) end
            else begin Pfid^.PfKind := Formal; OpenScope(FormalBlock) end;
            OpenStackFrame
        end;
    Accept(Ident);
    if (Symbol = LeftParent) and AlreadyDeclared
    then begin
            SemanticError(140); DuplicateParameterScope; AlreadyDeclared := false
        end;
    if PfClass = Proc
    then begin
            if Symbol = LeftParent
            then begin
                    FormalParameterList([Semicolon] + Context);
                    Pfid^.Formals := FormalList
```

```
                    end
             else if not AlreadyDeclared then Pfid^.Formals := nil;
             if not AlreadyDeclared and (HeadingKind = Actual)
             then SaveParameterScope
          end
      else begin
             if Symbol = LeftParent
             then begin
                    FormalParameterList([Colon, Semicolon] + Context);
                    Pfid^.Formals := FormalList
                 end
             else if not AlreadyDeclared then Pfid^.Formals := nil;
             if not AlreadyDeclared and (HeadingKind = Actual)
             then SaveParameterScope;
             if Symbol = Colon
             then begin
                    AcceptSymbol;
                    if Symbol = Ident
                    then begin
                           if AlreadyDeclared then SemanticError(141);
                           SearchId([Types], TypeId);
                           FuncType := TypeId^.IdType;
                           if FuncType <> Unknown
                           then if FuncType^.Form in
                                      [Scalars, SubRanges, Pointers]
                                 then Pfid^.IdType := FuncType
                                 else SemanticError(142)
                        end;
                    Accept(Ident)
                 end
             else if not AlreadyDeclared then SemanticError(143)
          end;
       CheckContext(Context)
   end { pfheading };
procedure CheckDirective(Word: AlfaHead);
   begin
     if Word = 'FORWARD         '
     then BlockKind := Forwerd else SemanticError(154)
   end { checkdirective };
procedure ForwardBlock;
   begin
     with BlockId^ do
        begin
          if Forwrd then SemanticError(144);
          Forwrd := true; Declaration := StartOfSymbol
        end
   end { forwardblock };
begin { pfdeclaration }
```

```
        PfHeading(BlockContext + [Semicolon], Actual, BlockId); Accept(Semicolon);
        BlockKind := Local;
        if Symbol = Ident
        then begin
                CheckDirective(Spelling.Head);
                if BlockKind = Forwerd then ForwardBlock;
                AcceptSymbol; Accept(Semicolon); CheckContext(BlockContext)
            end
        else begin
                RestoreScope(BlockId^.FormalScope); RestoreStackFrame;
                with BlockId^ do
                  begin
                    EntryLabel := CodeBody; OpenCodeSpace(EntryLabel);
                    CodeBody := EntryLabel; Forwrd := false;
                    if Klass = Func
                    then begin
                            Assignable := true; Assigned := false; SetAddressFor(BlockId)
                        end
                  end;
                repeat
                  { for syntax error recovery }

                  Block(Semicolon, BlockId); Accept(Semicolon);
                  CheckNextOrContext([BeginSy, ProcSy, FuncSy], BlockContext)
                until Symbol in [BeginSy, ProcSy, FuncSy];
                with BlockId^ do
                  if Klass = Func
                  then begin
                          Assignable := false;
                          if not Assigned then SemanticError(146)
                      end;
                FileScope(BlockId); CloseCodeSpace; CloseStackFrame; DisposeScope;
                CloseScope
            end
    end { pfdeclaration };
{
```

10.8 Variable analysis.

Variable analysis is carried out by one of two procedures:

(i)   Selector, which is called when the table entry for the initial variable identifier has already been located; or

(ii)   Variable, which is called when no preliminary identifier checking has occurred.

In either case the type of the variable is left in the global variable VarType. Additional information on the accessibility of the variable is left in the following global flags:

SimpleVar   the variable is a simple variable

PackedVar   the variable is a component of a packed structure

TagVar   the variable is a tag field

NewRecVar   the variable is a complete record created by 'new'

When TagVar is true, the global VntSelector holds a pointer to the the type descriptor for the variant part containing the tag field.

```
}
    procedure Expression(ExpContext: SetOfSymbols); forward;

    procedure Selector(SelectContext: SetOfSymbols; VarIdEntry: IdEntry);
      var LocalType: TypEntry; LocalId: IdEntry;
          LowerBound, UpperBound: ObjectValue;
      begin
        PackedVar := false; SimpleVar := true; TagVar := false; NewRecVar := false;
        with VarIdEntry^ do
          begin
            LocalType := IdType;
            case Klass of
              Vars :
                if Conformant(LocalType)
                then StackReference(true, VarAddress)
                else StackReference((VarKind = VarParam), VarAddress);
              Field :
                begin
                  SimpleVar := false; TagVar := Tag; WithReference(LevelFound);
                  with Display[LevelFound] do
                    begin
                      PackedVar := FieldsPacked;
                      with RecordType^ do
                        if VarPart <> nil
                        then if VariantField(VarPart, VarIdEntry)
                             then VariantChecks(VarPart, VarIdEntry);
                      if TagVar
                      then VntSelector :=
                              TaggedVarPart(RecordType^.VarPart, VarIdEntry)
                    end;
                  FieldReference(Offset, TagVar)
                end;
              Func :
                if PfDecKind = Predefined
                then SemanticError(147)
                else if PfKind = Formal
                     then SemanticError(148)
                     else if Assignable
                          then begin StackReference(false, Result); Assigned := true end
                          else SemanticError(149)
          end
```

```
        end;
    if VarIdEntry^.Klass = Func
    then CheckContext(SelectContext)
    else CheckContext(SelectSymbols + SelectContext);
    while Symbol in SelectSymbols do
      begin
        NewRecVar := false;
        case Symbol of
          LeftBracket :
            begin
              repeat
                if not Conformant(LocalType)
                then EnsureFormIs(Arrays, LocalType);
                AcceptSymbol; Expression([Comma, RightBracket] + SelectContext);
                EnsureOrdinal(ExpType);
                with LocalType^ do
                  if Compatible(IndexOf(LocalType), ExpType)
                  then begin
                        if Form = CAPSchema
                        then WithSchema(LocalType, IndexedCAPReference)
                        else begin
                              GetBounds(InxType, LowerBound, UpperBound);
                              IndexedReference
                                (PackedArray, LowerBound, UpperBound,
                                    AelType^.Representation)
                            end;
                        PackedVar := PackingOf(LocalType)
                      end
                  else SemanticError(160);
                LocalType := ElementOf(LocalType)
              until Symbol <> Comma;
              Accept(RightBracket)
            end;
          Period :
            begin
              EnsureFormIs(Records, LocalType);
              PackedVar := LocalType^.PackedRecord; AcceptSymbol;
              if Symbol = Ident
              then begin
                    SearchLocalId(LocalType^.FieldScope, LocalId);
                    if LocalId = nil
                    then begin SemanticError(100); LocalType := Unknown end
                    else begin
                          with LocalType^ do
                            if VarPart <> nil
                            then if VariantField(VarPart, LocalId)
                                then VariantChecks(VarPart, LocalId);
                          with LocalId^ do
                            begin
                              TagVar := Tag;
```

```
                                if TagVar
                                then VntSelector :=
                                        TaggedVarPart
                                          (LocalType^.VarPart, LocalId);
                                FieldReference(Offset, TagVar);
                                LocalType := IdType
                             end
                       end
                  end;
               Accept(Ident)
            end;
         Arrow :
            begin
               if LocalType <> Unknown
               then with LocalType^ do
                     if Form = Pointers
                     then begin
                             LocalType := DomainType; PackedVar := false;
                             NewRecVar := (LocalType^.Form = Records);
                             PnterReference
                          end
                     else if Form = Files
                          then begin
                                  LocalType := FelType;
                                  PackedVar := PackedFile;
                                  BufferReference
                                    (PackedVar, TextFile,
                                       FelType^.Representation)
                               end
                          else SemanticError(161);
               AcceptSymbol
            end
      end;
      SimpleVar := false; CheckContext(SelectSymbols + SelectContext)
   end;
   VarType := LocalType
end { selector };
procedure Variable(Context: SetOfSymbols);
   var VarId: IdEntry;
   begin
      if Symbol = Ident
      then SearchId([Vars, Field], VarId) else VarId := DummyVarId;
      Accept(Ident); Selector(Context, VarId);
      if SimpleVar then Threaten(VarId)
   end { variable };
```

{

10.9 Procedure and function call analysis.

Procedure and function calls are processed by procedure Call and its subprocedures CallStandard and CallUserDefined as follows.

The procedure CallStandard analyses calls to all the required (standard) functions and procedures of Pascal. A variety of ad-hoc techniques are employed to check the number and validity of the actual parameters.

The procedure CallUserDefined analyses calls to procedures and functions declared within the program. The analysis of actual parameters is controlled by the formal list which is attached to the procedure or function's IdRecord. Actual-formal correspondence is established on the basis of position and is checked using the attributes held in the formal list, by one of the procedures ActualValue, ActualVariable, ActualProcedure, and ActualFunction. The first two also check conformance of actual array parameters passed to a conformant array schema.

}

```
    procedure Call(CallContext: SetOfSymbols; Pfid: IdEntry);
      procedure CallStandard(WhichPf: StdProcFuncs);
        { Analyses all calls on standard procedures and functions }
        var First, Last: ObjectValue;
        procedure ResetOrRewrite;
          { Analyses parameter list for reset or rewrite }
          begin
            Variable([RightParent] + CallContext); EnsureFormIs(Files, VarType);
            SelectFile(VarType); FileOperation(WhichPf); DiscardFile
          end { fileprocedures };
        procedure GetOrPut;
          { Analyses the parameter list for get or put }
          begin
            Variable([RightParent] + CallContext); EnsureFormIs(Files, VarType);
            SelectFile(VarType); FileOperation(WhichPf); DiscardFile
          end { getorput };
        procedure SelectInput;
          { Default action when read, readln, eof or eoln
            is called without an explicit textfile parameter }
          begin
            if InputFile = nil
            then SemanticError(232)
            else with InputFile^ do
                begin
                    StackReference((VarKind = VarParam), VarAddress);
                    SelectFile(TextType)
```

```
            end
      end { selectinput };
procedure SelectOutput;

   { Default action when write or writeln is
   called without an explicit textfile parameter }
   begin
      if OutputFile = nil
      then SemanticError(233)
      else with OutputFile^ do
            begin
               StackReference((VarKind = VarParam), VarAddress);
               SelectFile(TextType)
            end
   end { selectoutput };
procedure ReadProcedure;

   { Analyses parameter list of read or readln. }
   label 1;

   var FileDetermined: Boolean; FileType: TypEntry;

   procedure InputVariable;

      { Analyses any parameter of read or readln,
        including the optional initial textfile }
      procedure SimpleRead;
         begin
            with FileType^ do
            begin
               ReadBuffer; CheckAssignment(VarType, FelType);
               Assign(VarType^.Representation); FileOperation(Getp)
            end
         end { simpleread };
      procedure NumericRead;
         begin
            if Compatible(VarType, RealType)
            then ReadNumeric(RealKind)
            else if Compatible(VarType, IntType)
                  then begin
                          ReadNumeric(IntKind);
                          CheckAssignment(VarType, IntType)
                       end
                  else SemanticError(163);
            Assign(VarType^.Representation)
         end { numericread };

      begin { inputvariable }
         Variable([Comma, RightParent] + CallContext);
         if VarType^.Form = Files
         then if FileDetermined
```

```
                then SemanticError(162)
                else begin
                        case WhichPf of
                          Readp :
                            if Symbol <> Comma then Error(24, StartOfSymbol);
                          ReadInp :
                            if not Compatible(VarType, TextType)
                            then SemanticError(177)
                        end;
                        FileType := VarType; SelectFile(FileType)
                      end
          else begin
                if not FileDetermined
                then begin FileType := TextType; SelectInput end;
                if (FileType = TextType) and
                   not Compatible(VarType, CharType)
                then NumericRead else SimpleRead
              end;
          FileDetermined := true
        end { inputvariable };
    begin { readprocedure }
      FileDetermined := false;
      while true do
        begin
          InputVariable;
          if Symbol <> Comma then goto 1;
          AcceptSymbol
        end;
      1:
        if WhichPf = ReadInp then ReadLayout;
      DiscardFile
    end { readprocedure };
procedure WriteProcedure;
  { Analyses parameter list of write or writeln }
  label 1;
  var FileDetermined: Boolean; FileType: TypEntry;
  procedure OutputValue;
    { Analyses any parameter of write or writeln, including the optional
      initial textfile. Assumes that Expression leaves a file variable
      operand in reference form, without attempting to "dereference" it. }
    var Expl Type: TypEntry; WriteKind: OutputKind; Format: FormatKind;
```

```
procedure WriteOtherFile;
  begin
    with FileType^ do
      begin
        CheckAssignment(FelType, Exp1Type); WriteBuffer;
        FileOperation(Putp)
      end
  end { writeotherfile };
procedure WriteTextFile;
  begin
    if Compatible(Exp1Type, CharType)
    then WriteKind := CharKind
    else if Compatible(Exp1Type, IntType)
        then WriteKind := IntKind
        else if Compatible(Exp1Type, RealType)
            then WriteKind := RealKind
            else if Compatible(Exp1Type, BoolType)
                then WriteKind := BoolKind
                else if String(Exp1Type)
                    then WriteKind := StringKind
                    else begin
                        SemanticError(164);
                        WriteKind := DefaultKind
                      end;
    if Symbol = Colon
    then begin
        AcceptSymbol;
        Expression([Comma, Colon, RightParent] + CallContext);
        if not Compatible(ExpType, IntType) then SemanticError(165);
        if Symbol = Colon
        then begin
            AcceptSymbol;
            Expression([Comma, RightParent] + CallContext);
            if not Compatible(ExpType, IntType)
            then SemanticError(166);
            if not Compatible(Exp1Type, RealType)
            then SemanticError(167);
            Format := Fixed
          end
        else Format := Floating
      end
    else Format := Default;
    case WriteKind of
      IntKind, RealKind, CharKind, BoolKind :
        WriteScalars(WriteKind, Format);
      StringKind : WriteString(Exp1Type^.InxType^.Max, Format);
      DefaultKind :
    end
  end { writetextfile };
```

```
begin { outputvalue }
  Expression([Comma, Colon, RightParent] + CallContext);
  Exp1Type := ExpType;
  if Exp1Type^.Form = Files
  then if FileDetermined
        then SemanticError(162)
        else begin
              case WhichPf of
                Writep :
                  if Symbol <> Comma then Error(24, StartOfSymbol);
                Writelnp :
                  if not Compatible(VarType, TextType)
                  then SemanticError(178)
              end;
              FileType := Exp1Type; SelectFile(FileType)
            end
  else begin
        if not FileDetermined
        then begin FileType := TextType; SelectOutput end;
        if FileType = TextType then WriteTextFile else WriteOtherFile
      end;
  FileDetermined := true
end { outputvalue };
begin { writeprocedure }
  FileDetermined := false;
  while true do
    begin
      OutputValue;
      if Symbol <> Comma then goto 1;
      AcceptSymbol
    end;
  1:
  if WhichPf = Writelnp
  then begin StackConstant(LineFeed); WriteLayout end;
  DiscardFile
end { writeprocedure };
procedure PageProcedure;

  { Analyses parameter list of page. }
  begin
    Variable([RightParent] + CallContext);
    if Compatible(VarType, TextType)
    then begin
          SelectFile(TextType); StackConstant(PageThrow); WriteLayout;
          DiscardFile
        end
    else SemanticError(168)
  end;
```

```
procedure CheckArray(PackingRequired: Boolean);
  begin
    if VarType^.Form <> CAPSchema then EnsureFormIs(Arrays, VarType);
    if PackingRequired <> PackingOf(VarType)
    then if PackingRequired then SemanticError(169) else SemanticError(170)
  end { checkarray };
procedure Repack(WhichOp: StdProcFuncs; UpType, PkType: TypEntry);
  var UpIndex, PkIndex, UpElem, Pkelem: TypEntry;
      UpRep, Pkrep: TypeRepresentation;
      PkLow, PkHigh, UpLow, UpHigh: ObjectValue;
  begin
    UpIndex := IndexOf(UpType); PkIndex := IndexOf(PkType);
    UpElem := ElementOf(UpType); Pkelem := ElementOf(PkType);
    if not Identical(UpElem, Pkelem)
    then SemanticError(171)
    else begin
         GetBounds(UpIndex, UpLow, UpHigh);
         GetBounds(PkIndex, PkLow, PkHigh);
         UpRep := UpElem^.Representation;
         Pkrep := Pkelem^.Representation;
         if Conformant(UpType)
         then if Conformant(PkType)
             then CAPCAPOp
                      (WhichOp, UpType^.LowBdAddress,
                         UpType^.HighBdAddress, UpType^.Representation,
                           UpRep, Pkrep, PkType^.LowBdAddress,
                              PkType^.HighBdAddress)
             else CAPArrayOp
                      (WhichOp, UpType^.LowBdAddress,
                         UpType^.HighBdAddress, UpType^.Representation,
                           UpRep, Pkrep, PkLow, PkHigh)
         else if Conformant(PkType)
             then ArrayCAPOp
                      (WhichOp, UpLow, UpHigh, UpRep, Pkrep,
                         PkType^.LowBdAddress, UpType^.HighBdAddress)
             else ArrayArrayOp
                      (WhichOp, UpLow, UpHigh, UpRep, Pkrep, PkLow,
                         PkHigh)
       end
  end { repack };
procedure PackProcedure;
  var UnpackedType, PackedType: TypEntry;
  begin
    Variable(CallContext + [Comma, RightParent]); CheckArray(false);
    UnpackedType := VarType; Accept(Comma);
    Expression(CallContext + [Comma, RightParent]); EnsureOrdinal(ExpType);
    if not Compatible(ExpType, IndexOf(UnpackedType))
```

```
      then SemanticError(172);
      Accept(Comma); Variable(CallContext + [RightParent]); CheckArray(true);
      PackedType := VarType; Repack(Packp, UnpackedType, PackedType)
   end { packprocedure };
procedure UnpackProcedure;
   var UnpackedType, PackedType: TypEntry;
   begin
      Variable(CallContext + [Comma, RightParent]); CheckArray(true);
      PackedType := VarType; Accept(Comma);
      Variable(CallContext + [Comma, RightParent]); CheckArray(false);
      UnpackedType := VarType; Accept(Comma);
      Expression(CallContext + [RightParent]); EnsureOrdinal(ExpType);
      if not Compatible(ExpType, IndexOf(UnpackedType))
      then SemanticError(172);
      Repack(Unpackp, UnpackedType, PackedType)
   end { unpackprocedure };
procedure HeapProcedure;
   { Analyses parameter list for new or dispose. }
   label 1;
   var ThisVarPart, ThisVariant: TypEntry; TagVal: ObjectValue;
       TagValType: TypEntry; StructureKnown: Boolean;
   begin
      ThisVarPart := nil; StructureKnown := true;
      if WhichPf = Newp
      then Variable([Comma, RightParent] + CallContext)
      else begin
            Expression([Comma, RightParent] + CallContext);
            VarType := ExpType
         end;
      EnsureFormIs(Pointers, VarType);
      with VarType^ do
        begin
          HeapRequest(DomainType^.Representation);
          if DomainType^.Form = Records
          then ThisVarPart := DomainType^.VarPart
        end;
      while Symbol = Comma do
        begin
          AcceptSymbol;
          InConstant
            ([Comma, RightParent] + CallContext, TagValType, TagVal);
          EnsureOrdinal(TagValType);
          if StructureKnown
          then if ThisVarPart = nil
              then begin SemanticError(173); StructureKnown := false end
              else if Compatible(ThisVarPart^.TagType, TagValType)
                  then begin
```

```
                        ThisVariant := ThisVarPart^.FirstVariant;
                        while ThisVariant <> nil do
                          with ThisVariant^ do
                            if SameValue(VariantValue, TagVal)
                            then begin
                                    TailorRequest
                                        (ThisVarPart^.Representation,
                                         Representation);
                                    ThisVarPart := SubVarPart; goto 1
                                 end
                            else ThisVariant := NextVariant;
                          SemanticError(173); StructureKnown := false
                        end
                      else begin SemanticError(174); StructureKnown := false end;
              1:
          end;
        HeapOperation(WhichPf)
      end { heapprocedure };

  begin { callstandard }
    if Symbol = LeftParent
    then begin
            AcceptSymbol;
            if Pfid^.Klass = Proc
            then { standard procedure with parameters }
                    case WhichPf of
                      Getp, Putp : GetOrPut;
                      Resetp, Rewritep : ResetOrRewrite;
                      Readlnp, Readp : ReadProcedure;
                      Writelnp, Writep : WriteProcedure;
                      Pagep : PageProcedure;
                      Newp, Disposep : HeapProcedure;
                      Packp : PackProcedure;
                      Unpackp : UnpackProcedure
                    end
            else { standard function with an argument }
                begin
                  Expression([RightParent] + CallContext);
                  case WhichPf of
                    Absf, Sqrf :
                      if Compatible(ExpType, IntType)
                      then IntegerFunction(WhichPf)
                      else if Compatible(ExpType, RealType)
                          then RealFunction(WhichPf)
                          else begin SemanticError(109); ExpType:=IntType end;
                    Oddf :
                      begin
                        if not Compatible(ExpType, IntType)
                        then SemanticError(107);
```

```
                    IntegerFunction(Oddf); ExpType := BoolType
                  end;
                Succf, Predf :
                  begin
                    EnsureOrdinal(ExpType); IntegerFunction(WhichPf);
                    GetBounds(ExpType, First, Last);
                    RangeCheck(First, Last)
                  end;
                Ordf :
                  begin
                    EnsureOrdinal(ExpType); IntegerFunction(Ordf);
                    ExpType := IntType
                  end;
                Chrf :
                  begin
                    if not Compatible(ExpType, IntType)
                    then SemanticError(107);
                    RangeCheck(MinCharValue, MaxCharValue);
                    IntegerFunction(Chrf); ExpType := CharType
                  end;
                Truncf, Roundf :
                  begin
                    if not Compatible(ExpType, RealType)
                    then SemanticError(108);
                    RealFunction(WhichPf); ExpType := IntType
                  end;
                Sinf, Cosf, Expf, Lnf, Sqrtf, Arctanf :
                  begin
                    if Compatible(ExpType, IntType)
                    then FloatInteger(TopOfStack)
                    else if not Compatible(ExpType, RealType)
                         then SemanticError(109);
                    RealFunction(WhichPf); ExpType := RealType
                  end;
                Eoff :
                  begin
                    EnsureFormIs(Files, ExpType); SelectFile(ExpType);
                    FileFunction(Eoff); DiscardFile; ExpType := BoolType
                  end;
                Eolnf :
                  begin
                    if not Compatible(ExpType, TextType)
                    then SemanticError(176);
                    SelectFile(TextType); FileFunction(Eolnf); DiscardFile;
                    ExpType := BoolType
                  end
              end
            end;
        Accept(RightParent)
    end
```

```
        else { parameterless procedure or function call }
            if WhichPf in [Readlnp, Writelnp, Pagep, Eolnf, Eoff]
            then begin
                    case WhichPf of
                        Readlnp :
                            begin SelectInput; ReadLayout; DiscardFile end;
                        Writelnp :
                            begin
                                SelectOutput; StackConstant(LineFeed); WriteLayout;
                                DiscardFile
                            end;
                        Pagep :
                            begin
                                SelectOutput; StackConstant(PageThrow); WriteLayout;
                                DiscardFile
                            end;
                        Eolnf, Eoff :
                            begin
                                SelectInput; FileFunction(WhichPf); DiscardFile;
                                ExpType := BoolType
                            end
                    end
                end
            else Error(20, StartOfSymbol)
    end { callstandard };
procedure CallUserDefined;
    { Analyses all calls to user defined procedures and functions }
    var ThisFormal: FormalEntry; LastActual: TypEntry; ToBePassed: Boolean;
    procedure PfIdentifier(PfIdent: IdEntry);
        var CodeOfBody: BlockLabel;
        begin
            with PfIdent^ do
                if PfKind = Actual
                then begin
                        CodeOfBody := CodeBody; StackActualBlock(CodeOfBody);
                        CodeBody := CodeOfBody
                    end
                else StackFormalBlock(FAddress)
        end { pfidentifier };
    procedure ActualProcedure;
        var ActualId: IdEntry;
        begin
            if Symbol = Ident
            then begin
                    SearchId([Proc], ActualId);
                    if ActualId^.PfDecKind = Predefined
                    then SemanticError(180)
```

```
                    else if not Congruent(ThisFormal^.ItsFormals, ActualId^.Formals)
                        then SemanticError(182)
                        else begin PfIdentifier(ActualId); PassBlock end
                end;
            Accept(Ident); CheckContext([Comma, RightParent] + CallContext)
        end { actualprocedure };

    procedure ActualFunction;

        var ActualId: IdEntry;

        begin
            if Symbol = Ident
            then begin
                    SearchId([Func], ActualId);
                    if ActualId^.PfDecKind = Predefined
                    then SemanticError(181)
                    else if not Congruent(ThisFormal^.ItsFormals, ActualId^.Formals)
                            or not Identical(ActualId^.IdType, ThisFormal^.FormalType)
                        then SemanticError(183)
                        else begin PfIdentifier(ActualId); PassBlock end
                end;
            Accept(Ident); CheckContext([Comma, RightParent] + CallContext)
        end { actualfunction };

    procedure CheckConformance(Actual, Formal: TypEntry);

        var InxLow, InxHigh, ActLow, ActHigh: ObjectValue;

        begin
            if (Actual <> Unknown) and (Formal <> Unknown)
            then if not Conformant(Formal) or
                    not (Actual^.Form in [Arrays, CAPSchema])
                then SemanticError(251)
                else if not Compatible(IndexOf(Actual), IndexOf(Formal)) or
                        (PackingOf(Actual) <> PackingOf(Formal))
                    then SemanticError(251)
                    else begin
                            if ToBePassed
                            then begin
                                    GetBounds(IndexOf(Formal), InxLow, InxHigh);
                                    if Conformant(Actual)
                                    then with Actual^ do
                                            PassCAPBoundPair
                                                (LowBdAddress, HighBdAddress,
                                                    InxLow, InxHigh, Representation)
                                    else begin
                                            GetBounds
                                                (IndexOf(Actual), ActLow, ActHigh);
                                            PassArrayBoundPair
                                                (ActLow, ActHigh, InxLow, InxHigh,
                                                    Actual^.AelType^.Representation,
                                                    Actual^.PackedArray)
                                    end
```

```
                                       end;
                           if MultiLevel(Formal)
                           then CheckConformance
                                    (ElementOf(Actual), ElementOf(Formal))
                           else begin
                                    if ElementOf(Actual) <> ElementOf(Formal)
                                    then SemanticError(251);
                                    ToBePassed := false
                                end
                       end
        end { checkconformance };
procedure ActualVariable;
    begin
        Variable([Comma, RightParent] + CallContext);
        if PackedVar then SemanticError(184);
        if TagVar then SemanticError(185);
        if NewRecVar then TailoredFactorCheck(VarType^.Representation);
        with ThisFormal^ do
            if Conformant(FormalType)
            then begin
                    CheckConformance(VarType, FormalType);
                    if not Identical(LastActual, VarType)
                    then SemanticError(252) else LastActual := VarType
                end
            else if not Identical(VarType, FormalType) then SemanticError(186);
        PassReference(MayBeInsecure)
    end { actualvariable };
procedure ActualValue;
    begin
        Expression([Comma, RightParent] + CallContext);
        if ThisFormal <> nil
        then with ThisFormal^ do
                if Conformant(FormalType)
                then if Conformant(ExpType)
                        then SemanticError(253)
                        else if EmbeddedFile(ExpType)
                            then SemanticError(150)
                            else begin
                                    CheckConformance(ExpType, FormalType);
                                    if not Identical(LastActual, ExpType)
                                    then SemanticError(252)
                                    else LastActual := ExpType;
                                    MakeAuxiliary(ExpType^.Representation);
                                    PassReference(Secure)
                                end
                else begin
                        CheckAssignment(FormalType, ExpType);
                        PassValue(FormalType^.Representation)
```

```
                        end
        end { actualvalue };
    procedure NewArraySchema;
        begin
            LastActual := Unknown; ToBePassed := true; StartBoundPairs;
            ThisFormal := ThisFormal^.Next
        end { newarrayschema };
    begin { calluserdefined }
        PfIdentifier(Pfid); ThisFormal := Pfid^.Formals;
        OpenParameterList(Pfid^.Klass);
        if Symbol = LeftParent
        then begin
                repeat
                    { for each actual parameter }
                    AcceptSymbol;
                    if ThisFormal <> nil
                    then begin
                            if ThisFormal^.Parm = BoundParm then NewArraySchema;
                            with ThisFormal^ do
                                case Parm of
                                    ValueParm : ActualValue;
                                    VarParm : ActualVariable;
                                    ProcParm : ActualProcedure;
                                    FuncParm : ActualFunction
                                end
                        end
                    else begin
                            SemanticError(187);

                            { for recovery purposes ... }

                            ActualValue
                        end;
                    if ThisFormal <> nil then ThisFormal := ThisFormal^.Next
                until Symbol <> Comma;
                Accept(RightParent)
            end;
        if ThisFormal <> nil then SemanticError(187);
        CloseParameterList; CallBlock;
        if Pfid^.Klass = Func
        then begin
                TakeResult(Pfid^.IdType^.Representation); ExpType := Pfid^.IdType
            end
    end { calluserdefined };
    begin { call }
        if Pfid^.PfDecKind = Predefined
        then CallStandard(Pfid^.PfIndex) else CallUserDefined
    end { call };
```

{

10.10 Expression analysis.

Expression analysis is carried out by the procedure SubExpression, which leaves the type of the expression analysed in the global ExpType. In practice it is called by one of two routes:

(i)   when an assignable value is required as result it is called via the procedure Expression;

(ii)   when a Boolean condition is required (by a control statement) it is called via the procedure BooleanExpression.

These differ in the code generation interface calls they produce as explained in chapter 5.

}

```
    procedure SubExpression(ExpContext: SetOfSymbols);
      var LeftType: TypEntry; RelOperator: OpType;
      procedure SimpleExpression(SimExpContext: SetOfSymbols);
        var LeftType: TypEntry; Sign, AddOperator: OpType; Signed: Boolean;
        procedure PlusMinusMul(FirstOpType: TypEntry; Operator: OpType);
          { This procedure performs semantic analysis of operators +,-, and *.
            It assumes the operand types are given by FirstOpType and ExpType
            respectively, and resets ExpType to describe the result. }
        begin
          if (FirstOpType^.Form = Sets) or (ExpType^.Form = Sets)
          then begin
              if Compatible(FirstOpType, ExpType)
              then begin
                  if ExpType = Unknown then ExpType := FirstOpType
                  end
              else begin SemanticError(191); ExpType := EmptyType end;
              BinarySetOperation(Operator)
            end
          else if Compatible(FirstOpType, IntType) and
              Compatible(ExpType, IntType)
            then begin ExpType := IntType; BinaryIntegerOperation(Operator) end
            else begin
                if Compatible(FirstOpType, IntType)
                then begin
                    FirstOpType := RealType; FloatInteger(NextToTop)
                  end;
                if Compatible(ExpType, IntType)
                then begin ExpType := RealType; FloatInteger(TopOfStack) end;
                if Compatible(FirstOpType, RealType) and
                  Compatible(ExpType, RealType)
                then ExpType := RealType
                else begin SemanticError(190); ExpType := IntType end;
                BinaryRealOperation(Operator)
              end
        end { plusminusmul };
```

```
procedure Term(TermContext: SetOfSymbols);
  var LeftType: TypEntry; MulOperator: OpType;
  procedure Factor(FactorContext: SetOfSymbols);
    var FirstId: IdEntry;
    procedure SetConstructor;
      label 1;
      var BaseNow, SetType: TypEntry;
      begin
        AcceptSymbol; BaseNow := Unknown; SetType := EmptyType;
        StackConstant(EmptyValue);
        if Symbol = RightBracket
        then AcceptSymbol
        else begin
              while true do
                begin
                  Expression([Comma, Thru, RightBracket] + FactorContext);
                  EnsureOrdinal(ExpType);
                  if (BaseNow = Unknown) and (ExpType <> Unknown)
                  then begin
                        BaseNow := ExpType; NewType(SetType, Sets);
                        with SetType^ do
                          begin
                            FormOfSet := Constructed;
                            BaseType := BaseNow
                          end;
                        SetRepresentationFor(SetType)
                      end
                  else if not Compatible(BaseNow, ExpType)
                      then SemanticError(192);
                  if Symbol = Thru
                  then begin
                        AcceptSymbol;
                        Expression
                          ([Comma, RightBracket] + FactorContext);
                        EnsureOrdinal(ExpType);
                        if not Compatible(BaseNow, ExpType)
                        then SemanticError(192);
                        RangeSet(SetType^.Representation)
                      end
                  else SingletonSet(SetType^.Representation);
                  BinarySetOperation(Plus);
                  if Symbol <> Comma then goto 1;
                  AcceptSymbol
                end;
              1: Accept(RightBracket)
            end;
        ExpType := SetType
      end { setconstructor };
```

```
begin { factor }
  CheckNextOrContext(FacBegSys, FactorContext);
  if Symbol in FacBegSys
  then begin
      case Symbol of
        Ident :
          begin
            SearchId([Consts, Vars, Field, Bound, Func], FirstId);
            AcceptSymbol;
            case FirstId^.Klass of
              Consts, Bound :
                with FirstId^ do
                  begin
                    if Klass = Consts
                    then StackConstant(Values)
                    else begin
                        StackReference(false, BdAddress);
                        DeReference(IdType^.Representation)
                      end;
                    ExpType := IdType
                  end;
              Vars, Field :
                begin
                  Selector(FactorContext, FirstId);
                  if VarType^.Form <> Files
                  then begin
                      if NewRecVar
                      then TailoredFactorCheck
                            (VarType^.Representation);
                      if Conformant(VarType)
                      then WithSchema
                            (VarType, CAPDeReference)
                      else DeReference(VarType^.Representation);
                      if FirstId^.Klass = Field
                      then UndefinedVariableCheck
                      else if (FirstId^.VarKind <> ValueParam)
                          and
                          not Includes(ControlVars, FirstId)
                        then UndefinedVariableCheck
                    end;
                  if VarType^.Form = SubRanges
                  then ExpType := VarType^.RangeType
                  else ExpType := VarType
                end;
              Func :
                begin Call(FactorContext, FirstId) end
          end
      end;
```

```
            IntConst :
              begin
                StackConstant(Constant.Value); ExpType := IntType;
                AcceptSymbol
              end;
            RealConst :
              begin
                StackConstant(Constant.Value); ExpType := RealType;
                AcceptSymbol
              end;
            CharConst :
              begin
                StackConstant(Constant.Value); ExpType := CharType;
                AcceptSymbol
              end;
            StringConst :
              begin
                StackConstant(Constant.Value); StringType(ExpType);
                AcceptSymbol
              end;
            NilSy :
              begin
                StackConstant(NilValue); ExpType := NilType;
                AcceptSymbol
              end;
            LeftParent :
              begin
                AcceptSymbol;
                SubExpression([RightParent] + FactorContext);
                Accept(RightParent)
              end;
            NotSy :
              begin
                AcceptSymbol; Factor(FactorContext);
                if Compatible(ExpType, BoolType)
                then NegateABoolean else SemanticError(106);
                ExpType := BoolType
              end;
            LeftBracket : SetConstructor
          end;
          CheckContext(FactorContext)
        end
  else ExpType := Unknown
end { factor };
```

```
      begin { term }
        Factor([MulOp] + FacBegSys + TermContext);
        if (Symbol = MulOp) and (Operator = AndOp)
        then BinaryBooleanOperation(AndOp, true);
        while (Symbol = MulOp) or (Symbol in FacBegSys) do
          begin
            LeftType := ExpType;
            if Symbol = MulOp
            then MulOperator := Operator else MulOperator := NotOp;
            Accept(MulOp); Factor([MulOp] + FacBegSys + TermContext);
            case MulOperator of
              Mul : PlusMinusMul(LeftType, Mul);
              Rdiv :
                begin
                  if Compatible(LeftType, IntType)
                  then begin FloatInteger(NextToTop); LeftType := RealType end;
                  if Compatible(ExpType, IntType)
                  then begin FloatInteger(TopOfStack); ExpType := RealType end;
                  if not (Compatible(LeftType, RealType) and
                          Compatible(ExpType, RealType))
                  then SemanticError(193);
                  ExpType := RealType; BinaryRealOperation(Rdiv);
                  ExpType := RealType
                end;
              Idiv, Imod :
                begin
                  if not (Compatible(LeftType, IntType) and
                          Compatible(ExpType, IntType))
                  then SemanticError(194);
                  BinaryIntegerOperation(MulOperator); ExpType := IntType
                end;
              AndOp :
                begin
                  if not (Compatible(LeftType, BoolType) and
                          Compatible(ExpType, BoolType))
                  then SemanticError(195);
                  BinaryBooleanOperation(AndOp, false); ExpType := BoolType
                end;
              NotOp : ExpType := Unknown
            end { case }
          end
      end { term };
    begin { simple expression }
      if (Symbol = AddOp) and (Operator in [Plus, Minus])
      then begin Signed := true; Sign := Operator; AcceptSymbol end
      else Signed := false;
      Term([AddOp] + SimExpContext);
```

```
        if Signed
        then if Compatible(ExpType, IntType)
            then begin
                    if Sign = Minus then NegateAnInteger
                 end
            else if Compatible(ExpType, RealType)
                then begin
                        if Sign = Minus then NegateAReal
                     end
                else begin SemanticError(196); ExpType := Unknown end;
        if (Symbol = AddOp) and (Operator = OrOp)
        then BinaryBooleanOperation(OrOp, true);
        while Symbol = AddOp do
          begin
            LeftType := ExpType; AddOperator := Operator; AcceptSymbol;
            Term([AddOp] + SimExpContext);
            case AddOperator of
              Plus : PlusMinusMul(LeftType, Plus);
              Minus : PlusMinusMul(LeftType, Minus);
              OrOp :
                begin
                  if not (Compatible(LeftType, BoolType) and
                          Compatible(ExpType, BoolType))
                  then SemanticError(195);
                  BinaryBooleanOperation(OrOp, false); ExpType := BoolType
                end
            end { case }
          end
    end { simple expression };
begin { subexpression }
   SimpleExpression([RelOp] + ExpContext);
   if Symbol = RelOp
   then begin
           ExcludeConditions; LeftType := ExpType; RelOperator := Operator;
           if RelOperator = InOp then EnsureOrdinal(LeftType);
           AcceptSymbol; SimpleExpression(ExpContext); ExcludeConditions;
           if RelOperator = InOp
           then begin
                   EnsureFormIs(Sets, ExpType);
                   if Compatible(LeftType, ExpType^.BaseType)
                   then SetComparison(InOp) else SemanticError(197)
                end
           else begin
                   if not Compatible(LeftType, ExpType)
                   then { may be real/integer mix }
                           if Compatible(LeftType, IntType)
                           then begin
                                   FloatInteger(NextToTop); LeftType := RealType
                                end
```

```
                    else if Compatible(ExpType, IntType)
                      then begin
                              FloatInteger(TopOfStack);
                              ExpType := RealType
                           end;
                 if Compatible(LeftType, ExpType)
                 then case LeftType^.Form of
                      Scalars, SubRanges :
                        if Compatible(LeftType, RealType)
                        then RealComparison(RelOperator)
                        else OrdinalComparison(RelOperator);
                      Pointers :
                        if RelOperator in [LtOp, LeOp, GtOp, GeOp]
                        then SemanticError(199)
                        else PointerComparison(RelOperator);
                      Sets :
                        if RelOperator in [LtOp, GtOp]
                        then SemanticError(200)
                        else SetComparison(RelOperator);
                      Arrays :
                        if not String(LeftType)
                        then SemanticError(201)
                        else StringComparison
                                (RelOperator, LeftType^.InxType^.Max);
                      CAPSchema : SemanticError(254);
                      Records, Files : SemanticError(202)
                    end
                 else SemanticError(198)
               end;
            ExpType := BoolType
         end
   end { subexpression };
procedure Expression;
   begin SubExpression(ExpContext); ExcludeConditions end { expression };
procedure BooleanExpression(CondContext: SetOfSymbols);
   begin
      SubExpression(CondContext);
      if not Compatible(ExpType, BoolType) then SemanticError(106)
   end { booleanexpression };
```

{

10.11 Statement analysis.

Analysis of the different Pascal statements is carried out by subprocedures of the procedure Statement called within StatementSequence.

The semantic processing of statement labels is implemented by the procedures Statement, NestedStatement and GotoStatement as described in chapter 9.

The procedure ForStatement must check whether a for-statement control-variable is threatened by an assigning reference in any procedure or function declared in the same block. The procedure Threaten examines every assigning reference, and maintains for each block scope an identifier-set Threatened of simple variables declared in that scope, but assigned within one of the (block) scopes contained by it. The for-statement analyser checks that each control-variable does not belong to the threatened set for its scope.

The control-variable is protected from rogue-assignments within the for loop, by placing it in the identifier-set ControlVars, prior to analysis of the body of the for-statement. Assigning references vetted by the procedure Threaten are permitted only if the destination variable is not a member of ControlVars. The control-variable is removed from the set when analysis of the for-statement is complete.

}

```
    procedure StatementSequence(Context: SetOfSymbols); forward;
    procedure Statement(Context: SetOfSymbols);
      var FirstId: IdEntry;
      procedure Assignment(VarId: IdEntry);
        var LVarType, LVarPart: TypEntry;
        begin
          Selector([Becomes] + Context, VarId);
          if NewRecVar then TailoredFactorCheck(VarType^.Representation);
          if SimpleVar then Threaten(VarId);
          LVarType := VarType;
          if TagVar then LVarPart := VntSelector else LVarPart := nil;
          Accept(Becomes); Expression(Context); CheckAssignment(LVarType, ExpType);
          if LVarPart <> nil
          then AssignTag(LVarPart^.Representation)
          else Assign(LVarType^.Representation)
        end { assignment };
    procedure NestedStatement(Context: SetOfSymbols);
      begin OpenLabelDepth; Statement(Context); CloseLabelDepth end;
    procedure GotoStatement;
      var LabelFound: LabelEntry;
      begin
        Accept(GotoSy);
        if Symbol = IntConst
```

```
            then begin
                    CheckLabel(LabelFound);
                    LabelJump(LabelFound^.LabelledCode, LevelFound)
                end;
            Accept(IntConst)
        end { gotostatement };
procedure CompoundStatement;
    begin Accept(BeginSy); StatementSequence([EndSy]+Context); Accept(EndSy) end;
procedure IfStatement;
    var ForFalseAction, FollowingStatement: CodeLabel;
    begin
        FutureCodeLabel(FollowingStatement); Accept(IfSy);
        BooleanExpression([ThenSy, ElseSy] + Context);
        FutureCodeLabel(ForFalseAction); JumpOnFalse(ForFalseAction);
        Accept(ThenSy); NestedStatement([ElseSy] + Context);
        if Symbol = ElseSy
        then begin
                Jump(FollowingStatement); NextIsCodeLabel(ForFalseAction);
                AcceptSymbol; NestedStatement(Context)
            end
        else NextIsCodeLabel(ForFalseAction);
        NextIsCodeLabel(FollowingStatement)
    end { ifstatement };
procedure CaseStatement;
    label 9;
    type Casentry = ^CaseRec;
        CaseRec =
            record
                CaseValue: ObjectValue;
                NextCase: Casentry
            end;
    var CaseType: TypEntry; FirstCase, ThisCase, NextCase: Casentry;
        FollowingStatement: CodeLabel;
    procedure NewCaseLabel;
        var LabelType: TypEntry; LabelValue: ObjectValue;
            ThisCase, LastCase: Casentry;
        begin
            InConstant([Comma, Colon] + Context, LabelType, LabelValue);
            EnsureOrdinal(LabelType);
            if LabelType <> Unknown
            then if Compatible(LabelType, CaseType)
                then begin
                        ThisCase := FirstCase; LastCase := nil;
                        while ThisCase <> nil do
                            begin
                                if SameValue(ThisCase^.CaseValue, LabelValue)
```

```
                         then SemanticError(210);
                         LastCase := ThisCase; ThisCase := ThisCase^.NextCase
                       end;
                     new(ThisCase);
                     with ThisCase^ do
                       begin
                         CaseValue := LabelValue; NextIsCase(LabelValue);
                         NextCase := nil
                       end;
                     if LastCase = nil
                     then FirstCase := ThisCase
                     else LastCase^.NextCase := ThisCase
                   end
             else SemanticError(211)
      end { newcaselabel };

   begin { casestatement }
      FutureCodeLabel(FollowingStatement); Accept(CaseSy);
      Expression([OfSy, Comma, Colon] + Context); CaseType := ExpType;
      EnsureOrdinal(CaseType); OpenCase; Accept(OfSy); FirstCase := nil;
      repeat
         while true do
            begin
               NewCaseLabel;
               if Symbol <> Comma then goto 9;
               AcceptSymbol
            end;
         9: Accept(Colon); NestedStatement([Semicolon, EndSy] + Context);
         Jump(FollowingStatement);
         if Symbol = Semicolon then AcceptSymbol
      until (Symbol = EndSy) or (Symbol in Context);
      Accept(EndSy); CloseCase; NextCase := FirstCase;
      while NextCase <> nil do
         begin
            ThisCase := NextCase; NextCase := ThisCase^.NextCase;
            dispose(ThisCase)
         end;
      NextIsCodeLabel(FollowingStatement)
   end { casestatement };

procedure WhileStatement;

   var ToTestCondition, FollowingStatement: CodeLabel;

   begin
      FutureCodeLabel(FollowingStatement); Accept(WhileSy);
      NewCodeLabel(ToTestCondition); FlowPoint(Source.Position.LineNumber);
      BooleanExpression([DoSy] + Context); JumpOnFalse(FollowingStatement);
      Accept(DoSy); NestedStatement(Context); Jump(ToTestCondition);
      NextIsCodeLabel(FollowingStatement)
   end { whilestatement };
```

```
procedure RepeatStatement;
   var ThisStatement: CodeLabel;
   begin
      NewCodeLabel(ThisStatement); Accept(RepeatSy);
      StatementSequence([UntilSy] + Context);
      FlowPoint(Source.Position.LineNumber); Accept(UntilSy);
      BooleanExpression(Context); JumpOnFalse(ThisStatement)
   end { repeatstatement };

procedure ForStatement;
   var ForVarId: IdEntry; ForVarType: TypEntry; ForMin, ForMax: ObjectValue;
      Increasing: Boolean;
   begin
      Accept(ForSy);
      if Symbol = Ident
      then begin
               SearchId([Vars], ForVarId); ForVarType := ForVarId^.IdType;
               if LevelFound < BlockLevel
               then SemanticError(220)
               else if Includes(Display[BlockLevel].Threatened, ForVarId)
                     then SemanticError(222)
                        else if Includes(ControlVars, ForVarId)
                              then SemanticError(225)
                                 else if not Ordinal(ForVarType)
                                       then begin
                                                SemanticError(110); ForVarType := Unknown
                                             end;
               with ForVarId^ do
                  begin
                     if VarKind <> LocalVar then SemanticError(221);
                     StackReference(false, VarAddress)
                  end
            end
      else ForVarType := Unknown;
      GetBounds(ForVarType, ForMin, ForMax); Accept(Ident);
      CheckContext([Becomes, ToSy, DoSy] + Context); Accept(Becomes);
      Expression([ToSy, DoSy] + Context);
      if not Compatible(ForVarType, ExpType) then SemanticError(223);
      if Symbol = ToSy
      then Increasing := (Operator = Plus) else Increasing := true;
      Accept(ToSy); Expression([DoSy] + Context);
      if not Compatible(ForVarType, ExpType) then SemanticError(224);
      OpenFor(Increasing, ForMin, ForMax); Accept(DoSy);
      Include(ControlVars, ForVarId); NestedStatement(Context); CloseFor;
      Exclude(ControlVars, ForVarId)
   end { forstatement };
```

```
procedure WithStatement;
  { Analysis of the iterative record-variable-list is implemented
    recursively, to handle the implied nested scopes correctly }
  begin
    AcceptSymbol
      { accepts WithSy on initial call, Comma on subsequent recursive calls };
    Variable([Comma, DoSy] + Context); EnsureFormIs(Records, VarType);
    OpenScope(RecordScope); OpenWith(ScopeLevel);
    with Display[ScopeLevel] do
      begin
        Locals := VarType^.FieldScope; RecordType := VarType;
        FieldsPacked := VarType^.PackedRecord
      end;
    if Symbol = Comma
    then WithStatement
    else begin Accept(DoSy); NestedStatement(Context) end;
    CloseWith; CloseScope
  end { withstatement };

begin { statement }
  if Symbol = IntConst
  then begin DefineLabel; AcceptSymbol; Accept(Colon) end;
  CheckContext(StatBegSys + [Ident] + Context);
  if Symbol in StatBegSys + [Ident]
  then begin
        FlowPoint(Source.Position.LineNumber); OpenLabelDepth;
        case Symbol of
          Ident :
            begin
              SearchId([Vars, Field, Func, Proc], FirstId); AcceptSymbol;
              if FirstId^.Klass = Proc
              then Call(Context, FirstId) else Assignment(FirstId)
            end;
          GotoSy : GotoStatement;
          BeginSy : CompoundStatement;
          IfSy : IfStatement;
          CaseSy : CaseStatement;
          WhileSy : WhileStatement;
          RepeatSy : RepeatStatement;
          ForSy : ForStatement;
          WithSy : WithStatement
        end;
        CloseLabelDepth; CheckContext(Context)
      end
  else FlowPoint(Source.Position.LineNumber)
end { statement };
```

```
    procedure StatementSequence {context : setofsymbols};
      begin
      Statement([Semicolon] + StatBegSys + Context);
        while (Symbol = Semicolon) or (Symbol in StatBegSys) do
          begin Accept(Semicolon); Statement([Semicolon] + StatBegSys + Context) end
      end { statementsequence };
    procedure StatementPart;
      begin
      if BlockLevel = GlobalLevel
      then begin
            EnterProgram(ProgId, Source.Position.LineNumber); VerifyProgParams
          end
      else EnterPfBody(BlockIdEntry, Source.Position.LineNumber);
      PresetBlock; InitLabelDepth; FlowPoint(Source.Position.LineNumber);
      repeat { for syntax error recovery }
        Accept(BeginSy); StatementSequence(BlockBegSys + [EndSy]); Accept(EndSy)
      until (Symbol = BlockFollower) or (Symbol in BlockBegSys);
      PostSetBlock;
      if BlockLevel = GlobalLevel
      then LeaveProgram
      else with BlockIdEntry^ do
            if Klass = Func
            then LeaveFunction(Result, IdType^.Representation) else LeaveProcedure
      end { statementpart };
  begin { block }
    BlockContext := BlockBegSys + StatBegSys - [CaseSy]; StartSet(ControlVars);
    FutureStatementLabel(FinalPart);
    repeat
      if Symbol = LabelSy then LabelDeclarationPart;
      if Symbol = ConstSy then ConstDefinitionPart;
      if Symbol = TypeSy then TypeDefinitionPart;
      if Symbol = VarSy then VarDeclarationPart;
      while Symbol in [ProcSy, FuncSy] do PfDeclaration;
      CheckNextOrContext(StatBegSys, BlockBegSys)
    until Symbol in StatBegSys;
    StatementPart; DsposeSet(ControlVars)
  end { block };
begin { programme }
  StartList(Externals); OpenScope(ActualBlock); OpenStackFrame; ProgramHeading;
  Accept(Semicolon); EntryLabel := ProgId^.ProgBody; OpenCodeSpace(EntryLabel);
  ProgId^.ProgBody := EntryLabel;
  repeat { for syntax error recovery }
    Block(Period, ProgId)
  until Symbol = Period;
  FileScope(ProgId); CloseCodeSpace; CloseStackFrame; DisposeScope; CloseScope;
  DisposeList(Externals)
end { programme };
```

{

CHAPTER 11

Code Generator Overview

The code generator transforms the set of code-generation interface calls made during program analysis into a code-byte stream for direct execution on the P-machine. This transformation is achieved by simulating all operations defined at interface level on a compile-time evaluation stack, and delaying actual code generation until the context of an expression or reference is fully known. Such a "delayed" code-generation strategy is both useful for a wide variety of target machine architectures, and necessary for the implementation of the more complex runtime checks.

The P-machine itself is described separately within its own free-standing definition, but aspects relevant to the code generation process are included in Chapter 2 as a set of constant definitions describing machine parameters (prefixed MC), and the P-machine instruction set.

Overall, the code generator can be summarised as follows.

Chapter 12 defines the representations of all data types, and provides a high-level interface to the generator procedures for type-specific intialisation, finalisation, and value inspection.

Chapter 13 contains procedures for storage management and runtime address assignment, and provides high-level support for block initialisation and finalisation.

Chapter 14 provides utilities for the evaluation of target machine object values corresponding to literal constants, and for the limited manipulation of these values that the analyser requires. In addition, certain useful global object values are initialised here.

Chapter 15 contains the low-level facilities necessary to format and generate the CodeFile containing the executable object program.

Chapters 16 and 17 implement the compile-time stack model of the target machine and simulate all reference and binary operations defined in the code-generation interface. Throughout the simulation, a tree representation of each expression is built, in which the internal nodes define operations, and the left and right sub-trees define the operands. Each leaf node is either a reference to a stored operand, or a self-defining constant operand containing an embedded object value.

Component references and expressions are stored on the compile-time stack until the context of code-generation is identified as:

(a)   a Boolean expression evaluation;

(b)   the start or end of a case-statement, for-statement, or with-statement;

(c)   a procedure or function call;

(d)   an assignment statement.

For example, within the context of the assignment statement

     v := a+b+c ;

the compile-time evaluation stack contains:

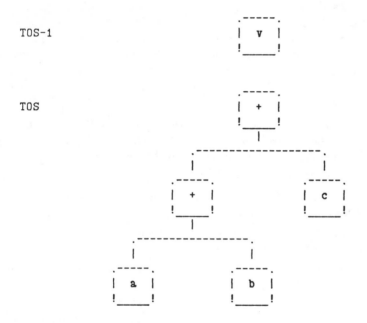

Chapter 18 contains the procedures for generating equivalent P-code instruction sequences from the reference and expression trees built on the evaluation stack. Thus, expression evaluation code is generated by simple traversal of the expression tree in which the left and right subtrees are evaluated as operands, followed by the appropriate P-machine operation P-code. Reference evaluation is equivalent to traversal of a degenerate tree and results in the generation of appropriate store-access code. Chapter 18 also contains low-level support for all P-code emission, and for the generation and fix-up of jump instructions.

Chapters 19 to 23 provide for code-generation of higher-level constructs such as assignment statements, with-statements, standard procedures, case-statements, for-statements, and procedure/function calls. Chapter 24 provides support for program parameter passing.

Chapters 25 and 26 respectively provide for low-level support for undefined variable detection, and the generation of internal type-specific procedures for generalised variable initialisation and value inspection.

Chapter 27 contains procedures necessary to generate the code and data maps that constitute the compiler's interface to the Postmortem Generator.

Chapter 28 controls the phased initialisation of all data-structures and global variables used by the generator.

The following procedures are utilities used throughout the code generator. PredictedError is used to report runtime errors predicted at compile-time; MCSetBit, MCGetBit, and MCSet-Byte provide bit and byte access on the host compiling machine. They rely on logical over-laying of the variants of MCWordForm by the host Pascal processor, and assume that impli-cit changes of variant do not cause variant re-initialisation or variant errors!

```
}
procedure PredictedError(Code: Scalar);
   begin Error(Code + PredictedBase, StartOfSymbol) end;
procedure MCSetBit(var Word: MCWordForm; BitIndex: MCBitIndex);
   begin
      { recast(word, asbits) }
      if IndexedFromLeft
      then Word.WBits[MCMaxBitNum - BitIndex] := 1 else Word.WBits[BitIndex] := 1
   end { mcsetbit };
procedure MCGetBit(Word: MCWordForm; BitIndex: MCBitIndex;
                        var ResultBit: MCBit);
   begin
      { recast(word, asbits) }
      if IndexedFromLeft
      then ResultBit := Word.WBits[MCMaxBitNum - BitIndex]
      else ResultBit := Word.WBits[BitIndex]
   end { mcgetbit };
procedure MCSetByte(var Word: MCWordForm; ByteIndex: MCByteIndex;
                        DataByte: MCByte);
   begin
      { recast(word, asbytes) }
      if IndexedFromLeft
      then Word.WBytes[MCMaxByteNum - ByteIndex] := DataByte
      else Word.WBytes[ByteIndex] := DataByte
   end { mcsetbyte };
```

{

CHAPTER 12

Data Representations

Data representations are specified by the Representation field of the TypeRecord. This itself is a record of type TypeRepresentation whose fields are used as follows:

(1) WordSize is a word-measure of the storage requirement for the type. BitSize is an equivalent bit-measure for types that can be packed.

(2) Kind provides an alternative data classification, relevant to various needs of the code-generator.

(3) Min and Max define the minimum and maximum values of an ordinal type and are used to generate range-checking code.

(4) CheckValue contains a representation of the "undefined value" for scalar types and optimisable structured types. For other structured types, the entry points of internally compiled procedures performing type-specific initialisation, finalisation, and value inspection are recorded in the fields PresetCode, PostSetCode, and CheckCode.

(5) Selector holds the field-offset of the selector associated with a record variant-part, and is used in the generation of checking code for variant-field access and variant (re-) selection.

The procedures in this chapter are grouped into those dealing with basic data representations, augmented representations and standard representations. The following utilities are used by the first of these groups.
}

```
procedure Validate(var DataSize: Scalar);
  begin
    if DataSize > MCMaxMemWord
    then begin SystemError(2); DataSize := 0 end
  end { validate };
function WordsFor(Units, UnitsPerWord: Scalar): Scalar;
  var Words: Scalar;
  begin
    Words := Units div UnitsPerWord;
    if (Units mod UnitsPerWord) <> 0
    then WordsFor := Words + 1 else WordsFor := Words
  end { wordsfor };
```

```pascal
function BitsFor(Decimal: MCScalar): MCBitRange;
  var Bits: MCBitRange;
  begin
    Bits := 0;
    repeat Bits := Bits + 1; Decimal := Decimal div 2 until Decimal = 0;
    BitsFor := Bits
  end { bitsfor };
function PowerOf2(Index: MCBitIndex): Scalar;
  var Decimal: Scalar;
  begin
    Decimal := 1;
    while Index > 0 do
      begin Decimal := 2 * Decimal; Index := Index - 1 end;
    PowerOf2 := Decimal
  end { powerof2 };
procedure SetCheckValue(var Representation: TypeRepresentation);
  begin
    with Representation, CheckValue do
      begin
        Multiple := WordSize; Defined := false;
        if (Kind = ForScalar) and (Checks in Requested)
        then if BitSize < MCBitsPerWord
             then begin
                    if BitSize < MCBitsPerWord - 1
                    then begin Defined := true; Magnitude := PowerOf2(BitSize) end;
                    BitSize := BitSize + 1
                  end
      end
  end { setcheckvalue };
function Cardinality(OrdinalType: TypEntry): integer;
  var TypeMin, TypeMax: ObjectValue;
  begin
    GetBounds(OrdinalType, TypeMin, TypeMax);
    Cardinality := Range(TypeMin, TypeMax)
  end { cardinality };
function VariantFiles(VariantList: TypEntry): Boolean;
  var AnyFiles: Boolean; ThisVariant: TypEntry;
  begin
    AnyFiles := false; ThisVariant := VariantList;
    while (ThisVariant <> nil) and (not AnyFiles) do
      if EmbeddedFile(ThisVariant)
      then AnyFiles := true else ThisVariant := ThisVariant^.NextVariant;
    VariantFiles := AnyFiles
  end { variantfiles };
{
```

12.1 Basic Representations

The representation of each user-defined type is set by a call to the procedure SetRepresentationFor made once the type has been fully-defined. The settings for each of the representation fields depend upon a number of criteria which may be summarised as follows:

(1) Scalar Types

The Min and Max fields are set directly from the bounding values associated with the type.
A scalar whose Min is non-negative is potentially packable into a bits field whose width is
set to the minimum required to store the value Max. If runtime checks are being generated
the CheckValue field is set to the smallest power of 2 larger than Max, and BitSize is
increased to accommodate this value. Thus the type

primary = (violet, indigo, blue, green, yellow, orange, red)

has a representation denoted by:

WordSize = 1; BitSize = 4; CheckValue = 8; Min = 0; Max = 6.

When runtime checks are suppressed, BitSize would be 3 and CheckValue would not be
required.

(2) Pointer Types

If checks are being generated the wordsize is set to 2, and to 1 otherwise. All other fields are
irrelevant. BitSize is set to MCBitsPerWord to ensure pointers are never packed.

(3) Set Types

For a given base-type whose bounds are BaseMin and BaseMax, sets are allocated as if their
actual base-type was the subrange 0..BaseMax. Sets are implemented as bit-maps using
(MCBitsPerWord-1) bits for member storage in each word. This leaves the most significant
bit free to denote an "undefined" set word. The special instructions of the P-machine
require that a set must never be packed, and accordingly BitSize is set to MCBitsPerWord to
achieve that effect. To handle set constructors where the base-type is integer, an actual
basetype defined by the subrange 0..MCMaxSet is used. Base types whose minimum is negative, or whose maximum exceeds MCMaxSet are always rejected. The set type:

set of 'a'..'z'

has a representation:

WordSize = 4; BitSize = MCBitsPerWord; Min = 98; Max = 123

where the Min and Max are the ASCII display codes derived from the base-type and used to
generate the set-assignment check.

(4) Array Types

Storage for unpacked arrays is calculated according to the number of elements and the size
of each. For packed arrays the WordSize is reduced according to the number of elements
that can be packed per word. Thus, given the subrange:

range = 0..63

whose representation is:

WordSize = 1; BitSize = 7; CheckValue = 64; Min = 0; Max = 63

the array type:

packed array [1..8] of range

occupies 2 words which are indexed by the P-machine as follows:

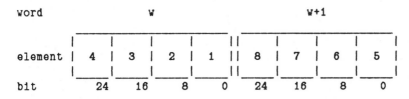

```
word                    w                          w+1

          _____   __   _____
         |    |    |    |    |   |  |  |    |    |    |    |
element  | 4  | 3  | 2  | 1  |   || | 8  | 7  | 6  | 5  |
         |____|____|____|____|   |  |  |____|____|____|____|
bit        24   16    8    0        24   16    8    0
```

Notice the actual indexed element size is taken to be (MCBitsPerWord div ElementsPer-Word) which is 8 rather than 7. This has the dual effect of avoiding unused word portions and spreading each element into a more efficiently accessed machine byte without loss of packing density.

Packed arrays may occupy partwords if the number of elements is less than ElementsPer-Word. The representation of:

packed array [1..2] of range

is

WordSize = 1; BitSize = 16

The criteria for augmenting the array representation with specific preset, postset and value-checking procedures are examined for each array type by a call to procedure AugmentRepresentationFor. A more detailed discussion of these criteria is deferred to Section 12.2.

(5) Conformant Array Types

By definition, the static store requirement of a conformant array type cannot be known at compile-time. However, a call is made to SetRepresentationFor to set the storage requirement for each bound-pair block in such a way that the block for the outer-most dimension effectively encloses blocks for the inner dimensions. Individually each block occupies 3 machine words arranged as follows:

```
        |-------------|
        | lower bound |   w
        |-------------|
        | upper bound |   w+1
        |-------------|
        |    size     |   w+2
        |-------------|
```

For an unpacked schema, the third word holds the size of an actual array element. For a packed schema the third word holds the size of the actual array itself.

The two-dimensional array schema:

     array [l1..u1: integer] of array [l2..u2: integer] of real

is represented by two adjacent bound-pair blocks utilised as follows:

```
|-------------|
|     l1      |  w
|-------------|
|     u1      |  w+1
|-------------|
|    size1    |  w+2
|-------------|
|     l2      |  w+3
|-------------|
|     u2      |  w+4
|-------------|
|    size2    |  w+5
|-------------|
```

At runtime size2=1 and size1 = u2-l2+1. The inner block has a representation WordSize of 3 and the outer block a WordSize of 6.

(6) Record Types

The aggregate representation for a record is computed from the sum of its fixed-part representation, and its variant-part representation. For an unpacked record fixed fields are assigned consecutive offsets from the record base. Thus:

     record i, j: integer; a: array [1..2] of real end

has a representation WordSize = 6 with the fields assigned word offsets 0 for i, 1 for j, and 2 for a.

Storage for variant records is overlaid so that the fraction of storage corresponding to the variant-part as a whole reduces to that required for the largest variant. In addition a control word is required if run-time checks are being generated. Thus:

    record
      fixed: integer;
      case tag: boolean of
        false: (a, b: real);
        true: (c: array [1..3] of real)
    end

has a maximum storage requirement of:

     $2 + \max (4, 6) = 8$ words

The need for a control word increases this to 6 words. The fields are assigned offsets to correspond with the following picture:

```
    |---------|            |---------|
    | control |     0      | control |
    |---------|            |---------|
    |  fixed  |     1      |  fixed  |
    |---------|            |---------|
    |   tag   |     2      |   tag   |
    |---------|            |---------|
    |    a    |     3      |  c[1]   |
    |---------|            |---------|
    |    b    |     5      |  c[2]   |
    |---------|            |---------|
                    7      |  c[3]   |
                           |---------|

     tag = false        tag = true
```

The representation of a variant-part is accumulated by processing each distinct variant in turn. Recursively, the representation of each variant is derived from its local fixed part and its nested variant part. In addition, the CheckValue of each variant representation is set to the selector value associated with the variant. This is derived either from the case constant labelling the variant or, in the case of multiple labels, from an independent ordinal value that identifies each distinct variant. Finally the representation of the variant part is augmented with procedures to select, preset and postset the individual variants.

Storage for packed records is reduced by packing those fields whose representation BitSize is less than MCBitsPerWord. Fields are packed from the most significant end of the P-machine word in order of declaration. If a field cannot be packed within the remaining portion of a word, packing recommences at bit 0 of the following word, and the preceding field is "spread" to include the unused portion. Thus the fields of

packed record i: 0..1; a: packed array [1..2] of 0..100; j: 0..7; k: integer end;

are assigned as follows:

```
bit used      14        16        2      offset
           |-----------------------|
           |   j   |    a    | |1|      0
           |-----------------------|
           |          k            |      1
           |-----------------------|
```

Note that j which needs only 4 bits has been spread into a field of 14 bits since k needs a full word.

As with arrays, the representation may be augmented with type-specific code generated by the call to AugmentRepresentationFor. The use of the control word when checks have been requested is explained in Chapter 26 where this type-specific code is generated.

(7)   File Types

All file types are represented by a block of 5 words which holds information required to open the file, and a file "descriptor" which identifies the associated physical file thereafter. Information is preset into this block by a type-specific preset procedure generated by the call to AugmentRepresentationFor and allows a file buffer to be allocated from the heap when the file is opened. If the file type is the standard type text, a corresponding postset procedure is generated to close the file and discard the buffer. This postset procedure is shared for all other file types.

}

procedure AugmentRepresentationFor(TheType: TypEntry); forward;

procedure SetRepresentationFor {TheType : TypEntry};

   var TheMax, TheMin: ObjectValue; BitsNeeded, ElsPerWord: MCBitRange;
      WordsNeeded, FirstOffset: Scalar; Members: MCScalar; Packing: Boolean;
      ThisRepresentation: TypeRepresentation;

   procedure AllocateLevel(FixedPart: IdEntry; VariantPart: TypEntry;
                   ThisLevel, StartWord: Scalar; StartBits: MCBitRange;
                   var MaxWordsize: Scalar; **var** MaxBitSize: MCBitRange);

   var WordFree, ThisVarWordSize: Scalar; BitsFree, ThisVarBitSize: MCBitRange;
      LastField, ThisField: IdEntry; LastVariant, ThisVariant: TypEntry;
      SelectorValue: MCIntegerForm; MultipleLabels: Boolean;

   procedure SpreadLastField;
     begin
      if LastField $<>$ **nil**
      then begin
           with LastField^.Offset **do**
             if BitOffset $= 0$
             then begin PartWord := false; WordSize := 1 **end**
             else BitSize := MCBitsPerWord - BitOffset;
           WordFree := WordFree + 1; BitsFree := MCBitsPerWord;
           LastField := **nil**
        end
      else if BitsFree $<>$ MCBitsPerWord
        then begin WordFree := WordFree + 1; BitsFree := MCBitsPerWord **end**
     end { spreadlastfield };

   procedure SpreadSelector;
     var SelectorMustSpread: Boolean; FirstActualField: IdEntry;
     begin
      with VariantPart^ **do**
        begin
        SelectorMustSpread := true; ThisVariant := FirstVariant;

        { with checks on, start each field-list on a
          word boundary in order to pack preset-values }

        if not (Checks **in** Requested)
        then while (ThisVariant $<>$ **nil**) **and** SelectorMustSpread **do**

```
                    with ThisVariant^ do
                      begin
                        if SubFixedPart <> nil
                        then FirstActualField := SubFixedPart
                        else if SubVarPart = nil
                            then FirstActualField := nil
                            else FirstActualField := SubVarPart^.TagField;
                        if FirstActualField <> nil
                        then if FirstActualField^.IdType <> Unknown
                            then with FirstActualField^.IdType^.Representation do
                                if WordSize = 1
                                then if BitSize <= BitsFree
                                    then SelectorMustSpread := false;
                        ThisVariant := NextVariant
                      end;
              if SelectorMustSpread then SpreadLastField
          end
  end { spreadselector };

procedure Allocate(FieldEntry: IdEntry);
  var WordsNeeded: Scalar; BitsNeeded: MCBitRange;
  begin
    with FieldEntry^ do
      begin
        WordsNeeded := IdType^.Representation.WordSize;
        if Packing and (WordsNeeded = 1) and
          (IdType^.Representation.BitSize < MCBitsPerWord)
        then begin
              BitsNeeded := IdType^.Representation.BitSize;
              if BitsNeeded > BitsFree then SpreadLastField;
              with Offset do
                begin
                  WordOffset := WordFree; Level := ThisLevel;
                  PartWord := true; BitSize := BitsNeeded;
                  BitOffset := MCBitsPerWord - BitsFree
                end;
              BitsFree := BitsFree - BitsNeeded;
              if BitsFree = 0
              then begin
                    WordFree := WordFree + 1; BitsFree := MCBitsPerWord;
                    LastField := nil
                  end
              else LastField := FieldEntry
            end
        else begin
              if Packing then SpreadLastField;
              with Offset do
                begin
                  WordOffset := WordFree; Level := ThisLevel;
                  PartWord := false; WordSize := WordsNeeded
```

```
                   end;
               WordFree := WordFree + WordsNeeded; LastField := nil
            end
        end
    end { allocate };
begin { allocatelevel }
    WordFree := StartWord; BitsFree := StartBits; LastField := nil;
    ThisField := FixedPart;
    while ThisField <> nil do
        begin Allocate(ThisField); ThisField := ThisField^.NextField end;
    if VariantPart <> nil
    then begin
            if ThisLevel > MaxLevels then SystemError(8);
            with VariantPart^ do
                begin
                    if TagField <> nil then Allocate(TagField);
                    if SelectorField <> TagField then Allocate(SelectorField);
                    if Packing then SpreadSelector;
                    if BitsFree = MCBitsPerWord
                    then begin
                            MaxWordsize := WordFree; MaxBitSize := MCBitsPerWord
                        end
                    else begin
                            MaxWordsize := WordFree + 1;
                            MaxBitSize := MCBitsPerWord - BitsFree
                        end;
                    Representation := SelectorField^.IdType^.Representation;
                    with Representation do
                        begin Kind := ForSelector; Selector := SelectorField^.Offset end;
                    MultipleLabels :=
                        Cardinality(SelectorField^.IdType) < Cardinality(TagType);
                    if MultipleLabels then SelectorValue := 0
                end;
            LastVariant := Unknown; ThisVariant := VariantPart^.FirstVariant;
            while ThisVariant <> nil do
                with ThisVariant^ do
                    begin
                        if Distinct
                        then begin
                                AllocateLevel
                                    (SubFixedPart, SubVarPart, ThisLevel + 1, WordFree,
                                        BitsFree, ThisVarWordSize, ThisVarBitSize);
                                with Representation do
                                    begin
                                        WordSize := ThisVarWordSize;
                                        if ThisVarWordSize = 1
                                        then BitSize := ThisVarBitSize;
                                        Kind := ForVariant; CheckValue.Defined := true;
                                        if MultipleLabels
```

```
                        then begin
                                CheckValue.Magnitude := SelectorValue;
                                SelectorValue := SelectorValue + 1
                            end
                        else CheckValue.Magnitude := VariantValue.Ival
                      end;
                    if ThisVarWordSize > MaxWordsize
                    then begin
                            MaxWordsize := ThisVarWordSize;
                            MaxBitSize := ThisVarBitSize
                         end
                    else if ThisVarWordSize = MaxWordsize
                         then if ThisVarBitSize > MaxBitSize
                              then MaxBitSize := ThisVarBitSize;
                    LastVariant := ThisVariant
                  end
                else Representation := LastVariant^.Representation;
                ThisVariant := NextVariant
              end;
        AugmentRepresentationFor(VariantPart)
      end
  else begin
      if Packing and (WordFree > 0) then SpreadLastField;
      if BitsFree = MCBitsPerWord
      then begin
            MaxWordsize := WordFree;
            if MaxWordsize > 0
            then MaxBitSize := MCBitsPerWord else MaxBitSize := 0
          end
      else begin
            MaxWordsize := WordFree + 1;
            MaxBitSize := MCBitsPerWord - BitsFree
          end
      end
  end { allocatelevel };
begin { setrepresentationfor }
  if TheType <> Unknown
  then with TheType^ do
      case Form of
        Scalars :
          if ScalarKind = Declared
          then with Representation do
              begin
                Kind := ForScalar; GetBounds(TheType, TheMin, TheMax);
                BitSize := BitsFor(TheMax.Ival); Max := TheMax.Ival;
                ThisRepresentation := Representation;
                SetCheckValue(ThisRepresentation);
                Representation := ThisRepresentation
              end;
```

```
SubRanges :
  with Representation do
    begin
      Kind := ForScalar; Min := TheType^.Min.Ival;
      Max := TheType^.Max.Ival;
      if Min >= 0 then BitSize := BitsFor(Max);
      ThisRepresentation := Representation;
      SetCheckValue(ThisRepresentation);
      Representation := ThisRepresentation
    end;
Pointers : Representation := PointerRepresentation;
Sets :
  if BaseType <> Unknown
  then with Representation do
         begin
           Kind := ForSet;
           if (BaseType = IntType) and (FormOfSet = Constructed)
           then Max := MCMaxSet - 1
           else begin
                  GetBounds(BaseType, TheMin, TheMax);
                  if TheMin.Ival < 0
                  then SystemError(7) else Min := TheMin.Ival;
                  if TheMax.Ival >= MCMaxSet
                  then SystemError(6) else Max := TheMax.Ival
                end;
           WordSize := WordsFor(Max + 1, MCWordSetBits);
           ThisRepresentation := Representation;
           SetCheckValue(ThisRepresentation);
           Representation := ThisRepresentation
         end;
Arrays :
  if (AelType <> Unknown) and (InxType <> Unknown)
  then begin
         Members := Cardinality(InxType);
         if PackedArray and (AelType^.Representation.WordSize = 1)
         then begin
                ElsPerWord :=
                  MCBitsPerWord div AelType^.Representation.BitSize;
                WordsNeeded := WordsFor(Members, ElsPerWord)
              end
         else WordsNeeded :=
                Members * AelType^.Representation.WordSize;
         Validate(WordsNeeded);
         with Representation do
           begin
             Kind := ForArray; WordSize := WordsNeeded;
             if (WordsNeeded = 1) and PackedArray
             then BitSize :=
                    Members * (MCBitsPerWord div ElsPerWord);
```

```
                              if not StringConstant
                              then AugmentRepresentationFor(TheType)
                              end
                    end;
            CAPSchema :
               with Representation do
                  begin
                     Kind := ForCAP;
                     if CompType^.Form = CAPSchema
                     then WordSize :=
                              CompType^.Representation.WordSize + CAPBpSize
                     else WordSize := CAPBpSize
                  end;
            Records :
               begin
                  Packing := PackedRecord;
                  if VarPart = nil
                  then FirstOffset := 0
                  else FirstOffset :=
                          ord((Checks in Requested) or
                              VariantFiles(VarPart^.FirstVariant));
                  AllocateLevel(FixedPart, VarPart, 0, FirstOffset, MCBitsPerWord,
                              WordsNeeded, BitsNeeded);
                  Validate(WordsNeeded);
                  with Representation do
                     begin
                        if VarPart <> nil
                        then Kind := ForVntRecord else Kind := ForARecord;
                        WordSize := WordsNeeded;
                        if WordsNeeded = 1 then BitSize := BitsNeeded;
                        AugmentRepresentationFor(TheType)
                     end
               end;
            Files :
               with Representation do
                  begin
                     Kind := ForFile; WordSize := FileSize;
                     AugmentRepresentationFor(TheType)
                  end
         end
   end { setrepresentationfor };
{
```

12.2 Augmented Representations

In principle every type requires procedures to correctly preset, postset and check variables declared with that type. In practice, the model P-machine possesses special P-codes for presetting and checking arrays of words, and "manual" procedures are only required if the type has a manual component, or a packed component. Furthermore, files or types containing embedded files are the only types requiring a postset action.

Further optimisation is possible if a packed structure is contained entirely within a word. The representation of

packed array [1..2] of 0..63;

has WordSize = 1 and BitSize = 16. Clearly a variable of this type can be preset by storing the hexadecimal value 4040 to set each of the elements to the "undefined-value" 64. A manual preset procedure is not required. No such optimisation is possible for value-checking since an array of this type will be undefined if either of its elements is undefined. Consequently a manual checking procedure is required to check each array element in turn.

The scheme for generating manual preset and postset procedures has been extended to incorporate the implementation of value conformant arrays and variant records. The following utilities determine whether a given type requires manual pre- or postsetting or checking.

```
}
function APartWord(Representation: TypeRepresentation): Boolean;
  begin
    with Representation do
      APartWord := (WordSize = 1) and (BitSize < MCBitsPerWord)
  end { apartword };
function StructuredWord(Representation: TypeRepresentation): Boolean;
  begin
    with Representation do
      StructuredWord :=
        (WordSize = 1) and (BitSize <= MCBitsPerWord) and
        (Kind in [ForArray, ForARecord])
  end { structuredpartword };
function PackedElements(LocallyPacked: Boolean; Element: TypEntry): Boolean;
  begin
    with Element^ do
      PackedElements :=
        LocallyPacked and APartWord(Representation) and
        (Representation.BitSize <= MCBitsPerWord div 2)
  end { packedelements };
function PostsetByCall(TheType: TypEntry): Boolean;
  begin
    with TheType^ do
      case Form of
        Scalars, SubRanges, Pointers, Sets : PostsetByCall := false;
        Arrays, Records : PostsetByCall := EmbeddedFile(TheType);
        CAPSchema : PostsetByCall := ValueSchema;
        Files : PostsetByCall := true;
        VariantPart : PostsetByCall := VariantFiles(FirstVariant);
        Variant : PostsetByCall := false
      end
  end { postsetbybcall };
```

```
function PresetByCall(TheType: TypEntry): Boolean;
  var Manual: Boolean; Field: IdEntry;
  begin
    if not (Checks in Requested)
    then PresetByCall := PostsetByCall(TheType)
    else with TheType^ do
          case Form of
              Scalars, SubRanges, Pointers, Sets : PresetByCall := false;
              Arrays :
                PresetByCall :=
                  PresetByCall(AelType) or
                  ((Representation.WordSize > 1) and
                   (PackedElements(PackedArray, AelType) or
                    StructuredWord(AelType^.Representation)));
              CAPSchema : PresetByCall := ValueSchema;
              Records :
                if VarPart <> nil
                then PresetByCall := true
                else if Representation.WordSize > 1
                      then begin
                              Field := FixedPart; Manual := false;
                              while (Field <> nil) and (not Manual) do
                                with Field^ do
                                  if PresetByCall(IdType) or
                                     StructuredWord(IdType^.Representation) or
                                     Offset.PartWord
                                  then Manual := true else Field := NextField;
                              PresetByCall := Manual
                           end
                      else PresetByCall := false;
              Files, VariantPart : PresetByCall := true
          end
  end { presetbycall };
function CheckedByCall(TheType: TypEntry): Boolean;
  var Manual: Boolean; Field: IdEntry;
  begin
    if not (Checks in Requested) or EmbeddedFile(TheType)
    then CheckedByCall := false
    else with TheType^ do
          case Form of
              Scalars, SubRanges, Sets, Pointers : CheckedByCall := false;
              Arrays :
                CheckedByCall :=
                  CheckedByCall(AelType) or PackedElements(PackedArray, AelType);
              CAPSchema :
                CheckedByCall :=
                  (not ValueSchema) and
                  (CheckedByCall(CompType) or
                   PackedElements(PackedSchema, CompType));
```

```
          Records :
            if VarPart <> nil
            then CheckedByCall := true
            else begin
                   Field := FixedPart; Manual := false;
                   while (Field <> nil) and (not Manual) do
                     with Field^ do
                        if CheckedByCall(IdType) or Offset.PartWord
                        then Manual := true else Field := NextField;
                   CheckedByCall := Manual
                 end;
          VariantPart, Variant : CheckedByCall := false
        end
  end { checkedbycall };
{
```

The following procedures generate manual procedures for a given type. To hide low-level
details of code-generation, their bodies have been deferred to Chapter 26. In each case, however, the procedure is responsible for recording the entry point of the manual procedure in
the representation field of the TypeRecord.

```
}
procedure PresetAnArray(ArrayType: TypEntry); forward;
procedure PostsetAnArray(ArrayType: TypEntry); forward;
procedure CheckAnArray(ArrayType: TypEntry); forward;
{
```

The procedures AcceptACAP and ReleaseACAP are used to generate procedures that manually create and dispose the auxiliary variable associated with a value conformant array-
parameter. The procedure CheckACAP generates a procedure to check for undefined elements within a variable conformant array parameter.

```
}
procedure AcceptACAP(CAPType: TypEntry); forward;
procedure ReleaseACAP(CAPType: TypEntry); forward;
procedure CheckACAP(CAPType: TypEntry); forward;
{
```

The procedures PresetARecord, PostsetARecord, and CheckARecord generate manual procedures for a record-type. PostSetARecord is called only if the record contains an embedded
file.

```
}
procedure PresetARecord(RecordType: TypEntry); forward;
procedure PostsetARecord(RecordType: TypEntry); forward;
procedure CheckARecord(RecordType: TypEntry); forward;
{
```

The procedures GenerateActivator, and GeneratePassivator generate the activator and passivator procedures associated with a variant part. Conceptually, for a given tagtype:

tagtype = (one, two, three)

the activator derived from:

case tag: tagtype of
one: (a: real);
two: (i, j: integer);
three: (f: text)

presets the fields of the newly selected variant according to the new selector value. The passivator is required to postset (close) the file variable f in either of the tag-value transitions three to one or three to two.

The third procedure GenerateSelector generates a manual variant selection procedure which is called whenever the tag value changes to check and implement the variant (re-)selection. Further details of these activator, passivator and selector procedures generated for a given variant part are to be found in Section 26.3.
}

procedure GenerateActivator(PartType: TypEntry); forward;
procedure GeneratePassivator(PartType: TypEntry); forward;
procedure GenerateSelector(PartType: TypEntry); forward;
{

The procedure PresetaFile is called for every file-type to generate a manual presetting (opening) procedure. The procedure PostsetaFile is used to generate a corresponding postsetting (closing) procedure. In practice it is called only for text files, and shared for all subsequent file types.
}

procedure PresetAFile(FileType: TypEntry); forward;
procedure PostSetAFile(FileType: TypEntry); forward;
{

The following procedures are responsible for augmenting the representation and setting the CheckValue for structured types as required. For single word types with embedded structure such as:

packed array [1..2] of 0..63;

the procedure StructuredCheckValue is called to derive the preset value (hex 4040) for the entire array. A variable of this type can then be preset efficiently by storing this value into the assigned storage word.
}

procedure ResetPresetBuffer;
  begin
    with PresetBuffer **do**
      begin Shift := 0; BitsFree := MCBitsPerWord; Buffer.WValue := 0 **end**
  end { resetpresetbuffer };

```
procedure FlushBuffer(var PresetValue: MachineValue);
  begin
    with PresetValue do
      begin
        Multiple := 1; Defined := true; Magnitude := PresetBuffer.Buffer.WValue
      end;
    ResetPresetBuffer
  end { flushbuffer };
procedure PresetPartWord(PartSize: MCBitRange; PresetValue: MachineValue);
  var PartValue: MCWordForm; i: MCBitIndex; Bit: MCBit;
  begin
    PartValue.WValue := PresetValue.Magnitude;
    with PresetBuffer do
      begin
        for i := 0 to PartSize - 1 do
          begin
            MCGetBit(PartValue, i, Bit);
            if Bit <> 0 then MCSetBit(Buffer, Shift + i)
          end;
        Shift := Shift + PartSize; BitsFree := BitsFree - PartSize
      end
  end { presetpartword };
procedure PresetStructuredWord(FieldType: TypEntry; FieldSize: MCBitRange);
  var PartSize: MCBitRange; Members, Count: Scalar; PartField: IdEntry;
  begin
    with FieldType^ do
      case Form of
        Arrays :
          begin
            Members := Cardinality(InxType); PartSize := FieldSize div Members;
            for Count := 1 to Members do
              with AelType^.Representation do PresetPartWord(PartSize, CheckValue)
          end;
        Records :
          begin
            PartField := FixedPart;
            while PartField <> nil do
              with PartField^ do
                begin
                  if Offset.PartWord
                  then PartSize := Offset.BitSize else PartSize := MCBitsPerWord;
                  with IdType^.Representation do
                    PresetPartWord(PartSize, CheckValue);
                  PartField := PartField^.NextField
                end
          end
      end
  end { presetstructuredword };
```

```
procedure StructuredCheckValue(TheType: TypEntry);
   var ThisRepresentation: TypeRepresentation; PresetValue: MachineValue;
   begin
      with TheType^ do
        begin
           ThisRepresentation := Representation;
           if StructuredWord(ThisRepresentation)
           then begin
                   ResetPresetBuffer;
                   PresetStructuredWord(TheType, ThisRepresentation.BitSize);
                   FlushBuffer(PresetValue); ThisRepresentation.CheckValue := PresetValue
                end
           else SetCheckValue(ThisRepresentation);
           Representation := ThisRepresentation
        end
   end { structuredcheckvalue };
procedure AugmentRepresentationFor {TheType : TypEntry};
   var SelectorNeeded: Boolean;
   begin
      with TheType^ do
        case Form of
          Arrays :
             begin
                StructuredCheckValue(TheType);
                if PresetByCall(TheType) then PresetAnArray(TheType);
                if PostsetByCall(TheType) then PostsetAnArray(TheType);
                if CheckedByCall(TheType) then CheckAnArray(TheType)
             end;
          CAPSchema :
             begin
                if PresetByCall(TheType) then AcceptACAP(TheType);
                if PostsetByCall(TheType) then ReleaseACAP(TheType);
                if CheckedByCall(TheType) then CheckACAP(TheType)
             end;
          Records :
             begin
                StructuredCheckValue(TheType);
                if PresetByCall(TheType) then PresetARecord(TheType);
                if PostsetByCall(TheType) then PostsetARecord(TheType);
                if CheckedByCall(TheType) then CheckARecord(TheType)
             end;
          Files :
             begin
                PresetAFile(TheType);
                if TheType = TextType
                then PostSetAFile(TheType)
                else with Representation do
                        PostsetCode := TextType^.Representation.PostsetCode
             end;
```

```
            VariantPart :
              begin
                SelectorNeeded := false;
                if PresetByCall(TheType)
                then begin GenerateActivator(TheType); SelectorNeeded := true end;
                if PostsetByCall(TheType)
                then begin GeneratePassivator(TheType); SelectorNeeded := true end;
                if SelectorNeeded then GenerateSelector(TheType)
              end
          end
    end { augmentrepresentationfor };
```

{

The procedure AugmentSchema is used during block entry code generation in Chapter 15 to trigger the generation of manual code for conformant array parameters. For efficiency reasons these procedures must be local to the procedure containing the conformant array declaration and their generation is delayed until processing of the procedure statement part is about to begin. The function EnvelopeUsed is a diagnostic used retrospectively by the manual code generation procedures.

}

```
procedure AugmentSchema(TheType: TypEntry);
  begin
    with TheType^ do
      begin
        if CompType^.Form = CAPSchema then AugmentSchema(CompType);
        if FirstIndex or (not ValueSchema) then AugmentRepresentationFor(TheType)
      end
  end { augmentschema };
function EnvelopeUsed(Representation: TypeRepresentation; Action: TypeActions):
          Boolean;
  begin
    with Representation do
      case Kind of
        ForScalar, ForReal, ForString, ForPnter, ForSet, ForOther :
          EnvelopeUsed := false;
        ForArray, ForARecord, ForVntRecord, ForCAP, ForFile :
          case Action of
            Presets : EnvelopeUsed := PresetCode.EntryOffset <> 0;
            Postsets : EnvelopeUsed := PostsetCode.EntryOffset <> 0;
            ValueChecks : EnvelopeUsed := CheckCode.EntryOffset <> 0
          end
      end
  end { envelopeused };
```

```
{
```

Constant expression operands are assigned representations which must be updated to reflect the results of folded integer and set operations. The following procedure is called to re-compute the result representation following compile-time set-arithmetic:

```
}
procedure SetBaseLimits(var SetRep: TypeRepresentation; SetConstant: ObjectValue);
   var SetWord: WordEntry; Temp: MCIntegerForm;
   procedure Adjust(var Limit: MCIntegerForm; SetWord: MCWordForm;
                      Delta, BitIndex: integer);
      var BitValue: MCBit;
      begin
        repeat
          MCGetBit(SetWord, BitIndex, BitValue);
          if BitValue = 0 then Limit := Limit + Delta;
          BitIndex := BitIndex + Delta
        until BitValue <> 0
      end { adjust };
   begin
     with SetRep do
       begin
         Min := 0; Max := 0; SetWord := SetConstant.Setval;
         if SetWord <> nil
         then begin
                while SetWord^.Word.WValue = 0 do
                  begin
                    Min := Min + MCWordSetBits; SetWord := SetWord^.Next
                  end;
                Max := Min + MCMaxSetBit; Temp := Min;
                Adjust(Temp, SetWord^.Word, +1, 0); Min := Temp;
                while SetWord^.Next <> nil do
                  begin
                    Max := Max + MCWordSetBits; SetWord := SetWord^.Next
                  end;
                Temp := Max; Adjust(Temp, SetWord^.Word, -1, MCMaxSetBit);
                Max := Temp
              end
       end
   end { setbaselimits };
{
```

12.3 Standard Representations

The representations for the standard types integer, real, Boolean and char are held in global variables IntegerRepresentation, RealRepresentation, BooleanRepresentation and Char-Representation and initialised by the procedure InitRepresentations. With the exception of reals, the scalar standard types occupy a single P-machine word. Reals are allocated one or

more words, depending on the value of MCRealsize. In addition InitRepresentations com-
poses the value of DefaultRepresentation which is used as the base of all other representations. The variable PointerRepresentation is used for all pointer types.
}

```
procedure InitRepresentations;
  begin
    with DefaultRepresentation do
      begin
        WordSize := 1; BitSize := MCBitsPerWord; Kind := ForOther; Min := 0;
        Max := 0; PresetCode := DefaultLabel; PostsetCode := DefaultLabel;
        CheckCode := DefaultLabel; Selector := DefaultOffset
      end;
    SetCheckValue(DefaultRepresentation);

    { set the standard representations }

    EmptyRepresentation := DefaultRepresentation;
    with EmptyRepresentation do
      begin Kind := ForSet; WordSize := 0; BitSize := 0 end;
    SetCheckValue(EmptyRepresentation);
    RealRepresentation := DefaultRepresentation;
    with RealRepresentation do
      begin Kind := ForReal; WordSize := MCRealSize end;
    SetCheckValue(RealRepresentation);
    BooleanRepresentation := DefaultRepresentation;
    with BooleanRepresentation do
      begin Kind := ForScalar; BitSize := 1; Max := 1 end;
    SetCheckValue(BooleanRepresentation);
    CharRepresentation := DefaultRepresentation;
    with CharRepresentation do
      begin
        Kind := ForScalar; BitSize := MCBitsPerByte; Max := MCMaxChar;
        if Checks in Requested
        then with CheckValue do
                begin Defined := true; Magnitude := MCUndefinedChar end
      end;
    IntegerRepresentation := DefaultRepresentation;
    with IntegerRepresentation do
      begin Kind := ForScalar; Max := MCMaxint; Min := -MCMaxint end;
    SetCheckValue(IntegerRepresentation);
    PointerRepresentation := DefaultRepresentation;
    with PointerRepresentation do
      begin
        Kind := ForPnter;
        if Checks in Requested then WordSize := 2
      end;
    SetCheckValue(PointerRepresentation)
  end { initrepresentations };
```

{

CHAPTER 13

Static Storage Management

The static storage required by a procedure, function or program block is calculated at compile-time by recording:

(1) the storage required by local variables, formal parameters, and function results;

(2) the storage required by temporaries used internally by the generated code;

(3) the storage required to preserve "extended references";

as the block is analysed.

Storage for local variables and parameters is allocated using the WordSize field of the variable type's representation. The run-time addresses allocated reflect the order of declaration. Thereafter, temporaries may be allocated during analysis of the statement-part of the block to avoid repeated address or expression evaluation.

To preserve vulnerable references to file buffer variables, dynamic variables, and record variant fields made in the context of a with-statement or in passing an actual-variable parameter, a "lock stack" is embedded within each stack frame. The static storage requirement for the lock stack is calculated from the maximum depth of the lock stack recorded during analysis of the statement part. Storage for the lock stack is reserved after the last temporary.

The general layout of the run-time stack-frames is:

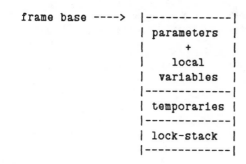

```
frame base ---->   |-------------|
                   | parameters  |
                   |      +      |
                   |    local    |
                   |  variables  |
                   |-------------|
                   | temporaries |
                   |-------------|
                   | lock-stack  |
                   |-------------|
```

13.1 Stack Frame Management

The requirements for local-variable, temporary, and lock-stack storage of each block are logged in fields of a corresponding FrameRecord as the block is analysed. In particular:

(1)   NextOffset is the word offset of the next available storage word in the stack frame.

(2)   LockDepth and MaxDepth are respectively the current depth, and maximum depth to date of the lock stack.

(3)   Local variables requiring manual initialisation and finalisation are recorded as anonymous items in the lists PresetList and PostsetList.

(4)   Value conformant arrays are accumulated in the list CAPlist. Corresponding entries in the PresetList and PostsetList are made after the code for handling the auxiliary variable has been generated.

Since temporary and lock stack storage cannot be accumulated until the statement part of a block, its frame record must be preserved while nested local blocks are processed. Frame records for all open blocks are therefore held within a frame stack referenced by the variable TopFrameEntry.

To enable non-local variable access, each nested stack frame is identified by the value of the global variable FrameLevel. FrameLevel is incremented by each call to OpenStackFrame and decremented accordingly by CloseStackFrame.

The stack of nested frame records is maintained by the following procedures:

```
}
procedure StartManuals(var List: ManualList); forward;
procedure OpenStackFrame;
  var TopFrame: FrameEntry;
  begin
    FrameLevel := FrameLevel + 1; new(TopFrame);
    with TopFrame^ do
      begin
        NextOffset := FirstOffset; LockDepth := 0; MaxDepth := 0;
        StartManuals(PresetList); StartManuals(PostsetList); StartList(CAPList);
        Next := TopFrameEntry
      end;
    TopFrameEntry := TopFrame
  end { openstackframe };
procedure CloseStackFrame;
  var TopFrame: FrameEntry;
  begin
    TopFrame := TopFrameEntry;
    with TopFrame^ do
      begin DisposeList(CAPList); TopFrameEntry := Next end;
    dispose(TopFrame); FrameLevel := FrameLevel - 1
  end { closestackframe };
```

```
procedure SaveStackFrame;
  begin
    with Display[ScopeLevel] do
      begin
        SavedFrame := TopFrameEntry; TopFrameEntry := TopFrameEntry^.Next
      end;
    FrameLevel := FrameLevel - 1
  end { savestackframe };
procedure RestoreStackFrame;
  begin
    with Display[ScopeLevel] do
      begin SavedFrame^.Next := TopFrameEntry; TopFrameEntry := SavedFrame end;
    FrameLevel := FrameLevel + 1
  end { restorestackframe };
procedure InitFrames;
  begin
    FrameLevel := 0; new(TopFrameEntry);
    with TopFrameEntry^ do
      begin
        NextOffset := FirstOffset; LockDepth := 0; MaxDepth := 0;
        StartManuals(PresetList); StartManuals(PostsetList); Next := nil
      end
  end { initframes };
{
```

The following procedures enable the allocation of variable and lock-stack locations within the current stack frame:

```
}
procedure Acquire(Amount: WordRange; var Address: RuntimeAddress);
  begin
    with TopFrameEntry^ do
      begin
        Address.BlockLevel := FrameLevel; Address.WordOffset := NextOffset;
        NextOffset := NextOffset + Amount
      end
  end { acquire };
procedure PushLock;
  begin
    with TopFrameEntry^ do
      begin
        LockDepth := LockDepth + 1;
        if LockDepth > MaxDepth then MaxDepth := LockDepth
      end
  end { pushlock };
procedure PopLocks(OldDepth: Scalar);
  begin with TopFrameEntry^ do LockDepth := OldDepth end;
```

{

13.2 Storage and Address Allocation

Storage and address allocation are performed for each declared variable by a call to the procedure SetAddressFor. Each variable and function IdRecord carries with it a field of type RuntimeAddress whose internal fields BlockLevel and WordOffset respectively locate the variable within a nested stack frame at a particular word offset from the start of the frame. SetAddressFor calls the procedure SelectManuals to decide if the allocated variable should be added to the Pre- or PostsetList.

The procedure SetBoundPairBlockFor is called to allocate storage for the bound pair block associated with each conformant array schema, and to map the associated bound-identifiers onto the first and second words of the block.

}

```
procedure SelectManual(Action: TypeActions; var List: ManualList;
                       LocalId: IdEntry); forward;

procedure SetAddressFor {VarId : IdEntry};
   var Address: RuntimeAddress; WordsNeeded: WordRange;
   begin
     with VarId^ do
       case Klass of
         Vars :
           begin
             if (VarKind = VarParam) or (IdType^.Form = CAPSchema)
             then WordsNeeded := 1
             else WordsNeeded := IdType^.Representation.WordSize;
             Acquire(WordsNeeded, Address); VarAddress := Address;
             if VarKind <> VarParam
             then with TopFrameEntry^ do
                     if Conformant(IdType)
                     then AppendId(CAPList, VarId)
                     else if VarKind = LocalVar
                         then begin
                                 SelectManual(Presets, PresetList, VarId);
                                 SelectManual(Postsets, PostsetList, VarId)
                              end
           end;
         Proc, Func :
           if PfKind = Formal
           then begin Acquire(2, Address); FAddress := Address end
           else begin
                   WordsNeeded := IdType^.Representation.WordSize;
                   Acquire(WordsNeeded, Address); Result := Address
                end
       end
   end { setaddressfor };
```

procedure SetBoundPairBlockFor { LowBound, HighBound : IdEntry };
  var Address: RuntimeAddress;
  begin
    Acquire(CAPBpSize, Address); LowBound^.BdAddress := Address;
    with Address **do** WordOffset := WordOffset + 1;
    HighBound^.BdAddress := Address
  end { setboundpairblock };
function SameAddress(Addr1, Addr2: RuntimeAddress): Boolean;
  begin
    SameAddress :=
      (Addr1.BlockLevel = Addr2.BlockLevel) **and**
      (Addr1.WordOffset = Addr2.WordOffset)
  end { SameAddress };
{

13.3 Variable Initialisation and Finalisation

If runtime checks have been requested, each local variable must be preset on entry to any block such that its value is initially "undefined". This is achieved in one of three ways:

(1) The P-machine automatically presets each new stack frame so that every storage location therein holds a default undefined pattern. This suffices for all scalar local variables and for all unpacked structured types except files.

(2) For structured variables occupying a single word but with embedded packed structure such as:

    var a: packed array [1..2] of char

in-line code is generated to deposit the structured check value into the bitfields occupied by a[1] and a[2].

(3) For file-types and all other types which must be preset manually by type-specific procedures, code is generated to call the preset procedure, passing the appropriate variable address as parameter.

Given the variable declarations:

    i, j: integer;
    b: Boolean;
    a: array [1..100, 1..100] of real;
    r: record c: char; s: 0..10; t: (on, off) end;
    s: set of char;

the automatic presetting undertaken by the P-machine is sufficient to initialise every variable. Given the declarations:

    r: packed record b1, b2: boolean end;
    s: record l: 0..255; t: packed array [0..255] of char end;
    f: text;

manual code would be required to preset r in-line, and to preset s and f by calling the precompiled type-presetting procedure.

Presetting code is generated prior to code for the statement part of a block. File variables, or variables containing embedded file components, also need post-setting code which must be executed prior to leaving a block. An internally declared statement label FinalPart is sited at the start of the post-setting code-sequence by a call to NextIsStatementLabel. As explained in Chapter 22, this ensures that code will be generated to void the lock stack, thereby discarding all references extended within the current block. The declaration and siting of FinalPart is achieved by calls to FutureStatementlabel and NextIsStatementLabel made from procedures Block and PostsetBlock in Chapter 10.

On exiting a block by means of a non-local goto, care must be taken to finalise all active blocks nested within the destination global block.

The procedure SelectManual is used by SetAddressFor and by PresetRecord to determine if a variable or field should be added to a corresponding Pre- or PostsetList. As these lists are built, items of similar shape are merged to achieve optimization when variables of the same type are declared together.

For example, given

    var r1, r2, r3: packed record b1, b2: boolean end;

the two preset values for b1 and b2 can be combined into a composite value, and this value can be preset repeatedly into the consecutive word locations for r1, r2 and r3.

The manual preset and postset lists are built by procedures:

}
```
procedure StartManuals { var List : ManualList };
   begin List.FirstEntry := nil; List.LastEntry := nil end { StartManuals };
procedure AppendManual(var List: ManualList; Entry: ManualEntry);
   begin
     with List do
       begin
         if FirstEntry = nil
         then FirstEntry := Entry else LastEntry^.NextItem := Entry;
         LastEntry := Entry
       end
   end { appendmanual };
procedure CreateItem(Representation: TypeRepresentation; var Item: ManualEntry);
   begin
     new(Item);
     with Item^ do
       begin
         ItsRepresentation := Representation; ItsOffset := DefaultOffset; Repeated := 1;
         NextItem := nil
       end
   end { createitem };
```

```
procedure SetItemShape(Item: ManualEntry; ItsClass: IdClass);
  begin
    with Item^ do
      if ItsClass = Field
      then ItsShape :=
              ItemShapes[ItsOffset.PartWord, StructuredWord(ItsRepresentation)]
      else if StructuredWord(ItsRepresentation)
          then ItsShape := WordStructure else ItsShape := Word
  end { setitsshape };
procedure SetItemCode(Item: ManualEntry; ItsClass: IdClass; Action: TypeActions);
  begin
    with Item^ do
      begin
        case Action of
          Presets, ValueChecks :
            if EnvelopeUsed(ItsRepresentation, Action)
            then ItsCode := Indirect
            else if not (Checks in Requested)
                then ItsCode := None
                else if ItsClass = Field
                    then ItsCode := Inline
                    else if ItsShape = WordStructure
                        then ItsCode := Inline else ItsCode := None;
          Postsets :
            if EnvelopeUsed(ItsRepresentation, Postsets)
            then ItsCode := Indirect else ItsCode := None
        end
      end
  end { setitemcode };
function SameWordSize(r1, r2: TypeRepresentation): Boolean;
  begin SameWordSize := r1.WordSize = r2.WordSize end;
function SameCheckValues(r1, r2: TypeRepresentation): Boolean;
  begin SameCheckValues := r1.CheckValue.Magnitude = r2.CheckValue.Magnitude end;
function SameLabels(l1, l2: BlockLabel): Boolean;
  begin
    SameLabels := (l1.BlockLevel = l2.BlockLevel) and (l1.EntryOffset = l2.EntryOffset)
  end { samelabels };
procedure SelectManual { Action: TypeActions; var List: ManualList;
                         LocalId : IdEntry };
  var NewItem: ManualEntry;
  procedure AbsorbManual;
    var Merging: Boolean;
    begin
      Merging := false;
```

```
    if List.LastEntry <> nil
    then with List.LastEntry^ do
            if ItsCode = NewItem^.ItsCode
            then case ItsCode of
                    Indirect :
                        if ItsRepresentation.Kind <> ForCAP
                        then case Action of
                                Presets :
                                    Merging :=
                                        SameLabels
                                            (ItsRepresentation.PresetCode,
                                                NewItem^.ItsRepresentation.PresetCode);
                                Postsets :
                                    Merging :=
                                        SameLabels
                                            (ItsRepresentation.PostsetCode,
                                                NewItem^.ItsRepresentation.PostsetCode);
                                ValueChecks :
                                    Merging :=
                                        SameLabels
                                            (ItsRepresentation.CheckCode,
                                                NewItem^.ItsRepresentation.CheckCode)
                            end;
                    Inline :
                        if ItsShape = NewItem^.ItsShape
                        then case ItsShape of
                                Word :
                                    Merging :=
                                        SameWordSize
                                            (ItsRepresentation, NewItem^.ItsRepresentation);
                                WordStructure :
                                    Merging :=
                                        SameCheckValues
                                            (ItsRepresentation, NewItem^.ItsRepresentation);
                                PartWrd, PartWrdStructure : Merging := false
                            end;
                    None : Merging := true
                end;
        if Merging
        then begin
                with List.LastEntry^ do Repeated := Repeated + 1;
                dispose(NewItem)
            end
        else AppendManual(List, NewItem)
    end { absorbmanual };
begin { selectmanual }
    with LocalId^ do
        begin
            CreateItem(IdType^.Representation, NewItem);
```

```
        with NewItem^ do
          if Klass = Field
          then ItsOffset := Offset else ItsOffset.WordOffset := VarAddress.WordOffset;
          SetItemShape(NewItem, Klass); SetItemCode(NewItem, Klass, Action);
          AbsorbManual
      end
  end { selectmanual };
procedure DisposeManuals(var List: ManualList);
  var OldEntry: ManualEntry;
  begin
    with List do
      while FirstEntry <> nil do
        begin
          OldEntry := FirstEntry; FirstEntry := OldEntry^.NextItem; dispose(OldEntry)
        end;
      List.LastEntry := nil
  end { disposemanuals };
{
```

The generation of manual preset and postset code is triggered by calls to the procedures InitialiseVariables and FinaliseVariables. Variables requiring manual pre- or postset code are treated as fields of a conceptual record and transformed into anonymous items identified by a field offset deduced from the runtime address. Preset code is emitted by the procedure PresetManuals according to the contents of the PresetList. The PostsetList is processed similarly by procedure PostsetManuals. Details of PresetManuals and PostsetManuals are deferred to Chapter 25.

```
}
procedure PresetManuals(ManualScope: DispRange; List: ManualList); forward;
procedure PostsetManuals(ManualScope: DispRange; List: ManualList); forward;
procedure SelectCAPS(Action: TypeActions);
  var CAPEntry: ListEntry;
  begin
    with TopFrameEntry^ do
      begin
        CAPEntry := CAPList.FirstEntry;
        while CAPEntry <> nil do
          begin
            case Action of
              Presets : SelectManual(Presets, PresetList, CAPEntry^.Id);
              Postsets : SelectManual(Postsets, PostsetList, CAPEntry^.Id)
            end;
            CAPEntry := CAPEntry^.Next
          end
      end
  end { selectcaps };
```

```
procedure InitializeVariables;
  var FrameBase: RuntimeAddress;
  begin
    with TopFrameEntry^ do
      begin
        SelectCAPS(Presets); FrameBase.BlockLevel := FrameLevel;
        FrameBase.WordOffset := FirstOffset; StackReference(false, FrameBase);
        OpenWith(FrameLevel); PresetManuals(FrameLevel, PresetList); CloseWith;
        DisposeManuals(PresetList)
      end
  end { initialisevariables };
procedure FinalizeVariables;
  var FrameBase: RuntimeAddress;
  begin
    with TopFrameEntry^ do
      begin
        SelectCAPS(Postsets); FrameBase.BlockLevel := FrameLevel;
        FrameBase.WordOffset := FirstOffset; StackReference(false, FrameBase);
        OpenWith(FrameLevel); PostsetManuals(FrameLevel, PostsetList); CloseWith;
        DisposeManuals(PostsetList)
      end
  end { finalizevariables };
```

{

CHAPTER 14

Object Value Manipulation

This chapter implements the interface procedures for creating and manipulating literal object values at compile-time, as defined in Section 5.3.

The overriding consideration in determining how these are implemented is the distinction between the representation of primitive values such as integers, reals etc. on the host compiling machine and that to be used on the target machine on which compiled programs are run. For many compilers the host and target machines are identical and the distinction is not important, but for cross compilers it is essential that the distinction be maintained and that conversion from host to target representations occur at the correct points.

In this version of the Model Implementation the following assumptions are made.

(a)   The integer range of the target machine is no greater than that of the host machine.

(b)   The floating point representations of the host and target machines are identical.

(c)   The character set representations of the host and target machines are identical.

With these assumptions the type ObjectValue, which is used to represent target machine literal values, is easily defined: all ordinal target values are held as a host integer subrange; real target values are held as a host real; string, set and pointer values which may extend over several target words are held as linked lists of target word images. In the case of strings, which may not occupy an integral multiple of words a length in bytes is also maintained.

The following procedures isolate the points at which mapping of host to target values occur:
}
procedure SetIval(HostInteger: integer; var Value: ObjectValue);
  begin
    with Value do
      begin
        Kind := IntValue; Ival := HostInteger;
        WordSize := IntegerRepresentation.WordSize
      end
  end { setival };

```
procedure SetRval(HostReal: real; var Value: ObjectValue);
  begin
    with Value do
      begin
        Kind := RealValue; Rval := HostReal;
        WordSize := RealRepresentation.WordSize
      end
  end { setrval };
procedure SetBval(HostBoolean: Boolean; var Value: ObjectValue);
  begin
    with Value do
      begin Kind := BoolValue; Ival := ord(HostBoolean); WordSize := 1 end
  end { setbval };
function MapChar(HostCh: char): MCByte;
  begin MapChar := ord(HostCh) end;
```

{

The procedure Evaluate carries out the conversion of source literal images in character form
to the target values they denote. In addition to the assumptions listed above the following
version of Evaluate makes the assumption that a host integer provides sufficient accuracy for
accumulating the value of the mantissa in a real constant. For many host machines this
would not be acceptable and an augmented mantissa representation would be necessary. It
is important, however, to avoid accumulating mantissa values as host reals, since inaccuracies
introduced during the accumulation may significantly degrade the accuracy of the final
mantissa obtained. The strategy below uses real arithmetic only to compute a power-of-10
scale factor required for the final scaling operation. Accuracy may be further increased by
using table look-up to obtain the power of 10 required.

}

```
procedure Evaluate {var SourceValue : ValueDetails};
  var Index: integer; ByteIndex: MCByteIndex; Ivalu, Scale, Exponent: integer; Rvalu: real;
      StringWord, Element: WordEntry; Negative, Overflow: Boolean;
  procedure AddDigitTo(var Number: integer);
    var Digit: 0..9;
    begin
      Digit := ord(SourceValue.String[Index]) - ord('0');
      Overflow :=
        Overflow or (Number > MCMaxintDiv10) or
        ((Number = MCMaxintDiv10) and (Digit > MCMaxintMod10));
      if not Overflow then Number := Number * 10 + Digit
    end { AddDigitTo };
```

```
function PowerOf10(n: integer): real;
  var Factor, Power: real;
  begin
    Factor := 10.0; Power := 1.0;
    repeat
      if odd(n) then Power := Power * Factor;
      Factor := sqr(Factor); n := n div 2
    until n = 0;
    PowerOf10 := Power
  end { powerof10 };
begin { evaluate }
  with SourceValue do
    case Kind of
      OrdValue : SetIval(Ival, Value);
      CharValue :
        with Value do
          begin Kind := CharValue; WordSize := 1; Ival := MapChar(String[1]) end;
      StringValue :
        with Value do
          begin
            Kind := StringValue; Stringval := nil; Index := 1; ByteIndex := 0;
            while Index <= SourceValue.Length do
              begin
                if ByteIndex = 0
                then begin
                       new(Element);
                       with Element^ do
                         begin Word.WValue := 0; Next := nil end;
                       if Stringval = nil
                       then Stringval := Element
                       else StringWord^.Next := Element;
                       StringWord := Element
                     end;
                with StringWord^ do
                  MCSetByte(Word, ByteIndex, MapChar(String[Index]));
                ByteIndex := (ByteIndex + 1) mod MCBytesPerWord;
                Index := Index + 1
              end;
            Length := SourceValue.Length;
            WordSize := WordsFor(Length, MCBytesPerWord)
          end;
      IntValue :
        begin
          Ivalu := 0; Overflow := false;
          for Index := 1 to Length do AddDigitTo(Ivalu);
          if Overflow
          then begin PredictedError(47); Value := MaxintValue end
          else SetIval(Ivalu, Value)
        end;
```

```
RealValue :
  begin
    Ivalu := 0; Scale := 0; Overflow := false; Index := 1;
    String[Length + 1] := ' ';
    while String[Index] in ['0'..'9'] do
      begin
        AddDigitTo(Ivalu);
        if Overflow then Scale := Scale + 1;
        Index := Index + 1
      end;
    if String[Index] = '.'
    then begin
            Index := Index + 1;
            while String[Index] in ['0'..'9'] do
              begin
                AddDigitTo(Ivalu);
                if not Overflow then Scale := Scale - 1;
                Index := Index + 1
              end
         end;
    if String[Index] = 'E'
    then begin
            Index := Index + 1; Negative := (String[Index] = '-');
            Exponent := 0;
            for Index := Index + 1 to Length do AddDigitTo(Exponent);
            if Negative
            then Scale := Scale - Exponent else Scale := Scale + Exponent
         end;
    if Scale = 0
    then Rvalu := Ivalu
    else if Scale < 0
            then Rvalu := Ivalu / PowerOf10(Scale)
            else Rvalu := Ivalu * PowerOf10(Scale);
    SetRval(Rvalu, Value)
  end
end
end { evaluate };
```

{

The following procedures implement the object value operators required by the analyser, within the assumptions listed above.

}

```
procedure NegateValue {var Value : ObjectValue};
  begin
    with Value do
      case Kind of
        OrdValue, IntValue : Ival := -Ival;
```

```
        BoolValue :
            case Ival of
                0 : Ival := 1;
                1 : Ival := 0
            end;
            RealValue : Rval := -Rval
        end
    end { negatevalue };
function SameValue {Value1,Value2 : ObjectValue ) : Boolean};
    begin SameValue := Value1.Ival = Value2.Ival end;
function OrderedValues {Value1,Value2 : ObjectValue ) : Boolean};
    begin OrderedValues := Value1.Ival < Value2.Ival end;
function Range {Min, Max: ObjectValue): integer};
```

{ Computes the range defined by two object values, as a host integer. The value maxint
  is returned for those values whose range cannot be represented by a host integer value. }

```
    var Finite: Boolean;
    begin
        if Max.Ival < 0 then Finite := true else Finite := (Max.Ival - maxint) < Min.Ival;
        if Finite then Range := Max.Ival - Min.Ival + 1 else Range := maxint
    end { range };
```

{

The procedure InitValues is called from within InitCodeGeneration to set up all predefined
object values which the generation interface provides.

}

```
procedure InitValues;
    begin
        SetIval(0, ZeroValue); SetIval(1, OneValue); SetIval(MCMaxint, MaxintValue);
        SetIval(0, MinCharValue); SetIval(MCMaxChar, MaxCharValue);
        SetIval(10, LineFeed); SetIval(12, PageThrow); SetIval(10, DefaultLayout);
        SetRval(0.0, ZeroReal); SetBval(false, FalseValue); SetBval(true, TrueValue);
        SetIval(0, DefaultValue); SetIval(0, MinLabValue); SetIval(9999, MaxLabValue);
        with NilValue do
            begin Kind := PntrValue; Pval := nil; WordSize := 0 end;
        with EmptyValue do
            begin Kind := SetValue; Setval := nil; WordSize := 0 end
    end { initvalues };
```

{

CHAPTER 15

Code File Emission

This chapter implements the creation and maintenance of ¨code-spaces¨, as defined in Section 5.4, together with the final output of the CodeFile which these create.

The ¨code-spaces¨, which correspond to blocks in the source program compiled, have nested lifetimes. A record of the currently open code-spaces is maintained as a code-space stack pointed to by the variable CurrentSpace. This stack is maintained by the procedures Open-CodeSpace and CloseCodeSpace defined below.

The output codefile is a file of target machine word images comprising:

(a) initial option words which transmit the chosen compile-time options to the run-time system;

(b) a sequence of code blocks, one for each code-space opened;

(c) an index to the program entry point within the final code-block, which represents a pseudo-block enclosing the program.

Item (a) is written during initialisation of the code file emitter. Items (b) and (c) form the addressable code-space of the program at run time and are written via the following procedure:

}

procedure FileWord(Word: MCWord);

  begin CodeFile^ := Word; put(CodeFile); CodeFileSize := CodeFileSize + 1 **end**;

{

Each code block consists of a set of data words and a stream of code bytes. Data words are allocated and indexed backward from the position of code byte 0, which acts as the base address of the code block.

The data words of a code-block are allocated and filled throughout the life time of the corresponding code-space. The partially completed data sets for all existing code-spaces are held in the array DataStack and indexed from the records of the code-space stack.

The stream of code bytes for the current code-space is accumulated in the array CodeBuffer.

The following procedures carry out the allocation and filling of data words and code bytes with these arrays.

}

```
procedure CodeByte(Byte: MCByte);
  begin
    if CodeCounter = CodeByteLimit
    then SystemError(3)
    else begin CodeBuffer[CodeCounter] := Byte; CodeCounter := CodeCounter + 1 end
  end { codebyte };
procedure FillByte(Index: CodeByteRange; Byte: MCByte);
  begin CodeBuffer[Index] := Byte end;
procedure WordOfBytes(Word: MCWordForm);
  var ByteIndex: MCByteIndex;
  begin
    { recast(word, asbytes) };
    for ByteIndex := 0 to MCMaxByteNum do CodeByte(Word.WBytes[ByteIndex])
  end { wordofbytes };
procedure Align;
  begin while CodeCounter mod MCBytesPerWord <> 0 do CodeByte(NoOperation) end;
procedure DataWord(Word: MCWordForm);
  begin
    if (DataCounter = DataWordLimit) or
       (DataCounter - CurrentBlock^.DataBase > MCMaxByte)
    then SystemError(4)
    else begin DataStack[DataCounter] := Word; DataCounter := DataCounter + 1 end
  end { dataword };
procedure FillWord(Offset: MCByte; Word: MCWordForm);
  begin with CurrentBlock^ do DataStack[DataBase + Offset] := Word end;
{
```

The hierarchy of access to code-blocks implied by program nesting is implemented by embedding the base address of a code block in the data words of the "enclosing" code block. A block label (which represents an accessible code block) is therefore represented by

(a)   a level number which enables the code block of the enclosing program block to be located, and

(b)   an offset to the data word of that block which holds the base address of the code block required.

The procedure FutureBlockLabel carries out the allocation of block labels on this basis.
}

```
procedure FutureBlockLabel {var L : BlockLabel };
  var DataEntry: MCWordForm;
  begin
    L.BlockLevel := FrameLevel;
    L.EntryOffset := DataCounter - CurrentBlock^.DataBase + 1;
    DataEntry.Linked := false; DataEntry.Address := 0; DataWord(DataEntry)
  end { futureblocklevel };
```

{

The procedures OpenCodeSpace and CloseCodeSpace carry out the necessary housekeeping on the code-space stack, the allocation and filling of data words reserved for special purposes, and the output of data words and code bytes to the code file itself. CloseCodeSpace also includes a call to the forward procedure EndOfBody which enables the Code Map Emitter (Chapter 27) to record the necessary information on the code block filed.

}

```
procedure EndOfBody(CodeSize, DataSize: Scalar); forward;
procedure OpenCodeSpace {var L : BlockLabel};
    var ThisBlock: BlockPtr;
    begin
      if CurrentBlock <> nil then CurrentBlock^.EntryLabel := L;
      new(ThisBlock);
      with ThisBlock^ do
        begin DataBase := DataCounter; Next := CurrentBlock end;
      DataStack[DataCounter + ParamsOffset].WValue := TopFrameEntry^.NextOffset;
      DataStack[DataCounter + SerialOffset].WValue := 0;
      DataCounter := DataCounter + HeaderSize; CurrentBlock := ThisBlock
    end { opencodespace };

procedure CloseCodeSpace;
    var CodeSize: CodeRange; Adjustment: CodeAddress; ThisBlock: BlockPtr;
        Index: integer; EntryPoint, Buffer: MCWordForm; ByteIndex: MCByteIndex;
    begin
      with CurrentBlock^ do
        begin
          if CodeIsToBeGenerated then Align;
          CodeSize := CodeCounter div MCBytesPerWord;
          Adjustment := (CodeFileSize + DataCounter - DataBase) * MCBytesPerWord;
          DataStack[DataBase + LocalsOffset].WValue :=
            TopFrameEntry^.NextOffset - DataStack[DataBase + ParamsOffset].WValue;
          DataStack[DataBase + LocksOffset].WValue :=
            TopFrameEntry^.MaxDepth * LockSize;
          EndOfBody(CodeSize, DataCounter - DataBase);
          for Index := DataCounter - 1 downto DataBase + HeaderSize do
            with DataStack[Index] do
              if Linked then FileWord(Address + Adjustment) else FileWord(Address);
          FileWord(DataStack[DataBase + SerialOffset].WValue);
          FileWord(DataStack[DataBase + LocksOffset].WValue);
          FileWord(DataStack[DataBase + LocalsOffset].WValue);
          FileWord(DataStack[DataBase + ParamsOffset].WValue);
          { save entry-point address }
          EntryPoint.Linked := false; EntryPoint.Address := CodeFileSize;
```

```
        ByteIndex := 0;
        for Index := 0 to CodeCounter - 1 do
          begin
            Buffer.WBytes[ByteIndex] := CodeBuffer[Index];
            ByteIndex := (ByteIndex + 1) mod MCBytesPerWord;
            if ByteIndex = 0
            then begin { recast(buffer, asvalue) } ; FileWord(Buffer.WValue) end
          end;
        DataCounter := DataBase; CodeCounter := 0
      end;
    ThisBlock := CurrentBlock; CurrentBlock := ThisBlock^.Next;
    if CurrentBlock <> nil
    then with CurrentBlock^ do FillWord(EntryLabel.EntryOffset - 1, EntryPoint);
    dispose(ThisBlock)
  end { closecodespace };
```
{

Initialisation and finalisation of the overall code filing process is carried out by the procedures InitEmitter and EndEmitter. This includes output of the option words to the start of the code file, the creation of an initial code-space which corresponds to a pseudo-block surrounding the compiled program, and output of the number of data words created by this pseudo-block (which determines the position of the program block entry within it).
}

```
procedure InitEmitter;
  var Option: OptionType;
  begin
    CodeIsToBeGenerated := true; rewrite(CodeFile);
    for Option := Listing to Other do
      begin
        case Option of
          Listing, Margin, Other : CodeFile^ := 0;
          Checks, PMDump : CodeFile^ := ord(Option in Requested);
          Level : CodeFile^ := OptionValue[Option]
        end;
        put(CodeFile)
      end;
    CodeCounter := 0; DataCounter := 0; CodeFileSize := 0; CurrentBlock := nil;
    OpenCodeSpace(DefaultLabel)
  end { initemitter };
procedure EndEmitter;
  var DataSize: MCByte;
  begin
    with CurrentBlock^ do DataSize := DataCounter - DataBase;
    CloseCodeSpace; FileWord(DataSize)
  end { endemitter };
```

{

CHAPTER 16

Variable Reference Generation

16.1 A Delayed Code Generation Strategy

The analyser uses the code generation interface to signal the required program actions as a sequence of "post fix" operations. With a simple stack machine as target, these calls can output a corresponding sequence of stack manipulation code directly. With this simple strategy, however, difficulties arise in the generation of efficient code for optimised P-machines, and in the implementation of run-time checks.

In the Model Compiler, therefore, the interface calls made by the analyser construct tree representations of each variable reference and expression evaluation required, delaying actual code generation until the context of the reference or evaluation is established.

This delayed code generation is achieved using a stack, referenced by the variable TopStack-Entry, to simulate the evaluation-stack contents of a simple stack machine during execution of the operations implied by the interface call sequence. Each operand value or variable reference on this stack is represented by a record of type StackNode.

In the case of operand values this record is the root of a tree of stacknodes defining the computation required to obtain the operand value. Each internal node in the tree is of variant Operation, and denotes a value-producing operation whose operands are represented by appended subtrees. Each leaf node, which represents a primary operand, is of variant Reference, denoting a variable access, or of variant AConstant, denoting an explicit constant value. (The variants Address and Result are used to describe references and operands after evaluation code has been generated.)

The generation of stack nodes of variants Operation and AConstant is described in Chapter 17. In this chapter the form and generation of variable references is considered.

16.2 Stacked References

A stack node representing a variable reference is the head of a list of such nodes (linked by the field AccessList), each representing an access step. The list holds the access steps in reverse order, i.e. the head record represents the last step in the access sequence. The tail record defines a base address within the run-time data stack from which all subsequent address calculations derive. Each access record then implies calculation from this base address of a word or part-word address, using some or all of the following:

(a)   indirection, as indicated by the field Indirect;

(b)   indexing by a list of index expression values, pointed to by the field Indices for word references or by the field Index for part-word references;

(c)   further word address adjustment by the field Adjustment.

Multiple access records are generated when the necessary address calculation cannot be achieved by a single step defined as above, or when access checks must be applied at a particular step of the address calculation. The access to every file variable occurring in a file buffer reference, to every dynamic variable, and to every record variable in a tag- or variant-field reference, is tagged as "vulnerable" to ensure that a separate access record remains available for the addition of subsequently determined access checks.

The access checks applicable to the (intermediate) address implied by any access record, are represented as a list of ancillary checks, pointed to by the field CheckList of the record. Each entry on the list is a record of type AncillaryRecord whose tag field WhichOp defines one of the following ancillary check operations.

(1)   WhichOp=CheckSelector: access to a field of a tagged record variant is checked by verifying that the SeclectorField associated with the variant-part holds the Selector-Value associated with the variant. This check is appended by the procédure CheckTaggedVariant.

(2)   WhichOp=SetSelector: access to a field of an untagged record variant is accompanied by implicit variant (re) selection. The TagValue associated with the variant, and the record base address are passed as parameters to an internally compiled selector procedure which implements the variant (re) selection. The mechanisms involved in this process are discussed in detail in Section 26.3. This check is appended by the procedure CheckUntaggedVariant.

(3)   WhichOp=CheckIfActive: the "undefined" check for a tag-field is implemented by checking a "variant-active" flag in the control word of the record. The field Selector-Level identifies the bit position of this flag. The control word is discussed in detail in Section 26.3. This check is appended by the procedure UndefinedVariableCheck.

(4)   WhichOp=SetALock: a reference must be protected to guarantee its existence for the duration of a with-statement body or procedure activation. LockWord contains the word-offset of the lock relative to the base-address defined by the current access list entry, and LockBit specifies the lock bit position within the lock-word. Reference protection is discussed in detail in Section 18.3. This check is appended by procedure ExtendReferences.

(5)   WhichOp=CheckIfNew: a dynamic variable used as a factor is checked for creation by the extended form of new. This check is appended by the procedure TailoredFactorCheck.

(6)   WhichOp=CheckFile: in this implementation, file buffers are allocated dynamically on the first reset or rewrite operation. Accordingly, an existence check is required to trap any attempt to access the buffer variable prior to a reset or rewrite. Such a check is not required by the Standard but by the implementation-dependent buffer allocation strategy.

Subsequent sections of this chapter define basic utilities for the creation and maintenance of stacked references and implement the interface procedures defined in Section 5.5.

16.3 Ancillary Check List Maintenance

The following procedures enable the creation and maintenance of the ancillary check lists attached to stack nodes of form reference:

```
}
procedure StartAncillaries(var List: AncillaryList);
  begin List.FirstEntry := nil; List.LastEntry := nil end;
procedure AppendEntry(var List: AncillaryList; NewEntry: AncillaryEntry);
  begin
    with List do
      begin
        if FirstEntry = nil
        then FirstEntry := NewEntry else LastEntry^.Next := NewEntry;
        LastEntry := NewEntry
      end
  end { appendentry };
function CheckCount(List: AncillaryList): Scalar;
  var Entry: AncillaryEntry; Count: Scalar;
  begin
    Count := 0; Entry := List.FirstEntry;
    while Entry <> nil do
      begin Count := Count + 1; Entry := Entry^.Next end;
    CheckCount := Count
  end { checkcount };
{
```

16.4 Evaluation Stack Maintenance

The following procedures enable creation and maintenance of the evaluation stack itself:

```
}
procedure GetEntry(var Entry: StackEntry);
  begin
    new(Entry);
    with Entry^ do
      begin
        NextNode := nil; RunError := 0; Vulnerable := false;
        StartAncillaries(CheckList); DataRep := DefaultRepresentation; DataBytes := 0
      end
  end { getentry };
```

```
procedure FreeEntry(Entry: StackEntry);
  var NextWord, ThisWord: WordEntry;
  begin
    with Entry^ do
      if Kind = AConstant
      then with TheConst do
              if Kind in [SetValue, StringValue]
              then begin
                     if Kind = SetValue
                     then NextWord := Setval else NextWord := Stringval;
                     while NextWord <> nil do
                       begin
                         ThisWord := NextWord; NextWord := ThisWord^.Next;
                         dispose(ThisWord)
                       end
                   end;
      dispose(Entry)
  end { freeentry };
procedure Push(Entry: StackEntry);
  begin Entry^.NextNode := TopStackEntry; TopStackEntry := Entry end;
procedure Pop(var Entry: StackEntry);
  begin Entry := TopStackEntry; TopStackEntry := Entry^.NextNode end;
procedure InitStack;
  begin TopStackEntry := nil end;
{
```

16.5 Reference Creation and Manipulation

The following utility procedures simplify creation of maintenance of (access lists of) reference records.
}

```
procedure GetReference(var NewEntry: StackEntry);
  begin
    GetEntry(NewEntry);
    with NewEntry^ do
      begin
        Kind := Reference; BaseAddress := DefaultAddress; Adjustment := 0;
        Level := 0; Indirect := false; AccessList := nil; Class := VarRef;
        PartOfWord := false; Indexed := false
      end
  end { getreference };
```

```
procedure ReferencePartWord(var Entry: StackEntry);
  begin
    with Entry^ do
      begin
        PartOfWord := true; BitOffset := 0; BitSize := 0; OnByteBoundary := false;
        IndexedPartWord := false
      end
  end { refpartword };
procedure PushNewAccess(var Entry: StackEntry; ForAPartWord: Boolean);
  var NewEntry: StackEntry;
  begin
    GetReference(NewEntry);
    with NewEntry^ do
      begin
        AccessList := Entry;
        if ForAPartWord then ReferencePartWord(NewEntry)
      end;
    Entry := NewEntry
  end { pushnewaccess };
procedure PreserveAccess(var Entry: StackEntry);
  begin PushNewAccess(Entry, Entry^.PartOfWord) end;
procedure PartWordReference(var Entry: StackEntry);
  begin
    with Entry^ do
      if Kind <> Reference
      then PushNewAccess(Entry, true)
      else if PartOfWord
          then begin
                OnByteBoundary := false;
                if IndexedPartWord then PushNewAccess(Entry, true)
              end
          else if Indexed
              then PushNewAccess(Entry, true) else ReferencePartWord(Entry)
  end { partwordreference };
{
```

16.6 Simple References

The interface procedure StackReference, which creates the base reference from which more complex access lists are built, is trivially implemented using the preceding utilities:

```
}
```

```
procedure StackReference {Indirct: Boolean; Location: RuntimeAddress};
   var NewEntry: StackEntry;
   begin
      if CodeIsToBeGenerated
      then begin
            GetReference(NewEntry);
            with NewEntry^ do
               begin BaseAddress := Location; Indirect := Indirct end;
            Push(NewEntry)
         end
   end { stackreference };
{
```

16.7 Indexed References

The IndexedReference operation, for indexing normal arrays, is carried out as follows:

(a)   the index value is checked for range, using the CheckRange procedure defined in
       Chapter 17.

(b)   if the index value is constant a direct adjustment of the array reference is made to
       address the element required, otherwise the index value is appended to the appropriate
       index list for delayed index code generation.

The IndexedCAPReference operation for indexing conformant arrays is simpler in that no
special treatment of constant indices is possible and the nature of the existing array reference
is known. A corresponding procedure CheckCAPRange defined in Chapter 17 is used to
check the index value range in this case.

```
}
procedure CheckRange(Min, Max: MCIntegerForm; CheckNumber: Scalar); forward;
procedure IndexedReference {PackedArray: Boolean;
                            LowBound, HighBound: ObjectValue;
                            Element: TypeRepresentation};
   var Entry, ArrayIndex: StackEntry; ConstIndex, PackedElement: Boolean;
       ThisIndex: IndexEntry; NormalisedIndex: MCIntegerForm;
       ElsPerWord: 2..MCBitsPerWord;
   begin
      if CodeIsToBeGenerated
      then begin
            CheckRange(LowBound.Ival, HighBound.Ival, 1); Pop(ArrayIndex);
            if ArrayIndex^.Kind = AConstant
            then begin
                  ConstIndex := true;
                  NormalisedIndex := ArrayIndex^.TheConst.Ival - LowBound.Ival;
                  FreeEntry(ArrayIndex)
               end
            else begin
                  ConstIndex := false; new(ThisIndex);
```

```
              with ThisIndex^ do
                begin
                  TheIndex := ArrayIndex; Next := nil; CAPIndex := false;
                  Lower := LowBound.Ival; Upper := HighBound.Ival
                end
            end;
        Pop(Entry);
        if Entry^.Vulnerable then PreserveAccess(Entry);
        with Element do
          if WordSize > 1
          then PackedElement := false
          else PackedElement :=
                PackedArray and (BitSize <= MCBitsPerWord div 2);
        if PackedElement then PartWordReference(Entry);
        with Entry^ do
          if PackedElement
          then begin
                  ElsPerWord := MCBitsPerWord div Element.BitSize;
                  BitSize := MCBitsPerWord div ElsPerWord;
                  if ConstIndex
                  then begin
                          Adjustment :=
                            Adjustment + NormalisedIndex div ElsPerWord;
                          BitOffset :=
                            BitOffset + (NormalisedIndex mod ElsPerWord) * BitSize
                      end
                  else begin
                          IndexedPartWord := true;
                          OnByteBoundary := (ElsPerWord = MCBytesPerWord);
                          ThisIndex^.Factor := ElsPerWord; Index := ThisIndex
                      end
              end
          else begin
                  if ConstIndex
                  then Adjustment :=
                          Adjustment + NormalisedIndex * Element.WordSize
                  else begin
                          Adjustment :=
                            Adjustment - LowBound.Ival * Element.WordSize;
                          ThisIndex^.Factor := Element.WordSize;
                          if Indexed
                          then ThisIndex^.Next := Indices else Indexed := true;
                          Indices := ThisIndex
                      end
              end;
        Entry^.DataRep := Element; Push(Entry)
      end
end { indexedreference };
```

```
procedure CheckCAPRange(LowBoundAddress, HighBoundAddress:
                                RuntimeAddress); forward;
procedure IndexedCAPReference { PackedSchema: Boolean;
                                LowBoundAddress,
                                HighBoundAddress: RuntimeAddress;
                                BoundPairRepresentation,
                                Component: TypeRepresentation };
  { The parameter BoundPairRepresentation is not used in this implementation. }
  var Entry, ArrayIndex: StackEntry; ThisIndex: IndexEntry; PackedComponent: Boolean;
    ElsPerWord: 2..MCBitsPerWord;
begin
  if CodeIsToBeGenerated
  then begin
        if Checks in Requested
        then CheckCAPRange(LowBoundAddress, HighBoundAddress);
        Pop(ArrayIndex); new(ThisIndex);
        with ThisIndex^ do
          begin
            TheIndex := ArrayIndex; Next := nil; CAPIndex := true;
            BpAddress := LowBoundAddress
          end;
        Pop(Entry);
        with Component do
          if WordSize > 1
          then PackedComponent := false
          else PackedComponent :=
                PackedSchema and (BitSize <= MCBitsPerWord div 2);
        if PackedComponent then PartWordReference(Entry);
        with Entry^ do
          if PackedComponent
          then begin
                ElsPerWord := MCBitsPerWord div Component.BitSize;
                OnByteBoundary := (ElsPerWord = MCBytesPerWord);
                BitSize := MCBitsPerWord div ElsPerWord;
                IndexedPartWord := true; ThisIndex^.Factor := ElsPerWord;
                Index := ThisIndex
              end
          else begin
                if Indexed then ThisIndex^.Next := Indices else Indexed := true;
                Indices := ThisIndex
              end;
        Push(Entry)
      end
end { indexedcapreference };
{
```

16.8 Field References

A field reference involves adjustment of the record address by the word or part-word offset of the field. In practice this is complicated by the following:

(a)   if the field is a tag field, the record access is vulnerable to a check arising from a subsequent tag field assignment;

(b)   if the field is a variant field a cascade of variant checks may have been generated by a preceding call to VariantChecks.

VariantChecks generates this cascade by recursive identification of the variant in which the field lies from the outermost variant level. At each level the action required is either to check or to reset the corresponding selector value, depending on whether the variant part does or does not have an explicit tag field. Accordingly, the procedures CheckUntaggedVariant and CheckTaggedVariant append appropriate entries on the CheckList for the record-variable reference.

```
}
procedure CheckUntaggedVariant(SelectorRep: TypeRepresentation;
                                VariantValue: ObjectValue);
  var CheckEntry: AncillaryEntry; RecordEntry: StackEntry;
  begin
    if CodeIsToBeGenerated and (SelectorRep.CheckCode.EntryOffset <> 0)
    then begin
          Pop(RecordEntry); new(CheckEntry);
          with CheckEntry^ do
            begin
              Next := nil; WhichOp := SetSelector;
              Selector := SelectorRep.CheckCode; TagValue := VariantValue.Ival
            end;
          AppendEntry(RecordEntry^.CheckList, CheckEntry); Push(RecordEntry)
        end
  end { checkuntaggedvariant };
procedure CheckTaggedVariant(SelectorRep, VariantRep: TypeRepresentation);
  var CheckEntry: AncillaryEntry; RecordEntry: StackEntry;
  begin
    if CodeIsToBeGenerated and (Checks in Requested)
    then begin
          Pop(RecordEntry); new(CheckEntry);
          with CheckEntry^ do
            begin
              Next := nil; WhichOp := CheckSelector;
              SelectorField := SelectorRep.Selector;
              SelectorValue := VariantRep.CheckValue.Magnitude
            end;
          AppendEntry(RecordEntry^.CheckList, CheckEntry); Push(RecordEntry)
        end
  end { checktaggedvariant };
```

```
procedure VariantChecks {VarPart: TypEntry; FieldId: IdEntry};
   var LocalVariant: TypEntry;
   begin
     if VarPart^.TagField <> FieldId
     then begin
             LocalVariant := VarPart^.FirstVariant;
             while not VariantField(LocalVariant, FieldId) do
                LocalVariant := LocalVariant^.NextVariant;
             with VarPart^ do
                if TagField = nil
                then CheckUntaggedVariant(Representation, LocalVariant^.VariantValue)
                else CheckTaggedVariant(Representation, LocalVariant^.Representation);
             with LocalVariant^ do
                if SubVarPart <> nil
                then if VariantField(SubVarPart, FieldId)
                        then VariantChecks(SubVarPart, FieldId)
          end
   end { variantchecks };
procedure FieldReference { Field: FieldOffset; TagField: Boolean };
   var Entry: StackEntry;
   begin
     if CodeIsToBeGenerated
     then begin
             Pop(Entry);
             if TagField or (Entry^.CheckList.FirstEntry <> nil)
             then Entry^.Vulnerable := true;
             if Entry^.Vulnerable or (Entry^.Kind = Address) then PreserveAccess(Entry);
             if Field.PartWord then PartWordReference(Entry);
             with Entry^ do
               begin
                 if Field.PartWord
                 then begin
                         BitSize := Field.BitSize; BitOffset := BitOffset + Field.BitOffset
                      end;
                 Adjustment := Adjustment + Field.WordOffset; Level := Field.Level
               end;
             if TagField then Entry^.Class := TagRef;
             Push(Entry)
          end
   end { fieldreference };
```

{

16.9 Pointer and File Buffer References

Pointer and file buffer references, except those to text files, both involve indirection. The procedure IndirectReference implements those aspects of indirection common to pointer and file references.

In the case of file buffer references the indirection is via a buffer pointer embedded within the file record, which points to a sliding buffer window within the associated transfer buffer itself.

In the case of text files the file buffer is maintained as a character field of the file record itself, so a BufferReference is equivalent to a FieldReference.

The access created by a pointer reference, and the file record access involved in a buffer reference are always vulnerable to subsequent access checks. In particular, buffer-variable references are accompanied by an existence check as described in 16.2 above.

}

```
procedure IndirectReference(APointer: Boolean);
    var Entry: StackEntry;
    begin
      if CodeIsToBeGenerated
      then begin
            Pop(Entry);
            with Entry^ do
              begin
                if not (Vulnerable or Indirect or PartOfWord or Indexed or
                        (AccessList <> nil))
                then with BaseAddress do WordOffset := WordOffset + Adjustment
                else PreserveAccess(Entry)
              end;
            with Entry^ do
              begin
                Adjustment := 0; Indirect := true;
                if APointer
                then begin
                        Class := PnterRef;
                        if Checks in Requested then Vulnerable := true
                     end
              end;
            Push(Entry)
         end
   end { indirectreference };
```

procedure PnterReference;
  begin if CodeIsToBeGenerated **then** IndirectReference(true) **end**;
procedure BufferReference { PackedFile, TextFile: Boolean; Element: TypeRepresentation };
  { The parameters PackedFile and Element are not used in this implementation. }
  var Entry: StackEntry; CheckEntry: AncillaryEntry;
  begin
    if CodeIsToBeGenerated
    then begin
          Pop(Entry);
          if (Checks **in** Requested) **and** Entry^.Vulnerable **then** PreserveAccess(Entry);
          Entry^.Class := FileRef; new(CheckEntry);
          with CheckEntry^ **do**
            begin Next := **nil**; WhichOp := CheckFile **end**;
          AppendEntry(Entry^.CheckList, CheckEntry); Entry^.Vulnerable := true;
          Push(Entry); FieldReference(BufferOffset, false);
          if not TextFile **then** IndirectReference(false)
        end
  end { bufferreference };
{

16.10 Reference Testing

The following function enables subsequent chapters to test whether a reference is simple, i.e.
is a word access involving no indexing, pointer chasing, or access checking code.
}
function SimpleReference(Entry: StackEntry): Boolean;
  begin
    with Entry^ **do**
      if Kind <> Reference
      then SimpleReference := false
      else SimpleReference :=
            (AccessList = **nil**) **and not** PartOfWord **and not** Indexed **and**
            not (Indirect **and** (Class = PnterRef))
  end { simplereference };

{

CHAPTER 17

Expression Evaluation

This chapter defines the procedures used to construct the tree of stack nodes that represents an expression evaluation.

17.1 Primary Operands

The primary operands in expression trees are

(a)   variable values obtained from variable accesses, and

(b)   constant values appearing in the program text.

The interface procedure DeReference represents the conversion of a variable reference to the corresponding value. In building expressions trees, however, no explicit conversion is involved, the variable representation is merely added to the existing variable reference for use in subsequent delayed code generation.

The procedure CAPDeReference represents the special case of dereferencing a conformant array for assignment to another conformant array of identical size and shape. In this case an operation node is created with the references to the array and the associated bound pair block as parameters.

}

```
procedure DeReference { Representation: TypeRepresentation };
   var TopEntry: StackEntry;
   begin
     if CodeIsToBeGenerated
     then begin
           Pop(TopEntry); TopEntry^.DataRep := Representation; Push(TopEntry)
         end
   end { dereference };
procedure CAPDeReference {PackedSchema: Boolean ;
                          LowBoundAddress,
                          HighBoundAddress: RuntimeAddress;
                          BoundPairRepresentation,
                          ComponentRepresentation: TypeRepresentation};
   { The parameter HighBoundAddress is not used in this implementation. }
   var ValueEntry: StackEntry; ElementsPacked: Boolean;
```

```
    begin
      if CodeIsToBeGenerated
      then begin
            with ComponentRepresentation do
              if WordSize > 1
              then ElementsPacked := false
              else ElementsPacked :=
                    PackedSchema and (BitSize <= MCBitsPerWord);
            GetEntry(ValueEntry);
            with ValueEntry^ do
              begin
                DataRep := ComponentRepresentation; Kind := Operation;
                OpForm := CAPLoad; Pop(CAPEntry);
                CAPEntry^.DataRep := BoundPairRepresentation;
                CAPPacked := ElementsPacked; BpAddress := LowBoundAddress
              end;
            Push(ValueEntry)
          end
    end { capdereference };
{
```

Constant operands are generated by the interface procedure StackConstant, which creates a constant stack node holding the constant's object value, together with a representation appropriate to the value concerned.

```
}
procedure StackConstant { ConstValue : ObjectValue };
  var ConstEntry: StackEntry; ConstRep: TypeRepresentation;
  begin
    if CodeIsToBeGenerated
    then begin
          with ConstValue do
            begin
              ConstRep := DefaultRepresentation; ConstRep.WordSize := WordSize;
              case Kind of
                IntValue, BoolValue, CharValue :
                  with ConstRep do
                    begin Kind := ForScalar; Min := Ival; Max := Ival end;
                RealValue : ConstRep.Kind := ForReal;
                SetValue :
                  begin
                    ConstRep.Kind := ForSet; SetBaseLimits(ConstRep, ConstValue)
                  end;
                StringValue : ConstRep.Kind := ForString;
                PntrValue : ConstRep.Kind := ForPnter
              end
            end;
          GetEntry(ConstEntry);
          with ConstEntry^ do
```

```
          begin
            Kind := AConstant; TheConst := ConstValue; DataRep := ConstRep
          end;
        Push(ConstEntry)
      end
  end { stackconstant };
{
```

17.2 Operand Value Checks

Primary, intermediate and final values in an expression are subject to value checks of various kinds, if requested. These are implemented as follows.

Undefined variable value checks are handled by the procedure UndefinedVariableCheck. For tag fields these are implemented using an access check which tests whether a variant of the corresponding variant part is active, since the tag value itself may have been preset if created by the extended form of ¨new¨, even though the tag field is still deemed to be undefined. For all other variables the undefined value check is implicit in the subsequent load operation, and UndefinedVariableCheck indicates this by recording the appropriate error code in the operand record.

A dynamically accessed record occurring as an expression factor is subject to a check that it has not been created by the extended form of ¨new¨. This is handled by TailoredFactorCheck again using the access check mechanism.

Ordinal values are subject to range checks in many contexts, which are signalled either explicitly by the interface procedure RangeCheck, or implicitly from within other generative operations. To reduce the number of checks involved, all other generators for ordinal operations perform range analysis to determine the implied range of the result value from the known ranges of the operands. The procedure CheckRange uses this implied range to determine whether a run-time check is necessary, and if so adds an appropriate check operation to the operand tree, for subsequent code generation.

The procedure SetCheck handles checks on the range of members in a set value in a similar manner, exploiting range analysis performed by set arithmetic generators.
}

```
procedure UndefinedVariableCheck;
  var Reference, RecordEntry: StackEntry; CheckEntry: AncillaryEntry;
  begin
    if CodeIsToBeGenerated and (Checks in Requested)
    then begin
        Pop(Reference);
        if Reference^.Class = TagRef
        then begin
            RecordEntry := Reference^.AccessList; new(CheckEntry);
            with CheckEntry^ do
              begin
                Next := nil; WhichOp := CheckIfActive;
```

```
                    SelectorLevel := Reference^.Level
                end;
            AppendEntry(RecordEntry^.CheckList, CheckEntry)
        end
    else Reference^.RunError := 43;
    Push(Reference)
  end
end { undefinedvariablecheck };
procedure TailoredFactorCheck { Representation: TypeRepresentation };
  var RecordEntry: StackEntry; CheckEntry: AncillaryEntry;
  begin
    if CodeIsToBeGenerated and (Checks in Requested)
    then begin
        Pop(RecordEntry); new(CheckEntry);
        with CheckEntry^ do
          begin Next := nil; WhichOp := CheckIfNew end;
        AppendEntry(RecordEntry^.CheckList, CheckEntry);
        PushNewAccess(RecordEntry, false); Push(RecordEntry)
      end
  end { tailoredfactorcheck };
procedure CheckRange { Min, Max: MCIntegerForm; CheckNumber: Scalar };
  var Expression, CheckedEntry: StackEntry; CheckedRange: RangeEntry;
      ActualMin, ActualMax: MCIntegerForm;
  begin
    Pop(Expression);
    with Expression^ do
      begin
        ActualMin := DataRep.Min; ActualMax := DataRep.Max;
        if (Max < ActualMin) or (ActualMax < Min)
        then begin
            PredictedError(CheckNumber);
            if Kind = AConstant then TheConst.Ival := Min
          end
      end;
    if CodeIsToBeGenerated and (Checks in Requested) and
      ((ActualMin < Min) or (Max < ActualMax))
    then begin
        new(CheckedRange);
        with CheckedRange^ do
          begin Lower := Min; Upper := Max; CAPBounds := false end;
        GetEntry(CheckedEntry);
        with CheckedEntry^ do
          begin
            RunError := CheckNumber;
            if ActualMin > Min
            then DataRep.Min := ActualMin else DataRep.Min := Min;
            if ActualMax < Max
            then DataRep.Max := ActualMax else DataRep.Max := Max;
```

```
                    Kind := Operation; OpGroup := AnInteger; OpForm := RangeChk;
                    CheckKind := SubrangeChecks; RequiredRange := CheckedRange;
                    EntryToCheck := Expression
                  end;
                Push(CheckedEntry)
             end
        else Push(Expression)
    end { checkrange };
procedure RangeCheck { Min, Max: ObjectValue };

   var CheckNumber: Scalar;

   begin
     if CodeIsToBeGenerated
     then begin
             case ContextOfCheck of
                IsSucc : CheckNumber := 38;
                IsPred : CheckNumber := 39;
                IsUnknown : CheckNumber := 49
             end;
             CheckRange(Min.Ival, Max.Ival, CheckNumber);
             ContextOfCheck := IsUnknown
          end
   end { rangecheck };
procedure CheckCAPRange { LowBoundAddress,
                          HighBoundAddress: RuntimeAddress };

   { The parameter HighBoundAddress is not used in this implementation. }

   var Expression, CheckedEntry: StackEntry; CheckedRange: RangeEntry;

   begin
     Pop(Expression); new(CheckedRange);
     with CheckedRange^ do
       begin CAPBounds := true; BpAddress := LowBoundAddress end;
     GetEntry(CheckedEntry);
     with CheckedEntry^ do
       begin
         RunError := 1; DataRep.Min := Expression^.DataRep.Min;
         DataRep.Max := Expression^.DataRep.Max; Kind := Operation;
         OpGroup := AnInteger; OpForm := RangeChk; CheckKind := SubrangeChecks;
         RequiredRange := CheckedRange; EntryToCheck := Expression
       end;
     Push(CheckedEntry)
   end { checkcaprange };
procedure SetCheck { Min, Max: ObjectValue };

   var Expression, CheckedEntry: StackEntry; CheckedRange: RangeEntry;
       CheckIsNeeded: Boolean; ActualMin, ActualMax: MCIntegerForm;

   begin
     if CodeIsToBeGenerated
     then begin
```

```
               Pop(Expression);
               with Expression^ do
                  begin ActualMin := DataRep.Min; ActualMax := DataRep.Max end;
               if (ActualMin < Min.Ival) or (Max.Ival < ActualMax)
               then begin
                      CheckIsNeeded := true;
                      with Expression^ do
                        if Kind = AConstant
                        then begin
                               if TheConst.Setval <> nil then PredictedError(50);
                               CheckIsNeeded := false; DataRep.Min := Min.Ival;
                               DataRep.Max := Max.Ival
                             end;
                      if CheckIsNeeded and (Checks in Requested)
                      then begin
                             new(CheckedRange);
                             with CheckedRange^ do
                               begin Lower := Min.Ival; Upper := Max.Ival end;
                             GetEntry(CheckedEntry);
                             with CheckedEntry^ do
                               begin
                                 RunError := 50;
                                 if ActualMin > Min.Ival
                                 then DataRep.Min := ActualMin
                                 else DataRep.Min := Min.Ival;
                                 if ActualMax < Max.Ival
                                 then DataRep.Max := ActualMax
                                 else DataRep.Max := Max.Ival;
                                 Kind := Operation; OpGroup := ASet;
                                 OpForm := RangeChk; CheckKind := MemberChecks;
                                 RequiredRange := CheckedRange;
                                 EntryToCheck := Expression
                               end;
                             Push(CheckedEntry)
                           end
                        else Push(Expression)
                   end
               else Push(Expression)
           end
   end { setcheck };
{
```

17.3 Compile-time Arithmetic

The generators used for arithmetic operations have a number of similar characteristics:

(a)   as indicated above, all ordinal and set arithmetic generators perform range analysis to determine the range of the result from the known ranges of the operands;

(b)   when the operands involved in ordinal and set operations are constant the operation is
      "folded", i.e. carried out at compile-time, to avoid the use of any run-time code;

(c)   in all other cases generation results in the creation of a stack node of variant Opera-
      tion, with subtrees representing the operands involved, for subsequent code generation.

Range analysis and the folding of operations with constant operands both require the ability
to perform safe object machine arithmetic at compile-time, i.e. without the risk of host arithmetic overflow. The following procedure enables such arithmetic to be performed:

```
}
procedure ConstArith(Operator: OpType; Left, Right: MCIntegerForm;
                     var Result: MCIntegerForm);
  var StoredMod: 0..MCMaxint;
  begin
    with Overflow do
      begin Occurred := false; Positive := false end;
    case Operator of
      Plus, Minus :
        begin
          if Operator = Minus then Right := -Right;
          if (Left > 0) and (Right > 0)
          then Overflow.Occurred := (Left > MCMaxint - Right);
          if (Left < 0) and (Right < 0)
          then Overflow.Occurred := (Left < -MCMaxint - Right);
          if Overflow.Occurred
          then Overflow.Positive := (Left > 0) else Result := Left + Right
        end;
      Mul :
        if Right = 0
        then Result := 0
        else if abs(Left) > MCMaxint div abs(Right)
             then begin
                    Overflow.Occurred := true;
                    Overflow.Positive :=
                      (Left > 0) and (Right > 0) or (Left < 0) and (Right < 0)
                  end
             else Result := Left * Right;
      Idiv :
        if Right = 0 then Overflow.Occurred := true else Result := Left div Right;
      Imod :
        if Right <= 0
        then Overflow.Occurred := true
        else begin
               StoredMod := abs(Left) mod Right;
               if (StoredMod = 0) or (Left > 0)
               then Result := StoredMod else Result := Right - StoredMod
             end
    end
  end { constarith };
```

{

17.4 Generic procedures for negation and comparison

The negation operators for integer, real, and Boolean values, and the comparison operators
for all values types, require common code generation patterns which are provided by the following procedures. Note that the number of distinct cases dealt with in comparisons is
reduced by operand interchange for $>$ and $>=$, thus equivalencing them to $<$ and $<=$.

}

```
procedure Negate(Group: OperandKind);
   var Argument, ResultEntry: StackEntry; Result: ObjectValue;
       ResultRep: TypeRepresentation;
   begin
     if CodeIsToBeGenerated
     then begin
           Pop(Argument);
           if Argument^.Kind = AConstant
           then begin
                 Result := Argument^.TheConst; NegateValue(Result);
                 FreeEntry(Argument); StackConstant(Result)
               end
           else begin
                 ResultRep := Argument^.DataRep;
                 if Group = AnInteger
                 then with Argument^.DataRep do
                         begin ResultRep.Min := -Max; ResultRep.Max := -Min end;
                 GetEntry(ResultEntry);
                 with ResultEntry^ do
                   begin
                     DataRep := ResultRep; Kind := Operation; OpGroup := Group;
                     OpForm := Unary; UnaryEntry := Argument;
                     UnaryOp := NegateOp
                   end;
                 Push(ResultEntry)
               end
         end
   end { negate };
procedure Compare(Operator: OpType; Group: OperandKind);
   var ResultEntry: StackEntry;
   begin
     GetEntry(ResultEntry);
     with ResultEntry^ do
       begin
         DataRep := BooleanRepresentation; Kind := Operation; OpGroup := Group;
         OpForm := Binary;
         if Operator in [GtOp, GeOp]
         then begin
```

```
                    Pop(LeftEntry); Pop(RightEntry);
                    if Operator = GtOp then BinaryOp := LtOp else BinaryOp := LeOp
                  end
              else begin Pop(RightEntry); Pop(LeftEntry); BinaryOp := Operator end
            end;
          Push(ResultEntry)
       end { compare };
{
```

17.5 Integer/Ordinal Arithmetic

Generation of integer or ordinal arithmetic operations is handled by the following procedures. All are characterised by range analysis to determine result ranges, and folding of
operators with constant operands.

```
}
procedure SelectCheck(EntryToCheck: StackEntry; CheckNumber: Scalar);
  begin
    if EntryToCheck^.Kind = Operation
    then with EntryToCheck^ do
            if OpForm = RangeChk then RunError := CheckNumber
  end { selectcheck };
procedure IntegerFunction { WhichFunc: StdProcFuncs };
  var Argument, ResultEntry: StackEntry; Result: ObjectValue;
  procedure SetResultLimits(var OldRep, NewRep: TypeRepresentation);
    var NewMin, NewMax: MCIntegerForm;
    begin
      if WhichFunc in [Absf, Sqrf, Succf, Predf]
      then begin
              with OldRep do
                case WhichFunc of
                  Absf, Sqrf :
                    begin
                      if Min >= 0
                      then begin NewMin := Min; NewMax := Max end
                      else if Max >= 0
                          then begin
                                  if -Min > Max then NewMax := -Min;
                                  NewMin := 0
                              end
                          else begin NewMax := -Min; NewMin := -Max end;
                      if WhichFunc = Sqrf
                      then begin
                              ConstArith(Mul, NewMin, NewMin, NewMin);
                              if Overflow.Occurred then PredictedError(32);
                              ConstArith(Mul, NewMax, NewMax, NewMax)
                          end
```

```
                    end;
                 Succf :
                    begin
                       ConstArith(Plus, Min, 1, NewMin);
                       if Overflow.Occurred then NewMin := Min;
                       ConstArith(Plus, Max, 1, NewMax);
                       if Overflow.Occurred then NewMax := Max
                    end;
                 Predf :
                    begin
                       ConstArith(Minus, Max, 1, NewMax);
                       if Overflow.Occurred then NewMax := Max;
                       ConstArith(Minus, Min, 1, NewMin);
                       if Overflow.Occurred then NewMin := Min
                    end
               end;
            NewRep := OldRep;
            with NewRep do
               begin Min := NewMin; Max := NewMax end
         end
   else case WhichFunc of
         Oddf : NewRep := BooleanRepresentation;
         Ordf, Chrf : NewRep := OldRep
      end
   end { setresultlimits };

begin { integerfunction }
   if CodeIsToBeGenerated
   then begin
         Pop(Argument);
         if Checks in Requested
         then if WhichFunc in [Succf, Predf, Chrf]
               then case WhichFunc of
                     Succf : ContextOfCheck := IsSucc;
                     Predf : ContextOfCheck := IsPred;
                     Chrf : SelectCheck(Argument, 37)
                  end;
         if Argument^.Kind = AConstant
         then begin
               Result := Argument^.TheConst;
               with Result do
                  case WhichFunc of
                     Absf : Ival := abs(Ival);
                     Sqrf :
                        begin
                           ConstArith(Mul, Ival, Ival, Ival);
                           if Overflow.Occurred then PredictedError(32)
                        end;
                     Succf :
                        begin
```

```
                              ConstArith(Plus, Ival, 1, Ival);
                              if Overflow.Occurred then PredictedError(38)
                           end;
                        Predf :
                           begin
                              ConstArith(Minus, Ival, 1, Ival);
                              if Overflow.Occurred then PredictedError(39)
                           end;
                        Oddf :
                           begin Ival := ord(odd(Ival)); Kind := BoolValue end;
                        Ordf : Kind := IntValue;
                        Chrf : Kind := CharValue
                     end;
                  FreeEntry(Argument); StackConstant(Result)
               end
         else begin
               GetEntry(ResultEntry);
               with ResultEntry^ do
                  begin
                     SetResultLimits(Argument^.DataRep, DataRep);
                     Kind := Operation; OpGroup := AnInteger;
                     OpForm := Standard; StdOp := WhichFunc;
                     StdEntry := Argument
                  end;
               Push(ResultEntry)
            end
      end
   end { integerfunction };
procedure NegateAnInteger;
   begin if CodeIsToBeGenerated then Negate(AnInteger) end;
procedure BinaryIntegerOperation { Operator: OpType };
   var LeftOperand, RightOperand: StackEntry; Result: ObjectValue;
       ResultVal: MCIntegerForm; ResultEntry: StackEntry;
   procedure SetResultLimits;
      var LeftMin, LeftMax, RightMin, RightMax, ResultMin, ResultMax, SavedMin:
            MCIntegerForm;
          UfCount, OfCount: MCIntegerForm;
      procedure TryMin(PossibleMin: MCIntegerForm);
         begin if PossibleMin < ResultMin then ResultMin := PossibleMin end;
      procedure TryMax(PossibleMax: MCIntegerForm);
         begin if ResultMax < PossibleMax then ResultMax := PossibleMax end;
      procedure TryProduct(Bound1, Bound2: MCIntegerForm);
         var Product: MCIntegerForm;
         begin
            ConstArith(Mul, Bound1, Bound2, Product);
```

```
      if Overflow.Occurred
      then if Overflow.Positive
          then begin OfCount := OfCount + 1; ResultMax := MCMaxint end
          else begin UfCount := UfCount + 1; ResultMin := -MCMaxint end
      else begin TryMin(Product); TryMax(Product) end
   end { tryproduct };
procedure TryQuotient(Bound1, Bound2: MCIntegerForm);
   var Quotient: MCIntegerForm;
   begin
      ConstArith(Idiv, Bound1, Bound2, Quotient);
      TryMin(Quotient); TryMax(Quotient)
   end { tryquotient };
begin { setresultlimits }
   with LeftOperand^.DataRep do
      begin LeftMin := Min; LeftMax := Max end;
   with RightOperand^.DataRep do
      begin RightMin := Min; RightMax := Max end;
   case Operator of
      Plus, Minus :
        begin
          if Operator = Minus
          then begin
                  SavedMin := RightMin; RightMin := -RightMax;
                  RightMax := -SavedMin
               end;
          ConstArith(Plus, LeftMin, RightMin, ResultMin);
          if Overflow.Occurred
          then if Overflow.Positive
               then PredictedError(47) else ResultMin := -MCMaxint;
          ConstArith(Plus, LeftMax, RightMax, ResultMax);
          if Overflow.Occurred
          then if Overflow.Positive
               then ResultMax := MCMaxint else PredictedError(47)
        end;
      Mul :
        begin
          ResultMin := MCMaxint; ResultMax := -MCMaxint;
          OfCount := 0; UfCount := 0;
          TryProduct(LeftMin, RightMin); TryProduct(LeftMin, RightMax);
          TryProduct(LeftMax, RightMin); TryProduct(LeftMax, RightMax);
          if (OfCount = 4) or (UfCount = 4) then PredictedError(47)
        end;
      Idiv :
        begin
          ResultMin := MCMaxint; ResultMax := -MCMaxint;
          if RightMin <> 0
          then begin
                  TryQuotient(LeftMin, RightMin); TryQuotient(LeftMax, RightMin)
```

```
                    end;
            if RightMax <> 0
            then begin
                    TryQuotient(LeftMin, RightMax); TryQuotient(LeftMax, RightMax)
                    end;
            if (RightMin <= 0) and (RightMax >= 0)
            then begin
                    if RightMin < 0
                    then begin
                            TryQuotient(LeftMin, -1); TryQuotient(LeftMax, -1)
                        end;
                    if RightMax > 0
                    then begin TryQuotient(LeftMin, 1); TryQuotient(LeftMax, 1) end;
                    if (RightMin = 0) and (RightMax = 0) then PredictedError(45)
                end
        end;
    Imod :
        if (LeftMin = LeftMax) and (RightMin = RightMax)
        then begin
                ResultMin := LeftMin mod RightMin; ResultMax := ResultMin
            end
        else begin
                ResultMin := 0;
                if (LeftMin < 0) or (LeftMax >= RightMax)
                then ResultMax := RightMax - 1 else ResultMax := LeftMax
            end
    end;
    with ResultEntry^ do
        begin DataRep.Min := ResultMin; DataRep.Max := ResultMax end
    end { setresultlimits };
begin { binaryintegeroperation }
    if CodeIsToBeGenerated
    then begin
            Pop(RightOperand); Pop(LeftOperand);
            if (LeftOperand^.Kind = AConstant) and
                (RightOperand^.Kind = AConstant)
            then begin
                    ConstArith
                        (Operator, LeftOperand^.TheConst.Ival,
                            RightOperand^.TheConst.Ival, ResultVal);
                    if Overflow.Occurred
                    then begin
                            case Operator of
                                Plus, Minus, Mul : PredictedError(47);
                                Idiv : PredictedError(45);
                                Imod : PredictedError(46)
                            end;
                            ResultVal := MCMaxint
                        end;
```

```
                    SetIval(ResultVal, Result); StackConstant(Result);
                    FreeEntry(LeftOperand); FreeEntry(RightOperand)
                end
            else begin
                if Operator = Imod
                then begin
                        Push(RightOperand); CheckRange(1, MCMaxint, 46);
                        Pop(RightOperand)
                     end;
                GetEntry(ResultEntry);
                with ResultEntry^ do
                  begin
                    DataRep := IntegerRepresentation; SetResultLimits;
                    Kind := Operation; OpGroup := AnInteger; OpForm := Binary;
                    LeftEntry := LeftOperand; RightEntry := RightOperand;
                    BinaryOp := Operator
                  end;
                Push(ResultEntry)
                end
            end
    end { binaryintegeroperation };
procedure OrdinalComparison { operator: optype };
    var RightOperand, LeftOperand: StackEntry; Result: ObjectValue; Bval: Boolean;
    begin
      if CodeIsToBeGenerated
      then if (TopStackEntry^.Kind = AConstant) and
              (TopStackEntry^.NextNode^.Kind = AConstant)
          then begin
                  Pop(RightOperand); Pop(LeftOperand);
                  with LeftOperand^ do
                    case Operator of
                      LtOp : Bval := TheConst.Ival < RightOperand^.TheConst.Ival;
                      LeOp : Bval := TheConst.Ival <= RightOperand^.TheConst.Ival;
                      GeOp : Bval := TheConst.Ival >= RightOperand^.TheConst.Ival;
                      GtOp : Bval := TheConst.Ival > RightOperand^.TheConst.Ival;
                      NeOp : Bval := TheConst.Ival <> RightOperand^.TheConst.Ival;
                      EqOp : Bval := TheConst.Ival = RightOperand^.TheConst.Ival
                    end;
                  SetBval(Bval, Result); FreeEntry(LeftOperand);
                  FreeEntry(RightOperand); StackConstant(Result)
              end
          else Compare(Operator, AnInteger)
    end { ordinalcomparison };
{
```

17.6 Real Arithmetic

Real arithmetic is more simply handled, in that no range analysis is possible, and no folding with constant operands is attempted.

```
}
procedure FloatInteger { StackPosition: StackTop };
   var ResultEntry, Argument, SavedEntry: StackEntry;
   begin
     if CodeIsToBeGenerated
     then begin
            SavedEntry := nil;
            if StackPosition = TopOfStack
            then Pop(Argument)
            else begin Pop(SavedEntry); Pop(Argument) end;
            GetEntry(ResultEntry);
            with ResultEntry^ do
              begin
                DataRep := RealRepresentation; Kind := Operation;
                OpGroup := AnInteger; OpForm := Unary; UnaryOp := FloatOp;
                UnaryEntry := Argument
              end;
            Push(ResultEntry);
            if SavedEntry <> nil then Push(SavedEntry)
          end
   end { floatinteger };
procedure RealFunction { WhichFunc: StdProcFuncs };
   var ResultEntry: StackEntry;
   begin
     if CodeIsToBeGenerated
     then begin
            GetEntry(ResultEntry);
            with ResultEntry^ do
              begin
                if WhichFunc in [Truncf, Roundf]
                then DataRep := IntegerRepresentation
                else DataRep := RealRepresentation;
                Kind := Operation; OpGroup := AReal; OpForm := Standard;
                StdOp := WhichFunc; Pop(StdEntry)
              end;
            Push(ResultEntry)
          end
   end { realfunction };
procedure NegateAReal;
   begin if CodeIsToBeGenerated then Negate(AReal) end;
procedure BinaryRealOperation { RealOperator: OpType };
   var LeftOperand, RightOperand, ResultEntry: StackEntry;
```

```
begin
  if CodeIsToBeGenerated
  then begin
        Pop(RightOperand); Pop(LeftOperand); GetEntry(ResultEntry);
        with ResultEntry^ do
          begin
            DataRep := RealRepresentation; Kind := Operation;
            OpGroup := AReal; OpForm := Binary; RightEntry := RightOperand;
            LeftEntry := LeftOperand; BinaryOp := RealOperator
          end;
        Push(ResultEntry)
      end
end { binaryrealoperation };
procedure RealComparison { Operator: OpType };
  begin if CodeIsToBeGenerated then Compare(Operator, AReal) end;
{
```

17.6 Boolean Arithmetic

The IfFalseConditional and IfTrueConditional instructions of the P-machine enable fast, simple code sequences using jump out logic for sequences of "and" or "or" operators. For delayed code generation these are represented as an operation node of form Condition which points to a chain of the operands involved. With these P-code instructions no problems arise with jump out conditions in any context, so the interface procedure ExcludeConditions is redundant.

```
}
procedure NegateABoolean;
  begin if CodeIsToBeGenerated then Negate(ABoolean) end;
procedure BinaryBooleanOperation { Operator: OpType; FirstOperation: Boolean };
  var Entry, ListEntry, Index: StackEntry;
  begin
    if CodeIsToBeGenerated
    then begin
          Pop(Entry); Entry^.NextNode := nil;
          if FirstOperation
          then begin
                GetEntry(ListEntry);
                with ListEntry^ do
                  begin
                    DataRep := BooleanRepresentation; Kind := Operation;
                    OpForm := Condition;
                    if Operator = OrOp
                    then Jump := IfTrueConditional
                    else Jump := IfFalseConditional;
                    OpList := Entry
                  end
              end
```

```
            else begin
                    Pop(ListEntry); Index := ListEntry^.OpList;
                    while Index^.NextNode <> nil do Index := Index^.NextNode;
                    Index^.NextNode := Entry
                end;
            Push(ListEntry)
        end
  end { binarybooleanoperation };
procedure ExcludeConditions;
  begin end;
{
```

17.7 Set Arithmetic

Set arithmetic is handled by the procedures BinarySetOperation and SetComparison in a manner similar to that used for scalar types. In addition, however, set arithmetic involves the construction of sets, by the procedures SingletonSet and RangeSet in conjunction with the union operation implemented by BinarySetOperation.

Because all constructed sets, even those which are entirely constant, are handled in this way, it is essential that all possible "folding" of set operations is carried out at compile-time. To this end, the procedure ConstSetOperation implements the complete range of set-producing operators for operands held as object values.

```
}
procedure ConstSetOperation(var SetResult: ObjectValue; Left, Right: ObjectValue;
                               Operator: OpType);
    var Index, LastNonZero: Scalar; ResultSet: MCWordForm;
        LeftList, RightList: WordEntry; Result: ObjectValue;
        LeftVal, RightVal: MCIntegerForm;

    procedure PushSet(Part: MCWordForm);

        var SetPart, NextPart: WordEntry;

        begin
          new(SetPart);
          with SetPart^ do
            begin Word := Part; Next := nil end;
          with Result do
            begin
              WordSize := WordSize + 1;
              if Setval = nil
              then Setval := SetPart
              else begin
                      NextPart := Setval;
                      while NextPart^.Next <> nil do NextPart := NextPart^.Next;
                      NextPart^.Next := SetPart
                  end
            end
        end { pushset };
```

```
procedure SetFrame(Element: MCIntegerForm);
  var Empty: MCWordForm;
  begin
    Empty.WValue := 0;
    repeat PushSet(Empty); Element := Element - MCWordSetBits until Element < 0
  end { setframe };
procedure FindWord(Element: MCIntegerForm; var Entry: WordEntry);
  var NextPart: WordEntry;
  begin
    NextPart := Result.Setval;
    while Element >= MCWordSetBits do
      begin NextPart := NextPart^.Next; Element := Element - MCWordSetBits end;
    Entry := NextPart;
  end { findword };
procedure SetElement(Element: MCIntegerForm);
  var Part: WordEntry; Bit: MCSetBits;
  begin
    FindWord(Element, Part); Bit := Element mod MCWordSetBits;
    with Part^ do MCSetBit(Word, Bit)
  end { setelement };
procedure CopySurplus(Surplus: WordEntry);
  begin
    while Surplus <> nil do
      begin PushSet(Surplus^.Word); Surplus := Surplus^.Next end
  end { copysurplus};
procedure FreeList(FirstWord: WordEntry);
  var NextWord: WordEntry;
  begin
    while FirstWord <> nil do
      begin
        NextWord := FirstWord^.Next; dispose(FirstWord); FirstWord := NextWord
      end
  end { freelist };
procedure ReduceResult(NewSize: MCIntegerForm);
  var NextEntry: WordEntry; i: MCIntegerForm;
  begin
    if NewSize = 0
    then begin FreeList(Result.Setval); Result := EmptyValue end
    else with Result do
            if WordSize <> NewSize
            then begin
                    NextEntry := Setval;
                    for i := 1 to NewSize - 1 do NextEntry := NextEntry^.Next;
```

```
                    FreeList(NextEntry^.Next); NextEntry^.Next := nil;
                    WordSize := NewSize
                 end
      end { reduceresult };

begin { constsetoperation }
   Result := EmptyValue;
   if Operator in [SingleOp, RangeOp]
   then begin LeftVal := Left.Ival; RightVal := Right.Ival end
   else begin LeftList := Left.Setval; RightList := Right.Setval end;
   case Operator of
      SingleOp, RangeOp :
         if LeftVal <= RightVal
         then begin
                 SetFrame(RightVal);
                 for Index := LeftVal to RightVal do SetElement(Index)
              end;
      Plus :
         begin
            while (LeftList <> nil) and (RightList <> nil) do
               begin
                  ResultSet.WSet := LeftList^.Word.WSet + RightList^.Word.WSet;
                  PushSet(ResultSet); LeftList := LeftList^.Next;
                  RightList := RightList^.Next
               end;
            if LeftList <> nil then CopySurplus(LeftList) else CopySurplus(RightList)
         end;
      Mul :
         begin
            LastNonZero := 0;
            while (LeftList <> nil) and (RightList <> nil) do
               begin
                  ResultSet.WSet := LeftList^.Word.WSet * RightList^.Word.WSet;
                  PushSet(ResultSet);
                  if ResultSet.WSet <> [] then LastNonZero := Result.WordSize;
                  LeftList := LeftList^.Next; RightList := RightList^.Next
               end;
            ReduceResult(LastNonZero)
         end;
      Minus :
         begin
            LastNonZero := 0;
            while (LeftList <> nil) and (RightList <> nil) do
               begin
                  ResultSet.WSet := LeftList^.Word.WSet - RightList^.Word.WSet;
                  PushSet(ResultSet);
                  if ResultSet.WSet <> [] then LastNonZero := Result.WordSize;
                  LeftList := LeftList^.Next; RightList := RightList^.Next
               end;
            if LeftList <> nil then CopySurplus(LeftList) else ReduceResult(LastNonZero)
```

```
                end
           end;
         SetResult := Result
     end { constsetoperation };
procedure SingletonSet { SetRepresentation: TypeRepresentation };
     var Entry, ResultEntry: StackEntry; Result: ObjectValue;
     begin
        if CodeIsToBeGenerated
        then begin
                CheckRange(SetRepresentation.Min, SetRepresentation.Max, 62); Pop(Entry);
                if Entry^.Kind = AConstant
                then begin
                        ConstSetOperation
                          (Result, Entry^.TheConst, Entry^.TheConst, SingleOp);
                        StackConstant(Result); FreeEntry(Entry)
                      end
                else begin
                        GetEntry(ResultEntry);
                        with ResultEntry^ do
                          begin
                            DataRep := SetRepresentation; Kind := Operation;
                            OpGroup := ASet; OpForm := Unary; UnaryEntry := Entry
                          end;
                        Push(ResultEntry)
                      end
              end
     end { singletonset };
procedure RangeSet { SetRepresentation: TypeRepresentation };
     var LowBound, HighBound, ResultEntry: StackEntry; Result: ObjectValue;
     begin
        if CodeIsToBeGenerated
        then begin
                CheckRange(SetRepresentation.Min, SetRepresentation.Max, 62);
                Pop(HighBound);
                CheckRange(SetRepresentation.Min, SetRepresentation.Max, 62);
                Pop(LowBound);
                if (LowBound^.Kind = AConstant) and (HighBound^.Kind = AConstant)
                then begin
                        ConstSetOperation
                          (Result, LowBound^.TheConst, HighBound^.TheConst, RangeOp);
                        StackConstant(Result); FreeEntry(LowBound); FreeEntry(HighBound)
                      end
                else begin
                        GetEntry(ResultEntry);
                        with ResultEntry^ do
                          begin
                            DataRep := SetRepresentation; Kind := Operation;
                            OpGroup := ASet; OpForm := Binary; LeftEntry := LowBound;
```

```
                    RightEntry := HighBound; BinaryOp := RangeOp
                  end;
                Push(ResultEntry)
            end
      end
  end { rangeset };
function NullSet(Entry: StackEntry): Boolean;
  begin
    with Entry^ do
      if Kind <> AConstant
      then NullSet := false else NullSet := (TheConst.Setval = nil)
    end { nullset };
procedure BinarySetOperation { SetOperator: OpType };
  var ResultEntry, LeftOperand, RightOperand: StackEntry; Result: ObjectValue;
  procedure SetResultLimits;
    function MaxOf(a, b: MCScalar): MCScalar;
      begin if a >= b then MaxOf := a else MaxOf := b end;
    function MinOf(a, b: MCScalar): MCScalar;
      begin if a <= b then MinOf := a else MinOf := b end;
    begin { setresultlimits }
      with ResultEntry^.DataRep do
        begin
          Kind := ForSet;
          case SetOperator of
            Plus :
              begin
                Min :=
                  MinOf(LeftOperand^.DataRep.Min, RightOperand^.DataRep.Min);
                Max :=
                  MaxOf(LeftOperand^.DataRep.Max, RightOperand^.DataRep.Max)
              end;
            Mul :
              begin
                Min :=
                  MaxOf(LeftOperand^.DataRep.Min, RightOperand^.DataRep.Min);
                Max :=
                  MinOf(LeftOperand^.DataRep.Max, RightOperand^.DataRep.Max)
              end;
            Minus :
              begin
                Min := LeftOperand^.DataRep.Min;
                Max := LeftOperand^.DataRep.Max
              end
          end
        end
    end { setresultlimits };
```

```
begin { binarysetoperation }
  if CodeIsToBeGenerated
  then begin
        Pop(RightOperand); Pop(LeftOperand);
        if NullSet(LeftOperand)
        then begin
              FreeEntry(LeftOperand);
              if SetOperator = Plus
              then Push(RightOperand)
              else begin
                    StackConstant(EmptyValue); FreeEntry(RightOperand)
                  end
            end
        else if NullSet(RightOperand)
            then begin
                  if SetOperator in [Plus, Minus]
                  then Push(LeftOperand)
                  else begin
                        StackConstant(EmptyValue); FreeEntry(LeftOperand)
                      end
                end
            else if (RightOperand^.Kind = AConstant) and
                    (LeftOperand^.Kind = AConstant)
                then begin
                      ConstSetOperation
                        (Result, LeftOperand^.TheConst,
                            RightOperand^.TheConst, SetOperator);
                      StackConstant(Result); FreeEntry(LeftOperand);
                      FreeEntry(RightOperand)
                    end
                else begin
                      GetEntry(ResultEntry); SetResultLimits;
                      with ResultEntry^ do
                        begin
                          Kind := Operation; OpGroup := ASet;
                          OpForm := Binary; LeftEntry := LeftOperand;
                          RightEntry := RightOperand; BinaryOp := SetOperator
                        end;
                      Push(ResultEntry)
                    end
      end
end { binarysetoperation };
```

```
procedure SetComparison { SetOperator: OpType };
   var LeftOperand, RightOperand: StackEntry; Result: ObjectValue; Bval: Boolean;
   begin
     if CodeIsToBeGenerated
     then begin
            if (TopStackEntry^.Kind = AConstant) and
               (TopStackEntry^.NextNode^.Kind = AConstant)
            then begin
                   if SetOperator = GeOp
                   then begin
                          Pop(LeftOperand); Pop(RightOperand); SetOperator := LeOp
                        end
                   else begin Pop(RightOperand); Pop(LeftOperand) end;
                   if SetOperator = InOp
                   then with LeftOperand^ do
                          begin
                            ConstSetOperation
                               (TheConst, TheConst, TheConst, SingleOp);
                            SetOperator := LeOp
                          end;
                   case SetOperator of
                     LeOp :
                       if LeftOperand^.TheConst.WordSize >
                          RightOperand^.TheConst.WordSize
                       then Bval := false
                       else begin
                              ConstSetOperation
                                 (Result, LeftOperand^.TheConst,
                                    RightOperand^.TheConst, Minus);
                              Bval := (Result.Setval = nil)
                            end;
                     NeOp :
                       if LeftOperand^.TheConst.WordSize <>
                          RightOperand^.TheConst.WordSize
                       then Bval := true
                       else begin
                              ConstSetOperation
                                 (Result, LeftOperand^.TheConst,
                                    RightOperand^.TheConst, Minus);
                              Bval := (Result.Setval <> nil)
                            end;
```

```
            EqOp :
                if LeftOperand^.TheConst.WordSize <>
                    RightOperand^.TheConst.WordSize
                then Bval := false
                else begin
                        ConstSetOperation
                            (Result, LeftOperand^.TheConst,
                                RightOperand^.TheConst, Minus);
                        Bval := (Result.Setval = nil)
                    end
            end;
            SetBval(Bval, Result); StackConstant(Result);
            FreeEntry(LeftOperand); FreeEntry(RightOperand)
        end
    else Compare(SetOperator, ASet)
  end
end { setcomparision };
{
```

17.8 Pointer and String Comparison

Delayed code generation for all pointer and string comparisons is implemented as follows:
}

```
procedure PointerComparison { Operator: OpType };
  begin if CodeIsToBeGenerated then Compare(Operator, APointer) end;

procedure StringComparison { Operator: OpType; Length : ObjectValue };
  var LeftEntry, RightEntry: StackEntry;

  begin
    if CodeIsToBeGenerated
    then begin
            Pop(RightEntry); RightEntry^.DataBytes := Length.Ival;
            Pop(LeftEntry); LeftEntry^.DataBytes := Length.Ival;
            Push(LeftEntry); Push(RightEntry); Compare(Operator, AString)
        end
  end { stringcomparison };
```

{

CHAPTER 18

P-Code Assembly
and
Data Access Code Generation

This chapter defines the code generation utilities on which subsequent code generation procedures depend. The facilities provided include:

(a) basic P-code instruction assembly and storage;

(b) generation and fix-up of jump instructions;

(c) extended reference locking and release;

(d) generation of code to load the address implied by a reference held as an access list, together with the generation of ancillary access checks as described in Chapter 16;

(e) generation of code to load and check the value implied by an expression tree, as described in Chapter 17;

(f) temporary value storage and re-loading.

18.1 P-Code Instruction Assembly

The procedures which create and store P-code instructions (in the code buffer defined in Chapter 15) directly reflect the P-code formats dictated by the P-machine. Thus the procedures PCode0, PCode1, and Pcode2 generate class 1 instructions with 0, 1, and 2 operands respectively. In the latter cases the procedures make an automatic choice between the byte-operand or word-operand versions of the instruction required, according to the magnitude of the (first) operand.

Procedures PCode3 and PCode4 provide similar facilities for the generation of class 2 instructions, none of which take more than one operand.

The procedures InlineNumber, InlineReal and InlineWord generate the ConstX instructions which load literal values from the code itself. The procedure InlineMultipleConst is used to embed multi-word images in ConstMultiple and ConstRefMultiple instructions.

}

procedure Pcode0(Class1Instruction: Pcodes);

   begin CodeByte(Class1Instruction) **end**;

procedure PcodeAndWord(Class1Instruction: Pcodes; Operand: MCWord);

   var Buffer: MCWordForm;

```
   begin
      CodeByte(Class1Instruction); Buffer.WValue := Operand; WordOfBytes(Buffer)
   end { PcodeAndWord };
procedure Pcode1(Class1Instruction: Pcodes; Operand: MCWord);

   var Buffer: MCWordForm;

   begin
      if (Operand > MCMaxByte) or (Operand < 0)
      then begin
              Class1Instruction := succ(Class1Instruction); CodeByte(Class1Instruction);
              Buffer.WValue := Operand; WordOfBytes(Buffer)
           end
      else begin CodeByte(Class1Instruction); CodeByte(Operand) end
   end { pcode1 };
procedure Pcode2(Class1Instruction: Pcodes; Op1, Op2: MCWord);

   begin Pcode1(Class1Instruction, Op1); CodeByte(Op2) end;
procedure Pcode3(Class2Instruction: Pcodes);

   begin CodeByte(Escape); CodeByte(Class2Instruction - 256) end;
procedure Pcode4(Class2Instruction: Pcodes; Operand: MCWord);

   begin CodeByte(Escape); Pcode1(Class2Instruction - 256, Operand) end;
procedure InlineNumber(Number: MCIntegerForm);

   var Magnitude: MCIntegerForm;

   begin
      Magnitude := abs(Number);
      if Magnitude > MCMaxByte
      then Pcode1(ConstWord, Number)
      else begin
              if Magnitude >= 32
              then Pcode1(ConstWord, Magnitude) else Pcode0(Magnitude);
              if Number < 0 then Pcode0(NegateInteger)
           end
   end { inlinenumber };
procedure InLineReal(RealNumber: MCRealForm);

   var RealMap:
            record
              case Boolean of
                 false: (RealValue: MCRealForm);
                 true: (Words: array [1..MCRealSize] of MCWord)
            end;
       Buffer: MCWordForm; i: 1..MCRealSize;

   begin
      RealMap.RealValue := RealNumber;
      if MCRealSize = 1
      then begin
              Pcode0(succ(ConstWord)); Buffer.WValue := RealMap.Words[1];
```

```
                WordOfBytes(Buffer)
            end
        else begin
            Pcode1(ConstMultiple, MCRealSize); Align;
            for i := 1 to MCRealSize do
                begin Buffer.WValue := RealMap.Words[i]; WordOfBytes(Buffer) end
        end
    end { inlinereal };
procedure InlineWord(DataWord: WordEntry);

    var Buffer: MCWordForm;

    begin
        Buffer := DataWord^.Word; Pcode0(succ(ConstWord)); WordOfBytes(Buffer)
    end { inlineword };
procedure InlineMultipleConst(TheConst: ObjectValue);

    var NextWord: WordEntry;

    begin
        with TheConst do
            begin
                Align;
                if Kind = SetValue then NextWord := Setval else NextWord := Stringval;
                while NextWord <> nil do
                    begin WordOfBytes(NextWord^.Word); NextWord := NextWord^.Next end
            end
    end { inlinemultipleconst };
{
```

18.2 Generating Jump Instructions

All P-code jump instructions are two bytes long, the destination being specified either as a one byte relative offset, or indirectly via a data word indexed by a one byte data offset.

The interface type CodeLabel has two variants:

(a)   for expected code labels, i.e. those not yet sited, the LastReference field points to a chain of fix-up records which give the position and kind of forward jumps to the label;

(b)   for code labels already sited the field Address gives the byte position of the label within the current code block.

A label which is not reachable by a one-byte offset from all jumps that reference it is "linked", i.e. it is allocated a data word to hold its offset within the code block, for use by indirect "jump via" instructions.

The following procedures enable the generation and fix-up of jump instructions which reference code labels held in this way.
}

```
procedure LinkLabel(var TheLabel: CodeLabel; LabelAddress: CodeByteRange);
    var DataEntry: MCWordForm;
```

```
    begin
       DataEntry.Linked := true; DataEntry.Address := LabelAddress;
       TheLabel.LinkIndex := DataCounter - CurrentBlock^.DataBase + 1;
       TheLabel.Linked := true; DataWord(DataEntry)
    end { linklabel };
procedure PlantJump(var TheLabel: CodeLabel;
                        JumpAddress, LabelAddress: CodeByteRange;
                        Condition: JumpType);

    var OpCode: Pcodes; Operand: MCByte; Stride: integer;

    begin
       Stride := LabelAddress - JumpAddress - 2;
       if abs(Stride) > MCMaxByte
       then begin
              if Condition in [IfFalseConditional, IfTrueConditional]
              then SystemError(5)
              else begin
                     if not TheLabel.Linked then LinkLabel(TheLabel, LabelAddress);
                     Operand := TheLabel.LinkIndex;
                     if Condition = IfFalse
                     then OpCode := FJumpVia else OpCode := JumpVia
                   end
            end
       else begin
              if Stride < 0
              then if Condition = IfFalse
                     then OpCode := FJumpBack else OpCode := JumpBack
              else case Condition of
                     IfFalse : OpCode := FJumpForward;
                     IfFalseConditional : OpCode := FJumpConditional;
                     IfTrueConditional : OpCode := TJumpConditional;
                     Absolute : OpCode := JumpForward
                   end;
              Operand := abs(Stride)
            end;
       FillByte(JumpAddress, OpCode); FillByte(JumpAddress + 1, Operand)
    end { plantjump };
procedure FixUpJumps(var ThisLabel: CodeLabel; LabelSite: CodeByteRange);

    var ThisRef: FixUpEntry;

    begin
       with ThisLabel do
         while LastReference <> nil do
           begin
             ThisRef := LastReference;
             with ThisRef^ do PlantJump(ThisLabel, JumpAddress, LabelSite, JumpKind);
             LastReference := ThisRef^.Next; dispose(ThisRef)
           end
    end { fixupjumps };
```

```
procedure JumpTo(var TheLabel: CodeLabel; Condition: JumpType);
    var Fixup: FixUpEntry; Base: CodeByteRange;
  begin
    Base := CodeCounter; CodeByte(0); CodeByte(0);
    with TheLabel do
      if Expected
      then begin
            new(Fixup);
            with Fixup^ do
              begin
                JumpKind := Condition; JumpAddress := Base; Next := LastReference
              end;
            LastReference := Fixup
          end
      else PlantJump(TheLabel, Base, Address, Condition)
  end { jumpto };
{
```

18.3 Extended Reference Protection

A reference made to an actual variable parameter or to a record variable appearing in a
with-statement is "extended" for the duration of the procedure call or the body of the with-
statement. In most cases, the extension is conceptual, but references extended to file buffer
variables, record-variant fields, or dynamic variables, require actual protection to guard
against intervening motion on the file, variant reselection, or dynamic variable disposal. This
is achieved by associating each such variable with a "lock" which may be set whenever a
reference is extended. Thereafter, code is generated to check the lock prior to any operation
which could potentially destroy the reference. In particular:

(1)   Every file variable has a lock-bit embedded in the associated 5 word memory block.
       All code sequences generated from calls to reset, rewrite, put, and get, include a check
       that flags runtime error 306 if the lock-bit is set.

(2)   Every dynamic variable has a lock-bit embedded in the heap storage associated with
       the variable. All calls to dispose result in a check made internally by the P-machine,
       that flags runtime error 305 if the lock-bit is set.

(3)   Every record variant part has a lock-bit embedded in the control word. All variant
       reselections include a check that flags runtime error 302 if the lock-bit is set.

Locks are set by appending entries to the ancillary CheckList associated with the reference.
In the case of a reference made to a (nested) variant field, the CheckList will already have
one entry per level of nesting to check or set selector fields. Correspondingly, each active
variant is locked by appending entries to set the appropriate control word flags. Thereafter a
single lock is applied to the dynamic variable or the file variable as appropriate.

Each entry on the access list defines a base address from which the offset of the appropriate
lock word is measured. Entries are made on the CheckList by procedure ExtendReferences
but code generation is delayed until the reference is evaluated by procedure LoadAddress.

Multiple references extended to the same variable are handled by stacking each lock in turn on the lock-stack allocated within the current stack frame. When a lock is set, code is generated to push the current lock setting on the lock stack and then set the lock-bit. When an extended reference is discarded, code is generated to pop the lock stack, and restore the lock to its original setting.

Throughout program analysis, a compile-time record of the current lock stack depth is kept in the field LockDepth of the current FrameRecord. Prior to processing a with-statement or actual parameter-list, the value of LockDepth is saved and used when the context is closed to generate code to restore the lock stack to its original depth. The call to procedure PopLocks updates the compile-time record of the lock stack depth accordingly.
}

```
procedure ExtendReferences(Entry: StackEntry);
   var LockCount, LockingLevel: Scalar; ThisCheck: AncillaryEntry;
   procedure ApplyLock(LWord: Offsets; LBit: MCBitIndex);
      var CheckEntry: AncillaryEntry;
      begin
        new(CheckEntry);
        with CheckEntry^ do
           begin
             Next := nil; WhichOp := SetALock; LockWord := LWord; LockBit := LBit
           end;
        AppendEntry(Entry^.CheckList, CheckEntry); PushLock
      end { applylock };
   begin { extendreferences }
     if Checks in Requested
     then repeat
              if Entry^.Vulnerable
              then with Entry^ do
                      begin
                        ThisCheck := CheckList.FirstEntry; LockCount := 0;
                        while ThisCheck <> nil do
                           begin
                             if ThisCheck^.WhichOp in [CheckSelector, SetSelector]
                             then LockCount := LockCount + 1;
                             ThisCheck := ThisCheck^.Next
                           end;
                        for LockingLevel := 0 to LockCount - 1 do
                           ApplyLock(0, 3 * LockingLevel);
                        if Kind = Reference
                        then if Class = PnterRef
                                then ApplyLock(HeapLockOffset, HeapLockBit)
                                else if Class = FileRef
                                        then ApplyLock(FileLockOffset, FileLockBit)
                      end;
              Entry := Entry^.AccessList
           until Entry = nil
   end { extendreferences };
```

```
procedure DiscardReferences(OldDepth: Scalar);
  begin
    if Checks in Requested
    then with TopFrameEntry^ do
          begin
            if LockDepth > OldDepth then Pcode1(DiscardLocks, OldDepth);
            PopLocks(OldDepth)
          end
  end { discardreferences };
{
```

18.4 Stack Access and Block Calling Utilities

The following utilities are used to determine the appropriate method for accessing global, local and intermediate stack addresses and blocks, and enable the generation of code to address load, or store stack words, and to call code blocks.

```
}
procedure AdjustAddress(Delta: Offsets);
  begin
    if Delta <> 0
    then if Delta < 0
          then if Delta = -1 then Pcode0(AdjustM1) else Pcode1(AdjustMinus, -Delta)
          else if Delta = 1 then Pcode0(AdjustP1) else Pcode1(AdjustPlus, Delta)
  end { adjustaddress };
procedure AdjustLoad(Delta: Offsets);
  begin
    if Delta > 7
    then Pcode1(Index, Delta)
    else if Delta = 0 then Pcode0(LoadIndirect) else Pcode0(IndexShort + Delta - 1)
  end { adjustload };
procedure ModifyValue(Delta: MCIntegerForm);
  begin
    if Delta <> 0
    then if Delta < 0
          then if Delta = -1 then Pcode0(Dec1) else Pcode1(Decrement, -Delta)
          else if Delta = 1 then Pcode0(Inc1) else Pcode1(Increment, Delta)
  end { modifyvalue };
function AccessMethod(Level: AddressLevel): Accesses;
  begin
    if Level = GlobalLevel
    then AccessMethod := Global
    else if Level = FrameLevel
          then AccessMethod := Local
          else if Level = FrameLevel - 1
                then AccessMethod := Enclosing else AccessMethod := Intermediate
  end { accessmethod };
```

```
procedure AccessWord(WordLevel: AddressLevel; Delta: Offsets; Operation: AccessOps);
   var Adjustment: Offsets; OpCode: Pcodes; Negative: Boolean; Access: Accesses;
   begin
     if Delta < 0
     then begin Adjustment := Delta; Delta := 0; Negative := true;  end
     else Negative := false;
     Access := AccessMethod(WordLevel); OpCode := AccessCodes[Operation, Access];
     if Access = Intermediate
     then Pcode2(OpCode, Delta, FrameLevel - WordLevel)
     else if (Access = Local) and (Delta < 8)
         then Pcode0(OpCode - 8 + Delta) else Pcode1(OpCode, Delta);
     if Negative then AdjustAddress(Adjustment)
   end { accessword };
procedure EmitCall(BlockBase: BlockLabel);
   var CalledLevel, LevelOffset: AddressLevel; EntryPoint: MCByte;
   begin
     EntryPoint := BlockBase.EntryOffset; CalledLevel := BlockBase.BlockLevel;
     LevelOffset := FrameLevel - CalledLevel;
     if CalledLevel = GlobalLevel
     then Pcode1(CallGlobal, EntryPoint)
     else if LevelOffset > 1
         then Pcode2(CallOuter, LevelOffset, EntryPoint)
         else if LevelOffset = 1
             then Pcode1(Callevel, EntryPoint) else Pcode1(CallLocal, EntryPoint)
   end { emitcall };
{
```

18.5 Loading and Saving Addresses

The procedure LoadAddress is used to generate the code required to load the address implied by an access list, as defined in Chapter 16, and to carry out any ancillary access checks required at each access step.

The logic used by LoadAddress follows directly from the form of access lists defined in Chapter 13, and from the P-codes available for access operations. The procedure CheckAccess generates the code to apply any access checks required at each step.

The procedure SaveAddress is used to preserve an address for subsequent re-use if necessary, by acquiring temporary stack frame locations and generating code to store the address there.

An address saved in this way is represented by a stack record of variant Address.

```
}
procedure Load(Entry: StackEntry); forward;
procedure CheckAccess(var CheckList: AncillaryList);
   var CheckEntry, OldEntry: AncillaryEntry;
   begin
     CheckEntry := CheckList.FirstEntry;
```

```
      while CheckEntry <> nil do
        begin
          with CheckEntry^ do
            case WhichOp of
              CheckSelector :
                begin
                  Pcode0(DuplicateStack);
                  with SelectorField do
                    if PartWord
                    then begin
                            AdjustAddress(WordOffset); InlineNumber(BitSize);
                            InlineNumber(BitOffset); Pcode0(LoadPacked)
                         end
                    else AdjustLoad(WordOffset);
                  InlineNumber(SelectorValue); Pcode1(CheckVntField, SelectorField.Level)
                end;
              SetSelector :
                begin
                  Pcode0(MarkStack); Pcode1(LoadStack, FrameSize);
                  InlineNumber(TagValue); EmitCall(Selector)
                end;
              CheckIfActive :
                begin
                  Pcode0(DuplicateStack); Pcode1(LoadBit, 3 * SelectorLevel + 2);
                  Pcode1(TrapIfFalse, 43)
                end;
              CheckIfNew :
                begin Pcode0(DuplicateStack); Pcode0(CheckNew1) end;
              CheckFile :
                begin Pcode3(CheckBuffer) end;
              SetALock :
                begin
                  Pcode0(DuplicateStack); AdjustAddress(LockWord);
                  Pcode1(SetLock, LockBit)
                end
            end { case };
          OldEntry := CheckEntry; CheckEntry := CheckEntry^.Next; dispose(OldEntry)
        end;
      StartAncillaries(CheckList)
    end { checkaccess };
procedure LoadAddress(Entry: StackEntry);
  var StackedPartWord: Boolean; NextIndex, ThisIndex: IndexEntry;
  begin
    with Entry^ do
      begin
        case Kind of
          Reference :
            begin
              StackedPartWord := false;
```

```
{ load base word address }
if AccessList <> nil
then begin
        with AccessList^ do
          if ((Kind = Reference) and PartOfWord) or
             ((Kind = Address) and (not Loaded) and APartWord)
          then StackedPartWord := true;
        LoadAddress(AccessList);
        if Indirect
        then if (Class = PnterRef) and (Checks in Requested)
                then Pcode0(LoadPointer) else Pcode0(LoadIndirect);
        AdjustAddress(Adjustment); FreeEntry(AccessList);
        AccessList := nil
     end
else with BaseAddress do
        if Indirect
        then begin
                if (Class = PnterRef) and (Checks in Requested)
                then begin
                        AccessWord(BlockLevel, WordOffset, LoadRefOp);
                        Pcode0(LoadPointer)
                     end
                else AccessWord(BlockLevel, WordOffset, LoadOp);
                AdjustAddress(Adjustment)
             end
        else AccessWord
                (BlockLevel, WordOffset + Adjustment, LoadRefOp);
{ incorporate indices and/or partword offsets }
if PartOfWord
then if IndexedPartWord
     then begin
                with Index^ do
                  begin
                    if CAPIndex
                    then with BpAddress do
                            AccessWord
                                (BlockLevel, WordOffset, LoadRefOp);
                    Load(TheIndex);
                    if CAPIndex
                    then Pcode0(IndexPackdCAP)
                    else ModifyValue(-Lower);
                    if StackedPartWord
                    then Pcode1(IndexSubWord, Factor)
                    else if OnByteBoundary
                            then Pcode0(IndexByteRef)
                            else Pcode1(IndexPackedRef, Factor);
                    ModifyValue(BitOffset); FreeEntry(TheIndex);
                  end;
                dispose(Index)
```

```
                              end
                        else begin
                              InlineNumber(BitSize); InlineNumber(BitOffset);
                              if StackedPartWord then Pcode0(AdjustPackedRef)
                            end
                  else if Indexed
                      then begin
                            NextIndex := Indices;
                            repeat
                              ThisIndex := NextIndex;
                              with ThisIndex^ do
                                begin
                                  if CAPIndex
                                  then with BpAddress do
                                        AccessWord
                                          (BlockLevel, WordOffset, LoadRefOp);
                                  Load(TheIndex);
                                  if CAPIndex
                                  then Pcode0(IndexCAP)
                                  else if Factor = 1
                                        then Pcode0(AddAddress)
                                        else Pcode1(IndexRef, Factor);
                                  NextIndex := Next; FreeEntry(TheIndex)
                                end;
                              dispose(ThisIndex)
                            until NextIndex = nil
                          end
                  end;
            AConstant :
              begin
                Pcode1(ConstRefMultiple, TheConst.WordSize);
                InlineMultipleConst(TheConst)
              end;
            Address :
              if not Loaded
              then with TempAddress do
                    if APartWord
                    then begin
                          AccessWord(BlockLevel, WordOffset, LoadRefOp);
                          Pcode1(LoadMultiple, 3)
                        end
                    else AccessWord(BlockLevel, WordOffset, LoadOp)
          end;
          if CheckList.FirstEntry <> nil then CheckAccess(CheckList);
          Kind := Address; Vulnerable := false; Loaded := true
        end
end { loadaddress };
```

```
procedure SaveAddress(LocalBase: StackEntry);
   var SavedPartWord, IndexedRef: Boolean;
   begin
     with LocalBase^ do
       begin
         SavedPartWord := PartOfWord;
         if SavedPartWord
         then IndexedRef := IndexedPartWord else IndexedRef := Indexed;
         if (Indirect and (Class = PnterRef)) or (AccessList <> nil) or IndexedRef
         then begin
                 LoadAddress(LocalBase); Loaded := false;
                 if SavedPartWord
                 then begin
                         Acquire(3, TempAddress) {for packed-field pointer};
                         with TempAddress do
                            AccessWord(BlockLevel, WordOffset, LoadRefOp);
                         Pcode1(StoreMultiple, 3)
                      end
                 else begin
                         Acquire(1, TempAddress);
                         with TempAddress do
                            AccessWord(BlockLevel, WordOffset, StoreOp)
                      end;
                 APartWord := SavedPartWord
              end
       end
   end { saveaddress };
{
```

18.6 Evaluating Expressions

The procedure Load is used to generate the code required to load the result of evaluating an expression tree, as defined in Chapter 17.

The logic used by Load follows directly from the form of expression trees, the operations that they represent, and the P-codes available for their implementation. Range checks applicable to intermediate and final values are handled as explicit operations within the tree evaluation logic but the implicit undefined value checks applicable when a variable value is loaded are implemented by the auxiliary procedure CheckValue.

Because code generation for the file functions eof and eoln, and for numeric read operations, are included within expression trees, the following procedures are declared forward at this point, and implemented in Chapter 21 where the overall strategy for file manipulation is described.

```
}
procedure RestoreFile(IOFile: IOFileEntry); forward;
procedure LoadFileDescriptor; forward;
procedure DoFileChecks(FileOp: StdProcFuncs); forward;
```

```
procedure PostsetBuffer(FileOp: StdProcFuncs); forward;
procedure LoadCAPSize(ForPackedCAP: Boolean;
                            BoundPairBlock: RuntimeAddress); forward;
procedure CheckLoadedValue(Entry: StackEntry);
  procedure InLineCheck(DataSize: WordRange; ErrorCode: Scalar);
    begin
      if DataSize = 1
      then Pcode1(CheckTopDefined, ErrorCode)
      else begin
            Pcode0(DuplicateStack); InlineNumber(DataSize);
            Pcode1(CheckRepeated, ErrorCode)
          end
    end { inlinecheck };
  begin { checkloadedvalue }
    with Entry^.DataRep do
      if WordSize = 0
      then Pcode1(TrapError, 43)
      else case Kind of
            ForScalar, ForReal :
              if Entry^.PartOfWord
              then begin
                    InlineNumber(CheckValue.Magnitude);
                    Pcode1(CheckTopValue, Entry^.RunError)
                  end
              else InLineCheck(WordSize, Entry^.RunError);
            ForPnter : Pcode0(CheckPointer);
            ForArray, ForARecord, ForVntRecord :
              if CheckCode.EntryOffset <> 0
              then begin
                    Pcode0(MarkStack); Pcode1(LoadStack, FrameSize);
                    EmitCall(CheckCode)
                  end
              else InLineCheck(WordSize, Entry^.RunError);
            ForCAP :
              if CheckCode.EntryOffset <> 0
              then begin
                    Pcode0(MarkStack); Pcode1(LoadStack, FrameSize + 1);
                    EmitCall(CheckCode)
                  end
              else Pcode1(CheckCAP, Entry^.RunError);
            ForSet :
              if WordSize = 1
              then Pcode1(CheckTopDefined, Entry^.RunError)
              else begin
                    Pcode0(DuplicateStack); Pcode1(CheckWord, Entry^.RunError)
                  end
          end
  end { checkloadedvalue };
```

```
procedure Load {Entry : StackEntry};
  var CheckNeeded: Boolean;
  procedure DoBooleanOp;
    var ExitLabel: CodeLabel; ThisEntry, NextEntry: StackEntry;
    begin
      FutureCodeLabel(ExitLabel);
      with Entry^ do
        begin
          ThisEntry := OpList;
          while ThisEntry <> nil do
            begin
              NextEntry := ThisEntry^.NextNode; Load(ThisEntry);
              if NextEntry <> nil then JumpTo(ExitLabel, Jump);
              FreeEntry(ThisEntry); ThisEntry := NextEntry
            end
        end;
      NextIsCodeLabel(ExitLabel)
    end { dobooleanop };
  procedure DoUnaryOp;
    var OpCode: Pcodes;
    begin
      with Entry^ do
        begin
          Load(UnaryEntry);
          case OpGroup of
            AnInteger :
              if UnaryOp = NegateOp
              then OpCode := NegateInteger else OpCode := Float;
            AReal : OpCode := NegateReal;
            ABoolean : OpCode := NotOperation;
            ASet : OpCode := MakeSingletonSet
          end;
          Pcode0(OpCode); FreeEntry(UnaryEntry)
        end
    end { dounaryop };
  procedure DoBinaryOp;
    var Folded: Boolean;
    begin
      with Entry^ do
        begin
          case OpGroup of
            AnInteger :
              begin
                Folded := false;
```

```
                       if BinaryOp = Plus
                       then if RightEntry^.Kind = AConstant
                            then begin
                                    Load(LeftEntry);
                                    ModifyValue(RightEntry^.TheConst.Ival); Folded := true
                                 end
                            else begin
                                    if LeftEntry^.Kind = AConstant
                                    then begin
                                            Load(RightEntry);
                                            ModifyValue(LeftEntry^.TheConst.Ival);
                                            Folded := true
                                         end
                                 end
                       else if BinaryOp = Minus
                            then if RightEntry^.Kind = AConstant
                                 then begin
                                         Load(LeftEntry);
                                         ModifyValue(-RightEntry^.TheConst.Ival);
                                         Folded := true
                                      end;
                       if not Folded
                       then begin
                               Load(LeftEntry); Load(RightEntry); Pcode0(IntCodes[BinaryOp])
                            end
                  end;
               AReal :
                  begin
                     Load(LeftEntry); Load(RightEntry); Pcode0(RealCodes[BinaryOp])
                  end;
               APointer :
                  begin
                     Load(LeftEntry); Load(RightEntry);
                     if Checks in Requested
                     then Pcode0(PtrCodes[BinaryOp]) else Pcode0(IntCodes[BinaryOp])
                  end;
               AString :
                  begin
                     Load(LeftEntry); Load(RightEntry);
                     PcodeAndWord(StringCodes[BinaryOp], LeftEntry^.DataBytes)
                  end;
               ASet :
                  begin Load(LeftEntry); Load(RightEntry); Pcode0(SetCodes[BinaryOp]) end
            end;
         FreeEntry(LeftEntry); FreeEntry(RightEntry)
      end
end { dobinaryop };
```

```
procedure DoBlockCall;
  begin
    with Entry^ do
      begin
        FnBlockEntry^.CallToBeGenerated := true; Push(FnBlockEntry); CallBlock
      end
  end { doblockcall };
procedure DoSubrangeChecks;
  var MinTestNeeded, MaxTestNeeded: Boolean; Instruction: Pcodes;
  begin
    with Entry^ do
      begin
        Load(EntryToCheck);
        with RequiredRange^ do
          if CAPBounds
          then with BpAddress do
                  begin
                    AccessWord(BlockLevel, WordOffset, LoadOp);
                    AccessWord(BlockLevel, WordOffset + 1, LoadOp);
                    Instruction := CheckLimits
                  end
          else begin
                  if EntryToCheck^.DataRep.Min < Lower
                  then begin InlineNumber(Lower); MinTestNeeded := true end
                  else MinTestNeeded := false;
                  if Upper < EntryToCheck^.DataRep.Max
                  then begin InlineNumber(Upper); MaxTestNeeded := true end
                  else MaxTestNeeded := false;
                  Instruction := CheckCodes[MinTestNeeded, MaxTestNeeded]
               end;
        if Instruction <> NoOperation then Pcode1(Instruction, RunError);
        FreeEntry(EntryToCheck)
      end
  end { dorangecheck };
procedure DoTransferChecks;
  begin
    with Entry^ do
      begin
        Load(EntryToCheck);
        with RequiredRange^ do
          if CAPBounds
          then with BpAddress do AccessWord(BlockLevel, WordOffset + 1, LoadOp)
          else InlineNumber(Upper);
        with TransferRange^ do
          if CAPBounds
          then with BpAddress do
                  begin
                    AccessWord(BlockLevel, WordOffset + 1, LoadOp);
```

```
                    AccessWord(BlockLevel, WordOffset, LoadOp); Pcode0(SubInteger)
                end
            else InlineNumber(Upper - Lower);
            Pcode0(SubInteger); Pcode1(CheckUpper, RunError); FreeEntry(EntryToCheck)
        end
    end { dotransferchecks };
procedure DoMembershipChecks;
    begin
        with Entry^ do
            begin
                Load(EntryToCheck);
                with RequiredRange^ do
                    if Lower <> 0
                    then begin
                            InlineNumber(Lower); InlineNumber(Upper);
                            Pcode1(CheckSetLimits, RunError)
                        end
                    else begin InlineNumber(Upper); Pcode1(CheckSetUpper, RunError) end;
                FreeEntry(EntryToCheck)
            end
    end { domembershipchecks };
procedure DoReadOp;
    begin
        with Entry^ do
            begin
                if Checks in Requested then DoFileChecks(Readp);
                LoadFileDescriptor;
                case Mode of
                    IntKind : Pcode3(ReadInteger);
                    RealKind : Pcode3(ReadReal)
                end;
                if Checks in Requested then PostsetBuffer(Readp)
            end
    end { doreadop };
procedure DoCAPLoad;
    begin
        with Entry^ do
            begin
                CheckNeeded := (CAPEntry^.RunError <> 0); LoadAddress(CAPEntry);
                LoadCAPSize(CAPPacked, BpAddress);
                if CheckNeeded then CheckLoadedValue(Entry);
                FreeEntry(CAPEntry)
            end
    end { docapload };
```

```
procedure DoStandardOp;
  begin
    with Entry^ do
      begin
        case OpGroup of
          AnInteger :
            begin
              Load(StdEntry);
              case StdOp of
                Absf : Pcode0(AbsInteger);
                Sqrf : Pcode0(SquareInteger);
                Oddf : Pcode0(OddInteger);
                Succf : Pcode0(Inc1);
                Predf : Pcode0(Dec1);
                Ordf, Chrf :
              end;
              FreeEntry(StdEntry)
            end;
          AReal :
            begin
              Load(StdEntry);
              case StdOp of
                Absf : Pcode0(AbsReal);
                Sqrf : Pcode0(SquareReal);
                Truncf : Pcode0(TruncateReal);
                Roundf : Pcode0(RoundReal);
                Sinf : Pcode3(Sine);
                Cosf : Pcode3(Cosine);
                Expf : Pcode3(NaturalExp);
                Lnf : Pcode3(NaturalLog);
                Sqrtf : Pcode3(SquareRoot);
                Arctanf : Pcode3(ArcTangent)
              end;
              FreeEntry(StdEntry)
            end;
          AFile :
            begin
              RestoreFile(IOEntry);
              if Checks in Requested then DoFileChecks(StdOp);
              LoadFileDescriptor;
              case StdOp of
                Eolnf : Pcode3(EndOfLine);
                Eoff : Pcode3(EndOfFile)
              end;
              DiscardFile
            end
        end
      end
  end { dostandardop };
```

```
begin { load }
   with Entry^ do
      case Kind of
         Reference :
            begin
               CheckNeeded := (Entry^.RunError <> 0);
               if PartOfWord
               then begin
                      LoadAddress(Entry);
                      if OnByteBoundary
                      then Pcode0(LoadByte) else Pcode0(LoadPacked);
                      if CheckNeeded then CheckLoadedValue(Entry)
                    end
               else if DataRep.WordSize > 1
                  then begin
                         LoadAddress(Entry);
                         if CheckNeeded then CheckLoadedValue(Entry);
                         with DataRep do
                           if Kind = ForSet
                           then Pcode1(LoadSet, WordSize)
                           else if (Kind = ForVntRecord) and (Checks in Requested)
                                 then begin
                                        Pcode0(PurgeLocks);
                                        Pcode1(LoadMultiple, WordSize - 1)
                                      end
                                 else Pcode1(LoadMultiple, WordSize)
                       end
                  else begin
                         if Indexed
                         then begin LoadAddress(Entry); Pcode0(LoadIndirect) end
                         else if AccessList <> nil
                            then begin
                                   LoadAddress(AccessList);
                                   if Indirect
                                   then if (Class = PnterRef) and
                                           (Checks in Requested)
                                        then Pcode0(LoadPointer)
                                        else Pcode0(LoadIndirect);
                                   AdjustLoad(Adjustment); FreeEntry(AccessList)
                                 end
                            else with BaseAddress do
                                   if Indirect
                                   then begin
                                          if (Class = PnterRef) and
                                             (Checks in Requested)
                                          then begin
                                                 AccessWord
                                                   (BlockLevel, WordOffset,
                                                     LoadRefOp);
                                                 Pcode0(LoadPointer)
```

```
                                                end
                                   else AccessWord
                                           (BlockLevel, WordOffset, LoadOp);
                                   AdjustLoad(Adjustment)
                                end
                          else AccessWord
                                   (BlockLevel, WordOffset + Adjustment,
                                       LoadOp);
                      if CheckNeeded then CheckLoadedValue(Entry)
                  end
    end;
BlockRef : ;
Result : ;
Address :
    begin
        if not Loaded then LoadAddress(Entry);
        Pcode0(LoadIndirect)
    end;
AConstant :
    with TheConst do
        case Kind of
            IntValue, BoolValue, CharValue : InlineNumber(TheConst.Ival);
            RealValue : InLineReal(TheConst.Rval);
            StringValue :
                if WordSize > 1
                then begin
                        Pcode1(ConstMultiple, WordSize); InlineMultipleConst(TheConst)
                    end
                else InlineWord(TheConst.Stringval);
            SetValue :
                if WordSize = 0
                then InlineNumber(0)
                else if WordSize > 1
                    then begin
                            Pcode1(ConstSet, WordSize); InlineMultipleConst(TheConst)
                        end
                    else InlineWord(TheConst.Setval);
            PntrValue :
                begin
                    InlineNumber(0);
                    if Checks in Requested then InlineNumber(0)
                end
        end;
Operation :
    case OpForm of
        Unary : DoUnaryOp;
        Binary : DoBinaryOp;
        Condition : DoBooleanOp;
        BlockCall : DoBlockCall;
```

```
        RangeChk :
          case CheckKind of
            SubrangeChecks : DoSubrangeChecks;
            TransferChecks : DoTransferChecks;
            MemberChecks : DoMembershipChecks
          end;
        ReadOp : DoReadOp;
        CAPLoad : DoCAPLoad;
        Standard : DoStandardOp
      end
    end;
  Entry^.Kind := Result
end { load };
{
```

18.6 Saving and Reloading Values

The procedure SaveValue is used to save a loaded expression result for subsequent re-use, in a temporary location acquired for the purpose, and to create a reference record for the temporary. The procedure LoadValue is used to reload a result saved in this way, or to load the value of a constant expression (which would not be saved). LoadValue does not alter the stack record describing the value to be loaded, so that multiple (re-) loading operations may be applied.
}

```
procedure SaveValue(ExpValue: StackEntry);
  begin
    with ExpValue^ do
      begin
        Kind := Reference; Indirect := false; Class := VarRef; AccessList := nil;
        Acquire(1, BaseAddress); Adjustment := 0; PartOfWord := false;
        Indexed := false;
        with BaseAddress do AccessWord(BlockLevel, WordOffset, StoreOp)
      end
  end { savevalue };
procedure LoadValue(TempEntry: StackEntry);
  begin
    with TempEntry^ do
      if Kind = AConstant
      then InlineNumber(TheConst.Ival)
      else with BaseAddress do
             if Indirect
             then begin
                    AccessWord(BlockLevel, WordOffset, LoadOp);
                    AdjustLoad(Adjustment)
                  end
             else AccessWord(BlockLevel, WordOffset + Adjustment, LoadOp)
  end { loadvalue };
```

{

CHAPTER 19

Code Generation
For Assignments

Assignment code is generated by the procedures Assign and AssignTag. For normal assignments the procedure Assign distinguishes the following cases:

(a) assignment of entire conformant arrays is carried out by the special P-code MoveCAP, using the conformant array value representation generated by the LoadCAP operation within the expression tree;

(b) assignment of addressable multiword values is carried out by the store-to-store P-code, Move;

(c) assignment of evaluated sets or multiword values is carried out by the P-codes StoreSet or StoreMultiple;

(d) assignment of word or part-word variables is carried out by loading and storing the value concerned, using the most efficient storage P-codes available.

Tagfield assignment is different in that, if checks have been requested or the variant part involved contains an embedded file, a call must be generated to the selector-updating procedure within the augmented representation. Otherwise normal assignment code is used.

}

```
procedure Assign { VarRep: TypeRepresentation };
   var Expression, Variable: StackEntry; CheckNeeded: Boolean;
   function AString(Entry: StackEntry): Boolean;
     begin
       with Entry^ do
         if Kind <> AConstant
         then AString := false else AString := TheConst.Kind = StringValue
     end { astring };
```

```
begin { assign }
  if CodeIsToBeGenerated
  then begin
        Pop(Expression); Pop(Variable);
        if VarRep.Kind = ForCAP
        then begin Load(Expression); LoadAddress(Variable); Pcode0(MoveCAP) end
        else if (VarRep.WordSize > 1) or (VarRep.Kind = ForSet)
            then with Expression^ do
                  if (Kind in [Reference, Address]) or AString(Expression)
                  then begin
                        if Kind = Reference
                        then CheckNeeded := (Expression^.RunError <> 0)
                        else CheckNeeded := false;
                        LoadAddress(Expression);
                        if CheckNeeded then CheckLoadedValue(Expression);
                        LoadAddress(Variable);
                        with VarRep do
                          if (Kind = ForVntRecord) and (Checks in Requested)
                          then begin
                                Pcode0(SampleAndPurge);
                                Pcode1(Move, WordSize - 1)
                              end
                          else Pcode1(Move, WordSize)
                      end
                  else begin
                        Load(Expression); LoadAddress(Variable);
                        if VarRep.Kind = ForSet
                        then Pcode1(StoreSet, VarRep.WordSize)
                        else Pcode1(StoreMultiple, VarRep.WordSize)
                      end
            else begin
                  Load(Expression);
                  with Variable^ do
                    if PartOfWord
                    then begin
                          LoadAddress(Variable);
                          if OnByteBoundary
                          then Pcode0(StoreByte) else Pcode0(StorePacked)
                        end
                    else if Indexed or Indirect or (AccessList <> nil)
                        then begin
                              LoadAddress(Variable); Pcode0(StoreIndirect)
                            end
                        else with BaseAddress do
                              AccessWord
                                (BlockLevel, WordOffset + Adjustment, StoreOp)
                  end;
        FreeEntry(Expression); FreeEntry(Variable)
      end
end { assign };
```

```
procedure AssignTag { SelectorRep: TypeRepresentation };
   var RecordEntry, TagEntry, Expression: StackEntry; CodeOfBody: BlockLabel;
   begin
     if CodeIsToBeGenerated
     then if SelectorRep.CheckCode.EntryOffset <> 0
          then begin
                  Pop(Expression); Pop(TagEntry);
                  RecordEntry := TagEntry^.AccessList;
                  CodeOfBody := SelectorRep.CheckCode;
                  StackActualBlock(CodeOfBody); OpenParameterList(Proc);
                  Push(RecordEntry); PassReference(Secure);
                  Push(Expression); PassValue(Expression^.DataRep);
                  CloseParameterList; CallBlock;
                  FreeEntry(TagEntry)
               end
          else Assign(SelectorRep)
   end { assigntag };
```

{

CHAPTER 20

Code Generation
for
With Statements

The set of records addressed by currently open with-statements is held as a "with-stack", pointed to by the variable TopWithEntry, and maintained by the procedures OpenWith and CloseWith.

OpenWith creates an extended reference to the record variable, generates code if necessary to save its address in temporary storage, and pushes a new entry onto the with-stack holding the variable reference and a unique "with-base" key generated by the analyser.

Subsequent calls to WithReference use the key value supplied by the analyser to locate the corresponding reference in the with-stack, and re-create it on the operand/reference stack for use by the subsequent call to FieldReference.

At the end of a with-statement the procedure CloseWith releases any locks set by the extended reference and pops the with-stack.

}

```
procedure OpenWith { WithBase: DispRange };
   var LocalBase: StackEntry; ThisEntry: WithEntry;
   begin
      if CodeIsToBeGenerated
      then begin
            new(ThisEntry);
            with ThisEntry^ do
               begin
                  BaseNum := WithBase; OldDepth := TopFrameEntry^.LockDepth;
                  Pop(LocalBase); ExtendReferences(LocalBase); SaveAddress(LocalBase);
                  Entry := LocalBase; Next := TopWithEntry
               end;
            TopWithEntry := ThisEntry
         end
   end { openwith };
```

```
procedure WithReference { WithBase: DispRange };
  var BaseEntry: WithEntry; NewBase: StackEntry;
  begin
    if CodeIsToBeGenerated
    then begin
          BaseEntry := TopWithEntry;
          while BaseEntry^.BaseNum <> WithBase do
            BaseEntry := BaseEntry^.Next;
          GetEntry(NewBase); NewBase^ := BaseEntry^.Entry^; Push(NewBase)
        end
  end { withreference };
procedure CloseWith;
  var ThisEntry: WithEntry;
  begin
    if CodeIsToBeGenerated
    then begin
          ThisEntry := TopWithEntry;
          with ThisEntry^ do
            begin
              DiscardReferences(OldDepth); FreeEntry(Entry); TopWithEntry := Next
            end;
          dispose(ThisEntry)
        end
  end { closewith };
procedure InitWith;
  begin TopWithEntry := nil end;
```

CHAPTER 21

Code Generation
for
Standard Procedures

This chapter contains the code generation procedures for the standard input/output procedures, for pack and unpack, and for new and dispose. The remaining arithmetic functions are implemented by dedicated P-codes.

21.1 File Selection

All input/output operations are performed with respect to an argument file "selected" as appropriate from Input, Output or the standard procedure parameter list. Details of the selected file are provided by the call to procedure SelectFile and stored for the duration of the I/O operation in the fields of a record of type IOFileRecord. In particular, FileType is the TypeEntry for the argument file type, and FileEntry is the file variable reference. The statement:

write (f, eof(g))

indicates that I/O operations may be nested, and so the IOFileRecords are preserved in a stack whose top-most node is referenced by the global variable SelectedFile. Furthermore, the delayed code-generation strategy employed to evaluate an expression such as:

eof(g) or eof(h) or eof(i)

requires that the selected file for each function must be preserved, and restored immediately prior to code generation for the function call. The following procedures satisfy those requirements by maintaining a stack of selected files onto which entries are pushed prior to any input/output code generation, and popped when code-generation is complete. Delayed evaluation of the functions eof and eoln is provided for by procedures SaveFile and RestoreFile.

procedure CheckManuals(ManualScope: DispRange; List: ManualList); forward;

```
procedure SelectFile { FType: TypEntry };
    var IOFile: IOFileEntry;
    begin
      if CodeIsToBeGenerated
      then begin
              new(IOFile);
              with IOFile^ do
                begin
                  FileType := FType; Pop(FileEntry); SaveAddress(FileEntry);
                  Next := SelectedFile
                end;
              SelectedFile := IOFile
          end
    end { selectfile };
procedure GetIOBase(var BaseEntry: StackEntry);
    begin GetEntry(BaseEntry); BaseEntry^ := SelectedFile^.FileEntry^ end;
procedure SaveFile(var IOFile: IOFileEntry);
    begin
      new(IOFile);
      with IOFile^ do
        begin FileType := SelectedFile^.FileType; GetIOBase(FileEntry); Next := nil end
    end { savefile };
procedure RestoreFile {IOFile: IOFileEntry};
    begin IOFile^.Next := SelectedFile; SelectedFile := IOFile end;
procedure DiscardFile;
    var IOFile: IOFileEntry;
    begin
      if CodeIsToBeGenerated
      then begin
              IOFile := SelectedFile;
              with IOFile^ do
                begin FreeEntry(FileEntry); SelectedFile := Next end;
              dispose(IOFile)
          end
    end { discardfile };
procedure InitIO;
    begin SelectedFile := nil end;
{
```

21.2 File-Checks

Operations on a file-variable are subject to run-time checks to verify that the file variable is defined, that its mode and position are consistent with the intended input/output operation, and that no reference is currently extended to the file buffer variable. These checks are performed by the procedures FileVariableCheck, FileModeCheck, FilePosition and

CheckLockedFile respectively.

In addition, the pre-assertions for the put operation require that the buffer-variable be checked against the "undefined" value. This is achieved by creating a degenerate manual list containing a single item corresponding to the file buffer variable. Conceptually, this "buffer item" is regarded as a field of the file variable and code to check the undefined variable is generated using the representation field of the file element type.

The post-assertions for read, readln, reset, and get require that the buffer-variable be reset to the "undefined" value if the operation leaves the file positioned at end of file. The post-assertions for all write operations require the buffer variable be reset unconditionally. This is achieved by creating a degenerate manual list containing a single buffer item and calling procedure PresetManuals to generate code to reset the buffer variable to the "modified" value.

Code generation for the file-checks required by the pre-assertions for a given I/O operation is triggered by calling procedure DoFileChecks immediately prior to generating code for the input/output operation itself.

Note that since:

> writeln (f, e1, e2, e3)

is defined as equivalent to:

> write(f, e1); write(f, e2); write(f, e3); writeln(f)

the pre- and post-assertions for write must be verified by making a call to DoFileChecks for each implied component write statement.

}

```
procedure LoadFileReference;
   var FileEntry: StackEntry;
   begin
     GetIOBase(FileEntry);
     if FileEntry^.Kind = Address then PushNewAccess(FileEntry, false);
     Push(FileEntry)
   end { loadfilereference };
procedure LoadFileAddress;
   var FileEntry: StackEntry;
   begin
     GetIOBase(FileEntry); LoadAddress(FileEntry); FreeEntry(FileEntry)
   end { loadfileaddress };
procedure LoadFileDescriptor;
   var FileEntry: StackEntry;
   begin
     GetIOBase(FileEntry); FileEntry^.DataRep := IntegerRepresentation;
     Load(FileEntry); FreeEntry(FileEntry)
   end { loadfiledescriptor };
```

```
procedure FileVariableCheck(FileOp: StdProcFuncs);
  begin
    LoadFileDescriptor;
    case FileOp of
      Resetp : Pcode1(TrapIfFalse, 13);
      Getp, Readp, Readlnp : Pcode1(TrapIfFalse, 15);
      Putp, Pagep, Writep, Writelnp : Pcode1(TrapIfFalse, 10);
      Eoff : Pcode1(TrapIfFalse, 40);
      Eolnf : Pcode1(TrapIfFalse, 41)
    end
  end { filevariablecheck };
procedure FileModeCheck(Mode: FileModes);
  begin
    LoadFileDescriptor;
    if Mode = Inspection then Pcode3(CheckReadMode) else Pcode3(CheckWriteMode)
  end { filemodecheck };
procedure FilePositionCheck(FileOp: StdProcFuncs);
  begin
    LoadFileDescriptor; Pcode3(EndOfFile);
    case FileOp of
      Getp, Readp, Readlnp : Pcode1(TrapIfTrue, 16);
      Eolnf : Pcode1(TrapIfTrue, 42)
    end
  end { filepositioncheck };
procedure CheckLockedFile;
  var FileEntry: StackEntry;
  begin
    LoadFileReference; Pop(FileEntry);
    with FileEntry^ do Adjustment := Adjustment + FileLockOffset;
    LoadAddress(FileEntry); Pcode1(LoadBit, FileLockBit); Pcode1(TrapIfTrue, 6);
    FreeEntry(FileEntry)
  end { checklockedfile };
procedure CheckUndefinedBuffer;
  var ChecksList: ManualList; BufferItem: ManualEntry;
  begin
    StartManuals(ChecksList);
    with SelectedFile^.FileType^ do
      begin
        CreateItem(FelType^.Representation, BufferItem);
        SetItemShape(BufferItem, Field); SetItemCode(BufferItem, Field, ValueChecks);
        AppendManual(ChecksList, BufferItem); LoadFileReference;
        FieldReference(BufferOffset, false);
        if not TextFile then IndirectReference(false);
        OpenWith(FrameLevel); CheckManuals(FrameLevel, ChecksList); CloseWith
      end;
    DisposeManuals(ChecksList)
  end { checkundefinedbuffer };
```

```
procedure PostsetBuffer {FileOp: StdProcFuncs};
  var PresetList: ManualList; BufferItem: ManualEntry; ExitLabel: CodeLabel;
  begin
    FutureCodeLabel(ExitLabel); StartManuals(PresetList);
    with SelectedFile^.FileType^ do
      begin
        if FileOp in [Resetp, Getp, Readp, Readlnp]
        then begin
                LoadFileDescriptor; Pcode3(EndOfFile); JumpTo(ExitLabel, IfFalse)
            end;
        CreateItem(FelType^.Representation, BufferItem);
        SetItemShape(BufferItem, Field); SetItemCode(BufferItem, Field, Presets);
        AppendManual(PresetList, BufferItem); LoadFileReference;
        FieldReference(BufferOffset, false);
        if not TextFile then IndirectReference(false);
        OpenWith(FrameLevel); PresetManuals(FrameLevel, PresetList); CloseWith
      end;
    DisposeManuals(PresetList); NextIsCodeLabel(ExitLabel)
  end { postsetbuffer };
procedure DoFileChecks {FileOp: StdProcFuncs};
  begin
    case FileOp of
      Resetp :
        begin FileVariableCheck(Resetp); CheckLockedFile end;
      Rewritep : CheckLockedFile;
      Getp, Readp, Readlnp :
        begin
          FileVariableCheck(FileOp); FileModeCheck(Inspection);
          FilePositionCheck(FileOp); CheckLockedFile
        end;
      Putp, Pagep, Writep, Writelnp :
        begin
          FileVariableCheck(FileOp); FileModeCheck(Generation);
          if FileOp = Putp then CheckUndefinedBuffer;
          CheckLockedFile
        end;
      Eoff : FileVariableCheck(Eoff);
      Eolnf :
        begin FileVariableCheck(Eolnf); FilePositionCheck(Eolnf) end
    end
  end { dofilechecks };
{
```

21.3 Input/Output Operations

The following procedures generate code for all standard I/O procedures. For text files binary/decimal conversion is carried out by the appropriate P-codes. For non-text files read(f, v) is treated as:

> v := f^; get(f))

and write(f, v) as:

> f^ := v; put(f)

The procedure WriteLayout is used to generate appropriate P-codes for both page and writeln, depending upon an implicitly stacked format control value. The functions eolnf and eof are implemented by calls to FileFunction, with code generation being delayed until the expression value is required.

```
}
procedure FileOperation {Which: StdProcFuncs};
   begin
      if CodeIsToBeGenerated
      then begin
              if Checks in Requested then DoFileChecks(Which);
              case Which of
                 Resetp : begin LoadFileAddress; Pcode3(ResetFile) end;
                 Rewritep : begin LoadFileAddress; Pcode3(RewriteFile) end;
                 Getp : begin LoadFileDescriptor; Pcode3(GetFile) end;
                 Putp : begin LoadFileDescriptor; Pcode3(PutFile) end
              end;
              if Checks in Requested then PostsetBuffer(Which)
           end
   end { fileoperation };
procedure ReadBuffer;
   begin
      if CodeIsToBeGenerated
      then with SelectedFile^ do
              begin
                 LoadFileReference;
                 with FileType^ do
                    begin
                       BufferReference(PackedFile, TextFile, FelType^.Representation);
                       DeReference(FelType^.Representation)
                    end;
                 { buffer postset performed by subsequent get }
              end
   end { readbuffer };
procedure WriteBuffer;
   var Expression: StackEntry;
   begin
      if CodeIsToBeGenerated
```

```
        then with SelectedFile^ do
                begin
                    Pop(Expression);
                    if Checks in Requested then SelectCheck(Expression, 18);
                    with FileType^ do
                        begin
                            LoadFileReference;
                            BufferReference(PackedFile, false, FelType^.Representation);
                            Push(Expression); Assign(FelType^.Representation)
                        end;
                    { buffer postset performed by subsequent put }
                end
    end { writebuffer };
procedure ReadNumeric {ReadMode: InputKind};
    var ReadEntry: StackEntry;
    begin
        if CodeIsToBeGenerated
        then begin
                GetEntry(ReadEntry);
                with ReadEntry^ do
                    begin
                        Kind := Operation; OpForm := ReadOp; Mode := ReadMode;
                        case ReadMode of
                            IntKind : DataRep := IntegerRepresentation;
                            RealKind : DataRep := RealRepresentation
                        end
                    end;
                Push(ReadEntry)
            end
    end { readnumeric };
procedure WriteScalars {WriteMode: OutputKind; Format: FormatKind};
    var Expression, TotalWidth, FracDigits: StackEntry;
    begin
        if CodeIsToBeGenerated
        then begin
                if Format = Fixed
                then begin CheckRange(1, MCMaxint, 58); Pop(FracDigits) end;
                if Format <> Default
                then begin CheckRange(1, MCMaxint, 58); Pop(TotalWidth) end
                else begin
                        new(TotalWidth); TotalWidth^ := DefaultWidth^;
                        if WriteMode = CharKind then TotalWidth^.TheConst.Ival := 1
                    end;
                Pop(Expression);
                if Checks in Requested then DoFileChecks(Writep);
                Load(Expression); Load(TotalWidth);
                if Format = Fixed then Load(FracDigits);
                LoadFileDescriptor;
```

```
            case WriteMode of
              IntKind : Pcode3(WriteInteger);
              RealKind :
                if Format = Fixed
                then Pcode3(WriteFixedReal) else Pcode3(WriteFloatedReal);
              CharKind : Pcode3(WriteCharacter);
              BoolKind : Pcode3(WriteBoolean);
              StringKind, DefaultKind :
            end;
            if Checks in Requested then PostsetBuffer(Writep);
            if Format = Fixed then FreeEntry(FracDigits);
            FreeEntry(TotalWidth); FreeEntry(Expression)
          end
  end { writescalars };
procedure WriteString {ActualLength: ObjectValue; Format: FormatKind};

  var Expression, TotalWidth: StackEntry; StringSize: MCScalar;

  begin
    if CodeIsToBeGenerated
    then begin
          if Format = Default then StackConstant(ActualLength);
          CheckRange(1, MCMaxint, 58); Pop(TotalWidth); Pop(Expression);
          if Checks in Requested then DoFileChecks(Writep);
          StringSize := ActualLength.Ival;
          if StringSize > MCBytesPerWord
          then LoadAddress(Expression) else Load(Expression);
          InlineNumber(StringSize); Load(TotalWidth); LoadFileDescriptor;
          Pcode3(WriteCString);
          if Checks in Requested then PostsetBuffer(Writep);
          FreeEntry(Expression); FreeEntry(TotalWidth)
        end
  end { writestring };
procedure ReadLayout;

  begin
    if CodeIsToBeGenerated
    then begin
          if Checks in Requested then DoFileChecks(Readlnp);
          LoadFileDescriptor; Pcode3(ReadLine);
          if Checks in Requested then PostsetBuffer(Readlnp)
        end
  end { readlayout };
procedure WriteLayout;

  var Formatter: StackEntry;

  begin
    if CodeIsToBeGenerated
    then begin
          Pop(Formatter);
          if Checks in Requested then DoFileChecks(Writelnp);
```

```
                LoadFileDescriptor;
                with Formatter^ do
                  if SameValue(TheConst, LineFeed)
                  then Pcode3(WriteLine) else Pcode3(PageFile);
                if Checks in Requested then PostsetBuffer(Writelnp);
                FreeEntry(Formatter)
              end
      end { writelayout };
procedure FileFunction {WhichFunc: StdProcFuncs};
  var FuncEntry: StackEntry;
  begin
    if CodeIsToBeGenerated
    then begin
          GetEntry(FuncEntry);
          with FuncEntry^ do
            begin
              DataRep := BooleanRepresentation; Kind := Operation;
              OpGroup := AFile; OpForm := Standard; StdOp := WhichFunc;
              SaveFile(IOEntry)
            end;
          Push(FuncEntry)
        end
  end { filefunction };
{
```

21.4 Pack and Unpack

The Model Compiler allows pack and unpack operations to be performed between conformant as well as ordinary arrays. In general, given:

    a: array [lu..hu] of T;
    z: packed array [lp..hp] of T;

either transfer operation must be checked to verify that no element of the source array is undefined, and that the indexing expression satisfies:

    lu <=i<= hu   (errors D26, D29)
          i<= hu - (hp-lp)   (errors D28, D31)

If neither array is conformant, the parameters to these range checks are known at compile-time. If either or both arrays are conformant, code is generated to access the bounds from the bound-pair blocks. These checks are generated in the usual way by post-fixing a range-checking operator to the index expression-tree.

Special P-codes are used by the P-machine to perform the transfer operation. If runtime checks have been selected, variants of these P-codes are employed which additionally check for undefined source elements using the CheckValue extracted from the source array TypeRepresentation.

}

```
procedure LoadCAPEls(BoundPairBlock: RuntimeAddress);
  begin
    with BoundPairBlock do
      begin
        AccessWord(BlockLevel, WordOffset + 1, LoadOp);
        AccessWord(BlockLevel, WordOffset, LoadOp);
      end;
    Pcode0(SubInteger); Pcode0(Inc1)
  end { loadcapels };
procedure LoadCAPSize {ForPackedCAP: Boolean; BoundPairBlock: RuntimeAddress};
  begin
    with BoundPairBlock do
      if ForPackedCAP
      then AccessWord(BlockLevel, WordOffset + 2, LoadOp)
      else begin AccessWord(BlockLevel, WordOffset, LoadRefOp); Pcode0(SizeCAP) end
  end { loadcapsize };
procedure EmitTransfer(Which: StdProcFuncs; ElementsPerWord: MCBitRange);
  var Instruction: Pcodes;
  begin
    Instruction := TransferCodes[Checks in Requested, Which = Unpackp];
    Pcode4(Instruction, ElementsPerWord)
  end { emittransfer };
function ConstantIndex: Boolean;
  begin with TopStackEntry^ do ConstantIndex := Kind = AConstant end;
procedure ArrayArrayOp {Which: StdProcFuncs;
                        UpLowBound, UpHighBound: ObjectValue;
                        UnpackedRep, PackedRep: TypeRepresentation;
                        PkLowBound,PkHighBound: ObjectValue};
  var PackedBase, UnpackedBase: StackEntry; PackedEls: MCScalar;
      Convertible, ConstIndex: Boolean; ElsPerWord: 2..MCBitsPerWord;
  begin
    if CodeIsToBeGenerated
    then begin
         if Which = Packp then Pop(PackedBase);
         PackedEls := PkHighBound.Ival - PkLowBound.Ival + 1;
         if ConstantIndex
         then begin
              CheckRange
                (UpLowBound.Ival, UpHighBound.Ival,
                 26 + 3 * ord(Which = Unpackp));
              CheckRange
                (-MCMaxint, UpHighBound.Ival - PackedEls + 1,
                 28 + 3 * ord(Which = Unpackp));
              ConstIndex := true
              end
         else ConstIndex := false;
```

```
        with PackedRep do
          if WordSize > 1
          then Convertible := false
          else Convertible := (BitSize <= MCBitsPerWord div 2);
        if CodeIsToBeGenerated
        then begin
                IndexedReference(false, UpLowBound, UpHighBound, UnpackedRep);
                Pop(UnpackedBase);
                if (Checks in Requested) and (not ConstIndex)
                then with UnpackedBase^.Indices^ do
                        begin
                          SelectCheck(TheIndex, 26 + 3 * ord(Which = Unpackp));
                          Push(TheIndex);
                          CheckRange
                            (-MCMaxint, UpHighBound.Ival - PackedEls + 1, 1);
                          Pop(TheIndex);
                          SelectCheck(TheIndex, 28 + 3 * ord(Which = Unpackp))
                        end;
                if Which = Unpackp then Pop(PackedBase);
                if Convertible
                then begin
                        LoadAddress(UnpackedBase); LoadAddress(PackedBase);
                        InlineNumber(PackedEls);
                        ElsPerWord := MCBitsPerWord div PackedRep.BitSize;
                        if (Which = Unpackp) and (Checks in Requested)
                        then InlineNumber(PackedRep.CheckValue.Magnitude);
                        EmitTransfer(Which, ElsPerWord)
                     end
                else begin
                        if Which = Packp
                        then LoadAddress(UnpackedBase)
                        else LoadAddress(PackedBase);
                        if Which = Packp
                        then LoadAddress(PackedBase)
                        else LoadAddress(UnpackedBase);
                        Pcode1(Move, PackedEls * PackedRep.WordSize)
                     end;
                FreeEntry(UnpackedBase); FreeEntry(PackedBase)
             end
        end
    end { arrayarrayop };
procedure CheckArrayCAPTransfer(LowBound, HighBound: MCIntegerForm;
                                CAPBpAddress: RuntimeAddress);

  var IndexEntry, CheckedEntry: StackEntry; IndexRange, LimitedRange: RangeEntry;
  begin
    Pop(IndexEntry); new(IndexRange);
    with IndexRange^ do
      begin Lower := LowBound; Upper := HighBound; CAPBounds := false end;
```

```
      new(LimitedRange);
      with LimitedRange^ do
         begin CAPBounds := true; BpAddress := CAPBpAddress end;
      GetEntry(CheckedEntry);
      with CheckedEntry^ do
         begin
            RunError := 1; DataRep.Min := IndexEntry^.DataRep.Min;
            DataRep.Max := IndexEntry^.DataRep.Max; Kind := Operation;
            OpGroup := AnInteger; OpForm := RangeChk; CheckKind := TransferChecks;
            RequiredRange := IndexRange; TransferRange := LimitedRange;
            EntryToCheck := IndexEntry
         end;
      Push(CheckedEntry)
   end { checkarraycaptransfer };
procedure ArrayCAPOp {Which: StdProcFuncs;
                        UpLowBound, UpHighBound: ObjectValue;
                        UnpackedRep, PackedRep: TypeRepresentation;
                        PkLowBoundAddress, PkHighBoundAddress: RuntimeAddress};
   { The parameter PkHighBoundAddress is not used in this implementation. }
   var CAPPackedBase, UnpackedBase, IndexEntry: StackEntry; Convertible: Boolean;
      ElsPerWord: 2..MCBitsPerWord;
begin
   if CodeIsToBeGenerated
   then begin
         if Which = Packp then Pop(CAPPackedBase);
         if ConstantIndex
         then begin
               Pop(IndexEntry); Load(IndexEntry); SaveValue(IndexEntry);
               Push(IndexEntry)
            end;
         with PackedRep do
            if WordSize > 1
            then Convertible := false
            else Convertible := (BitSize <= MCBitsPerWord div 2);
         IndexedReference(false, UpLowBound, UpHighBound, UnpackedRep);
         Pop(UnpackedBase);
         if (Checks in Requested)
         then with UnpackedBase^.Indices^ do
                  begin
                     SelectCheck(TheIndex, 26 + 3 * ord(Which = Unpackp));
                     Push(TheIndex);
                     CheckArrayCAPTransfer
                        (-MCMaxint, UpHighBound.Ival, PkLowBoundAddress);
                     Pop(TheIndex);
                     SelectCheck(TheIndex, 28 + 3 * ord(Which = Unpackp))
                  end;
         if Which = Unpackp then Pop(CAPPackedBase);
```

```
                    if Convertible
                    then begin
                            LoadAddress(UnpackedBase); LoadAddress(CAPPackedBase);
                            LoadCAPEls(PkLowBoundAddress);
                            ElsPerWord := MCBitsPerWord div PackedRep.BitSize;
                            if (Which = Unpackp) and (Checks in Requested)
                            then InlineNumber(PackedRep.CheckValue.Magnitude);
                            EmitTransfer(Which, ElsPerWord)
                         end
                    else begin
                            if Which = Packp
                            then LoadAddress(UnpackedBase) else LoadAddress(CAPPackedBase);
                            LoadCAPSize(true, PkLowBoundAddress);
                            if Which = Packp
                            then LoadAddress(CAPPackedBase) else LoadAddress(UnpackedBase);
                            Pcode0(MoveCAP)
                         end;
                    FreeEntry(CAPPackedBase); FreeEntry(UnpackedBase)
                 end
    end { arraycapop };
procedure CheckCAPArrayTransfer(CAPBpAddress: RuntimeAddress;
                                LowBound, HighBound: MCIntegerForm);
    var IndexEntry, CheckedEntry: StackEntry; IndexRange, LimitedRange: RangeEntry;
    begin
       Pop(IndexEntry); new(IndexRange);
       with IndexRange^ do
         begin CAPBounds := true; BpAddress := CAPBpAddress end;
       new(LimitedRange);
       with LimitedRange^ do
         begin Lower := LowBound; Upper := HighBound; CAPBounds := false end;
       GetEntry(CheckedEntry);
       with CheckedEntry^ do
         begin
           RunError := 1; DataRep.Min := IndexEntry^.DataRep.Min;
           DataRep.Max := IndexEntry^.DataRep.Max; Kind := Operation;
           OpGroup := AnInteger; OpForm := RangeChk; CheckKind := TransferChecks;
           RequiredRange := IndexRange; TransferRange := LimitedRange;
           EntryToCheck := IndexEntry
         end;
       Push(CheckedEntry)
    end { checkcaparrraytransfer };
procedure CAPArrayOp {Which: StdProcFuncs;
                      UpLowBoundAddress, UpHighBoundAddress: RuntimeAddress;
                      BpRep, UnpackedRep, PackedRep: TypeRepresentation;
                      PkLowBound, PkHighBound: ObjectValue };
    var PackedBase, CAPUnpackedBase: StackEntry; Convertible: Boolean;
        PackedEls: MCScalar; ElsPerWord: 2..MCBitsPerWord;
```

```
    begin
      if CodeIsToBeGenerated
      then begin
            if Which = Packp then Pop(PackedBase);
            PackedEls := PkHighBound.Ival - PkLowBound.Ival + 1;
            with PackedRep do
              if WordSize > 1
              then Convertible := false
              else Convertible := (BitSize <= MCBitsPerWord div 2);
            IndexedCAPReference
              (false, UpLowBoundAddress, UpHighBoundAddress, BpRep, UnpackedRep);
            Pop(CAPUnpackedBase);
            if Checks in Requested
            then with CAPUnpackedBase^.Indices^ do
                    begin
                      SelectCheck(TheIndex, 26 + 3 * ord(Which = Unpackp));
                      Push(TheIndex);
                      CheckCAPArrayTransfer
                        (UpLowBoundAddress, PkLowBound.Ival, PkHighBound.Ival);
                      Pop(TheIndex);
                      SelectCheck(TheIndex, 28 + 3 * ord(Which = Unpackp))
                    end;
            if Which = Unpackp then Pop(PackedBase);
            if Convertible
            then begin
                    LoadAddress(CAPUnpackedBase); LoadAddress(PackedBase);
                    InlineNumber(PackedEls);
                    ElsPerWord := MCBitsPerWord div PackedRep.BitSize;
                    if (Which = Unpackp) and (Checks in Requested)
                    then InlineNumber(PackedRep.CheckValue.Magnitude);
                    EmitTransfer(Which, ElsPerWord)
                  end
            else begin
                    if Which = Packp
                    then LoadAddress(CAPUnpackedBase) else LoadAddress(PackedBase);
                    if Which = Packp
                    then LoadAddress(PackedBase) else LoadAddress(CAPUnpackedBase);
                    Pcode1(Move, PackedEls * PackedRep.WordSize)
                  end;
            FreeEntry(PackedBase); FreeEntry(CAPUnpackedBase)
          end
    end { caparrayop };
procedure CheckCAPCAPTransfer(CAP1BpAddress, CAP2BpAddress: RuntimeAddress);
  var IndexEntry, CheckedEntry: StackEntry; IndexRange, LimitedRange: RangeEntry;
  begin
    Pop(IndexEntry); new(IndexRange);
    with IndexRange^ do
      begin CAPBounds := true; BpAddress := CAP1BpAddress end;
```

```
      new(LimitedRange);
      with LimitedRange^ do
         begin CAPBounds := true; BpAddress := CAP2BpAddress end;
      GetEntry(CheckedEntry);
      with CheckedEntry^ do
         begin
            RunError := 1; DataRep.Min := IndexEntry^.DataRep.Min;
            DataRep.Max := IndexEntry^.DataRep.Max; Kind := Operation;
            OpGroup := AnInteger; OpForm := RangeChk; CheckKind := TransferChecks;
            RequiredRange := IndexRange; TransferRange := LimitedRange;
            EntryToCheck := IndexEntry
         end;
      Push(CheckedEntry)
   end { checkcapcaptransfer };
procedure CAPCAPOp {Which: StdProcFuncs;
                    UpLowBoundAddress, UpHighBoundAddress: RuntimeAddress;
                    BpRep, UnpackedRep, PackedRep: TypeRepresentation;
                    PkLowBoundAddress, PkHighBoundAddress: RuntimeAddress };
   { The parameter PkHighBoundAddress is not used in this implementation. }
   var CAPPackedBase, CAPUnpackedBase: StackEntry; Convertible: Boolean;
      ElsPerWord: 2..MCBitsPerWord;

begin
   if CodeIsToBeGenerated
   then begin
         if Which = Packp then Pop(CAPPackedBase);
         with PackedRep do
            if WordSize > 1
            then Convertible := false
            else Convertible := (BitSize <= MCBitsPerWord div 2);
         IndexedCAPReference
            (false, UpLowBoundAddress, UpHighBoundAddress, BpRep, UnpackedRep);
         Pop(CAPUnpackedBase);
         if Checks in Requested
         then with CAPUnpackedBase^.Indices^ do
                  begin
                     SelectCheck(TheIndex, 26 + 3 * ord(Which = Unpackp));
                     Push(TheIndex);
                     CheckCAPCAPTransfer
                        (UpLowBoundAddress, PkLowBoundAddress);
                     Pop(TheIndex);
                     SelectCheck(TheIndex, 28 + 3 * ord(Which = Unpackp))
                  end;
         if Which = Unpackp then Pop(CAPPackedBase);
         if Convertible
         then begin
               LoadAddress(CAPUnpackedBase); LoadAddress(CAPPackedBase);
               LoadCAPEls(PkLowBoundAddress);
               ElsPerWord := MCBitsPerWord div PackedRep.BitSize;
```

```
                    if (Which = Unpackp) and (Checks in Requested)
                    then InlineNumber(PackedRep.CheckValue.Magnitude);
                    EmitTransfer(Which, ElsPerWord)
                end
            else begin
                    if Which = Packp
                    then LoadAddress(CAPUnpackedBase)
                    else LoadAddress(CAPPackedBase);
                    LoadCAPSize(true, PkLowBoundAddress);
                    if Which = Packp
                    then LoadAddress(CAPPackedBase)
                    else LoadAddress(CAPUnpackedBase);
                    Pcode0(MoveCAP)
                end;
            FreeEntry(CAPPackedBase); FreeEntry(CAPUnpackedBase)
        end
    end { capcapop };
{
```

21.5 New/Dispose

The parameters to new and dispose are saved in fields of the global record variable HPRequests by one call to the procedure HeapRecord and zero or more subsequent calls to procedure TailorRequest. The effect of these is to preserve a reference to the pointer variable, and to chain the initial and subsequent tailored requests for heap storage on a linear list referenced by fields FirstReq and LastReq of HPRequests. Note that since the storage required for a variant record is the sum of its fixed part and largest variant, a call new(p) will in general over-allocate heap storage for all but the largest variant. A call new(p, c) however, will tailor storage exactly, if the variant labelled by c has no nested variants. Such tailoring is secure only if subsequent checks are generated to ensure the tag field is never set to a value other than c, and that p^ is never referenced in an assignment statement, or used as a factor.

The checks for consistency between new and dispose are generated by presetting the selector fields to the appropriate values after storage has been allocated. In addition, the preselection flags are set in the control word of the record to indicate the variant selectors are effectively "locked". Code for these checks is generated by procedure PreSelectVariants. Corresponding code to verify a subsequent dispose is generated by procedure CheckPreselectedVariants.

The P-machine automatically presets newly allocated heap storage so that each word is initially "undefined". For domain types that require manual presetting via generated code, the procedure PresetHeap will pass a preset list containing a single heap-item to the code-generating procedure PresetManuals. Domain types containing embedded files are similarly processed by procedure PostSetHeap.

Security against the use of "dangling" or "undefined" pointers is provided by a method described by Fischer and Leblanc whereby a "key" is embedded by the P-machine in both the pointer-variable, and the dynamic variable. Every pointer reference is subsequently

checked to ensure the keys match. On a dispose, the P-machine garbage collector erases the
heap key and dangling pointers are subsequently detected by key mismatch. This technique
is not totally secure since the erased key location may coincidentally re-acquire the same
value as actual data after re-allocation, but the probability of this happening is very low.

```
}
procedure PreservePtrReference(HeapOp: StdProcFuncs);
   var Entry: StackEntry; ResultSize: WordRange;
   begin
      with HpRequests do
         begin
            if HeapOp = Disposep
            then begin
                     Pop(Entry);
                     case Entry^.Kind of
                       Reference :
                          begin
                            PointerEntry := Entry;
                            with PointerEntry^ do
                               begin RunError := 0; DataRep := DefaultRepresentation end
                          end;
                       AConstant :
                          begin
                            PredictedError(3); FreeEntry(Entry); GetReference(PointerEntry)
                          end;
                       Operation :
                          begin
                            Load(Entry); ResultSize := PointerRepresentation.WordSize;
                            GetReference(PointerEntry);
                            with PointerEntry^ do
                               begin
                                 Acquire(ResultSize, BaseAddress);
                                 with BaseAddress do
                                 if ResultSize = 1
                                 then AccessWord(BlockLevel, WordOffset, StoreOp)
                                 else begin
                                          AccessWord(BlockLevel, WordOffset, LoadRefOp);
                                          Pcode1(StoreMultiple, ResultSize)
                                      end
                               end;
                            FreeEntry(Entry)
                          end
                  end
              end
            else Pop(PointerEntry);
            if Checks in Requested then SaveAddress(PointerEntry)
         end
   end { preserveptrreference };
```

```
procedure LoadPtrReference;
  var PtrEntry: StackEntry;
  begin
    GetEntry(PtrEntry); PtrEntry^ := HpRequests.PointerEntry^;
    if PtrEntry^.Kind = Address then PushNewAccess(PtrEntry, false);
    Push(PtrEntry)
  end { loadptrreference };
procedure LoadPtrAddress;
  var PtrEntry: StackEntry;
  begin
    LoadPtrReference; Pop(PtrEntry); LoadAddress(PtrEntry); FreeEntry(PtrEntry)
  end { loadptrentry };
procedure CheckDispose;
  begin
    with HpRequests do
      begin
        LoadPtrAddress; Pcode0(LoadPointer);
        if LastReq^.ReqLevel > 0
        then Pcode1(CheckDsp2, LastReq^.ReqLevel) else Pcode0(CheckDsp1)
      end
  end { checkdispose };
procedure CheckPreselectedVariants;
  var ThisReq: RequestEntry; SelectorEntry: StackEntry;
  begin
    with HpRequests do
      if FirstReq <> LastReq
      then begin
             ThisReq := FirstReq;
             repeat
               ThisReq := ThisReq^.Next;
               with ThisReq^ do
                 begin
                   LoadPtrReference; IndirectReference(false);
                   FieldReference(SelectorField, false); Pop(SelectorEntry);
                   Load(SelectorEntry); FreeEntry(SelectorEntry);
                   InlineNumber(SelectorValue); Pcode0(TestIEqual);
                   Pcode1(TrapIfFalse, 22)
                 end
             until ThisReq = LastReq
           end
  end { checkpreselectedvariants };
```

```
procedure PreselectVariants;
  var ThisReq: RequestEntry; CheckValue: ObjectValue; LockSettings: MCWordForm;
  procedure LoadFirstWord;
    var PtrEntry: StackEntry;
    begin
      LoadPtrReference; Pop(PtrEntry); PtrEntry^.DataRep.WordSize := 1;
      Load(PtrEntry); FreeEntry(PtrEntry)
    end { loadfirstword };
  begin
    with HpRequests do
      if FirstReq <> LastReq
      then begin
             LockSettings.WValue := 0; ThisReq := FirstReq;
             repeat
               ThisReq := ThisReq^.Next;
               with ThisReq^ do
                 begin
                   LoadPtrReference; IndirectReference(false);
                   FieldReference(SelectorField, false);
                   SetIval(SelectorValue, CheckValue); StackConstant(CheckValue);
                   Assign(IntegerRepresentation);
                   MCSetBit(LockSettings, 3 * ReqLevel - 2)
                 end
             until ThisReq = LastReq;
             { store preselection locks }
             InlineNumber(LockSettings.WValue); LoadFirstWord; Pcode0(StoreIndirect);
             { store request levels }
             InlineNumber(LastReq^.ReqLevel); LoadFirstWord; Pcode1(AdjustMinus, 2);
             Pcode0(StoreIndirect)
           end
  end { preselectvariants };

procedure PostsetHeap;
  var PostsetList: ManualList; HeapItem: ManualEntry;
  begin
    StartManuals(PostsetList);
    with HpRequests do
      begin
        CreateItem(FirstReq^.Request, HeapItem); SetItemShape(HeapItem, Vars);
        SetItemCode(HeapItem, Vars, Postsets); AppendManual(PostsetList, HeapItem);
        if HeapItem^.ItsCode <> None
        then begin
               LoadPtrReference; IndirectReference(false); OpenWith(FrameLevel);
               PostsetManuals(FrameLevel, PostsetList); CloseWith
             end
      end;
    DisposeManuals(PostsetList)
  end { postsetheap };
```

```
procedure PresetHeap;
  var PresetList: ManualList; HeapItem: ManualEntry;
  begin
    StartManuals(PresetList);
    with HpRequests do
      begin
        CreateItem(FirstReq^.Request, HeapItem); SetItemShape(HeapItem, Vars);
        SetItemCode(HeapItem, Vars, Presets); AppendManual(PresetList, HeapItem);
        if HeapItem^.ItsCode <> None
        then begin
              LoadPtrReference; IndirectReference(false); OpenWith(FrameLevel);
              PresetManuals(FrameLevel, PresetList); CloseWith
            end
      end;
    DisposeManuals(PresetList)
  end { presetheap };
procedure HeapRequest {Requested: TypeRepresentation};
  var ThisReq: RequestEntry;
  begin
    if CodeIsToBeGenerated
    then begin
          new(ThisReq);
          with ThisReq^ do
            begin Next := nil; Request := Requested; ReqLevel := 0 end;
          with HpRequests do
            begin FirstReq := ThisReq; LastReq := ThisReq end
        end
  end { heaprequest };
procedure TailorRequest {SelectorRep, SelectedRep: TypeRepresentation};
  var ThisReq: RequestEntry;
  begin
    if CodeIsToBeGenerated
    then with HpRequests do
          begin
            new(ThisReq);
            with ThisReq^ do
              begin
                Next := nil; Request := SelectedRep;
                ReqLevel := LastReq^.ReqLevel + 1;
                SelectorValue := SelectedRep.CheckValue.Magnitude;
                SelectorField := SelectorRep.Selector
              end;
            LastReq^.Next := ThisReq; LastReq := ThisReq
          end
  end { tailorrequest };
```

```
procedure HeapOperation {WhichPf: StdProcFuncs};
   var Amount: WordRange; ThisReq: RequestEntry;
  begin
    if CodeIsToBeGenerated
    then with HpRequests do
          begin
            PreservePtrReference(WhichPf);
            if (WhichPf = Disposep) and (Checks in Requested)
            then begin CheckDispose; CheckPreselectedVariants; PostsetHeap end;
            LoadPtrAddress; Amount := LastReq^.Request.WordSize;
            if WhichPf = Newp
            then Pcode1(New1, Amount) else Pcode1(Dispose1, Amount);
            if (WhichPf = Newp) and (Checks in Requested)
            then begin PresetHeap; PreselectVariants end;

            { now discard the requests }
            while FirstReq <> nil do
              begin
                ThisReq := FirstReq; FirstReq := ThisReq^.Next; dispose(ThisReq)
              end;
            FreeEntry(PointerEntry)
          end
  end { heapoperation };
```

{

CHAPTER 22

Code Generation
for
Control Structures

This chapter implements the interface procedures for the generation of control structures as defined in Section 5.10.

22.1 Code Labels and Jumps

The representation of code labels, the nature of jump instructions on the P-machine, and the fix-up mechanism used for forward jumps, were defined in Chapter 18. Using these, the interface procedures that bind code labels to corresponding points in the generated code stream, and generate the conditional and unconditional jumps required for basic control operations, are easily implemented as follows:

}

```
procedure NewCodeLabel {var L: CodeLabel};
  begin
    with L do
      begin Linked := false; Expected := false; Address := CodeCounter end
  end { newcodelabel };
procedure FutureCodeLabel {var L: CodeLabel};
  begin
    with L do
      begin Linked := false; Expected := true; LastReference := nil end
  end { futurecodelabel };
procedure NextIsCodeLabel {var L: CodeLabel};
  begin
    FixUpJumps(L, CodeCounter);
    with L do
      begin Expected := false; Address := CodeCounter end
  end { nextiscodelabel };
```

```
procedure JumpOnFalse {var Destination: CodeLabel};
   var BooleanEntry: StackEntry;
   begin
      if CodeIsToBeGenerated
      then begin
             Pop(BooleanEntry);
             with BooleanEntry^ do
                if Kind = AConstant
                then if TheConst.Ival = ord(true)
                      then { do nothing }
                      else JumpTo(Destination, Absolute)
                else begin Load(BooleanEntry); JumpTo(Destination, IfFalse) end;
             FreeEntry(BooleanEntry)
          end
   end { jumponfalse };
procedure Jump {var Destination: CodeLabel};
   begin if CodeIsToBeGenerated then JumpTo(Destination, Absolute) end;

{
```

22.2 Code Generation for Case Statements

For simple one-pass compilation, all case selection code is generated after the code for the case limbs involved. OpenCase, therefore, merely generates an unconditional jump to a future codelabel which is pushed with the selector expression onto a stack of case (statement) records to be recovered by the corresponding CloseCase.

During analysis of the case limbs the topmost case entry acts as the head of an ordered list of case label entries built by the sequence of call to NextIsCase. The case label entries record the code offset of the case limb corresponding to each case label in ascending case label order.

This list, together with the selector expression tree, enables the procedure CloseCase to generate the necessary case selection code. However, because the Pascal standard allows no limits to be imposed on the range of case labels involved, a simple jump table cannot always be used for case selection. CloseCase therefore partitions the ordered list of case label entries into a sequence of one or more sublists, each of which is suitable for selection through a corresponding sub-table. The maximum gap allowed between consecutive label entries in a subtable is chosen to minimise the overall code length that results.

This set of subtables is then built into a binary decision tree, by the function BuildTree, to enable the necessary subtable to be located by the minimum number of $<=$ tests on the selector value. The recursive procedure EmitCaseCode is then applied to this decision tree to generate the combination of comparisons and table-driven case jumps required. Note that subtables consisting of single case labels may arise and need special treatment to obtain acceptable selection code.

The procedure InitCase initialises the stack of case statement records during code generation initialisation.

```
}
procedure OpenCase;
  var ThisCase: CaseEntry;
  begin
    if CodeIsToBeGenerated
    then begin
            new(ThisCase);
            with ThisCase^ do
              begin
                Pop(Selector); FutureCodeLabel(CaseCode);
                JumpTo(CaseCode, Absolute); MinLabel := nil; MaxLabel := nil;
                Next := TopCaseEntry
              end;
            TopCaseEntry := ThisCase
         end
  end { opencase };
procedure NextIsCase {CaseConst: ObjectValue};
  label 9;
  var PreviousLabel, ThisLabel, FollowingLabel: CaseLabelEntry;
      NewLabel: MCIntegerForm;
  begin
    if CodeIsToBeGenerated
    then begin
            NewLabel := CaseConst.Ival; new(ThisLabel);
            with ThisLabel^ do
              begin
                LabelValue := NewLabel; LimbAddress := CodeCounter;
                NextLabel := nil
              end;
            with TopCaseEntry^ do
              begin
                if MinLabel = nil
                then begin MinLabel := ThisLabel; MaxLabel := ThisLabel end
                else begin
                        PreviousLabel := nil; FollowingLabel := MinLabel;
                        while FollowingLabel <> nil do
                          begin
                            if FollowingLabel^.LabelValue > NewLabel then goto 9;
                            PreviousLabel := FollowingLabel;
                            FollowingLabel := FollowingLabel^.NextLabel
                          end;
                        9:
                          if PreviousLabel = nil
                          then begin
                                  ThisLabel^.NextLabel := MinLabel;
                                  MinLabel := ThisLabel
                               end
```

```
                          else begin
                              ThisLabel^.NextLabel := FollowingLabel;
                              PreviousLabel^.NextLabel := ThisLabel;
                              if NewLabel >= MaxLabel^.LabelValue
                              then MaxLabel := ThisLabel
                          end
                  end
           end
       end
   end { nextiscase };
procedure CloseCase;
   type DecPtr = ^Decision;
       DecList = record First, Last: DecPtr; Length: Scalar end;
       DecKinds = (Test, Table);
       Decision =
           record
              NextInList: DecPtr;
              case Kind: DecKinds of
                 Test: (TestValue: MCIntegerForm; LePath, GtPath: DecPtr);
                 Table: (MinLabel, MaxLabel: CaseLabelEntry)
           end;
   var ThisCase: CaseEntry; SubCases: DecList; DecisionTree: DecPtr;
       TrapNeeded: Boolean;
   procedure Start(var List: DecList);
      begin with List do begin First := nil; Last := nil; Length := 0 end end;
   procedure Append(var List: DecList; Dec: DecPtr);
      begin
         with List do
            begin
               if First = nil then First := Dec else Last^.NextInList := Dec;
               Last := Dec; Last^.NextInList := nil; Length := Length + 1
            end
      end { append };
   procedure Remove(var List: DecList; var Dec: DecPtr);
      begin
         with List do
            begin
               Dec := First; First := Dec^.NextInList; Dec^.NextInList := nil;
               Length := Length - 1
            end
      end { remove };
   function SingleCase(DecNode: DecPtr): Boolean;
      begin
         with DecNode^ do
            if Kind <> Table
            then SingleCase := false else SingleCase := (MinLabel^.NextLabel = nil)
      end { singlecase };
```

```
function LabelGap(MinLab, MaxLab: MCIntegerForm): MCIntegerForm;
  var Finite: Boolean;
  begin
    if MaxLab < 0 then Finite := true else Finite := (MaxLab - maxint) < MinLab;
    if Finite then LabelGap := MaxLab - MinLab else LabelGap := maxint
  end { LabelGap };
procedure PartitionCases(LabelList: CaseLabelEntry; var TableList: DecList);
  var NextOne, ThisLabel: CaseLabelEntry; SubTable: DecPtr; MaxFound: Boolean;
  begin
    Start(TableList); ThisLabel := LabelList;
    while ThisLabel <> nil do
      begin
        new(SubTable);
        with SubTable^ do
          begin Kind := Table; MinLabel := ThisLabel end;
        MaxFound := false; NextOne := ThisLabel^.NextLabel;
          while (NextOne <> nil) and not MaxFound do
          if LabelGap(ThisLabel^.LabelValue, NextOne^.LabelValue) > MaxCaseGap
          then MaxFound := true
          else begin ThisLabel := NextOne; NextOne := ThisLabel^.NextLabel end;
          with ThisLabel^ do
          begin NextLabel := nil; SubTable^.MaxLabel := ThisLabel end;
        Append(TableList, SubTable); ThisLabel := NextOne
      end;
    TrapNeeded := SingleCase(SubTable)
  end { partitioncases };
function BuildTree(List: DecList): DecPtr;
  var SubList: DecList; SubTest, LastDec: DecPtr;
  function MaxValue(Dec: DecPtr): MCIntegerForm;
    begin
      with Dec^ do
        if Kind = Table
        then MaxValue := MaxLabel^.LabelValue
        else MaxValue := MaxValue(GtPath)
    end { maxvalue };
  begin { buildtree }
    if List.Length = 1
    then BuildTree := List.First
    else begin
            Start(SubList);
            while List.Length > 1 do
              begin
                new(SubTest);
                with SubTest^ do
                  begin
                    Kind := Test; Remove(List, LePath); Remove(List, GtPath);
```

```
                    TestValue := MaxValue(LePath)
                end;
            Append(SubList, SubTest)
          end;
        if List.Length <> 0
        then begin Remove(List, LastDec); Append(SubList, LastDec) end;
        BuildTree := BuildTree(SubList)
      end
  end { buildtree };
procedure EmitCaseCode(DecNode: DecPtr);
  var FailLabel: CodeLabel; CaseLabel, ThisLabel: CaseLabelEntry;
      LabelIndex: MCIntegerForm;
  procedure JumpToLimb(Destination: CodeByteRange; Condition: JumpType);
    var LimbLabel: CodeLabel;
    begin
      with LimbLabel do
        begin Linked := false; Expected := false; Address := Destination end;
      JumpTo(LimbLabel, Condition)
    end { jumptolimb };
  procedure TableWord(Datum: MCIntegerForm);
    var Buffer: MCWordForm;
    begin Buffer.WValue := Datum; WordOfBytes(Buffer) end { tableword };
  begin { emitcasecode }
    with DecNode^ do
      case Kind of
        Test :
          begin
            FutureCodeLabel(FailLabel);
            if not SingleCase(LePath)
            then begin
                LoadValue(TopCaseEntry^.Selector); InlineNumber(TestValue);
                Pcode0(TestILtOrEqual); JumpTo(FailLabel, IfFalse)
              end;
            EmitCaseCode(LePath); NextIsCodeLabel(FailLabel);
            EmitCaseCode(GtPath); dispose(LePath); dispose(GtPath)
          end;
        Table :
          begin
            LoadValue(TopCaseEntry^.Selector);
            if SingleCase(DecNode)
            then begin
                InlineNumber(MinLabel^.LabelValue); Pcode0(TestIUnequal);
                JumpToLimb(MinLabel^.LimbAddress, IfFalse)
              end
            else begin
                Pcode0(CaseJump); Align; TableWord(MinLabel^.LabelValue);
                TableWord(MaxLabel^.LabelValue); CaseLabel := MinLabel;
```

```
            for LabelIndex :=
                    MinLabel^.LabelValue to MaxLabel^.LabelValue do
            if LabelIndex = CaseLabel^.LabelValue
            then begin
                    TableWord(CaseLabel^.LimbAddress - CodeCounter);
                    ThisLabel := CaseLabel;
                    CaseLabel := CaseLabel^.NextLabel; dispose(ThisLabel)
                end
            else TableWord(0)
        end
      end
    end
  end { emitcasecode };
begin { closecase }
  if CodeIsToBeGenerated
  then begin
        with TopCaseEntry^ do
          begin
            NextIsCodeLabel(CaseCode); PartitionCases(MinLabel, SubCases);
            DecisionTree := BuildTree(SubCases);
            if not ((Selector^.Kind = AConstant) or SimpleReference(Selector))
            then begin Load(Selector); SaveValue(Selector) end;
            EmitCaseCode(DecisionTree);
            if TrapNeeded then Pcode1(TrapError, 51);
            dispose(DecisionTree); FreeEntry(Selector)
          end;
        ThisCase := TopCaseEntry; TopCaseEntry := TopCaseEntry^.Next;
        dispose(ThisCase)
      end
  end { closecase };
procedure InitCase;
  begin TopCaseEntry := nil end;
{
```

22.3 Code Generation for For-Statements

Entry and exit code sequences for for-statements are generated by procedures OpenFor and
CloseFor and communication between these two phases is achieved by embedding all necessary information in the fields of a ForRecord. Nested for-statements are handled by building
a stack of such records referenced by the variable TopForEntry.

This version of the Model Compiler generates minimal entry sequences by:

(1) Exploiting the results of range-analysis to eliminate the entry-check and assignment
     compatibility range-checks wherever possible.

(2) Exploiting the fact that range-checks are only necessary when the for-loop is entered to
     reduce each check to a single test with the appropriate limit for the initial or final
     expressions. These are performed by P-codes CheckForLower and CheckForUpper.

Minimal exit code sequences are generated by ensuring the final control variable value is available as a known constant, or by direct reference to a temporary storage location containing the value. The P-codes Inc1 and Dec1 are used to increment or decrement the control variable accordingly. Prior to exiting then for-statement, extra code is generated when checks have been selected, to postset the control variable to "undefined".
}

```
procedure OpenFor {Increasing: Boolean; ControlMin, ControlMax: ObjectValue};
  type LimitKinds = (Lower, Upper);
  var ThisFor: ForEntry; InitialEntry: StackEntry;
      EntryCode: (NoneNeeded, TestNeeded, JumpNeeded);
  function SimplyAccessed(Entry: StackEntry): Boolean;
    begin SimplyAccessed := (Entry^.Kind = AConstant) or SimpleReference(Entry) end;
  procedure CheckEntryCode(Low, High: StackEntry);
    begin
      if Increasing
      then if Low^.DataRep.Min > High^.DataRep.Max
          then EntryCode := JumpNeeded
          else if Low^.DataRep.Max > High^.DataRep.Min
              then EntryCode := TestNeeded else EntryCode := NoneNeeded
      else if Low^.DataRep.Max < High^.DataRep.Min
          then EntryCode := JumpNeeded
          else if Low^.DataRep.Min < High^.DataRep.Max
              then EntryCode := TestNeeded else EntryCode := NoneNeeded
    end { CheckEntryCode };
  procedure CheckLimit(Limit: StackEntry; Kind: LimitKinds; Error: Scalar);
    begin
      if Kind = Upper
      then begin
              if (ControlMax.Ival < Limit^.DataRep.Min)
              then PredictedError(Error)
              else if (ControlMax.Ival < Limit^.DataRep.Max)
                  then begin
                          LoadValue(Limit); InlineNumber(ControlMax.Ival);
                          Pcode1(CheckForUpper, Error)
                       end
          end
      else begin
              if (Limit^.DataRep.Max < ControlMin.Ival)
              then PredictedError(Error)
              else if (Limit^.DataRep.Min < ControlMin.Ival)
                  then begin
                          LoadValue(Limit); InlineNumber(ControlMin.Ival);
                          Pcode1(CheckForLower, Error)
                       end
          end
    end { checklimit };
```

```
begin { openfor }
  if CodeIsToBeGenerated
  then begin
          new(ThisFor);
          with ThisFor^ do
            begin
              Incrementing := Increasing; Pop(FinalEntry); Pop(InitialEntry);
              Pop(ControlVar);
              if {multi-instruction access}
                not SimplyAccessed(InitialEntry) or
                {side-effects of final might alter initial}
                (InitialEntry^.Kind <> AConstant) and
                not SimplyAccessed(FinalEntry))
              then begin Load(InitialEntry); SaveValue(InitialEntry) end;
              if {loop body might alter final}
                FinalEntry^.Kind <> AConstant
              then begin Load(FinalEntry); SaveValue(FinalEntry) end;
              CheckEntryCode(InitialEntry, FinalEntry);
              FutureCodeLabel(EndOfLoop);
              case EntryCode of
                JumpNeeded : JumpTo(EndOfLoop, Absolute);
                TestNeeded :
                  begin
                    if Increasing
                    then begin LoadValue(InitialEntry); LoadValue(FinalEntry) end
                    else begin LoadValue(FinalEntry); LoadValue(InitialEntry) end;
                    Pcode0(TestILtOrEqual); JumpTo(EndOfLoop, IfFalse)
                  end;
                NoneNeeded :
              end;
              if EntryCode <> JumpNeeded
              then begin
                      if Checks in Requested
                      then if Increasing
                              then begin
                                      CheckLimit(InitialEntry, Lower, 52);
                                      CheckLimit(FinalEntry, Upper, 53)
                                  end
                              else begin
                                      CheckLimit(InitialEntry, Upper, 52);
                                      CheckLimit(FinalEntry, Lower, 53)
                                  end;
                      LoadValue(InitialEntry);
                      with ControlVar^.BaseAddress do
                        AccessWord(BlockLevel, WordOffset, StoreOp)
                  end;
              NewCodeLabel(StartOfLoop); FreeEntry(InitialEntry);
              Next := TopForEntry
            end;
          TopForEntry := ThisFor
```

```
            end
      end { openfor };
procedure CloseFor;
   var ThisFor: ForEntry;
   begin
      if CodeIsToBeGenerated
      then begin
              with TopForEntry^ do
                begin
                  LoadValue(ControlVar); LoadValue(FinalEntry); Pcode0(TestIUnequal);
                  JumpTo(EndOfLoop, IfFalse); LoadValue(ControlVar);
                  if Incrementing then Pcode0(Inc1) else Pcode0(Dec1);
                  with ControlVar^.BaseAddress do
                     AccessWord(BlockLevel, WordOffset, StoreOp);
                  JumpTo(StartOfLoop, Absolute); NextIsCodeLabel(EndOfLoop);
                  if Checks in Requested
                  then begin
                          with ControlVar^.BaseAddress do
                             AccessWord(BlockLevel, WordOffset, LoadRefOp);
                          Pcode0(PresetWord)
                       end;
                  FreeEntry(FinalEntry); FreeEntry(ControlVar)
                end;
              ThisFor := TopForEntry; TopForEntry := TopForEntry^.Next;
              dispose(ThisFor)
           end
   end { closefor };
procedure InitFor;
   begin TopForEntry := nil end;
{
```

22.4 Statement Labels

The procedures FutureStatementLabel, NextIsStatementLabel, and LabelJump respectively handle the definition, siting, and referencing of all declared statement labels. Each such label is assigned a location in the data table which is subsequently filled with the appropriate branch address by NextIsStatementlabel. The data table location and the current block nesting level are recorded in the fields BlockLevel and EntryOffset of a StatementLabel record. Thereafter, all jumps to this label are made indirectly via this data-table entry using the JumpVia P-code for a local goto, or the JumpOut P-code for a non-local goto.

Note that whenever a label is sited, extra code is generated to discard dangling extended references that may result if the goto statement was situated in the body of a with-statement, or within a nested procedure. The P-code DiscardLocks is used to pop unwanted entries off the lock-stack until its depth coincides with that determined by the textual position of the statement label. This mechanism is also used to void the lock-stack prior to block-exit by defining an internal statement label to mark the start of a block finalisation code-sequence.

}

procedure FutureStatementLabel {var L: StatementLabel};
  begin FutureBlockLabel(L) **end**;

procedure NextIsStatementLabel {var L: StatementLabel};
  var DataEntry: MCWordForm;
  begin
    DataEntry.Linked := true; DataEntry.Address := CodeCounter;
    with L **do** FillWord(EntryOffset - 1, DataEntry);
    if CodeIsToBeGenerated **and** (Checks **in** Requested)
    then Pcode1(DiscardLocks, TopFrameEntry^.LockDepth)
  end { nextisstatementlabel };

procedure LabelJump {var Destination: StatementLabel; LabelLevel: DispRange};
  begin
    if CodeIsToBeGenerated
    then if LabelLevel = FrameLevel
        then Pcode1(JumpVia, Destination.EntryOffset)
        else Pcode2(JumpOut, FrameLevel - LabelLevel, Destination.EntryOffset)
  end { labeljump };

CHAPTER 23

Code Generation
for
Procedure and Function Calls

23.1 Delayed Code Generation in Procedure/Function Calls

In the implementation of procedure and function calls delayed code generation is used at two levels:

(a)   generation of parameter-passing code is delayed during analysis of the actual parameter list for both procedure and function calls, and

(b)   generation of parameter-passing and calling code for a function is further delayed until code generation for the complete expression in which the function call occurs.

Thus the procedures StackActualBlock and StackFormalBlock each push a stack record of variant BlockRef, which acts as the head of a list of actual parameter descriptors pointed to by the fields First and Last.

The stack record also holds the BlockLabel for an actual block, or the address of the block descriptor for a formal block, for use in subsequent calling or block passing code.
}

```
procedure StackActualBlock {var Body: BlockLabel};
   var BlockEntry: StackEntry;
   begin
     if CodeIsToBeGenerated
     then begin
          GetEntry(BlockEntry);
          with BlockEntry^ do
            begin
              Kind := BlockRef; CallToBeGenerated := true; First := nil;
              Last := nil; BlockKind := Actual; BlockBase := Body
            end;
          Push(BlockEntry)
        end
   end { stackactualblock };
procedure StackFormalBlock {FAddress: RuntimeAddress};
   var BlockEntry: StackEntry;
   begin
```

```
    if CodeIsToBeGenerated
    then begin
            GetEntry(BlockEntry);
            with BlockEntry^ do
              begin
                Kind := BlockRef; CallToBeGenerated := true; First := nil;
                Last := nil; BlockKind := Formal; FormalAddress := FAddress
              end;
            Push(BlockEntry)
        end
  end { stackformalblock };
{
```

23.2 Delayed Parameter Passing

The field CallToBeGenerated is initially true for both procedures and functions, but is set false for functions by the procedure OpenParameterList (to effect the further delay of calling-code generation, as explained in Section 23.4).

During parameter list analysis each actual parameter is appended to the list headed by the stacked block reference, by the procedure ExtendActualList which is called by the interface procedures PassBlock, PassValue and PassReference.

The interface procedure CloseParameterList has no role in this implementation strategy.

```
}
procedure OpenParameterList {ClassOfCall: IdClass};
  begin
    if CodeIsToBeGenerated
    then if ClassOfCall = Func then TopStackEntry^.CallToBeGenerated := false
  end { openparameterlist };
procedure ExtendActualList(ThisParam: StackEntry; ThisKind: ActualKind);
  var ThisEntry: ActualEntry;
  begin
    new(ThisEntry);
    with ThisEntry^ do
      begin
        Next := nil; Kind := ThisKind;
        case ThisKind of
          IsValue, IsRef, IsVar, IsBlock : ActualParam := ThisParam;
          IsBounds : BpList := nil
        end
      end;
    with TopStackEntry^ do
      begin
        if First = nil then First := ThisEntry else Last^.Next := ThisEntry;
        Last := ThisEntry
      end
  end { extendactuallist };
```

procedure PassValue {RepRequired: TypeRepresentation};

  var ActualParam: StackEntry;

  begin
    if CodeIsToBeGenerated
    then begin
        Pop(ActualParam);
        if Checks **in** Requested
        then if RepRequired.Kind = ForSet
            then SelectCheck(ActualParam, 8) **else** SelectCheck(ActualParam, 7);
        ExtendActualList(ActualParam, IsValue);
        TopStackEntry^.Last^.FormalRep := RepRequired
      end
  end { passvalue };

procedure PassReference {RefStatus: RefSecurity};

  var ActualParam: StackEntry;

  begin
    if CodeIsToBeGenerated
    then begin
        Pop(ActualParam);
        case RefStatus **of**
          Secure : ExtendActualList(ActualParam, IsRef);
          MayBeInsecure : ExtendActualList(ActualParam, IsVar)
        end
      end
  end { passreference };

procedure PassBlock;

  var BlockEntry: StackEntry;

  begin
    if CodeIsToBeGenerated
    then begin Pop(BlockEntry); ExtendActualList(BlockEntry, IsBlock) **end**
  end { passblock };

procedure CloseParameterList;

  begin end;
{

23.3 Conformant Array Parameters

Within the above scheme each conformant array parameter is passed as a reference, but the bound pairs are passed "before" the actual parameters corresponding to any conformant array schema (i.e. after the first actual reference has been created, but before the corresponding call to PassReference). The sequence of bound pairs passed are represented on the actual parameter list by a header for a secondary list of bound pairs, created by the interface procedure StartBoundPairs.

The procedure AppendBounds is used to extend this list, by each subsequent call to PassArrayBoundPair or PassCAPBoundPair.

```
}
procedure StartBoundPairs;
  begin if CodeIsToBeGenerated then ExtendActualList(nil, IsBounds) end;
procedure AppendBound(BoundPair: BpEntry);

  var LastBound: BpEntry;

  begin
    with TopStackEntry^.NextNode^.Last^ do
      if BpList = nil
      then BpList := BoundPair
      else begin
            LastBound := BpList;
            while LastBound^.Next <> nil do LastBound := LastBound^.Next;
            LastBound^.Next := BoundPair
          end
  end { appendbound };
procedure DisposeBounds(var Head: BpEntry);

  var ThisPair: BpEntry;

  begin
    while Head <> nil do
      begin ThisPair := Head; Head := ThisPair^.Next; dispose(ThisPair) end
  end { disposebounds };
procedure PassArrayBoundPair {ActualLowBound, ActualHighBound,
                                SchemaLowBound, SchemaHighBound: ObjectValue;
                                Element: TypeRepresentation;
                                ArrayPacked: Boolean};

  var ElementsPacked: Boolean; Words, Members: Scalar;
      ElsPerWord: MCBitRange; BoundPair: BpEntry;

  begin
    if CodeIsToBeGenerated
    then begin
          if Checks in Requested
          then if OrderedValues(ActualLowBound, SchemaLowBound) or
                  OrderedValues(SchemaHighBound, ActualHighBound)
              then PredictedError(59);
          if CodeIsToBeGenerated
          then begin
                Members := Range(ActualLowBound, ActualHighBound);
                with Element do
                  if WordSize > 1
                  then ElementsPacked := false
                  else ElementsPacked :=
                        ArrayPacked and (BitSize <= MCBitsPerWord div 2);
```

```
                if ElementsPacked
                then begin
                        ElsPerWord := MCBitsPerWord div Element.BitSize;
                        Words := WordsFor(Members, ElsPerWord)
                    end
                else Words := Element.WordSize;
                new(BoundPair);
                with BoundPair^ do
                  begin
                    Next := nil; CAPBounds := false;
                    Lower := ActualLowBound.Ival;
                    Upper := ActualHighBound.Ival; Size := Words
                  end;
                AppendBound(BoundPair)
              end
        end
  end { passarrayboundpair };
procedure PassCAPBoundPair {LowBoundAddress, HighBoundAddress: RuntimeAddress;
                            SchemaLowBound, SchemaHighBound : ObjectValue;
                            BoundPairRep: TypeRepresentation};

  { The parameter HighBoundAddress is not used in this implementation. }

  var BoundPair: BpEntry;

  begin
    if CodeIsToBeGenerated
    then begin
            new(BoundPair);
            with BoundPair^ do
              begin
                Next := nil; Lower := SchemaLowBound.Ival;
                Upper := SchemaHighBound.Ival; CAPBounds := true;
                BpAddress := LowBoundAddress; Size := BoundPairRep.WordSize
              end;
            AppendBound(BoundPair)
          end
  end { passcapboundpair };
procedure MakeAuxiliary {RepRequired: TypeRepresentation};
  begin end;
{
```

In this implementation, the copying of value conformant array parameters is carried out within the receiving block, as explained in Chapter 26, so the interface procedure MakeAuxiliary is redundant.

23.4 Generation of Calling Code

Calling code for both procedures and functions is generated by the procedure CallBlock. For procedures this occurs as the direct result of the corresponding interface call. For functions the interface call pushes an expression node representing the delayed function call onto the stack, but the subsequent application of Load to this node makes a further call to CallBlock, with the flag CallToBeGenerated reset to true, to generate the actual calling code.

The procedure LoadActuals generates the code required to load the actual parameters onto the runtime evaluation stack, by interpretation of the actual parameter descriptors appended to the block reference.

Since execution of a function call by the P-machine leaves the function result on the top of the evaluation stack, i.e. "loaded" the procedure TakeResult need only add the result representation to the expression node which denotes a call.
}

```
procedure LoadActuals(ThisActual: ActualEntry);
   var NextActual: ActualEntry; BoundPair: BpEntry;
   begin
     while ThisActual <> nil do
       begin
         with ThisActual^ do
           begin
             case Kind of
               IsValue :
                 begin
                   with FormalRep do
                     if Kind = ForSet
                     then begin Load(ActualParam); Pcode1(SetExpand, WordSize) end
                     else Load(ActualParam)
                 end;
               IsRef : LoadAddress(ActualParam);
               IsVar :
                 begin ExtendReferences(ActualParam); LoadAddress(ActualParam) end;
               IsBlock :
                 with ActualParam^ do
                   if BlockKind = Actual
                   then begin { load static link }
                         AccessWord(BlockBase.BlockLevel, 0, LoadRefOp);
                         Pcode1(ConstWord, BlockBase.EntryOffset)
                       end
                   else with FormalAddress do
                         begin
                           AccessWord(BlockLevel, WordOffset, LoadRefOp);
                           Pcode1(LoadMultiple, 2)
                         end;
```

```
                    IsBounds :
                      begin
                        BoundPair := BpList;
                        while BoundPair <> nil do
                          begin
                            with BoundPair^ do
                              if CAPBounds
                              then if Checks in Requested
                                    then begin
                                          with BpAddress do
                                            AccessWord(BlockLevel, WordOffset, LoadOp);
                                          InlineNumber(Lower); Pcode1(CheckLower, 59);
                                          with BpAddress do
                                            AccessWord
                                              (BlockLevel, WordOffset + 1, LoadOp);
                                          InlineNumber(Upper); Pcode1(CheckUpper, 59);
                                          with BpAddress do
                                            AccessWord
                                              (BlockLevel, WordOffset + 2, LoadOp)
                                        end
                                    else begin
                                          with BpAddress do
                                            AccessWord
                                              (BlockLevel, WordOffset, LoadRefOp);
                                          Pcode1(LoadMultiple, Size); DisposeBounds(Next)
                                        end
                              else begin
                                    InlineNumber(Lower); InlineNumber(Upper);
                                    InlineNumber(Size)
                                  end;
                            BoundPair := BoundPair^.Next
                          end
                      end
                end;
                if Kind = IsBounds
                then DisposeBounds(BpList) else FreeEntry(ActualParam);
                NextActual := Next
              end;
          dispose(ThisActual); ThisActual := NextActual
        end
  end { loadactuals };
procedure CallBlock;
  var CallEntry, BlockEntry: StackEntry; OldDepth: Scalar;
  begin
    if CodeIsToBeGenerated
    then begin
          Pop(BlockEntry);
```

```
              if BlockEntry^.CallToBeGenerated
              then begin
                      Pcode0(MarkStack);
                      with BlockEntry^ do
                        begin
                          OldDepth := TopFrameEntry^.LockDepth; LoadActuals(First);
                          if BlockKind = Actual
                          then EmitCall(BlockBase)
                          else with FormalAddress do
                                  begin
                                      AccessWord(BlockLevel, WordOffset, LoadRefOp);
                                      Pcode0(CallForml)
                                  end;
                          DiscardReferences(OldDepth)
                        end;
                      FreeEntry(BlockEntry)
                   end
              else begin
                      GetEntry(CallEntry);
                      with CallEntry^ do
                        begin
                          Kind := Operation; OpForm := BlockCall;
                          FnBlockEntry := BlockEntry
                        end;
                      Push(CallEntry)
                   end
            end
  end { callblock };
procedure TakeResult {Representation : TypeRepresentation};
  begin
    if CodeIsToBeGenerated then TopStackEntry^.DataRep := Representation
  end { takeresult };
{
```

23.5 Block Entry and Exit Code

All aspects of block entry concerning stack frame creation and initialisation are handled by the appropriate "block-call" P-codes. However, the diagnostics procedure StartOfBody is called to record the source-line number of the start of the block body on the Codemap file. For procedures or functions taking conformant array parameters, the procedure AugmentSchema is called to generate internal procedures for the implementation of value conformant arrays.

Stack house-keeping on block exit is likewise performed internally by the "block-exit" P-codes. Prior to leaving a function however, code is generated to load the function result and check that it is defined. P-codes EndFunction and EndMultiFunction are used depending upon whether the function has a single or multi-word result.

```
}
procedure StartOfBody(Serial: SerialRange; SourceLine: Scalar); forward;
procedure EnterProgram {ProgId: IdEntry; SourceLine: Scalar};
   begin StartOfBody(ProgId^.Serial, SourceLine) end;
procedure EnterPfBody {PfId: IdEntry; SourceLine: Scalar};
   var ThisFormal: FormalEntry;
   begin
     with Pfid^ do
       begin
         ThisFormal := Formals;
         while ThisFormal <> nil do
           with ThisFormal^ do
             begin
               if Parm = BoundParm then AugmentSchema(FormalType);
               ThisFormal := Next
             end;
         StartOfBody(Serial, SourceLine)
       end
   end { enterpfbody };
procedure LeaveProgram;
   begin
     if CodeIsToBeGenerated then Pcode0(HaltProgram)
   end { leaveprogram };
procedure LeaveProcedure;
   begin
     if CodeIsToBeGenerated then Pcode0(EndProcedure)
   end { leaveprocedure };
procedure LeaveFunction {Result: RuntimeAddress;
                         Representation: TypeRepresentation};
   var ResultEntry: StackEntry;
   begin
     if CodeIsToBeGenerated
     then begin
           StackReference(false, Result); DeReference(Representation); Pop(ResultEntry);
           if Checks in Requested then ResultEntry^.RunError := 48;
           Load(ResultEntry); FreeEntry(ResultEntry);
           with Representation do
             if WordSize = 1
             then Pcode0(EndFunction) else Pcode1(EndMultiFunction, WordSize)
         end
   end { leavefunction };
```

CHAPTER 24

Mapping Program Parameters

Pascal contains provision for the exchange of information between a program and its run time environment by means of program parameters. In practice most implementations (including the model implementation) provide only a skeleton frame work which is sufficient to map actual data files onto their respective program file variables. The P-machine contains a special P-code to enable a mapping between a named program parameter variable and a corresponding external entity to be established. No restriction on the parameter type is enforced but the P-code operates on the assumption that the entities involved are data files.

The following procedures are invoked to generate the parameter mapping code. Each formal parameter is denoted by its associated variable name and an ordinal position number which allows actual/formal correspondence to be established.

No means of returning information to the external environment (other than the semantics of file manipulation) is provided, and procedure ReturnProgParameter is consequently a dummy.

```
}
procedure OpenProgParameterList;
   begin if CodeIsToBeGenerated then ProgPmCount := 0 end;
procedure AcceptProgParameter {ParamId : IdEntry};

   var Size: 0..AlfaSize; i: AlfaIndex;

   begin
     if CodeIsToBeGenerated
     then with ParamId^ do
           begin
             with VarAddress do AccessWord(BlockLevel, WordOffset, LoadRefOp);
             Pcode3(MapProgParam);
             with Name do
               begin
                 Size := 0;
                 for i := 1 to AlfaSize do
                   if Head[i] <> ' ' then Size := Size + 1;
                 { count tail if necessary };
                 CodeByte(Size + 1); ProgPmCount := ProgPmCount + 1;
                 CodeByte(ProgPmCount);
```

```
                    for i := 1 to Size do CodeByte(ord(Head[i]));
                    { emit tail if necessary }
                end
            end
    end { acceptprogparameter };
procedure ReturnProgParameter {ParamId : IdEntry};
    begin  end;
procedure CloseProgParameterList;
    begin  end;
```

{

CHAPTER 25

Code Generation
for
Manual Operations

This chapter contains procedures for generating manual presetting, postsetting and value-checking operations from lists built by the procedure SelectManual. A manual operation is performed either directly by an in-line code sequence operating directly on one or more memory locations, or indirectly by passing the appropriate memory address as parameter to an internal type-specific procedure.

The procedures PresetMemory and CheckMemory provide for in-line presetting and checking of one or more memory locations. In each case the Multiple field of the Value parameter directs the choice between multi- or single word operations. The utility RunTimeError is used to generate conditional error reporting and is used by CheckMemory and many of the checking procedures discussed in the next chapter.

}

```
procedure RuntimeError(RunError: Scalar; Condition: JumpType);
    var CheckEntry: StackEntry;
    begin
      if CodeIsToBeGenerated
      then begin
            Pop(CheckEntry); Load(CheckEntry);
            case Condition of
              IfFalse : Pcode1(TrapIfFalse, RunError);
              IfTrue : Pcode1(TrapIfTrue, RunError);
              Absolute : Pcode1(TrapError, RunError)
            end;
            FreeEntry(CheckEntry)
         end
    end { runtimeerror };
procedure PresetMemory(Value: MachineValue);
    var BaseEntry: StackEntry; PresetValue: ObjectValue;
    begin
      if CodeIsToBeGenerated
      then with Value do
            if Defined
```

```
            then if Multiple = 1
                  then begin
                        SetIval(Magnitude, PresetValue); StackConstant(PresetValue);
                        Assign(IntegerRepresentation)
                      end
                  else begin
                        InlineNumber(Magnitude); Pop(BaseEntry);
                        LoadAddress(BaseEntry); Pcode1(StoreRepeated, Multiple);
                        FreeEntry(BaseEntry)
                      end
            else begin
                  Pop(BaseEntry); LoadAddress(BaseEntry);
                  if Multiple = 1
                  then Pcode0(PresetWord) else Pcode1(PresetRepeated, Multiple);
                  FreeEntry(BaseEntry)
                end
      end { presetmemory };
procedure CheckMemory(Value: MachineValue);
   var BaseEntry: StackEntry; CheckValue: ObjectValue;
   begin
      if CodeIsToBeGenerated
      then with Value do
            if Defined
            then begin
                  SetIval(Magnitude, CheckValue); StackConstant(CheckValue);
                  OrdinalComparison(EqOp); RuntimeError(43, IfTrue)
                end
            else begin
                  Pop(BaseEntry); LoadAddress(BaseEntry);
                  if Multiple > 1
                  then begin InlineNumber(Multiple); Pcode1(CheckRepeated, 43) end
                  else begin Pcode1(CheckWord, 43) end;
                  FreeEntry(BaseEntry)
                end
   end { checkmemory };
{
```

The procedure Perform generates calls to a type-specific procedure performing a manual operation indirectly. The operation, the procedure and kind of parameter, and the number of such calls are provided by fields of the parameter Action. A constant, InLineLimit, is used to choose between loop code which addresses each operand by indexing, or multiple in-line calls in which each operand is addressed incrementally. The current value of InLineLimit produces the most compact code sequence.

```
}
procedure Perform(Action: TypeSpecificAction);
   const InlineLimit = 5;
   var CodeEntry, BaseEntry: StackEntry; ProcedureCode: BlockLabel;
```

```
procedure DoCall;
  procedure PushCopy(OldEntry: StackEntry);
    var NewEntry: StackEntry;
    begin new(NewEntry); NewEntry^ := OldEntry^; Push(NewEntry) end;
  begin
    PushCopy(CodeEntry); OpenParameterList(Proc); PushCopy(BaseEntry);
    if Action.Invoked = WithValue
    then PassValue(Action.Representation) else PassReference(Secure);
    CloseParameterList; CallBlock
  end { docall };
procedure InlineCall(ElementSize: WordRange; Elements: Scalar);
  var CallIndex: Scalar;
  begin
    CallIndex := 0;
    while CallIndex < Elements do
      begin
        DoCall;
        with BaseEntry^ do
          if PartOfWord
          then BitOffset := BitOffset + BitSize
          else Adjustment := Adjustment + ElementSize;
        CallIndex := CallIndex + 1
      end
  end { inlinecall };
procedure IndexedCall(ElementSize: WordRange; Elements: Scalar);
  var Counter: RuntimeAddress; StartLoop, EndLoop: CodeLabel;
  procedure LoadCounter;
    begin with Counter do AccessWord(BlockLevel, WordOffset, LoadOp) end;
  procedure StoreInCounter;
    begin with Counter do AccessWord(BlockLevel, WordOffset, StoreOp) end;
  procedure IncrementCounter;
    begin LoadCounter; Pcode0(Inc1); StoreInCounter end;
  procedure CallByIndex;
    var ElsPerWord: MCBitRange; CallIndex: IndexEntry;
    begin
      new(CallIndex);
      with CallIndex^ do
        begin Pop(TheIndex); Next := nil; CAPIndex := false end;
      Pop(BaseEntry);
      with BaseEntry^ do
        if PartOfWord
        then begin
                ElsPerWord := MCBitsPerWord div BitSize;
                OnByteBoundary := (ElsPerWord = MCBytesPerWord);
```

```
                    BitSize := MCBitsPerWord div ElsPerWord;
                    IndexedPartWord := true; CallIndex^.Factor := ElsPerWord;
                    Index := CallIndex
                 end
              else begin
                    Indexed := true; CallIndex^.Factor := ElementSize; Indices := CallIndex
                 end;
           DoCall
        end { callbyindex };

     begin { indexedcall }
        Acquire(1, Counter); InlineNumber(0); StoreInCounter; FutureCodeLabel(EndLoop);
        NewCodeLabel(StartLoop); StackReference(false, Counter); CallByIndex;
        LoadCounter; InlineNumber(Elements - 1); Pcode0(TestIUnequal);
        JumpTo(EndLoop, IfFalse); IncrementCounter; JumpTo(StartLoop, Absolute);
        NextIsCodeLabel(EndLoop)
     end { indexedcall };

  begin { perform }
     if CodeIsToBeGenerated
     then with Action do
           begin
              case Request of
                 Presets : ProcedureCode := Representation.PresetCode;
                 Postsets : ProcedureCode := Representation.PostsetCode;
                 ValueChecks : ProcedureCode := Representation.CheckCode
              end;
              StackActualBlock(ProcedureCode); Pop(CodeEntry);
              if Multiple <= InlineLimit
              then begin
                    Pop(BaseEntry); InlineCall(Representation.WordSize, Multiple)
                 end
              else IndexedCall(Representation.WordSize, Multiple);
              FreeEntry(CodeEntry); FreeEntry(BaseEntry)
           end
  end { perform };
{
```

The generation of manual code is controlled by the procedures PresetManuals, PostsetManuals, and CheckManuals using the manual lists supplied as parameters.

PresetManuals triggers the generation of preset code for items classified as inline or indirect. For inline items sub-classified as part-words, additional processing is performed to pack their preset values into a composite word value. The appropriate generative procedure is then called with a reference to the item location available on the evaluation stack.
}

```
procedure PackItem(ThisItem: ManualEntry; var EndOfPack: Boolean);
   var Next: ManualEntry; BufferFull: Boolean;
   begin
     with ThisItem^ do
```

```
      begin
        with ItsRepresentation do
          case ItsShape of
            WordStructure :
              begin PresetPartWord(BitSize, CheckValue); BufferFull := true end;
            PartWrd, PartWrdStructure :
              begin
                PresetPartWord(ItsOffset.BitSize, CheckValue);
                BufferFull := (PresetBuffer.BitsFree = 0)
              end
          end;
        Next := NextItem;
        if Next = nil
        then EndOfPack := true
        else EndOfPack :=
                BufferFull or (ItsOffset.WordOffset <> Next^.ItsOffset.WordOffset)
      end
  end { packitem };
procedure PresetManuals {ManualScope: DispRange; List: ManualList},
    var PresetValue: MachineValue; FullWord: FieldOffset; ThisItem: ManualEntry;
        PackComplete: Boolean; Action: TypeSpecificAction;
  begin
    FullWord := DefaultOffset; ThisItem := List.FirstEntry; ResetPresetBuffer;
    while ThisItem <> nil do
      with ThisItem^ do
        begin
          case ItsCode of
            Indirect :
              begin
                with Action do
                  begin
                    Request := Presets; Representation := ItsRepresentation;
                    Invoked := WithRefnce; Multiple := Repeated
                  end;
                WithReference(ManualScope); FieldReference(ItsOffset, false);
                Perform(Action)
              end;
            Inline :
              begin
                if ItsShape = Word
                then begin
                        PresetValue := UndefinedValue;
                        PresetValue.Multiple := ItsRepresentation.CheckValue.Multiple;
                        PackComplete := true
                     end
                else begin
                        PackItem(ThisItem, PackComplete);
                        if PackComplete then FlushBuffer(PresetValue)
                     end;
```

```
                if PackComplete
                then begin
                        with PresetValue do Multiple := Multiple * Repeated;
                        FullWord.WordOffset := ItsOffset.WordOffset;
                        if PresetValue.Multiple > 0
                        then begin
                                WithReference(ManualScope);
                                FieldReference(FullWord, false);
                                PresetMemory(PresetValue)
                             end
                     end
             end;
          None :
          end;
          ThisItem := NextItem
        end
   end { presetmanuals };
{
```

PostsetManuals triggers the generation of postset code for file variables. Since these are always postset by procedure, only indirect items can ever occur on the manual list.

```
}
procedure PostsetManuals {ManualScope: DispRange; List: ManualList};
   var Action: TypeSpecificAction; ThisItem: ManualEntry;
   begin
      ThisItem := List.FirstEntry;
      while ThisItem <> nil do
        with ThisItem^ do
          begin
            case ItsCode of
              Indirect :
                begin
                  with Action do
                    begin
                      Request := Postsets; Representation := ItsRepresentation;
                      Invoked := WithRefrnce; Multiple := Repeated
                    end;
                  WithReference(ManualScope); FieldReference(ItsOffset, false);
                  Perform(Action)
                end;
              Inline, None :
            end;
            ThisItem := NextItem
          end
   end { postsetmanuals };
```

```
{
CheckManuals is called to generate value checking code for fields of a record or record vari-
ant.  The check may be either indirect or in line, but in the latter case the packing of part-
word check values is ruled out by the need to check each field individually.
}
procedure CheckManuals {ManualScope: DispRange; List: ManualList};

   var ThisItem: ManualEntry; Action: TypeSpecificAction; PresetValue: MachineValue;

   begin
      ThisItem := List.FirstEntry;
      while ThisItem <> nil do
         with ThisItem^ do
            begin
               case ItsCode of
                  Indirect :
                     begin
                        with Action do
                           begin
                              Request := ValueChecks; Representation := ItsRepresentation;
                              if Representation.WordSize > 1
                              then Invoked := WithRefrnce else Invoked := WithValue;
                              Multiple := Repeated
                           end;
                        WithReference(ManualScope); FieldReference(ItsOffset, false);
                        Perform(Action)
                     end;
                  Inline :
                     begin
                        if ItsShape = Word
                        then begin
                              PresetValue := UndefinedValue;
                              PresetValue.Multiple := ItsRepresentation.CheckValue.Multiple
                           end
                        else PresetValue := ItsRepresentation.CheckValue;
                        with PresetValue do Multiple := Multiple * Repeated;
                        if PresetValue.Multiple > 0
                        then begin
                              WithReference(ManualScope); FieldReference(ItsOffset, false);
                              CheckMemory(PresetValue)
                           end
                        else Pcode1(TrapError, 43)
                     end;
                  None :
               end;
               ThisItem := NextItem
            end
   end { checkmanuals };
```

{

CHAPTER 26

Code Generation
for
Augmented Type Representations

This chapter contains the generators for type-specific preset, postset and value checking code. The code produced by each generator takes the form of a procedure body whose entry point is recorded in the representation of the type concerned. The formal parameters of the generated procedures are declared internally within the respective generators by calls to the utility FormalParam. The kind and runtime address of each parameter are recorded in the fields of a descriptor of type LocalRecord. The utility StackParam is used in conjunction with this descriptor to address the parameter appropriately.

}

```
procedure FormalParm(FormalKind: ParmKind; var FormalEntry: LocalEntry;
                     FormalType: TypEntry);
  var WordsNeeded: WordRange;
  begin
    new(FormalEntry);
    with FormalEntry^ do
      begin
        if FormalKind = VarParm
        then LKind := VarParam else LKind := ValueParam;
        if LKind = VarParam
        then WordsNeeded := 1
        else WordsNeeded := FormalType^.Representation.WordSize;
        Acquire(WordsNeeded, LAddress)
      end
  end { formalparm };
procedure StackParm(ParmEntry: LocalEntry);
  begin with ParmEntry^ do StackReference((LKind = VarParam), LAddress) end;
```

{

26.1 The Array Type Generators

The procedures PresetAnArray, PostsetAnArray, and CheckAnArray generate pre-, postset, and value-checking code for a given array type. In each case the generated procedure takes a single variable parameter representing the array variable to be processed.

The procedure PresetAnArray is called for array types whose element-types are preset by procedure call, or for multi-word array types with packed sub-structure. In the first case the generated procedure body comprises repeated calls to the element preset procedure, and in the second case it comprises in-line preset code. Notice that in the latter case, elements-per-word preset values are packed into a word value, and the array preset on a word-by-word basis.

}
```
procedure PresetAnArray {ArrayType: TypEntry};
    var Entry: BlockLabel; ArrayVar: LocalEntry; ElementSize, ElsPerWord: MCBitRange;
        PresetValue: MachineValue; Action: TypeSpecificAction; Count: Scalar;
    begin
        FutureBlockLabel(Entry); OpenStackFrame;
        FormalParm(VarParm, ArrayVar, ArrayType); OpenCodeSpace(Entry);
        with ArrayType^ do
            begin
                Representation.PresetCode := Entry;
                if EnvelopeUsed(AelType^.Representation, Presets)
                then begin
                        with Action do
                            begin
                                Request := Presets; Representation := AelType^.Representation;
                                Invoked := WithRefrnce; Multiple := Cardinality(InxType)
                            end;
                        StackParm(ArrayVar); Perform(Action)
                    end
                else begin
                        if PackedArray
                        then begin
                                with AelType^ do
                                    ElsPerWord := MCBitsPerWord div Representation.BitSize;
                                    ElementSize := MCBitsPerWord div ElsPerWord
                                end
                        else begin
                                ElsPerWord := 1;
                                with AelType^ do ElementSize := Representation.BitSize
                            end;
                        ResetPresetBuffer;
                        for Count := 1 to ElsPerWord do
                            with AelType^.Representation do
                                PresetPartWord(ElementSize, CheckValue);
                        FlushBuffer(PresetValue);
                        PresetValue.Multiple := Representation.WordSize; StackParm(ArrayVar);
                        PresetMemory(PresetValue)
                    end
            end;
        LeaveProcedure; CloseCodeSpace; CloseStackFrame; dispose(ArrayVar)
    end { presetanarray };
```

{

Procedure PostsetAnArray is called to generate code for array types whose elements contain embedded file types. The body of the generated procedure therefore comprises repeated calls to the element postset procedure.

}

procedure PostsetAnArray {ArrayType: TypEntry};
   var Entry: BlockLabel; ArrayVar: LocalEntry; Action: TypeSpecificAction;
   begin
     FutureBlockLabel(Entry); OpenStackFrame;
     FormalParm(VarParm, ArrayVar, ArrayType); OpenCodeSpace(Entry);
     with ArrayType^ **do**
       begin
         Representation.PostsetCode := Entry;
         with Action **do**
           begin
             Request := Postsets; Representation := AelType^.Representation;
             Invoked := WithRefrnce; Multiple := Cardinality(InxType)
           end;
         StackParm(ArrayVar); Perform(Action)
       end;
     LeaveProcedure; CloseCodeSpace; CloseStackFrame; dispose(ArrayVar)
   end { postsetanarray };

{

Procedure CheckAnArray is called to generate code for array types whose elements are value-checked by procedure, or are part-words. In each case, the body of the generated procedure takes the form of a loop whose internally declared control variable ArrayIndex is used to index each element in turn. The code to check whether any element is undefined either takes the form of a call to the element-checking procedure passing the element value as parameter, or is a simple in-line check comparing the current element value with the predefined element CheckValue.

}

procedure CheckAnArray {ArrayType: TypEntry};
   var Entry: BlockLabel; ArrayVar: LocalEntry; LowBound, HighBound: ObjectValue;
     Action: TypeSpecificAction; ArrayIndex: RuntimeAddress;
   begin
     FutureBlockLabel(Entry); OpenStackFrame;
     with ArrayType^.Representation **do**
       if WordSize > 1
       then FormalParm(VarParm, ArrayVar, ArrayType)
       else FormalParm(ValueParm, ArrayVar, ArrayType);
     OpenCodeSpace(Entry);
     with ArrayType^ **do**
       begin
         Representation.CheckCode := Entry; Acquire(1, ArrayIndex);
         StackReference(false, ArrayIndex); GetBounds(InxType, LowBound, HighBound);

```
            StackConstant(LowBound); StackConstant(HighBound);
            OpenFor(true, LowBound, HighBound); StackParm(ArrayVar);
            StackReference(false, ArrayIndex); DeReference(InxType^.Representation);
            IndexedReference
                (PackedArray, LowBound, HighBound, AelType^.Representation);
            if EnvelopeUsed(AelType^.Representation, ValueChecks)
            then begin
                    with Action do
                      begin
                        Request := ValueChecks;
                        Representation := AelType^.Representation;
                        if Representation.WordSize > 1
                        then Invoked := WithRefrnce else Invoked := WithValue;
                        Multiple := 1
                      end;
                    Perform(Action)
                 end
            else CheckMemory(AelType^.Representation.CheckValue);
            CloseFor
          end;
      LeaveProcedure; CloseCodeSpace; CloseStackFrame; dispose(ArrayVar)
    end { checkanarray };
{
```

26.2 The Conformant Array Type Generators

The procedure AcceptACAP is called to generate code to create a local copy of an actual
value conformant array parameter, using storage acquired from the heap. The generated
procedure has a single variable parameter corresponding to the formal conformant array
variable. The generated body contains code to compute the word-size of the actual array
from the contents of the bound pair block, and then uses a special P-code to allocate heap,
copy the actual array, and overwrite the actual array address with the copy address.

```
}
procedure AcceptACAP {CAPType: TypEntry};
    var Entry: BlockLabel; ArrayVar: LocalEntry; ElementsPacked: Boolean;
    begin
      FutureBlockLabel(Entry); OpenStackFrame;
      FormalParm(VarParm, ArrayVar, CAPType); OpenCodeSpace(Entry);
      with CAPType^ do
        begin
          Representation.PresetCode := Entry;
          with CompType^.Representation do
            if WordSize > 1
            then ElementsPacked := false
            else ElementsPacked :=
                    PackedSchema and (BitSize <= MCBitsPerWord div 2);
```

```
        if CodeIsToBeGenerated
        then begin
                Pcode0(LoadShort); LoadCAPSize(ElementsPacked, LowBdAddress);
                Pcode0(DuplicateCAP)
            end
    end;
    LeaveProcedure; CloseCodeSpace; CloseStackFrame; dispose(ArrayVar)
  end { acceptacap };
{
```

The procedure ReleaseACAP is called to generate code to release the local copy of a value conformant array. The generated body calculates the size of the copy from the contents of the bound pair block, and makes use of a special P-code to release the allocated heap storage.

```
}
procedure ReleaseACAP {CAPType: TypEntry};
    var Entry: BlockLabel; ArrayVar: LocalEntry; ElementsPacked: Boolean;
    begin
        FutureBlockLabel(Entry); OpenStackFrame;
        FormalParm(VarParm, ArrayVar, CAPType); OpenCodeSpace(Entry);
        with CAPType^ do
          begin
            Representation.PostsetCode := Entry;
            with CompType^.Representation do
              if WordSize > 1
              then ElementsPacked := false
              else ElementsPacked :=
                    PackedSchema and (BitSize <= MCBitsPerWord div 2);
            if CodeIsToBeGenerated
            then begin
                    Pcode0(LoadShort); LoadCAPSize(ElementsPacked, LowBdAddress);
                    Pcode0(ReleaseCAP)
                end
        end;
        LeaveProcedure; CloseCodeSpace; CloseStackFrame; dispose(ArrayVar)
    end { releaseacap };
{
```

The procedure CheckACAP is called to generate code for variable conformant array schemas whose components are value-checked by procedure, or are part-words. The generated procedure has a single variable parameter corresponding to the formal conformant-array parameter. The body of the procedure comprises a for-loop whose internally declared control variable CAPIndex is used to index each component in turn. The code to check whether any component is undefined is either a call to the component-checking procedure with the component value passed as parameter, or is a simple in-line check that compares the component value with the predefined component CheckValue.

```
}
```

```
procedure CheckACAP {CAPType: TypEntry};
   var Entry: BlockLabel; CAPVar: LocalEntry; CAPIndex: RuntimeAddress;
      Lowest, Highest: ObjectValue; Action: TypeSpecificAction;
   procedure StackBound(BdAddress: RuntimeAddress);
      begin StackReference(false, BdAddress); DeReference(IntegerRepresentation) end;
   begin
      FutureBlockLabel(Entry); OpenStackFrame;
      FormalParm(VarParm, CAPVar, CAPType); OpenCodeSpace(Entry);
      with CAPType^ do
         begin
            Representation.CheckCode := Entry; Acquire(1, CAPIndex);
            StackReference(false, CAPIndex); StackBound(LowBdAddress);
            StackBound(HighBdAddress); GetBounds(IntType, Lowest, Highest);
            OpenFor(true, Lowest, Highest); StackParm(CAPVar);
            StackReference(false, CAPIndex); DeReference(InxSpec^.Representation);
            WithSchema(CAPType, IndexedCAPReference);
            if CheckedByCall(CompType)
            then begin
                     with Action do
                        begin
                           Request := ValueChecks;
                           Representation := CompType^.Representation;
                           if Representation.WordSize > 1
                           then Invoked := WithRefrnce else Invoked := WithValue;
                           Multiple := 1
                        end;
                     Perform(Action)
                 end
            else with CompType^ do CheckMemory(Representation.CheckValue);
            CloseFor
         end;
      LeaveProcedure; CloseCodeSpace; CloseStackFrame; dispose(CAPVar)
   end { checkacap };
{
```

26.3 The Generators for Record Variant (re) Selection

A secure implementation of record variant (re) selection requires:

(1) A control flag to indicate whether any variant of a variant part is "active". If not set, the tag-field (if any) is undefined.

(2) A "selector field" whose value uniquely identifies the currently active variant. Any attempt to access a variant associated with a different selector value must be reported.

(3) A control flag to indicate whether a variant of the variant part has been "preselected" by quoting its case-label in a call to the extended form of new. If set, any attempt to change the selector value must be reported as an error.

(4) A control flag to indicate a reference has been extended to any field of the active variant. If set, any attempt to change the selector value must be reported as an error.

(5) An "activator procedure" which presets all the local fields of a newly selected variant.

(6) A "passivator procedure" which postsets file-types embedded within the local fields of the active variant.

(7) A "selector procedure" which computes a selector-value from an associated value of the tag-type, checks the variant (re-) selection for consistency against the control flags, passivates the active variant if necessary, updates the selector value, and activates the newly selected variant.

In the model implementation, the first word of variant record storage is reserved for the control flags. Each nested variant part is assigned a level number starting at 0, and each variant part is assigned three control flags. For a given level l, these occupy bits as follows:

$$
\begin{array}{ll}
\text{Bit } 3*l & \text{extended reference flag} \\
\text{Bit } 3*l+1 & \text{pre-selection flag} \\
\text{Bit } 3*l+2 & \text{variant active flag}
\end{array}
$$

This leads to a system limit on the maximum depth to which variants can be nested given by MCBitsPerWord div 3. The control word is set to zero when the fixed-part of the record-variable is initialised.

Storage for the selector-field is allocated depending upon the assignment of case constants to individual variants. If no variant is multiply labelled, the case constants themselves uniquely identify the variants and the selector-field and tag-field (if any) occupy the same storage. Multiply labelled variants imply that a distinct selector field is always required. Thus in:

```
record
    case which: choice of
        one, two: (i: integer)
        three: (r: real)
    end
```

storage is allocated as follows:

```
    |----------|           |----------|
    | control  |           | control  |
    |----------|           |----------|
    |  which   |           |  which   |
    |----------|           |----------|
    | selector |           | selector |
    |  field   |           |  field   |
    |----------|           |----------|
    |    i     |           |    r     |
    |----------|           |----------|
   which = one, two       which = three
    selector = 1           selector = 0
```

The following utility procedures are used to clear, check, set, and reset the control flags

associated with a variant-part nested at a given level, and to activate or passivate a selected variant by calling the associated activator and passivator procedures.
}

```
function RecordBase: DispRange;
  begin RecordBase := TopWithEntry^.BaseNum end;
procedure StackRecordBase;
  var RecordEntry: StackEntry;
  begin
    GetEntry(RecordEntry); RecordEntry^ := TopWithEntry^.Entry^;
    if RecordEntry^.Kind = Address
    then PushNewAccess(RecordEntry, RecordEntry^.APartWord);
    Push(RecordEntry)
  end { stackrecordbase };
procedure LockBitReference(WOffset: WordRange; BOffset: MCBitIndex);
  var BitField: FieldOffset;
  begin
    with BitField do
      begin
        WordOffset := WOffset; Level := 0; PartWord := true; BitSize := 1;
        BitOffset := BOffset
      end;
    WithReference(RecordBase); FieldReference(BitField, false);
    DeReference(BooleanRepresentation)
  end { lockbitreference };
procedure TestActiveSelector(SelectorRep: TypeRepresentation);
  begin with SelectorRep do LockBitReference(0, 3 * Selector.Level + 2) end;
procedure LockedSelectorCheck(SelectorRep: TypeRepresentation);
  begin
    if Checks in Requested
    then begin
          with SelectorRep do LockBitReference(0, 3 * Selector.Level);
          RuntimeError(2, IfTrue)
        end
  end { lockedselectorcheck };
procedure PresetSelector(SelectorRep: TypeRepresentation);
  begin
    if CodeIsToBeGenerated
    then with SelectorRep do
            if Selector.Level = 0
            then begin
                  StackRecordBase; StackConstant(ZeroValue);
                  Assign(IntegerRepresentation)
                end
  end { presetselector };
```

```
procedure ActivateVariant(SelectorRep: TypeRepresentation);
   var ProcedureCode: BlockLabel;
   begin
     if CodeIsToBeGenerated
     then begin
             ProcedureCode := SelectorRep.PresetCode;
             StackActualBlock(ProcedureCode); OpenParameterList(Proc);
             StackRecordBase; PassReference(Secure); CloseParameterList; CallBlock;
             with SelectorRep do
                begin
                  LockBitReference(0, 3 * Selector.Level + 2); StackConstant(TrueValue);
                  Assign(BooleanRepresentation)
                end
          end
   end { activatevariant };
procedure PassivateVariant(SelectorRep: TypeRepresentation);
   var ExitLabel: CodeLabel; ProcedureCode: BlockLabel;
   begin
     if CodeIsToBeGenerated
     then begin
             FutureCodeLabel(ExitLabel); TestActiveSelector(SelectorRep);
             JumpOnFalse(ExitLabel); ProcedureCode := SelectorRep.PostsetCode;
             StackActualBlock(ProcedureCode); OpenParameterList(Proc);
             StackRecordBase; PassReference(Secure); CloseParameterList; CallBlock;
             with SelectorRep do LockBitReference(0, 3 * Selector.Level + 2);
             StackConstant(FalseValue); Assign(BooleanRepresentation);
             NextIsCodeLabel(ExitLabel)
          end
   end { passivatevariant };
{
```

CaseSelection is a utility procedure used to generate the selection code that forms the basis of the bodies of the activator and passivator procedures of a variant part. The procedure builds a list of potentially selectable variants and applies a generative procedure specified by the parameter Action to the SubFixedPart of each such variant. If checks are on, all variants will accumulate on this list, but if checks are off, only those variants containing embedded files will be considered. This leads to three basic forms of selection code:

(1)   If the selection list contains only one entry corresponding to a variant with corresponding selector value S, selection code takes the form:

```
          if selector = S then ...;
```

(2)   If the selection list holds a subset of the variants, selection code takes the form:

```
          if selector in [ Si, Sj, Sk] then
               case selector of
                    Si: ...;
                    Sj: ...;
                    Sk: ...
```

(3)   If the selection list holds all the variants then selection code takes the form:

```
case selector of
    S1: ...;
    S2: ...;
    ...
    Sn: ...
```

}
```
procedure CaseSelection(VarPart: TypEntry;
                        procedure Action(FixedPart: IdEntry; VariantPart: TypEntry));

   type SelectedEntry = ^SelectedRecord;
        SelectedRecord =
            record
               SelectVariant: TypEntry;
               SelectValue: ObjectValue;
               Next: SelectedEntry
            end;

   var SelectionList: record Length: Scalar; FirstEntry: SelectedEntry end;

   procedure StartSelectionList;

      begin SelectionList.Length := 0; SelectionList.FirstEntry := nil end;

   procedure BuildSelectionList;

      var ThisVariant: TypEntry; NewEntry: SelectedEntry;

      begin
         ThisVariant := VarPart^.FirstVariant;
         while ThisVariant <> nil do
            begin
               if ThisVariant^.Distinct
               then if (Checks in Requested) or EmbeddedFile(ThisVariant)
                  then with ThisVariant^ do
                           begin
                              new(NewEntry);
                              with NewEntry^ do
                                 begin
                                    SelectVariant := ThisVariant;
                                    SetIval(Representation.CheckValue.Magnitude, SelectValue)
                                 end;
                              with SelectionList do
                                 begin
                                    NewEntry^.Next := FirstEntry; FirstEntry := NewEntry;
                                    Length := Length + 1
                                 end
                           end;
               ThisVariant := ThisVariant^.NextVariant
            end
      end { buildselectionlist };
```

```
procedure AnalyseSelectionList;
  var ExitLabel: CodeLabel; Selected: SelectedEntry;
  procedure StackSelector;
    begin
      with VarPart^ do
        begin
          WithReference(FrameLevel); FieldReference(Representation.Selector, false);
          DeReference(SelectorField^.IdType^.Representation)
        end
    end { stackselector };
  procedure TestMembership;
    var SetType: TypEntry;
    begin
      StackSelector;
      with SelectionList do
        begin
          Selected := FirstEntry; StackConstant(EmptyValue); new(SetType);
          with SetType^ do
            begin
              Form := Sets; FormOfSet := Constructed; BaseType := IntType
            end;
          SetRepresentationFor(SetType);
          while Selected <> nil do
            with Selected^ do
              begin
                StackConstant(SelectValue); SingletonSet(SetType^.Representation);
                BinarySetOperation(Plus); Selected := Selected^.Next
              end
        end;
      SetComparison(InOp); JumpOnFalse(ExitLabel); dispose(SetType)
    end { testmembership };
  begin {analyseselectionlist }
    FutureCodeLabel(ExitLabel);
    with SelectionList do
      if Length = 1
      then with FirstEntry^ do
              begin
                StackSelector; StackConstant(SelectValue); OrdinalComparison(EqOp);
                JumpOnFalse(ExitLabel);
                with SelectVariant^ do Action(SubFixedPart, SubVarPart)
              end
      else begin
              if Length < Cardinality(VarPart^.SelectorField^.IdType)
              then TestMembership;
```

```
                StackSelector; OpenCase; Selected := FirstEntry;
                while Selected <> nil do
                  with Selected^ do
                    begin
                      NextIsCase(SelectValue);
                      with SelectVariant^ do Action(SubFixedPart, SubVarPart);
                      Jump(ExitLabel); Selected := Selected^.Next
                    end;
                  CloseCase
                end;
            NextIsCodeLabel(ExitLabel)
        end { analyseselectionlist };
    begin { caseselection } StartSelectionList; BuildSelectionList; AnalyseSelectionList end;
{
```

Code executed conditionally by the selection mechanism outlined above is generated by procedures PresetLevel, PostsetLevel, and CheckLevel. These procedures produce manual pre-, postset, and value-checking code for the fields of a given variant by passing manual lists to the procedures PresetManuals, PostsetMauals, and CheckManuals. Note:

(1) PresetLevel generates code to preset the fixed fields of a record, or record-variant. In addition if the outermost level of the record is being processed, code is generated by a call to PresetControlFlags to clear the control word.

(2) PostsetLevel generates code to postset the variant part of a given level, prior to postsetting its local fixed part.

(3) CheckLevel recursively reinvokes itself to ensure that the nested variant-parts of a given level are checked in addition to the fixed-part.

```
}
procedure PresetLevel(FixedPart: IdEntry; VariantPart: TypEntry);
  var ThisField: IdEntry; PresetList: ManualList;
  begin
    StartManuals(PresetList); ThisField := FixedPart;
    while ThisField <> nil do
      begin
        SelectManual(Presets, PresetList, ThisField); ThisField := ThisField^.NextField
      end;
    if VariantPart <> nil then PresetSelector(VariantPart^.Representation);
    PresetManuals(FrameLevel, PresetList); DisposeManuals(PresetList)
  end { presetlevel };
procedure PostsetLevel(FixedPart: IdEntry; VariantPart: TypEntry);
  var ThisField: IdEntry; PostsetList: ManualList;
  begin
    if VariantPart <> nil
    then if PostsetByCall(VariantPart)
       then PassivateVariant(VariantPart^.Representation);
```

```
      StartManuals(PostsetList); ThisField := FixedPart;
      while ThisField <> nil do
         begin
            SelectManual(Postsets, PostsetList, ThisField); ThisField := ThisField^.NextField
         end;
      PostsetManuals(FrameLevel, PostsetList); DisposeManuals(PostsetList)
   end { postsetlevel };
procedure CheckLevel(FixedPart: IdEntry; VariantPart: TypEntry);
   var ThisField: IdEntry; ChecksList: ManualList;
   begin
      StartManuals(ChecksList); ThisField := FixedPart;
      while ThisField <> nil do
         begin
            SelectManual(ValueChecks, ChecksList, ThisField);
            ThisField := ThisField^.NextField
         end;
      CheckManuals(FrameLevel, ChecksList); DisposeManuals(ChecksList);
      if VariantPart <> nil
      then with VariantPart^ do
            begin
               if CodeIsToBeGenerated then TestActiveSelector(Representation);
               RuntimeError(43, IfFalse); CaseSelection(VariantPart, CheckLevel)
            end
   end { checklevel };
{
```

The procedures GenerateActivator, GeneratePassivator, and GenerateSelector generate the activator, passivator and selector procedures that implement variant selection. The activator and passivator take a single variable parameter representing the record-variable in question. Their bodies are generated by calls to CaseSelection passing PresetLevel or PostsetLevel as an actual (generative) procedure parameter. GenerateSelector generates a selector procedure which is called whenever any variant of an untagged variant part is referenced, or whenever a value is assigned to the tag-field of a tagged variant part. The generated code deduces the new selector value implied by the tag value and when this is different from the current selector value, checks that the selection is neither inconsistent with preselection by new, nor prohibited by reference extension. The fields of the active variant are postset if necessary by calling the passivator procedure, then the tag and internal selector fields are updated, and the fields of the newly activated variant are preset by calling the activator procedure.

```
}
procedure GenerateActivator {parttype: typentry};
   var Entry: BlockLabel; RecordVar: LocalEntry;
   begin
      FutureBlockLabel(Entry); OpenStackFrame;
      FormalParm(VarParm, RecordVar, PartType); OpenCodeSpace(Entry);
      StackParm(RecordVar); OpenWith(FrameLevel);
```

```
      with PartType^ do
        begin
          Representation.PresetCode := Entry; CaseSelection(PartType, PresetLevel)
        end;
      CloseWith; LeaveProcedure; CloseCodeSpace; CloseStackFrame; dispose(RecordVar)
    end { generateactivator };
procedure GeneratePassivator {parttype: typentry};

  var Entry: BlockLabel; RecordVar: LocalEntry;

  begin
    FutureBlockLabel(Entry); OpenStackFrame;
    FormalParm(VarParm, RecordVar, PartType); OpenCodeSpace(Entry);
    StackParm(RecordVar); OpenWith(FrameLevel);
    with PartType^ do
      begin
        Representation.PostsetCode := Entry; CaseSelection(PartType, PostsetLevel)
      end;
    CloseWith; LeaveProcedure; CloseCodeSpace; CloseStackFrame; dispose(RecordVar)
  end { generatepassivator };
procedure PreselectionCheck(SelectorRep: TypeRepresentation);

  var ExitLabel: CodeLabel;

  begin
    if CodeIsToBeGenerated
    then begin
          FutureCodeLabel(ExitLabel);
          with SelectorRep do LockBitReference(0, 3 * Selector.Level + 1);
          JumpOnFalse(ExitLabel); WithReference(RecordBase);
          with SelectorRep do FieldReference(Selector, false);
          DeReference(SelectorRep); OrdinalComparison(NeOp);
          RuntimeError(19, IfTrue); NextIsCodeLabel(ExitLabel)
        end
  end { preselectioncheck };
procedure ReselectionCheck(SelectorRep: TypeRepresentation;
                           var ReturnLabel: CodeLabel);

  var ExitLabel: CodeLabel;

  begin
    if CodeIsToBeGenerated
    then begin
          FutureCodeLabel(ExitLabel); TestActiveSelector(SelectorRep);
          JumpOnFalse(ExitLabel); WithReference(RecordBase);
          with SelectorRep do FieldReference(Selector, false);
          DeReference(SelectorRep); OrdinalComparison(NeOp);
          JumpOnFalse(ReturnLabel); LockedSelectorCheck(SelectorRep);
          NextIsCodeLabel(ExitLabel)
        end
  end { reselectioncheck };
```

```
procedure GenerateSelector {PartType: TypEntry};
  var Entry: BlockLabel; RecordVar, TagValue: LocalEntry;
      SelectionValue: RuntimeAddress; SeparateTag: Boolean; ExitLabel: CodeLabel;
  procedure MapTagToSelectionValue;
    var ThisVariant: TypEntry; SelectorValue: ObjectValue; ExitLabel: CodeLabel;
    begin
      FutureCodeLabel(ExitLabel);
      with PartType^ do
        begin
          StackParm(TagValue); DeReference(TagType^.Representation); OpenCase;
          ThisVariant := FirstVariant; SelectorValue := ZeroValue;
          while ThisVariant <> nil do
            with ThisVariant^ do
              begin
                NextIsCase(VariantValue); StackReference(false, SelectionValue);
                SelectorValue.Ival := Representation.CheckValue.Magnitude;
                StackConstant(SelectorValue);
                Assign(PartType^.SelectorField^.IdType^.Representation);
                Jump(ExitLabel); ThisVariant := NextVariant
              end;
          CloseCase
        end;
      NextIsCodeLabel(ExitLabel)
    end { maptagtoselectionvalue };
  procedure StackSelectionValue;
    begin
      with PartType^ do
        if SeparateTag
        then begin
              StackReference(false, SelectionValue);
              DeReference(SelectorField^.IdType^.Representation)
            end
        else begin StackParm(TagValue); DeReference(TagType^.Representation) end
    end { stackselectionvalue };
  begin { generateselector }
    FutureBlockLabel(Entry); OpenStackFrame;
    FormalParm(VarParm, RecordVar, PartType);
    FormalParm(ValueParm, TagValue, PartType^.TagType); OpenCodeSpace(Entry);
    FutureCodeLabel(ExitLabel);
    with PartType^ do
      begin
        Representation.CheckCode := Entry;
        if Cardinality(SelectorField^.IdType) < Cardinality(TagType)
        then begin
              Acquire(1, SelectionValue); MapTagToSelectionValue;
              SeparateTag := true
            end
        else SeparateTag := false;
```

```
          StackParm(RecordVar); OpenWith(FrameLevel); StackSelectionValue;
          ReselectionCheck(Representation, ExitLabel);
          if Checks in Requested
          then begin StackSelectionValue; PreselectionCheck(Representation) end;
          if PostsetByCall(PartType) then PassivateVariant(Representation);
          if SeparateTag or (TagField = nil)
          then begin
                  WithReference(FrameLevel);
                  FieldReference(Representation.Selector, false); StackSelectionValue;
                  Assign(SelectorField^.IdType^.Representation)
               end;
          if TagField <> nil
          then begin
                  WithReference(FrameLevel); FieldReference(TagField^.Offset, false);
                  StackParm(TagValue); DeReference(TagType^.Representation);
                  Assign(TagType^.Representation)
               end;
          if PresetByCall(PartType) then ActivateVariant(Representation);
          CloseWith
       end;
     NextIsCodeLabel(ExitLabel); LeaveProcedure; CloseCodeSpace; CloseStackFrame;
     dispose(RecordVar); dispose(TagValue)
  end { generateselector };
{
```

26.4 The Record-Type Generators

The procedures PresetARecord, PostsetARecord and CheckARecord are called to generate pre-, postset, and value-checking code for a given record-type. In each case the generated procedure takes a single variable parameter representing the array variable to be processed.

The procedure PresetARecord is called for variant records, and for those record types whose fixed fields have packed substructure or contain embedded file components. The generator calls procedure PresetLevel to generate manual preset code for the fixed fields of the record. For a variant record, the control word will also be preset to zero.
}

```
procedure PresetARecord {RecordType: TypEntry};
  var Entry: BlockLabel; RecordVar: LocalEntry;
  begin
     FutureBlockLabel(Entry); OpenStackFrame;
     FormalParm(VarParm, RecordVar, RecordType); OpenCodeSpace(Entry);
     StackParm(RecordVar); OpenWith(FrameLevel);
     with RecordType^ do
        begin Representation.PresetCode := Entry; PresetLevel(FixedPart, VarPart) end;
     CloseWith; LeaveProcedure; CloseCodeSpace; CloseStackFrame; dispose(RecordVar)
  end { presetarecord };
{
```

The procedure PostsetRecord is called to generate postset code for record- types containing embedded file components.
}

procedure PostsetARecord {RecordType: TypEntry};

    var Entry: BlockLabel; RecordVar: LocalEntry;

    begin
        FutureBlockLabel(Entry); OpenStackFrame;
        FormalParm(VarParm, RecordVar, RecordType); OpenCodeSpace(Entry);
        StackParm(RecordVar); OpenWith(FrameLevel);
        with RecordType^ **do**
            begin Representation.PostsetCode := Entry; PostsetLevel(FixedPart, VarPart) **end**;
        CloseWith; LeaveProcedure; CloseCodeSpace; CloseStackFrame; dispose(RecordVar)
    end { postsetarecord };
{

The procedure CheckARecord is called to generate value-checking code for variant records, and for those record types whose fixed part contains packed sub-structure. Code is generated to manually check each fixed field in turn. If the record contains a variant-part, additional code is required to check the fixed fields of each nested variant.
}

procedure CheckARecord {RecordType: TypEntry};

    var Entry: BlockLabel; RecordVar: LocalEntry;

    begin
        FutureBlockLabel(Entry); OpenStackFrame;
        with RecordType^.Representation **do**
          if WordSize > 1
          then FormalParm(VarParm, RecordVar, RecordType)
          else FormalParm(ValueParm, RecordVar, RecordType);
        OpenCodeSpace(Entry); StackParm(RecordVar); OpenWith(FrameLevel);
        with RecordType^ **do**
            begin Representation.CheckCode := Entry; CheckLevel(FixedPart, VarPart) **end**;
        CloseWith; LeaveProcedure; CloseCodeSpace; CloseStackFrame; dispose(RecordVar)
    end { checkarecord };
{

26.5 The File-Type Generators

The procedures PresetAFile and PostsetAFile are called to generate pre- and postset code for file-variables. Each generated procedure takes a single variable parameter representing the actual file variable.

A file variable is represented by a block of five words which are manually preset as follows:

(1)   Word 0 is preset to zero to denote an ¨undefined¨ file-variable. When the corresponding file is opened by the P-machine, an identifying descriptor value is stored in this word.

(2)   Word 1 is preset to zero. Thereafter bit 0 is used as a lock bit which is set whenever a reference is extended to the buffer variable of the file.

(3)   Word 2 is preset to a code identifying the class of file:

Code	Class
1	textfile
2	wordfile
3	packedfile

The code allows an internal descriptor to be initialised by the P-machine when the file is opened. Thereafter, word 2 is used as the buffer variable for a text file, or as a pointer to the buffer variable for other file organisations.

(4)   When a file is opened, a buffer is allocated using available heap storage, and is used in all subsequent transfers to and from the file. Word 3 is preset with the required buffer-size. For text files the buffer-size is taken to be the value of a configurable constant DefaultBufferSize. For word-files, buffer size is set to a multiple of the element size. For packed files, the buffer size includes a requirement for a secondary buffer to hold the unpacked elements of the file, and a pointer word marking the last such element.

(5)   Word 4 is preset to the number of elements per word for a packed file, or to the element size for word and text files.

```
}
procedure PresetAFile {FileType: TypEntry};
    const UnknownId = 0; LockWord = 0;
    type FileClasses = (Notf, Textf, Wordf, Packedf);
    var Entry: BlockLabel; FileVar: LocalEntry; FileClass: FileClasses;
        BufferSize, Elements: WordRange; CanBePacked: Boolean;
        ElementRepresentation: TypeRepresentation;
    begin
        FutureBlockLabel(Entry); OpenStackFrame;
        FormalParm(VarParm, FileVar, FileType); OpenCodeSpace(Entry);
        with FileType^ do
            begin
                Representation.PresetCode := Entry;
                ElementRepresentation := FelType^.Representation;
                Elements := ElementRepresentation.WordSize;
                if TextFile
                then begin FileClass := Textf; BufferSize := DefaultBufferSize end
                else begin
                        if PackedFile
                        then with ElementRepresentation do
                                if WordSize > 1
                                then CanBePacked := false
                                else CanBePacked := BitSize <= MCBitsPerWord div 2
                        else CanBePacked := false;
```

```
              if CanBePacked
              then begin
                      FileClass := Packedf;
                      with ElementRepresentation do
                        Elements := MCBitsPerWord div BitSize;
                      BufferSize := DefaultBufferSize + Elements + 1
                    end
              else begin
                      FileClass := Wordf;
                      BufferSize := (DefaultBufferSize div Elements + 1) * Elements
                    end
            end;
        if CodeIsToBeGenerated
        then begin
                InlineNumber(UnknownId); InlineNumber(LockWord);
                InlineNumber(ord(FileClass)); InlineNumber(BufferSize);
                InlineNumber(Elements); Pcode0(LoadShort);
                Pcode1(StoreMultiple, FileSize)
              end
      end;
    LeaveProcedure; CloseCodeSpace; CloseStackFrame; dispose(FileVar)
  end { presetafile };
{
```

The procedure PostsetAFile is called to generate postset code for file types. The procedure is
called once for text files and thereafter the generated procedure suffices for all other file
types. A special P-code is used to close the P-machine file and release associated buffering
space.
}

```
procedure PostSetAFile {FileType: TypEntry};
  var Entry: BlockLabel; FileVar: LocalEntry;
  begin
    FutureBlockLabel(Entry); OpenStackFrame;
    FormalParm(VarParm, FileVar, FileType); OpenCodeSpace(Entry);
    with FileType^ do
      begin
        Representation.PostsetCode := Entry;
        if CodeIsToBeGenerated
        then begin Pcode0(LoadShort); Pcode3(CloseFile) end
      end;
    LeaveProcedure; CloseCodeSpace; CloseStackFrame; dispose(FileVar)
  end { postsetafile };
```

{

CHAPTER 27

Diagnostic File Generation

The code- and data-maps which comprise the interface to the Post-Mortem Generator program are implemented as serial files. The data-map is supplemented by a name-file which contains the identifier spelling of every named object on the data file. The code-map, data-map and name-files are generated when the boolean option PMDump has been selected.

27.1 The Code-Map File

The code-map is a file of records of type MapToken which allows an object program address to be related to a source program line number. Tokens are appended to this file by the procedure FileToken throughout analysis of the statement part of every block. The position of each new token on the file is recorded by global variable CodeMapIndex.

}
procedure FileToken(Token: MapToken);
   begin CodeMap^ := Token; put(CodeMap); CodeMapIndex := CodeMapIndex + 1 **end**;
{

Each statement-part generates a sequence of tokens beginning with a "StartBody" and ending with an "EndBody" token. The StartBody token contains a BlockSerial number identifying the program block, and a StartLine that identifies the source line containing the start of the statement part. The EndBody token marks the end of the token sequence for the block and contains additional information about the number of words of code and jump-table data for the block.

The StartBody and EndBody tokens embrace a sequence of zero or more FlowTokens. A FlowToken is appended to the code-map to mark the onset of code-generation for each new source line. The source line number and the relative code-byte offset from the base of the code-table are given by the values of the fields FlowLine and CodeOffset. FlowTokens are generated by the procedure FlowPoint which is called by the analyser prior to analysis of every statement. A variable LastFlowLine is therefore used to restrict the generation of FlowTokens to one per source-program line.

}

```
procedure StartOfBody {Serial: SerialRange; SourceLine: Scalar};
  var Token: MapToken;
  begin
    if CodeIsToBeGenerated and (PMDump in Requested)
    then begin
          with CurrentBlock^ do DataStack[DataBase + SerialOffset].WValue := Serial;
          BlockIndex := CodeMapIndex;
          with Token do
            begin
              Kind := StartBody; BlockSerial := Serial; StartLine := SourceLine
            end;
          FileToken(Token); LastFlowLine := SourceLine
        end
  end { startofbody };
procedure FlowPoint {SourceLine: Scalar};
  var Token: MapToken;
  begin
    if CodeIsToBeGenerated and (PMDump in Requested)
    then if SourceLine > LastFlowLine
        then begin
                with Token do
                  begin
                    Kind := FlowToken; FlowLine := SourceLine;
                    CodeOffset := CodeCounter
                  end;
                FileToken(Token); LastFlowLine := SourceLine
              end
  end { flowpoint };
procedure EndOfBody {CodeSize, DataSize: Scalar};
  var Token: MapToken;
  begin
    if CodeIsToBeGenerated and ((PMDump in Requested) or (CodeDump in Requested))
    then begin
            with Token do
              begin
                Kind := EndBody; JumpTableSize := DataSize;
                CodeTableSize := CodeSize
              end;
            FileToken(Token)
          end
  end { endofbody };
procedure InitCodeMap;
  begin rewrite(CodeMap); LastFlowLine := 0; CodeMapIndex := 0 end;
```

{

27.2 The Name File

Identifier spellings of all named objects on the data file are written onto a separate Name File. Each spelling is filed as a byte-string in which the first byte contains the length of the string. The byte-position of each byte-string is recorded in the global variable NameFileIndex. Generation of the Name File is controlled by the following procedures:

}

```
procedure PutByte(Byte: NameByte);
  begin NameFile^ := Byte; put(NameFile); NameFileIndex := NameFileIndex + 1 end;
procedure FileName(Name: Alfa);
  var Length: Scalar; Index: 1..AlfaSize; Trailer: AlfaEntry;
  procedure FileCh(c: char);
    begin if c <> ' ' then PutByte(ord(c)) end;
  begin
    Length := AlfaLength(Name); PutByte(Length);
    for Index := 1 to AlfaSize do FileCh(Name.Head[Index]);
    Trailer := Name.Tail;
    while Trailer <> nil do
      begin
        for Index := 1 to ChunkLength do FileCh(Trailer^.Chunk[Index]);
        Trailer := Trailer^.NextChunk
      end
  end { filename };
procedure InitNameFile;
  begin rewrite(NameFile); NameFileIndex := 0 end;
```

{

27.3 The Data File

The data file contains information necessary for the Post-Mortem Generator to:

(a)   map an object program data address onto a declared data item;

(b)   reconstruct a description of the data-item in source-language terms.

This information is filed by recording the contents of the Type and Identifier tables together with a block-identification for every procedure, function, and program block, in records of type DataObject. To preserve the compile-time linkages between the Identifier and Type tables, the various pointers are recast in terms of the serial numbers attached to each TypeRecord and IdRecord. Identifier spelling truncation is avoided by filing the spelling separately on the name-file and recording its position in the data-object record.

Every block scope gives rise to a sequence of elements on this file of the form:

   ... Type-Objects ... Identifier-Objects ... Block-Object

Both record and enumerated types will themselves give rise to sequences of identifier objects describing the fields of the record or the values of the type. The local variables, and parameters of a block are filed in reverse lexicographic order and each member of the sequence is serial-linked to its predecessor. The final block-object contains a serial-link to the last local identifier object-field, enabling the Post Mortem Generator to reproduce for each block-scope, a sorted list of local variable identifiers. Each object corresponding to a local-variable, record-field, or bound-identifier contains the associated runtime address or field offset, which together with the serial link to the appropriate type-object, allows the Post Mortem Generator to reconstruct the data-value in source-language terms. The following procedure controls the generation of the data file.
}

```
procedure PutData(var Object: DataObject);
    begin DataMap^ := Object; put(DataMap) end;
function IdSerialOf(Id: IdEntry): SerialRange;
    begin
        if Id = nil then IdSerialOf := NilSerial else IdSerialOf := Id^.Serial
    end { idserialof };
function TypeSerialOf(Typ: TypEntry): SerialRange;
    begin
        if Typ = nil then TypeSerialOf := NilSerial else TypeSerialOf := Typ^.Serial
    end { typeserialof };
procedure FileId {Id, NextId: IdEntry};
    var Object: DataObject; SerialOfNextId: SerialRange;
    begin
        if CodeIsToBeGenerated and (PMDump in Requested) and (Id <> nil)
        then begin
                SerialOfNextId := IdSerialOf(NextId);
                with Id^, Object do
                    begin
                        ObjSerial := Serial; ObjClass := Klass;
                        case Klass of
                            Consts :
                                begin
                                    ConstName := NameFileIndex; FileName(Id^.Name);
                                    ConstValue := Values; NextConst := SerialOfNextId
                                end;
                            Vars :
                                begin
                                    VarName := NameFileIndex; FileName(Id^.Name);
                                    VarType := TypeSerialOf(IdType);
                                    IsVarParam := (VarKind = VarParam);
                                    LocalAddress := VarAddress.WordOffset;
                                    NextLocalVar := SerialOfNextId
                                end;
```

```
            Bound :
              begin
                VarName := NameFileIndex; FileName(Id^.Name);
                VarType := TypeSerialOf(IdType); IsVarParam := false;
                LocalAddress := BdAddress.WordOffset
              end;
            Field :
              begin
                FieldName := NameFileIndex; FileName(Id^.Name);
                FieldType := TypeSerialOf(IdType); ObjOffset := Offset;
                NextField := SerialOfNextId
              end;
            Prog, Proc, Func :
              begin
                BlockName := NameFileIndex; FileName(Id^.Name);
                BlockBody := BlockIndex; FirstLocalVar := SerialOfNextId
              end
          end
        end;
      PutData(Object)
    end
  end { fileid };
procedure FileAType {TheType: TypEntry};
  var Low, High: ObjectValue; Object: DataObject;
  procedure FileFields(FirstField: IdEntry);
    var ThisField, NextField: IdEntry;
    begin
      ThisField := FirstField;
      while ThisField <> nil do
        begin
          NextField := ThisField^.NextField; FileId(ThisField, NextField);
          ThisField := NextField
        end
    end { filefields };
  procedure FileConsts(FirstConst: IdEntry);
    var ThisConst, NextConst: IdEntry;
    begin
      ThisConst := FirstConst;
      while ThisConst <> nil do
        begin
          NextConst := ThisConst^.SuccId; FileId(ThisConst, NextConst);
          ThisConst := NextConst
        end
    end { fileconsts };
```

```
begin { fileatype }
  if CodeIsToBeGenerated and (PMDump in Requested) and (TheType <> nil)
  then begin
        with TheType^, Object do
          begin
            ObjSerial := Serial; ObjClass := Types;
            ObjRepresentation := Representation; ObjForm := Form;
            case Form of
              Scalars :
                begin
                  ObjScalarKind := ScalarKind;
                  case ScalarKind of
                    Predefined :
                      if TheType = IntType
                      then StdType := IntStd
                      else if TheType = RealType
                              then StdType := RealStd
                              else if TheType = CharType
                                      then StdType := CharStd;
                    Declared :
                      begin
                        FileConsts(FirstConst);
                        ObjFirstConst := IdSerialOf(FirstConst)
                      end
                  end
                end;
              SubRanges :
                begin
                  ObjRangeType := TypeSerialOf(RangeType); ObjMin := Min;
                  ObjMax := Max
                end;
              Pointers : ObjDomain := TypeSerialOf(DomainType);
              Sets :
                begin
                  SetIsPacked := FormOfSet = IsPacked;
                  ObjBaseType := TypeSerialOf(BaseType)
                end;
              Arrays :
                begin
                  ArrayIsPacked := PackedArray; GetBounds(InxType, Low, High);
                  ObjLowBound := Low; ObjHighBound := High;
                  ObjAelType := TypeSerialOf(AelType);
                  ObjInxType := TypeSerialOf(InxType)
                end;
              CAPSchema :
                begin
                  SchemaIsPacked := PackedSchema;
                  ObjCompType := TypeSerialOf(CompType);
                  ObjInxSpec := TypeSerialOf(InxSpec);
                  ObjLowAddr := LowBdAddress.WordOffset;
```

```
                    ObjHighAddr := HighBdAddress.WordOffset
                  end;
                Records :
                  begin
                    FileFields(FixedPart); RecordIsPacked := PackedRecord;
                    ObjFixedPart := IdSerialOf(FixedPart);
                    ObjVarPart := TypeSerialOf(VarPart)
                  end;
                Files :
                  begin
                    FileIsPacked := PackedFile; FileIsText := TextFile;
                    ObjFelType := TypeSerialOf(FelType)
                  end;
                VariantPart :
                  begin
                    FileId(TagField, nil); ObjTagField := IdSerialOf(TagField);
                    ObjTagType := TypeSerialOf(TagType);
                    ObjFstVariant := TypeSerialOf(FirstVariant);
                    ObjSelector := SelectorField^.Offset
                  end;
                Variant :
                  begin
                    FileFields(SubFixedPart); VariantIsDistinct := Distinct;
                    ObjSubFixedPart := IdSerialOf(SubFixedPart);
                    ObjSubVarPart := TypeSerialOf(SubVarPart);
                    ObjNextVariant := TypeSerialOf(NextVariant);
                    ObjVariantValue := VariantValue
                  end
              end
            end;
          PutData(Object)
        end
  end { fileatype };
procedure InitDataMap;
  begin rewrite(DataMap) end;
```

{

The procedure InitDiagnostics ensures that the interface files are correctly initialised before compilation begins. Since all input/output to these files is performed in terms of the standard Pascal functions, no explicit file closure is necessary and procedure EndDiagnostics is consequently a dummy.

}

```
procedure InitDiagnostics;
  begin InitCodeMap; InitNameFile; InitDataMap end;
procedure EndDiagnostics;
  begin  end;
```

CHAPTER 28

Code Generator
Initialisation

The code-generator is initialised systematically on a module by module basis by a call to procedure InitCodeGeneration made from the compiler program body. However, a number of generator variables not associated with any module in particular are initialised here by procedures InitPCodes, InitDefaults, and InitOthers.

procedure InitPcodes;
  begin

```
IntCodes[Mul] := MultInteger;              RealCodes[Mul] := MultiplyReal;
IntCodes[Rdiv] := NoOperation;             RealCodes[Rdiv] := DivideReal;
IntCodes[AndOp] := NoOperation;            RealCodes[AndOp] := NoOperation;
IntCodes[Idiv] := DivInteger;              RealCodes[Idiv] := NoOperation;
IntCodes[Imod] := ModInteger;             RealCodes[Imod] := NoOperation;
IntCodes[Plus] := AddInteger;              RealCodes[Plus] := AddReal;
IntCodes[Minus] := SubInteger;            RealCodes[Minus] := SubtractReal;
IntCodes[OrOp] := NoOperation;             RealCodes[OrOp] := NoOperation;
IntCodes[LtOp] := TestILess;               RealCodes[LtOp] := TestRLess;
IntCodes[LeOp] := TestILtOrEqual;         RealCodes[LeOp] := TestRLtOrEqual;
IntCodes[GeOp] := NoOperation;             RealCodes[GeOp] := NoOperation;
IntCodes[GtOp] := NoOperation;             RealCodes[GtOp] := NoOperation;
IntCodes[NeOp] := TestIUnequal;           RealCodes[NeOp] := TestRUnequal;
IntCodes[EqOp] := TestIEqual;              RealCodes[EqOp] := TestREqual;
IntCodes[InOp] := NoOperation;             RealCodes[InOp] := NoOperation;
IntCodes[NotOp] := NoOperation;            RealCodes[NotOp] := NoOperation;
IntCodes[SingleOp] := NoOperation;        RealCodes[SingleOp] := NoOperation;
IntCodes[RangeOp] := NoOperation;         RealCodes[RangeOp] := NoOperation;
StringCodes[Mul] := NoOperation;          SetCodes[Mul] := SetIntersection;
StringCodes[Rdiv] := NoOperation;         SetCodes[Rdiv] := NoOperation;
StringCodes[AndOp] := NoOperation;        SetCodes[AndOp] := NoOperation;
StringCodes[Idiv] := NoOperation;         SetCodes[Idiv] := NoOperation;
StringCodes[Imod] := NoOperation;         SetCodes[Imod] := NoOperation;
StringCodes[Plus] := NoOperation;         SetCodes[Plus] := SetUnion;
StringCodes[Minus] := NoOperation;        SetCodes[Minus] := SetDifference;
StringCodes[OrOp] := NoOperation;         SetCodes[OrOp] := NoOperation;
StringCodes[LtOp] := TestSLess;           SetCodes[LtOp] := NoOperation;
```

```
    StringCodes[LeOp] := TestSLtOrEqual;        SetCodes[LeOp] := TestSubset;
    StringCodes[GeOp] := NoOperation;           SetCodes[GeOp] := NoOperation;
    StringCodes[GtOp] := NoOperation;           SetCodes[GtOp] := NoOperation;
    StringCodes[NeOp] := TestSUnequal;          SetCodes[NeOp] := TestSetUnequal;
    StringCodes[EqOp] := TestSEqual;            SetCodes[EqOp] := TestSetEqual;
    StringCodes[InOp] := NoOperation;           SetCodes[InOp] := InSet;
    StringCodes[NotOp] := NoOperation;          SetCodes[NotOp] := NoOperation;
    StringCodes[SingleOp] := NoOperation;       SetCodes[SingleOp] := MakeSingletonSet;
    StringCodes[RangeOp] := NoOperation;        SetCodes[RangeOp] := MakeRangeSet;
    PtrCodes[EqOp] := TestPEqual;               PtrCodes[NeOp] := TestPUnequal;

    AccessCodes[LoadOp, Local] := LoadLocal;
    AccessCodes[LoadOp, Enclosing] := LoadEnclosing;
    AccessCodes[LoadOp, Intermediate] := LoadIntermediate;
    AccessCodes[LoadOp, Global] := LoadGlobal;
    AccessCodes[StoreOp, Local] := StoreLocal;
    AccessCodes[StoreOp, Enclosing] := StoreEnclosing;
    AccessCodes[StoreOp, Intermediate] := StoreIntermediate;
    AccessCodes[StoreOp, Global] := StoreGlobal;
    AccessCodes[LoadRefOp, Local] := LoadRefLocal;
    AccessCodes[LoadRefOp, Enclosing] := LoadRefEnclosing;
    AccessCodes[LoadRefOp, Intermediate] := LoadRefIntermediate;
    AccessCodes[LoadRefOp, Global] := LoadRefGlobal;

    CheckCodes[false, false] := NoOperation;    CheckCodes[false, true] := CheckUpper;
    CheckCodes[true, false] := CheckLower;      CheckCodes[true, true] := CheckLimits;
    TransferCodes[false, false] := Pack;        TransferCodes[false, true] := Unpack;
    TransferCodes[true, false] := Packc;        TransferCodes[true, true] := Unpackc
  end { initpcodes };
procedure InitDefaults;
  begin
    with UndefinedValue do begin Defined := false; Multiple := 1 end;
    with BufferOffset do
      begin
        WordOffset := BufferVarOffset; Level := 0; PartWord := false; WordSize := 1
      end;
    with DefaultAddress do begin BlockLevel := 0; WordOffset := FirstOffset end;
    with DefaultOffset do
      begin WordOffset := 0; Level := 0; PartWord := false; WordSize := 1 end;
    with DefaultLabel do begin BlockLevel := 0; EntryOffset := 0 end
  end { initdefaults };
procedure InitOthers;
  begin
    StackConstant(ZeroValue); Pop(ZeroEntry);
    StackConstant(DefaultLayout); Pop(DefaultWidth);
    ItemShapes[false, false] := Word; ItemShapes[false, true] := WordStructure;
    ItemShapes[true, false] := PartWrd; ItemShapes[true, true] := PartWrdStructure;
    ContextOfCheck := IsUnknown
  end { initothers };
```

procedure InitCodeGeneration;
  begin
    InitPcodes; InitDefaults; InitValues; InitRepresentations; InitFrames; InitEmitter;
    InitStack; InitIO; InitWith; InitCase; InitFor; InitOthers
  end { initcodegeneration };

procedure EndCodeGeneration;
  begin EndEmitter **end**;

CHAPTER 29

The Driver Program

The compiler's main program body initialises each of the analyser and generator chapters in an appropriate order, and then calls the main analysis procedure Programme to carry out analysis and code generation for the source program input. On completion of this process, finalisation calls to appropriate chapters are made.

The global label 13 is provided for abnormal termination, and is positioned to carry out finalisation of the output listing only.

```
{

}
begin
    InitOptions;
    InitListing;
    InitCodeGeneration;
    InitDiagnostics;
    InitSymbol;
    InitSyntax;
    InitSemanticTables;

    Programme;

    EndDiagnostics;
    EndCodeGeneration;
    13: EndListing
end.
```

Index of
Major Procedures and Functions
in the Compiler

The following index lists all major procedures and functions used in the compiler, together with the page numbers needed to locate their definitions in this version of its text.

CHAPTER 30

P-machine Overview

{

This program provides an operational definition of the P-machine for executing object programs generated by the Model Compiler. The machine is characterised by its pure-stack architecture and its large repertoire of instructions tailored specifically towards an efficient and secure implementation of Standard Pascal. As with most high-level machine descriptions, no free-standing implementation of arithmetic functions has been attempted, and this version will inherit the real and integer arithmetic of its host. Moreover, no general implementation of program parameters can be expressed in Standard Pascal, and accordingly all communication with the external environment is channelled through the P-machine's own program heading which is as follows:

}

program Pmachine
(CodeFile, Input, Output, CorpseFile);

{

These input and output files have the following nature and purpose:

Pcode   is an input file containing the object program to be executed.

Input   is an input file providing an input medium for the executing program.

Output   is an output file providing an output medium for the executing program.

CorpseFile is an output file that contains the ¨corpse¨ of a program that terminated in error. The corpse file is passed to the Postmortem Generator program for subsequent error analysis.

The P-machine is modular in design, and comprises a Loader, Processor, Memory Manager, and Input/Output Manager. In addition, there are modules to provide support for file creation, instruction execution, and overall P-machine control. As with the Model Compiler, the modular structure is represented by organising the program as a series of code ¨chapters¨. However Standard Pascal constrains all declarations to be collected together within a single chapter which must then be read in conjuction with those that follow.

Chapter 32 provides overall P-machine control by reading the set of compile-time options from the header on the P-code file. The degree of runtime checking supported follows directly from the option values supplied. This chapter also provides for the generation of the CorpseFile and contains hooks for the system-dependent call to the Postmortem Generator.

Chapter 33 provides "micro-level" support for instruction execution.

Chapter 34 contains the Memory Manager, and provides stack and heap management for all program data and for I/O buffers. The module includes a simple garbage collector allowing effective re-utilisation of discarded heap storage.

Chapter 35 contains the machine Loader that reads the P-code file generated by the compiler.

Chapter 36 contains a number of utilities supporting integer, set and string arithmetic.

Chapter 37 contains the System File Interface, which implements standard I/O communication via the P-machine program parameters Input and Output, and defines a system-independent interface for more general file I/O.

Chapter 38 contains the Pascal I/O Manager, and provides support for all standard I/O functions. The I/O manager controls all transfers between the System File Interface and the corresponding file variables by means of I/O buffers acquired from the heap.

Chapter 39 contains the Processor that controls program execution. A program is run until normal termination, or an error occurs. In the latter case the Controller dumps the entire P-machine memory onto the CorpseFile, and calls the Postmortem Generator for subsequent analysis.

}

{

CHAPTER 31

Global Definitions
and Declarations

As in the Model Compiler, this chapter contains all of the global definitions and declarations on which the procedures in the subsequent chapters depend. In this chapter, only a brief indication of the overall nature of the constants, types and variables introduced is given, together with a reference to the chapter in which they are used. A more detailed explanation of the nature and purpose of each is given in the referenced chapter itself.

31.1 Another Global Label!

The global label 13 is used to terminate execution in the event of catastrophic P-machine failure.

}
label 13;
{

31.2 Global Constants

}
const
{

The following constants describe the model P-machine. Their values are strictly dependent on the host Pascal environment in which the model implementation is to run. An implementor must

1. Investigate how the host Pascal processor implements the packed-variable:

    HostWord : packed array[HostWordSize] of HostBit

    If HostWord[0] is mapped onto the most significant bit position, then set the constant IndexedFromLeft to the value true. Otherwise, set it to false.

2. Set the value of FormFeed so that chr(FormFeed) will throw a new printer page, or have an equivalent effect on the chosen output device.

3. Redefine the constants prefixed 'MC' for the host machine.

}

343

IndexedFromLeft= true;   { for host Pascal compiler }
FormFeed = 12;   { ASCII form-feed character }

MCBitsPerWord = 32;   { bits per memory-word }
MCWordSetBits = 31;   { bits per set-word }
MCBitsPerByte = 8;   { bits per memory-byte }
MCBytesPerWord = 4;   { mcbitsperword div mcbitsperbyte }
MCMaxBitnum = 31;   { mcbitsperword-1 }
MCMaxSetBit = 30;   { mcwordsetbits-1 }
MCMaxByteNum = 3;   { mcbytesperword-1 }

MCRealSize = 2;   { real size in words }
MCMaxByte = 255;   { max mc-byte value }
MCMaxInt = 2147483647;   { max mc-integer value }
MCMaxRealRoot = 46340.95;   { max real such that }
                                                { sqr(mcmaxrealroot)<=mcmaxint.0 }
MCMaxMemWord = 16383;   { max memory-word address }
MCMaxMemByte = 65535;   { max memory-byte address }

AlfaSize = 12;
MaxVariantLevel= 9;   { max variant nesting level }

{
The following constants define the opcode mnemonics used for P-code instructions within the
P-Machine. The form and effect of each instruction is defined in Chapter 39, together with
its implementation.
}
{ P-machine class 1 instructions }

cons0 = 0;	cons1 = 1;	cons2 = 2;	cons3 = 3;	cons4 = 4;
cons5 = 5;	cons6 = 6;	cons7 = 7;	cons8 = 8;	cons9 = 9;
cons10 = 10;	cons11 = 11;	cons12 = 12;	cons13 = 13;	cons14 = 14;
cons15 = 15;	cons16 = 16;	cons17 = 17;	cons18 = 18;	cons19 = 19;
cons20 = 20;	cons21 = 21;	cons22 = 22;	cons23 = 23;	cons24 = 24;
cons25 = 25;	cons26 = 26;	cons27 = 27;	cons28 = 28;	cons29 = 29;
cons30 = 30;	cons31 = 31;	consb = 32;	consw = 33;	conmb = 34;
conmw = 35;	crefb = 36;	crefw = 37;	csetb = 38;	csetw = 39;
lodl0 = 40;	lodl1 = 41;	lodl2 = 42;	lodl3 = 43;	lodl4 = 44;
lodl5 = 45;	lodl6 = 46;	lodl7 = 47;	lodlb = 48;	lodlw = 49;
lrf0 = 50;	lrf1 = 51;	lrf2 = 52;	lrf3 = 53;	lrf4 = 54;
lrf5 = 55;	lrf6 = 56;	lrf7 = 57;	lrflb = 58;	lrflw = 59;
stol0 = 60;	stol1 = 61;	stol2 = 62;	stol3 = 63;	stol4 = 64;
stol5 = 65;	stol6 = 66;	stol7 = 67;	stolb = 68;	stolw = 69;
lodgb = 70;	lodgw = 71;	lrfgb = 72;	lrfgw = 73;	stogb = 74;
stogw = 75;	lodeb = 76;	lodew = 77;	lrfeb = 78;	lrfew = 79;
stoeb = 80;	stoew = 81;	lodib = 82;	lodiw = 83;	lrfib = 84;
lrfiw = 85;	stoib = 86;	stoiw = 87;	lodin = 88;	indx1 = 89;
indx2 = 90;	indx3 = 91;	indx4 = 92;	indx5 = 93;	indx6 = 94;
indx7 = 95;	indxb = 96;	indxw = 97;	ixrfb = 98;	ixrfw = 99;
ixcap = 100;	stoin = 101;	adjpb = 102;	adjpw = 103;	adjpl = 104;
adjmb = 105;	adjmw = 106;	adjml = 107;	adadr = 108;	lodbt = 109;

lodpk = 110;   stobt = 111;   stopk = 112;   ixpkb = 113;   ixpcap = 114;
ixswb = 115;   adjpk = 116;   lodby = 117;   stoby = 118;   lbyrf = 119;
ibyrf = 120;   lodmb = 121;   lodmw = 122;   stomb = 123;   stomw = 124;
storb = 125;   storw = 126;   moveb = 127;   movew = 128;   szcap = 129;
mvcap = 130;   dpcap = 131;   rlcap = 132;   andop = 133;   notop = 134;
incrb = 135;   incrw = 136;   incr1 = 137;   decrb = 138;   decrw = 139;
decr1 = 140;   absint = 141;   negint = 142;   sqrint = 143;   addint = 144;
subint = 145;   mulint = 146;   divint = 147;   modint = 148;   oddint = 149;
eqint = 150;   neint = 151;   ltint = 152;   leint = 153;   chktv = 154;
chktd = 155;   chklm = 156;   chklw = 157;   chkup = 158;   chkcap = 159;
float = 160;   absrl = 161;   negrl = 162;   sqrl = 163;   addrl = 164;
subrl = 165;   mulrl = 166;   divrl = 167;   trurl = 168;   rndrl = 169;
eqrl = 170;   nerl = 171;   ltrl = 172;   lerl = 173;   lodptr = 174;
eqptr = 175;   neptr = 176;   eqstr = 177;   nestr = 178;   ltstr = 179;
lestr = 180;   lodset = 181;   stoset = 182;   sglset = 183;   rngset = 184;
setuni = 185;   setint = 186;   setdif = 187;   setexp = 188;   eqset = 189;
neset = 190;   leset = 191;   inset = 192;   chksl = 193;   chksu = 194;
jmpfw = 195;   jmpbk = 196;   jmpvia = 197;   jmpout = 198;   fjpfw = 199;
fjpbk = 200;   fjpvia = 201;   fjpcnd = 202;   tjpcnd = 203;   casejp = 204;
mark = 205;   calglo = 206;   calloc = 207;   callev = 208;   calotr = 209;
calfml = 210;   endp = 211;   endf = 212;   endmf = 213;   newp1b = 214;
newp1w = 215;   dspp1b = 216;   dspp1w = 217;   chkn1 = 218;   chkd1 = 219;
chkd2 = 220;   noop = 221;   preset = 222;   presrb = 223;   presrw = 224;
ldstk = 225;   dpstk = 226;   popstk = 227;   chkwd = 228;   chkrp = 229;
chkvf = 230;   trapp = 231;   trapt = 232;   trapf = 233;   setlk = 234;
dislk = 235;   pglk = 236;   smpglk = 237;   haltp = 238;   chkptr = 241;
chkflw = 242;   chkfup = 243;   escape = 255;

{ P-machine class 2 instructions }

chkrd = 0;   chkwr = 1;   rewrtf = 2;   resetf = 3;   eolnf = 4;
eoff = 5;   getf = 6;   rdint = 7;   rdrl = 8;   rdln = 9;
putf = 10;   wrchar = 11;   wrbool = 12;   wrstr = 13;   wrint = 14;
wrflt = 15;   wrfix = 16;   wrln = 17;   pagef = 18;   closef = 19;
pckpr = 20;   pckprc = 21;   Upkpr = 22;   upkprc = 23;   sinf = 24;
cosf = 25;   expf = 26;   logf = 27;   sqrtf = 28;   arctnf = 29;
mapp = 30;   chkbuf = 31;

{

The following constants define offsets used to access specific locations within the stack-frame headers and code-block headers used by the P-machine.

}

SLOffset = 1;   { |framebase-1|=staticlink }
CBOffset = 2;   { |framebase-2|=codebase }
DLOffset = 3;   { |framebase-3|=dynamiclink }
RAOffset = 4;   { |framebase-4|=returnaddress }
LDOffset = 5;   { |framebase-5|=lock-stack depth }
LTOffset = 6;   { |framebase-6|=lock-stack top }
FrameSize = 6;

```
ParamsOffset = 1;                    { |codebase-1| = parameter size }
LocalsOffset = 2;                    { |codebase-2| = stack size }
LocksOffset = 3;                     { |codebase-3| = lock-stack size }
SerialOffset = 4;                    { |codebase-4| = 0/pmd block serial }
FinalsOffset = 5;                    { |codebase-5| = finalisation ep }
```

{ constants used by the machine-controller, chapter 32 }

```
RuntimeBase = 300;                   { runtime errors: 301..400 }
SystemBase = 400;                    { system limit errors: 401..420 }
FatalBase = 420;                     { fatal errors: 421..450 }
```

{ constants used by the memory-manager, chapter 34 }

```
MinBlock = 64;                       { lower bound on free-space }
MinHeapBlock = 2;                    { lower bound on heap block size }
FreeList = MCMaxMemWord;             { [freelist] = next freeblock }
Null = 0;                            { null block pointer }
PointerSize = 2;                     { heap pointer size }
LockSize = 3;                        { lock-stack entry size }
HeapLockOffset = 2;                  { [heapaddress-2] = lock/level word }
HeapLockBit = MCMaxBitnum;           { heap lock bit in lock/level word }
HeapLevelByte = 0;                   { new1/new2 level in lock/level word }
```

{ constants used by the system file interface, chapter 37 }

```
MaxFileIndex = 16;                   { max file-index value }
UndefinedIndex = 0;                  { denotes "undefined" file variable }

BlankName = '        ';
```

{ constants used by the Pascal I/O manager, chapter 38 }

```
TextCode = 1;                        { textfile code }
WordCode = 2;                        { wordfile code }
PackedCode = 3;                      { packedfile code }
FileLockBit = 0;                     { set when buffer is referenced }
EofBit = 1;                          { save eof status }
EolBit = 2;                          { save eoln status }
MaxTextLine = 255;                   { max textfile line length }
   {
```

31.3 Global Types
```
}
```

type

{ types describing the model P-machine }

```
MCBit = 0..1;
MCByte = 0..MCMaxByte;
MCWord = integer;
MCScalar = 0..MCMaxInt;
MCInteger = integer;
```

```
MCReal = real;
MCBitRange = 0..MCBitsPerWord;
MCBitIndex = 0..MCMaxBitnum;
MCSetBits = 0..MCMaxSetBit;
MCBitArray = packed array [MCBitIndex] of MCBit;
MCByteIndex = 0..MCMaxByteNum;
MCByteArray = packed array [MCByteIndex] of MCByte;
MCWordSet = set of MCSetBits;

WordCast = (AsSet, AsBits, AsBytes, AsReal, AsValue);
MCWordForm = record
                case WordCast of
                    AsSet: (WSet: MCWordSet);
                    AsBits: (WBits: MCBitArray);
                    AsBytes: (WBytes: MCByteArray);
                    AsReal: (WReal: MCReal);
                    AsValue: (WValue: MCWord)
                end;

RealMap = record
                case Boolean of
                    false: (RealValue: MCReal);
                    true: (Word: array [1..MCRealSize] of MCWord)
                end;

WordRange = 0..MCMaxMemWord;
ByteRange = 0..MCMaxMemByte;
BitRange = MCBitRange;

Scalar = 0..maxint;

AlfaIndex = 1..AlfaSize;
Alfa = packed array [AlfaIndex] of char;

{ types required by the machine controller, chapter 32 }

OptionType = (Listing, Checks, PMDump, Level, Margin, Other);
Terminus = (Normal, RuntimeError, SystemLimit, Fatal);

{ type used by the memory manager, chapter 34 }

KeyValues = -MCMaxInt..+MCMaxInt;

{ types used by the system file interface, chapter 37 }

IndexRange = UndefinedIndex..MaxFileIndex;
FileStatus = (Detach, Retain);
IOmode = (ForReading, ForWriting);
IOTransfer = record ByteAmount: ByteRange; BitAmount: BitRange end;
```

```
{ types used by the Pascal I/O manager, chapter 38 }

PascFileMode = (NotSet, Inspection, Generation);
PascFileDescriptor = record
                       case Defined: Boolean of
                         false: ();
                         true:
                           (Mode: PascFileMode; EndOfFile: Boolean;
                            BufferSize, FirstWord: WordRange;
                            case TextFile: Boolean of
                              true:
                                (BufferWord: WordRange;
                                 BytePointer, LastByte: ByteRange);
                              false:
                                (PointerWord, LastWord: WordRange;
                                 case PackedFile: Boolean of
                                   false: (ComponentSize: WordRange);
                                   true:
                                     (WordPointer: WordRange;
                                      ElsPerWord: 2..MCBitsPerWord)))
                     end;
StringRange = 1..MaxTextLine;
TextString = record
               Length: 0..MaxTextLine; String: packed array [StringRange] of char
             end;
NumberForms = (IntForm, RealForm);
PrintedForms = (Floated, Fixed);
Number = record
           case Form: NumberForms of
             IntForm: (IntValue: MCInteger);
             RealForm:
               (RealValue: MCReal;
                case Format: PrintedForms of
                  Fixed: (FracDigits: MCWord);
                  Floated: (TotalWidth: MCWord))
         end;
{ types required by the arithmetic unit, chapter 36 }

OpType = (Plus, Minus, Mul, Idiv, Imod);
Operands = MCWord;
{
```

31.4 Global Variables

The global "variable" Undefined holds the represeantaion of an undefined P-machine
memory word. This value cannot be represented in Standard Pascal and is therefore constructed on a bit-by-bit basis by the procedure SetMCUndefined when the P-Machine is initialised.

}

var

Undefined: MCWord;

{ P-machine global memory }

Memory: **array** [WordRange] **of** MCWord;

{ P-machine global address registers }

ProgramCounter: ByteRange;
CodeBase: WordRange;
NewFrame, EnclosingFrame, CurrentFrame, GlobalFrame: WordRange;
StackTop, HeapTop: WordRange;
Address: MCWord;

{ P-machine global arithmetic registers }

RealResult, RealOperand, RealOp1, RealOp2: MCReal;
Result, Operand, Operand1, Operand2: Operands;

{ P-machine global set registers }

Element, Element1, Element2: MCWordForm;
SetDetails: **record** Size1, Size2, Subset, Stride: MCWord; Base1, Base2: WordRange **end**;

{ P-machine global condition code }

Overflowed: Boolean;

{ variables used by the machine controller, chapter 32 }

Control: **array** [OptionType] **of** MCWord;
Termination: Terminus;
ErrorCode: Scalar;
CorpseFile: **file of** MCWord;
ChecksOn: Boolean;

{ variable used by the memory manager, chapter 34 }

KeyValue: KeyValues;

{ variable used by the loader, chapter 35 }

CodeFile: **file of** MCWord;

{ variables used by the system file interface, chapter 37 }

FileIndex: MCWord;
InputId, OutputId: IndexRange;

{ variables used by the Pascal I/O manager, chapter 38 }

PascalFiles: **array** [IndexRange] **of** PascFileDescriptor;
NullTransfer: IOTransfer;

CHAPTER 32

P-Machine Control

Overall operation of the P-machine is controlled by reading values of the compile-time options from the first 8 words of the P-code file. In particular, the global variable ChecksOn will be set true if the program was compiled with the Boolean option Checks selected. Thereafter, this variable is used to control all aspects of the P-machine concerned with the detection of run-time errors.

Errors detected by the P-machine are classified as "run-time", "system", or "fatal" according to whether they derive from the executing program, from an internal P-machine system-limit, or from a corruption or malfunction of the P-machine itself. The following procedures select an error-code from an appropriate "base", and record the reason for termination in the global variable Termination.
}

```
procedure Error(CheckCode: Scalar);
   begin
      ErrorCode := CheckCode + RuntimeBase; Termination := RuntimeError; goto 13
   end { error };
procedure SystemError(SystemCode: Scalar);
   begin
      ErrorCode := SystemCode + SystemBase; Termination := SystemLimit; goto 13
   end { systemerror };
procedure FatalError(FatalCode: Scalar);
   begin
      ErrorCode := FatalCode + FatalBase; Termination := Fatal; goto 13
   end { fatalerror };
procedure InitController;
   var Option: OptionType;
   begin
      { initialise variables passed to PMD, in case of premature failure }
      ErrorCode := 0; ProgramCounter := 0; CurrentFrame := 0; GlobalFrame := 0;
      StackTop := 0; HeapTop := 0;
      for Option := Listing to Other do Control[Option] := 0;
      { now open the CodeFile and extract option settings }
      reset(CodeFile);
      if eof(CodeFile) then FatalError(4);
```

```
   for Option := Listing to Other do
      begin Control[Option] := CodeFile^; get(CodeFile) end;
   ChecksOn := Control[Checks] <> 0
  end { initcontroller };
{
```

Errors detected by the P-machine are analysed by passing all necessary information in a ''corpse-file'' to the Post-mortem Generator. This includes:

(a)   The error-code for subsequent error identification.

(b)   The values of global P-machine variables necessary for the production of a variable-dump.

(c)   Control information which indicates the values of the compile-time options Checks and PMDump.

(d)   The contents of the P-machine memory.

Control is then passed serially to the Post-mortem Generator for all subsequent error analysis. The means by which this is achieved is necessarily system-dependent.

```
}
procedure CallPMD;
  var Index: WordRange;
  procedure PutCorpseWord(Word: MCWord);
    begin CorpseFile^ := Word; put(CorpseFile) end;
  begin
    rewrite(CorpseFile);
    { dump the 8-word control block }
    PutCorpseWord(ErrorCode); PutCorpseWord(ProgramCounter);
    PutCorpseWord(CurrentFrame); PutCorpseWord(GlobalFrame);
    PutCorpseWord(StackTop); PutCorpseWord(HeapTop);
    PutCorpseWord(Control[Checks]); PutCorpseWord(Control[PMDump]);

    { dump the program corpse }
    for Index := 0 to MCMaxMemWord do
      begin CorpseFile^ := Memory[Index]; put(CorpseFile) end;

    { make system-dependent call to Postmortem Generator }
    writeln; writeln(' Runtime error ', ErrorCode: 3, ' occurred.');
    writeln(' Call Postmortem Generator.')
  end { callpmd };
{
```

The procedure EndController calls the procedure CallPMD for all programs that terminate abnormally.

```
}
procedure EndController;
  begin if Termination <> Normal then CallPMD end;
```

{

CHAPTER 33

P-Machine
Micro-Operations

The procedures in this chapter implement micro-operations upon which many of the higher-level instructions depend. They are grouped into three sections.

33.1 Part-Word Access

The following procedures are used to access and update memory on a bit or byte basis. Since the shift and mask operations normally associated with such accesses are not available in Standard Pascal, a familiar technique of employing a variant record MCWordForm as a type-recasting mechanism is used. Note the technique itself is non-standard since the variant-reselection implied by the recast strictly renders the variant-field undefined. For this reason, notional recast statements have been retained as comments.

}

```
procedure MCSetBit(var MachineWord: MCWordForm; BitIndex: MCBitIndex);
  begin
    { recast(machineword,asbits) }
    if IndexedFromLeft
    then MachineWord.WBits[MCMaxBitnum - BitIndex] := 1
    else MachineWord.WBits[BitIndex] := 1
  end { mcsetbit };

procedure MCClearBit(var MachineWord: MCWordForm; BitIndex: MCBitIndex);
  begin
    { recast(machineword,asbits) }
    if IndexedFromLeft
    then MachineWord.WBits[MCMaxBitnum - BitIndex] := 0
    else MachineWord.WBits[BitIndex] := 0
  end { mcclearbit };

procedure MCGetBit(MachineWord: MCWordForm; BitIndex: MCBitIndex;
                   var ResultBit: MCBit);
  begin
    { recast(machineword,asbits) }
    if IndexedFromLeft
    then ResultBit := MachineWord.WBits[MCMaxBitnum - BitIndex]
    else ResultBit := MachineWord.WBits[BitIndex]
  end { mcgetbit };
```

```
procedure MCSetByte(var MachineWord: MCWordForm; ByteIndex: MCByteIndex;
                    DataByte: MCByte);
  begin
    { recast(machineword,asbytes) }
    if IndexedFromLeft
    then MachineWord.WBytes[MCMaxByteNum - ByteIndex] := DataByte
    else MachineWord.WBytes[ByteIndex] := DataByte
  end { mcsetbyte };
procedure MCGetByte(MachineWord: MCWordForm; ByteIndex: MCByteIndex;
                    var ResultByte: MCByte);
  begin
    { recast(machineword,asbytes) }
    if IndexedFromLeft
    then ResultByte := MachineWord.WBytes[MCMaxByteNum - ByteIndex]
    else ResultByte := MachineWord.WBytes[ByteIndex]
  end { resultbyte };
{
```

The function MCEmptyField checks a bit-field on a bit-by-bit basis, and is used in the
implementation of run-time checks associated with set-assignment.
}

```
function MCEmptyField(MachineWord: MCWordForm; FirstBit, LastBit: MCBitRange):
        Boolean;
  var Bit: MCBit;
  begin
    Bit := 0;
    while (FirstBit <= LastBit) and (Bit = 0) do
      begin MCGetBit(MachineWord, FirstBit, Bit); FirstBit := FirstBit + 1 end;
    MCEmptyField := (Bit = 0)
  end { mcemptyfield };
{
```

33.2 Undefined Value Manipulation

The "undefined" P-machine word value cannot be represented in Standard Pascal and is
therefore constructed on a bit-by-bit basis and held in the global variable Undefined.
Thereafter, the test for undefined values is performed by function MCUndefined, although
the comparison of non-integer values implied is not necessarily operational. The procedures
PresetMemory and MemoryUndefined provide multi-word initialisation and checking.
}

```
procedure SetMCUndefined;
  var MachineWord: MCWordForm;
  begin
    MachineWord.WValue := 0; MCSetBit(MachineWord, MCMaxBitnum);
    Undefined := MachineWord.WValue
  end { setmcundefined };
```

```
function MCUndefined(Word: MCWord): Boolean;
   begin MCUndefined := (Word = Undefined) end;
procedure PresetMemory(Base, WordCount: WordRange);
   var i: WordRange;
   begin for i := Base to Base + WordCount - 1 do Memory[i] := Undefined end;
function MemoryUndefined(Base, WordCount: WordRange): Boolean;
   var i: WordRange;
   begin
      MemoryUndefined := false;
      for i := Base to Base + WordCount - 1 do
         if MCUndefined(Memory[i]) then MemoryUndefined := true
   end { memoryundefined };
{
```

33.3 Packing and Unpacking

The following procedures provide packing and unpacking required by the instructions implementing the standard procedures pack and unpack, and by the implementation of packed-
files. The procedures Packpc and Unpackpc additionally check each source value against the
appropriate undefined value and terminate execution with a run-time error if required.

```
}
procedure Packp(UnpackedBase, Elements, PackedBase: WordRange;
                ElsPerWord: BitRange);
   var RightMost, FieldSize, BitIndex: BitRange; UpIndex, PkIndex: WordRange;
       OpBuffer, IpBuffer: MCWordForm; Bit: MCBit;
   begin
      FieldSize := MCBitsPerWord div ElsPerWord; RightMost := 0; UpIndex := 0;
      PkIndex := 0; OpBuffer.WValue := 0;
      while UpIndex <> Elements do
         begin
            IpBuffer.WValue := Memory[UnpackedBase + UpIndex];
            for BitIndex := 0 to FieldSize - 1 do
               begin
                  MCGetBit(IpBuffer, BitIndex, Bit);
                  if Bit <> 0 then MCSetBit(OpBuffer, RightMost + BitIndex)
               end;
            RightMost := RightMost + FieldSize; UpIndex := UpIndex + 1;
            if UpIndex mod ElsPerWord = 0
            then begin
                    Memory[PackedBase + PkIndex] := OpBuffer.WValue;
                    PkIndex := PkIndex + 1; RightMost := 0; OpBuffer.WValue := 0
                 end
         end;
      if UpIndex mod ElsPerWord <> 0
      then Memory[PackedBase + PkIndex] := OpBuffer.WValue
   end { packp };
```

```
procedure Unpackp(PackedBase, UnpackedBase, Elements: WordRange;
                  ElsPerWord: BitRange);
   var RightMost, FieldSize, BitIndex: BitRange; UpIndex, PkIndex: WordRange;
      IpBuffer, OpBuffer: MCWordForm; Bit: MCBit;
   begin
      FieldSize := MCBitsPerWord div ElsPerWord; UpIndex := 0; PkIndex := 0;
      while UpIndex <> Elements do
         begin
            if UpIndex mod ElsPerWord = 0
            then begin
                    IpBuffer.WValue := Memory[PackedBase + PkIndex];
                    PkIndex := PkIndex + 1; RightMost := 0
                 end;
            OpBuffer.WValue := 0;
            for BitIndex := 0 to FieldSize - 1 do
               begin
                  MCGetBit(IpBuffer, BitIndex + RightMost, Bit);
                  if Bit <> 0 then MCSetBit(OpBuffer, BitIndex)
               end;
            Memory[UnpackedBase + UpIndex] := OpBuffer.WValue;
            RightMost := RightMost + FieldSize; UpIndex := UpIndex + 1
         end
   end { unpackp };
procedure Packpc(UnpackedBase, Elements, PackedBase: WordRange;
                 ElsPerWord: BitRange);
   var RightMost, FieldSize, BitIndex: BitRange; UpIndex, PkIndex: WordRange;
      IpBuffer, OpBuffer: MCWordForm; Bit: MCBit;
   begin
      FieldSize := MCBitsPerWord div ElsPerWord; RightMost := 0; UpIndex := 0;
      PkIndex := 0; OpBuffer.WValue := 0;
      while UpIndex <> Elements do
         begin
            IpBuffer.WValue := Memory[UnpackedBase + UpIndex];
            if MCUndefined(IpBuffer.WValue) then Error(27);
            for BitIndex := 0 to FieldSize - 1 do
               begin
                  MCGetBit(IpBuffer, BitIndex, Bit);
                  if Bit <> 0 then MCSetBit(OpBuffer, RightMost + BitIndex)
               end;
            RightMost := RightMost + FieldSize; UpIndex := UpIndex + 1;
            if UpIndex mod ElsPerWord = 0
            then begin
                    Memory[PackedBase + PkIndex] := OpBuffer.WValue;
                    PkIndex := PkIndex + 1; RightMost := 0; OpBuffer.WValue := 0
                 end
         end;
      if UpIndex mod ElsPerWord <> 0
      then Memory[PackedBase + PkIndex] := OpBuffer.WValue
   end { packpc };
```

```
procedure Unpackpc(PackedBase, UnpackedBase, Elements: WordRange;
                   CheckValue: MCWord; ElsPerWord: BitRange);
   var RightMost, FieldSize, BitIndex: BitRange; UpIndex, PkIndex: WordRange;
       IpBuffer, OpBuffer: MCWordForm; Bit: MCBit;
begin
   FieldSize := MCBitsPerWord div ElsPerWord; UpIndex := 0; PkIndex := 0;
   while UpIndex <> Elements do
      begin
         if UpIndex mod ElsPerWord = 0
         then begin
                 IpBuffer.WValue := Memory[PackedBase + PkIndex];
                 PkIndex := PkIndex + 1; RightMost := 0
              end;
         OpBuffer.WValue := 0;
         for BitIndex := 0 to FieldSize - 1 do
            begin
               MCGetBit(IpBuffer, BitIndex + RightMost, Bit);
               if Bit <> 0 then MCSetBit(OpBuffer, BitIndex)
            end;
         if OpBuffer.WValue = CheckValue then Error(30);
         Memory[UnpackedBase + UpIndex] := OpBuffer.WValue;
         RightMost := RightMost + FieldSize; UpIndex := UpIndex + 1
      end
end { unpackpc };
```

{

CHAPTER 34

Memory Management

The P-machine possesses a linear, unstructured, memory implemented as an array of words whose capacity is defined by the configurable constant MCMaxMemWord. In addition to direct indexing, bit and byte accessing is supported by the micro-functions in Chapter 33. Bits are numbered from 0 at the least significant end to MCMaxBitNum. Bytes are numbered correspondingly from 0 to MCMaxByteNum. Word capacity is given by MCBitsPerWord and MCBytesPerWord.

The loader reads the contents of the P-code file into low address memory. The remaining "free memory" is available for use as both a stack and heap. The following memory-map indicates the general layout of these three areas:

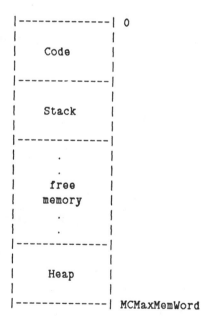

The remaining sections in this chapter deal with dynamic management of the stack and heap.

34.1 Acquisition and Control

Throughout program execution, the stack and heap acquire space from free memory. The following utilities monitor the growth of these structures and ensure that neither area will encroach on the other by an amount less than the configurable constant MinBlock. Should violation of this condition be anticipated, stack or heap overflow errors are reported.

```
}
function Safety(Request: WordRange): MCScalar;
   begin Safety := Request + MinBlock end;
procedure ClaimStack(Amount: WordRange);
   begin
      if StackTop + Safety(Amount) >= HeapTop then SystemError(11);
      StackTop := StackTop + Amount
   end { claimstack };
procedure FreeStack(Amount: WordRange);
   begin
      if StackTop - Amount < CurrentFrame - 1 then FatalError(2);
      StackTop := StackTop - Amount
   end { freestack };
procedure ClaimHeap(Amount: WordRange);
   begin
      if HeapTop - Safety(Amount) <= StackTop then SystemError(12);
      HeapTop := HeapTop - Amount
   end { claimheap };
procedure FreeHeap(Amount: WordRange);
   begin HeapTop := HeapTop + Amount end;
{
```

34.2 The Runtime Stack

All directly referenceable program data is held on a run-time stack. The stack is built from a series of stack-frames, each of which holds the local data of an active procedure, function or program block. The stack-frames are linked using the classic method of static and dynamic chains to provide non-local addressability and dynamic recovery of storage.

Each stack-frame has a six-word frame-header indexed negatively from the frame base. The contents of the header are as follows:

(1)   Word 1 holds the static link to the stack-frame of the enclosing block.

(2)   Word 2 holds the "code-base" of the code for the given block.

(3)   Word 3 holds the dynamic link to the stack-frame of the calling block.

(4)   Word 4 holds the return address to the code of the calling block.

(5)   Word 5 holds the current depth of the lock-stack, i.e. the number of entries.

(6)   Word 6 holds the address of the top-most lock-stack entry.

The static chain is supplemented by variables CurrentFrame, EnclosingFrame, and Global-Frame which in effect operate as a limited display by providing fast access to variables of the implied block. Variables belonging to blocks nested at intermediate levels are located using the static chain.

The layout and position of the current stack-frame are summarised in the diagram:

```
|--------------|
| Frame Header |
|--------------|<------ CurrentFrame
|  Parameters  |
|--------------|
|              |
|    Locals    |
|              |
|--------------|
| Temporaries  |
|--------------|
|  Lock Stack  |
|--------------|
|  Expression  |
|    Stack     |<------ StackTop
|      :       |
|    free      |
|   memory     |
```

The following procedures provide utilities for establishing a stack-frame header, and for locating the stack-frame of an enlosing block by following the static chain.
}
procedure SetFrameHeader;
   begin
      Memory[NewFrame - SLOffset] := EnclosingFrame;
      Memory[NewFrame - CBOffset] := CodeBase;
      Memory[NewFrame - DLOffset] := CurrentFrame;
      Memory[NewFrame - RAOffset] := ProgramCounter;
      Memory[NewFrame - LDOffset] := 0; Memory[NewFrame - LTOffset] := StackTop
   end { setframeheader };
function OuterFrame(FrameOffset: MCScalar): WordRange;
   var Index: MCScalar; FrameBase: WordRange;
   begin
      FrameBase := CurrentFrame;
      for Index := 1 **to** FrameOffset **do** FrameBase := Memory[FrameBase - SLOffset];
      OuterFrame := FrameBase
   end { outerframe };

{

The static part of each stack-frame contains storage for parameters, function results, local variables, and temporaries used by the generated code. Provision is also made for a "lock-stack" which is used to provide a general mechanism for applying and releasing reference locks. Each entry on the lock-stack is a three-word component comprising a lock-bit value, and a lock word-address/bit-offset pair. A lock is applied by pushing the current setting and lock location onto the lock-stack, and then setting the lock. A lock is released by popping the lock-stack entry and restoring the lock to the unstacked setting.

Both the lock-stack and local storage requirements that comprise the static part of a stack frame are computed at compile time and embedded in the generated code. During the creation of the stack-frame word 5 of the header is initialised to zero, and word 6 is set to the base of the lock-stack area. Locks are pushed onto the stack individually by the procedure PushLock and popped by the procedure PopLock.

}

```
procedure PushLock(LValue: MCBit; LWord: WordRange; LBit: BitRange);
    var LockTop, LockDepth: MCWord;
    begin
        LockDepth := Memory[CurrentFrame - LDOffset];
        LockTop := Memory[CurrentFrame - LTOffset]; Memory[LockTop + 1] := LValue;
        Memory[LockTop + 2] := LWord; Memory[LockTop + 3] := LBit;
        Memory[CurrentFrame - LDOffset] := LockDepth + 1;
        Memory[CurrentFrame - LTOffset] := LockTop + LockSize
    end { pushlock };
procedure PopLock(var LValue: MCBit; var LWord, LBit: MCWord);
    var LockTop, LockDepth: WordRange;
    begin
        LockDepth := Memory[CurrentFrame - LDOffset];
        LockTop := Memory[CurrentFrame - LTOffset]; LBit := Memory[LockTop];
        LWord := Memory[LockTop - 1]; LValue := Memory[LockTop - 2];
        Memory[CurrentFrame - LDOffset] := LockDepth - 1;
        Memory[CurrentFrame - LTOffset] := LockTop - LockSize
    end { poplock };
```

{

The top-most part of every stack-frame is used for expression evaluation, and operands are pushed and popped using the global variable StackTop. During function evaluation, the new stack frame is pushed on top of the current evaluation-stack. On exit from the function, the stack-frame is removed and the function result pushed as an expression operand. The following utilities provide for the pushing and popping of the evaluation stack.

}

```
procedure Push(Item: MCWord);
    begin StackTop := StackTop + 1; Memory[StackTop] := Item end;
```

```
procedure Pop(var Item: MCWord);
   begin Item := Memory[StackTop]; StackTop := StackTop - 1 end;
procedure PopOperands;
   begin Pop(Operand1); Pop(Operand2) end;
procedure PushLogical(Item: MCWordSet);
   var Gate: MCWordForm;
   begin Gate.WSet := Item; { recast(gate,asvalue) }; Push(Gate.WValue) end;
procedure PopLogical(var Item: MCWordSet);
   var Gate: MCWordForm;
   begin Pop(Gate.WValue); { recast(gate,asset) }; Item := Gate.WSet end;
procedure PushReal(Item: MCReal);
   var Gate: RealMap; i: 1..MCRealSize;
   begin
      Gate.RealValue := Item;
      for i := 1 to MCRealSize do Push(Gate.Word[i])
   end { pushreal };
procedure PopReal(var Item: MCReal);
   var Gate: RealMap; i: 1..MCRealSize;
   begin
      for i := MCRealSize downto 1 do Pop(Gate.Word[i]);
      Item := Gate.RealValue
   end { popreal };
procedure PopRealOperands;
   begin PopReal(RealOp1); PopReal(RealOp2) end;
procedure Spray(Pattern, WordBase: MCWord; WordCount: Scalar);
   begin
      while WordCount > 0 do
         begin
            Memory[WordBase + WordCount - 1] := Pattern;
            WordCount := WordCount - 1
         end
   end { spray };
procedure MoveWords(FromBase, ToBase, Size: WordRange);
   var Index: WordRange;
   begin
      if FromBase < ToBase
      then for Index := Size - 1 downto 0 do
              Memory[ToBase + Index] := Memory[FromBase + Index]
      else for Index := 0 to Size - 1 do
              Memory[ToBase + Index] := Memory[FromBase + Index]
   end { movewords };
```

```
procedure LoadWords(Base, Size: WordRange);
   var Too: WordRange;
   begin Too := StackTop + 1; ClaimStack(Size); MoveWords(Base, Too, Size) end;
procedure StoreWords(Base, Size: WordRange);
   begin FreeStack(Size); MoveWords(StackTop + 1, Base, Size) end;
{
```

34.3 Runtime Heap

Storage for file buffers and dynamic variables accessed via pointers is allocated on a run-time heap. Initially the heap is empty and grows by claiming "free" memory. As storage is dynamically released however, it is chained on a "free-list" for subsequent reallocation. The free-list contains linked blocks of inactive memory of known size. The diagram below shows three active (shaded) areas of memory interspersed with two chained inactive blocks. The highest memory word at address MaxMemWord is reserved for the head of the free-list.

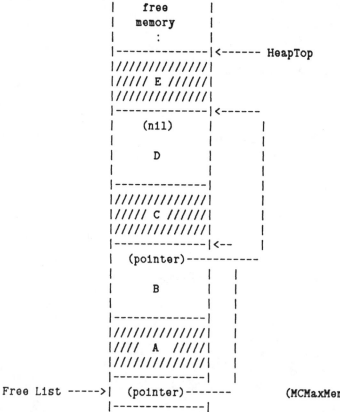

The procedure Acquire will allocate heap storage from the free-list if possible, but will call the procedure ClaimHeap in the event of the free-list being unable to satisfy the request. The global variable HeapTop defines the low address boundary of active heap storage.

```
}
procedure Acquire(Amount: WordRange; var Base: WordRange);
    var Current, Previous, Next, CurrentSize, SurplusBlock, Surplus: WordRange;
        Found: Boolean;
    begin
        if Amount < MinHeapBlock then Amount := MinHeapBlock;
        Current := FreeList; Found := false;
        repeat
            Previous := Current; Current := Memory[Current];
            if Current <> Null
            then begin
                    CurrentSize := Memory[Current + 1];
                    if CurrentSize >= Amount
                    then begin
                            Found := true; Next := Memory[Current];
                            Surplus := CurrentSize - Amount;
                            if Surplus = 0
                            then Memory[Previous] := Next
                            else begin
                                    SurplusBlock := Current + Amount;
                                    Memory[Previous] := SurplusBlock;
                                    Memory[SurplusBlock + 1] := Surplus;
                                    Memory[SurplusBlock] := Next
                                end
                        end
                end
        until (Current = Null) or Found;
        if not Found
        then begin ClaimHeap(Amount); Current := HeapTop end;
        Base := Current
    end { acquire };
{
```

Storage that is released is chained onto the free-list or returned to free memory depending upon its position in relation to the heap-top and the free-list. The procedure Release also performs simple garbage collection to ensure that whenever an active block is released, it is merged with any adjacent inactive blocks. Thus the allocated block C will be merged on release with both B and D to form a single aggregate chunk of inactive memory. Alternatively, if E were released it will be merged with D and the aggregate returned to free-memory.

}

```
procedure Release(Amount, Base: WordRange);
  var StartGarbage, EndGarbage, Current, EndCurrent, Previous: WordRange;
      Adjacent: Boolean;
  begin
    if Amount < MinHeapBlock then Amount := MinHeapBlock;
    StartGarbage := Base;
    if (StartGarbage < HeapTop) or (Base + Amount > MCMaxMemWord) or
       (Amount <= 0)
    then FatalError(3);
    EndGarbage := Base + Amount; Current := FreeList;
    repeat Previous := Current; Current := Memory[Current]
    until (Current = Null) or (Current <= EndGarbage);
    Adjacent := true;
    while (Current <> Null) and Adjacent do
      begin
        EndCurrent := Current + Memory[Current + 1];
        if (Current = EndGarbage) or (EndCurrent = StartGarbage)
        then begin
                Adjacent := true;
                if Current = EndGarbage
                then EndGarbage := EndCurrent
                else if EndCurrent = StartGarbage then StartGarbage := Current;
                Current := Memory[Current]
             end
        else Adjacent := false
      end;
    if StartGarbage > HeapTop
    then begin
            Memory[StartGarbage + 1] := EndGarbage - StartGarbage;
            Memory[StartGarbage] := Current; Memory[Previous] := StartGarbage
         end
    else begin FreeHeap(EndGarbage - StartGarbage); Memory[Previous] := Null end
  end { release };
{
```

The procedures Newp and Disposep provide a secure implementation of dynamic variables accessed via pointers by allocating extra storage for the implementation of run-time checks. Each dynamic variable is associated with a two-word header, the first word of which holds a unique key allocated in the range [-MCMaxint..+MCMaxint]. The second word is preset to zero but is subsequently used to hold a lock-bit and a monitoring count of the number of variant levels (if any) preselected by the extended form of new. The diagram shows how the pointer contents relate to the heap-storage.

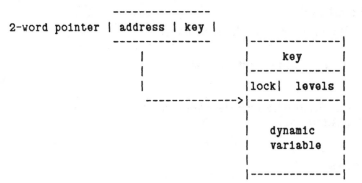

```
                 -----------------
2-word pointer | address | key |
                 -----------------        |--------------|
                       |                  |     key      |
                       |                  |--------------|
                       |                  |lock|  levels |
                        --------------->|--------------|
                                          |              |
                                          |   dynamic    |
                                          |   variable   |
                                          |              |
                                          |--------------|
```

When checks are on, code is generated by the Model Compiler to verify any pointer dereference by comparing the keys embedded within the pointer and the dynamic variable header.
When the variable is disposed code is generated to check the lock bit, and to check the levels
count for consistency. The procedure Disposep subsequently resets the header words to the
"undefined" value, enabling dereferences via dangling pointers to be caught by subsequent
key mismatch. Note that total security is not guaranteed, for subsequent repartitioning of
heap-storage coupled with the coincidental reconstruction of a previous key value as valid
data, could fool the dangling pointer check. However, such a situation, though not impossible is very unlikely.

The P-machine allocates key-values in the range of integers thereby leading to a system-limit
on the number of unique keys that can be generated. Since this limit is 2*MCMaxint+1, it
is not a serious implementation restriction.

}

procedure NewKeyValue;
  begin
    if KeyValue = MCMaxInt **then** SystemError(13) **else** KeyValue := KeyValue + 1
  end { newkeyvalue };

procedure Newp(Size: WordRange);
  var Amount, HeapAddress: WordRange; PtrAddress: MCWord;
  begin
    Amount := Size + 2 * ord(ChecksOn); Pop(PtrAddress);
    Acquire(Amount, HeapAddress);
    if ChecksOn
    then begin
        NewKeyValue; Memory[HeapAddress] := 0;
        Memory[HeapAddress + 1] := KeyValue; HeapAddress := HeapAddress + 2;
        PresetMemory(HeapAddress, Size); Memory[PtrAddress + 1] := KeyValue
      end;
    Memory[PtrAddress] := HeapAddress
  end { newp };

```
procedure Disposep(Size: WordRange);
   var Amount, HeapAddress: WordRange; PtrAddress: MCWord;
   begin
     Pop(PtrAddress); HeapAddress := Memory[PtrAddress];
     if ChecksOn
     then begin
             Amount := Size + 2; HeapAddress := HeapAddress - 2;
             PresetMemory(HeapAddress, 2)
          end
     else Amount := Size;
     Release(Amount, HeapAddress)
   end { disposep };
{
```
The following procedure initialises the memory manager by creating a null free-list and positioning the HeapTop pointer at the highest memory word. The first available key value is set to -MCMaxint.
```
}
procedure InitMemory;
   begin
     Memory[FreeList] := Null; HeapTop := MCMaxMemWord; KeyValue := -MCMaxInt
   end { initmemory };
```

{

CHAPTER 35

Object Program Format

The object program comprises a number of segments each of which derives from a compiled procedure, function, or program block. Each segment consists of a word-aligned jump-table followed by a word-aligned code-table. The boundary between these tables is referred to as the "code base" and marks the entry-point of the block. The code-table contains a stream of executable P-code bytes together with their in-line arguments. The jump-table contains the entry point addresses of all procedures local to the block, and also the code addresses of statement and code-labels situated within the block. Each jump-table also contains a five-word header which is indexed negatively from the code base. The contents of the header are as follows:

(1)   Word 1 contains the number of words of storage occupied by formal parameters.

(2)   Word 2 contains the number of words of storage occupied by local variables and temporaries.

(3)   Word 3 contains the number of words of storage occupied by the lock stack.

(4)   Word 4 contains a serial number identifying the block, which is used in analysis of the program "corpse" by the Post Mortem Generator.

(5)   Word 5 contains the code address of an internal label marking the start of finalisation code for the block.

When a block is activated, the contents of the header are used to construct the new stack frame. The code base address is placed in word 2 of the new stack frame header enabling access to the jump-table throughout the lifetime of the block. Non-local jumps are therefore implemented by locating the non-local stack frame via the static chain, and using word 2 of the frame header to locate the corresponding non-local jump-table.

The last segment of the file is degenerate and contains a jump-table corresponding to the pseudo-block surrounding the program. This jump-table contains the entry point addresses of internally compiled procedures to preset and postset text files, and the main program entry point addresses. The last word on the code file is an index into the jump-table location containing the program entry point.

The P-machine loader reads the P-code file into low address memory and initialises the run-time stack by creating stack frames for the pseudo-block and the global program block. For a P-code file containing n segments, the P-machine memory map immediately prior to execution is as follows:

```
    Word 0 |--------------|
           | Jump-Table 1 |
           |--------------|
           |              |
           | Code-Table 1 |
           |              |
           |--------------|

                   .
                   .
                   .

           |--------------|
           |Jump-Table n-1|
 ------->|--------------|<----- Program Code Base and Entry Point
 |   |   |              |
 |   |   |Code-Table n-1|
 |   |   |              |
 |   |   |--------------|
 |  ----| (Program EP)  |<----- (indexed from last word of code file)
 |      |              |
 |      | Jump-Table n |
 |      |              |
 |  --->|--------------|<----- Environment pseudo Code Base
 |  |   | haltp .....  |
 |  |   |--------------|
 |  |   |   Header 1   |
 |  |   |              |          Stack Frame Header for Pseudo-Block
 |  ----| (Code-base)  |
 |      |--------------|
 |      |   Header 2   |
 |      |              |          Stack Frame Header for Global Block
 --------| (Code-base)  |
         |--------------|<------ Global Frame for program data
         |              |
         | Global Data  |
         |      +       |
         | Temporaries  |
         |      +       |
         | Lock Stack   |
         |              |
         |--------------|<------ Stack Pointer
         |       .      |
         |       .      |
         |     free     |
               memory

}
```

```
procedure LoadProgram;
  var GlobalData, LockData, ProgramBase: WordRange; CodeWord: MCWordForm;
      Amount: Scalar; i: MCByteIndex;
begin
  { read codefile into memory }
  Amount := 0;
  while not eof(CodeFile) do
    begin
      Memory[Amount] := CodeFile^; Amount := Amount + 1;
      if Amount > MCMaxMemWord - MinBlock then FatalError(5);
      get(CodeFile)
    end;
  { locate code bases for pseudo- and program blocks }
  CodeBase := Amount - 1;
  ProgramBase := Memory[CodeBase - Memory[CodeBase]];

  { create dummy code-table for pseudo-block }
  with CodeWord do
    for i := 0 to MCMaxByteNum do WBytes[i] := haltp;
  { recast(codeword,asvalue) }
  Memory[CodeBase] := CodeWord.WValue;
  ProgramCounter := CodeBase * MCBytesPerWord;

  { create pseudo (environment) frame }
  EnclosingFrame := 0; CurrentFrame := 0; StackTop := 0;
  NewFrame := CodeBase + FrameSize + 1; SetFrameHeader;
  CurrentFrame := NewFrame;

  { create global frame as if called from environment }
  EnclosingFrame := CurrentFrame; CodeBase := ProgramBase;
  NewFrame := NewFrame + FrameSize; GlobalFrame := NewFrame;
  StackTop := NewFrame - 1;
  GlobalData :=
      Memory[ProgramBase - LocalsOffset] + Memory[ProgramBase - ParamsOffset];
  LockData := Memory[ProgramBase - LocksOffset]; ClaimStack(GlobalData);
  SetFrameHeader; ClaimStack(LockData);
  if ChecksOn and (GlobalData > 0) then PresetMemory(GlobalFrame, GlobalData);
  CurrentFrame := GlobalFrame;

  { set program counter for execution of program }
  ProgramCounter := ProgramBase * MCBytesPerWord
end { loadprogram };
```

{

CHAPTER 36

Data Representations
and
Arithmetic Utilities

The P-machine instruction-set provides for the manipulation of integer, real, Boolean, string, pointer, and set data according to the rules of the Pascal Standard. The machine representation of each of these data types is given below in terms of configurable constants.

(1) Integer data occupy a single P-machine word with values in the range [-MCMaxint..MCMaxint]. MCMaxint is given by $2**(MCBitsPerWord-1)-1$

(2) Real data occupy a number of P-machine words given by MCRealSize. The range and accuracy of real values is dependent upon the hardware hosting the P-machine.

(3) Boolean data occupy a single P-machine word. The value false is denoted by the integer value 0, and the value true by the integer value 1.

(4) String data occupy one or more P-machine words. Each word contains up to MCBytesPerWord character bytes, and each byte occupies MCBitsPerByte machine bits. The bytes in each word are numbered from 0 at the least significant end to MCMaxByteNum at the most significant end. The maximum word-size for string data is given by the maximum byte value MCMaxByte.

(5) Pointer data occupy two P-machine words. The low-address word contains a P-machine word-address, and the high-address word contains the check key.

(6) Set data have a dual representation depending upon whether the data is held in the static or dynamic part of the stack-frame. Sets are implemented as bitmaps in which MCWordSetBits in every word are available to represent a member of the set. To enable an "undefined" set-value to be constructed, the most significant bit is never used and MCWordSetBits = MCBitsPerWord-1. For a given base type whose bounds are BaseMin and BaseMax, sets are allocated storage as if their actual base-type were the subrange 0..BaseMax. Base types with negative lower bounds are not permitted.

When a set is pushed onto the stack, it is held in "reduced format" by truncating any high-order empty words and replacing them with a negative length-word. If the truncated length is one, the length-word is omitted. The empty set is represented by a single zero word on top of the stack. When a set result is popped, it is expanded to its static length prior to the store. The maximum word size of a set is limited to the maximum byte value MCMaxByte.

Integer and Real arithmetic are performed by host hardware. However all integer operations are pre-checked to determine whether overflow would occur. If runtime checking is requested the appropriate error is flagged. Otherwise the result is undefined. The following utilities check all integer operations and real-to-integer conversions against overflow.
}

```
procedure IntArith(Operator: OpType; Left, Right: Operands; var Result: MCWord);
    var Temp: MCWord; Overflows: Boolean;
    begin
      case Operator of
        Plus, Minus :
          begin
            Overflows := false;
            if Operator = Minus then Right := -Right;
            if (Left > 0) and (Right > 0)
            then Overflows := (Left > MCMaxInt - Right);
            if (Left < 0) and (Right < 0)
            then Overflows := (Left < -MCMaxInt - Right);
            if Overflows
            then begin if ChecksOn then Error(47) else Result := Undefined end
            else Result := Left + Right
          end;
        Mul :
          if Right = 0
          then Result := 0
          else if abs(Left) > MCMaxInt div abs(Right)
              then begin if ChecksOn then Error(47) else Result := Undefined end
              else Result := Left * Right;
        Idiv :
          if Right = 0
          then begin if ChecksOn then Error(45) else Result := Undefined end
          else if Right > 0
              then Result := Left div Right else Result := (-Left) div (-Right);
        Imod :
          if Right <= 0
          then begin if ChecksOn then Error(46) else Result := Undefined end
          else begin
              Temp := abs(Left) mod Right;
              if (Temp = 0) or (Left > 0)
              then Result := Temp else Result := Right - Temp
            end
      end
    end { intarith };
```

```
procedure Fix(Argument: MCReal; var Result: MCWord; var Overflow: Boolean);
   var Epsilon: MCReal;
   begin
      if abs(Argument) > MCMaxInt
      then Overflow := true
      else begin
            Result := trunc(Argument); Epsilon := Argument - Result;
            if Argument >= 0
            then Overflow := (Epsilon < 0) or (Epsilon > 1)
            else Overflow := (Epsilon <= -1) or (Epsilon > 0)
          end
   end { fix };
{
```

String comparisons are made with the following utilities which cater for strings whose length
is not a multiple of MCBytesPerWord.

```
}
function WordsFor(ByteAmount: ByteRange): WordRange;
   var WordAmount: WordRange;
   begin
      WordAmount := ByteAmount div MCBytesPerWord;
      if ByteAmount mod MCBytesPerWord <> 0
      then WordAmount := WordAmount + 1;
      WordsFor := WordAmount
   end { wordsfor };
function StringLess(StringLength: ByteRange): Boolean;
   label 1;
   var WordSize, Base1, Base2, Index: WordRange; ByteIndex: MCByteIndex;
       ChByte1, ChByte2: MCByte;
   begin
      WordSize := WordsFor(StringLength); Base2 := StackTop - WordSize + 1;
      Base1 := Base2 - WordSize;
      for Index := 0 to StringLength - 1 do
         begin
            ByteIndex := Index mod MCBytesPerWord;
            if ByteIndex = 0
            then begin
                  Element1.WValue := Memory[Base1]; Base1 := Base1 + 1;
                  Element2.WValue := Memory[Base2]; Base2 := Base2 + 1
                end;
            MCGetByte(Element1, ByteIndex, ChByte1);
            MCGetByte(Element2, ByteIndex, ChByte2);
            if ChByte1 <> ChByte2
            then begin StringLess := ChByte1 < ChByte2; goto 1 end
         end;
      StringLess := false; 1:
   end { stringless };
```

```
function StringEqual(StringLength: ByteRange): Boolean;
  label 1;
  var WordSize, Base1, Base2, Index: WordRange; ByteIndex: MCByteIndex;
      ChByte1, ChByte2: MCByte;
  begin
    WordSize := WordsFor(StringLength); Base2 := StackTop - WordSize + 1;
    Base1 := Base2 - WordSize;
    for Index := 0 to StringLength - 1 do
      begin
        ByteIndex := Index mod MCBytesPerWord;
        if ByteIndex = 0
        then begin
              Element1.WValue := Memory[Base1]; Base1 := Base1 + 1;
              Element2.WValue := Memory[Base2]; Base2 := Base2 + 1
            end;
        MCGetByte(Element1, ByteIndex, ChByte1);
        MCGetByte(Element2, ByteIndex, ChByte2);
        if ChByte1 <> ChByte2 then begin StringEqual := false; goto 1 end
      end;
    StringEqual := true; 1:
  end { stringequal };
{
```

The following utilities manipulate set values according to their truncated representations on the evaluation stack. The global variable SetDetails is used as a repository of information for two set operands, prior to executing a set-operation.

```
}
procedure SetElements(Base, Stride: WordRange);
  begin
    Element2.WValue := Memory[Base];
    Element1.WValue := Memory[Base + Stride]
    { recast(element1,asset) }
    { recast(element2,asset) }
  end { setelements };
procedure ExpandSet(StaticSize: WordRange);
  var CurrentSize: MCWord;
  begin
    Pop(CurrentSize);
    if CurrentSize >= 0
    then begin Push(CurrentSize); CurrentSize := 1 end
    else CurrentSize := -CurrentSize;
    if StackTop + Safety(StaticSize - CurrentSize) >= HeapTop then SystemError(11);
    while CurrentSize < StaticSize do
      begin Push(0); CurrentSize := CurrentSize + 1 end
  end { expandset };
```

```
procedure GetSetDetails;
  begin
    with SetDetails do
      begin
        Size1 := Memory[StackTop];
        if Size1 < 0
        then begin Size1 := -Size1; FreeStack(Size1) end
        else if Size1 > 0 then Size1 := 1;
        Base1 := StackTop; StackTop := StackTop - 1; Size2 := Memory[StackTop];
        if Size2 < 0
        then begin Size2 := -Size2; FreeStack(Size2) end
        else if Size2 > 0 then Size2 := 1;
        Base2 := StackTop; StackTop := StackTop - 1;
        if Size1 > Size2 then Subset := Size2 else Subset := Size1;
        if Subset = 0
        then if Size1 + Size2 > 0 then Subset := 1;
        Stride := Base1 - Base2
      end
  end { getsetdetails };
procedure PushSetSize(Size: WordRange);
  begin
    if Size = 0
    then Push(0)
    else if Size > 1 then Push(-Size)
  end { pushsetsize };
```

{

CHAPTER 37

System File InterFace

The implementation of file-variables requires some form of mapping between the variable and the corresponding physical file. In practice, such a mapping is system-dependent and cannot be given a generalised expression in Standard Pascal. In this version of the P-machine only communication via the standard text-files Input and Output is implemented, but an interface is defined for the system-dependent manipulation of other files.

The System File Interface provides for binding file variables to named physical files, for opening and closing files, and for file-block transfers, via by the procedures Bind, Open, Close, Getbytes, and PutBytes. For each of these procedures the file in question is identified by the global variable FileIndex, which is controlled by the Pascal File Manager in Chapter 38.

If FileIndex identifies either Input or Output, calls to Open and Close are ignored, and calls to GetBytes and PutBytes ensure the block transfer occurs using the P-machine program parameters Input and Output.
}

```
procedure InitSysFiles;
   begin { initialise any variables required } end;
procedure Bind(Name: Alfa);
   begin { Bind named physical file to current value of FileIndex } end;
procedure Open(Mode: IOmode);
   begin
      if (FileIndex <> InputId) and (FileIndex <> OutputId)
      then { if not file already bound to current value of FileIndex
            then bind a temporary file;
            open bound file in mode specified }
   end { open };
procedure Close(Status: FileStatus);
   begin
      if (FileIndex <> InputId) and (FileIndex <> OutputId)
      then { close file bound to current file index;
            if Status = Detach then unbind index }
   end { close };
```

```
procedure GetBytes(Buffer: WordRange; var Amount: IOTransfer; var EndFile: Boolean);
   var Base: WordRange; ByteBuffer: MCWordForm;
   begin
      Amount := NullTransfer;
      if FileIndex = InputId
      then begin
               EndFile := eof(Input);
               if not EndFile
               then with Amount do
                        begin
                           Base := Buffer; ByteBuffer.WValue := 0;
                           while not eoln(Input) do
                             begin
                               MCSetByte
                                  (ByteBuffer, ByteAmount mod MCBytesPerWord,
                                     ord(Input^));
                               ByteAmount := ByteAmount + 1;
                               if ByteAmount mod MCBytesPerWord = 0
                               then begin
                                       Memory[Base] := ByteBuffer.WValue;
                                       ByteBuffer.WValue := 0; Base := Base + 1
                                     end;
                               get(Input)
                             end;
                           if ByteAmount mod MCBytesPerWord <> 0
                           then Memory[Base] := ByteBuffer.WValue;
                           get(Input)
                        end
           end
      else { with file bound to current value of FileIndex do
                if no input records remain
                then EndFile := true
                else read next record to buffer area starting at Memory[Buffer]
                     and set Amount to size of record read }
   end { getbytes };
procedure PutBytes(Buffer: WordRange; Amount: IOTransfer);
   var Base: WordRange; Index: ByteRange; ByteIndex: MCByteIndex; CharByte: MCByte;
       ByteBuffer: MCWordForm;
   begin
      with Amount do
        if FileIndex = OutputId
        then begin
                Base := Buffer;
                for Index := 0 to ByteAmount - 1 do
                  begin
                    ByteIndex := Index mod MCBytesPerWord;
```

```
            if ByteIndex = 0
            then begin
                    ByteBuffer.WValue := Memory[Base]; Base := Base + 1
                 end;
            MCGetByte(ByteBuffer, ByteIndex, CharByte);
            Output^ := chr(CharByte); put(Output)
          end;
        writeln(Output)
      end
  else { with file bound to current value of FileIndex do
          write record of size specified by Amount
          from buffer area starting at Memory[Buffer] }
end { putbytes };
```

CHAPTER 38

Pascal I/O Management

The Pascal I/O Manager provides both high and low-level support for the instructions implementing the standard I/O functions.

Low-level support for I/O is provided by a buffering mechanism accompanied by the allocation of file-descriptors. Every file-variable in Pascal must be implicitly or explicitly initialised for I/O by a call to one of the standard procedures reset or rewrite. The first such call for a local file results in the allocation of a file descriptor, a file buffer, and a file index. Descriptors are allocated by a linear search of the descriptor array PascalFiles, which records the index-position of the first unallocated descriptor in the variable FileIndex. This value is embedded in word 0 of the file variable block, and is used thereafter to identify the file. The following utilities provide for the allocation and de-allocation of descriptors.
}

```
procedure AllocatePascalFile;
   var TypeCode, ElementSize: MCWord;
   begin
     with PascalFiles[FileIndex] do
       begin
         Defined := true; Mode := NotSet; EndOfFile := true;
         TypeCode := Memory[Address + 2]; BufferSize := Memory[Address + 3];
         ElementSize := Memory[Address + 4]; TextFile := (TypeCode = TextCode);
         if TextFile
         then BufferWord := Address + 2
         else begin
               PointerWord := Address + 2; PackedFile := (TypeCode = PackedCode);
               if PackedFile
               then ElsPerWord := ElementSize else ComponentSize := ElementSize
             end
       end
   end { allocatepascalfile };
procedure DeAllocatePascalFile;
   begin PascalFiles[FileIndex].Defined := false end;
```

```
procedure NextFileIndex;
  begin
    FileIndex := 1;
    while PascalFiles[FileIndex].Defined do
      FileIndex := succ(FileIndex) mod (MaxFileIndex + 1)
  end { nextfileindex };
```

{

When a file is opened, a buffer is allocated from the heap and used in all I/O transfers between the file and the addressable file buffer variable. The size of the buffer required is obtained from the file-variable block, where word 3 is preset with the storage requirement when the file variable is initialised. In addition word 2 of the block is preset with a code identifying the nature of the file, and word 4 with the element size in words. The descriptor fields BufferSize and FirstWord respectively hold the size of the allocated buffer and its start word address.

Three different buffer organisations are used depending upon whether the file variable is a text-file, an unpacked word file, or a packed file. These can be summarised as follows:

(1) For text files, the fields BytePointer and LastByte of the descriptor respectively hold the byte address of the current-component of the file, and the last byte of the buffer. Word 2 of the file variable memory block is used as the (unpacked) buffer variable, and its word-address is held in the descriptor field BufferWord.

(2) For an unpacked word file, the buffer variable is implemented by a 'window' that slides over the file-buffer. Word 2 of the file variable holds the word-address of the window and therefore functions as a pointer to the buffer-variable. The fields Pointer-Word and LastWord of the descriptor respectively hold the word-addresses of word 2 of the file variable, and the last buffer word. The field ComponentSize holds the word size of the current component of the file.

(3) Packed files use a two-level buffering scheme in which the primary file buffer is supplemented by a secondary buffer used for packing and unpacking components of the file. The capacity of the secondary buffer is determined from the number of file components that can be packed per word. A secondary pointer held in the memory word addressed by LastWord is used to mark undefined secondary buffer locations, arising when the last word of a packed-file contains less than elements-per-word packed components. This allows true end-of-file to be deduced correctly. The field WordPointer of the descriptor is the address of the primary buffer word from or into which transfer of packed components takes place.

Given these buffer/file organisations, the primitive operations of reset, rewrite, get, and put are performed by the following seven procedures.

}

```
procedure FillBuffer;
    var Amount: IOTransfer; Padding, FieldWidth: BitRange;
    begin
      with PascalFiles[FileIndex] do
        if TextFile
        then begin
                GetBytes(FirstWord, Amount, EndOfFile);
                BytePointer := FirstWord * MCBytesPerWord;
                LastByte := BytePointer + Amount.ByteAmount
             end
        else begin
                GetBytes(FirstWord, Amount, EndOfFile);
                LastWord := FirstWord + WordsFor(Amount.ByteAmount);
                if PackedFile
                then begin
                        Padding := Amount.BitAmount;
                        FieldWidth := MCBitsPerWord div ElsPerWord;
                        Memory[LastWord] := LastWord + Padding div FieldWidth;
                        WordPointer := FirstWord; Memory[PointerWord] := LastWord
                     end
                else Memory[PointerWord] := FirstWord
             end
    end { fillbuffer };
procedure FlushBuffer;
    var Amount: IOTransfer;
    begin
      Amount := NullTransfer;
      with PascalFiles[FileIndex] do
        if TextFile
        then begin
                Amount.ByteAmount := BytePointer - FirstWord * MCBytesPerWord;
                PutBytes(FirstWord, Amount);
                BytePointer := FirstWord * MCBytesPerWord
             end
        else begin
                with Amount do
                  if PackedFile
                  then begin
                          ByteAmount := (WordPointer - FirstWord) * MCBytesPerWord;
                          BitAmount := Memory[LastWord]
                       end
                  else ByteAmount :=
                          (Memory[PointerWord] - FirstWord) * MCBytesPerWord;
                PutBytes(FirstWord, Amount);
                if PackedFile
                then WordPointer := FirstWord else Memory[PointerWord] := FirstWord
             end
    end { flushbuffer };
```

```pascal
procedure GetFile;
    var ComponentPointer: WordRange; CharByte: MCByte; GetGate: MCWordForm;
    begin
      with PascalFiles[FileIndex] do
        if TextFile
        then begin
              if BytePointer = LastByte
              then FillBuffer else BytePointer := BytePointer + 1;
              if EndOfFile
              then { buffervar := undefined }
              else if BytePointer = LastByte
                  then Memory[BufferWord] := ord(' ')
                  else begin
                      GetGate.WValue :=
                        Memory[BytePointer div MCBytesPerWord];
                      MCGetByte
                        (GetGate, BytePointer mod MCBytesPerWord, CharByte);
                      Memory[BufferWord] := CharByte
                    end
          end
        else begin
              ComponentPointer := Memory[PointerWord];
              if PackedFile
              then begin
                  ComponentPointer := ComponentPointer - 1;
                  Memory[PointerWord] := ComponentPointer;
                  if ComponentPointer = Memory[LastWord]
                  then begin
                      if WordPointer = LastWord then FillBuffer;
                      if EndOfFile
                      then { buffervar := undefined }
                      else begin
                          Unpackp
                            (WordPointer, LastWord + 1, ElsPerWord,
                              ElsPerWord);
                          WordPointer := WordPointer + 1;
                          Memory[PointerWord] := LastWord + ElsPerWord
                        end
                    end
                end
              else begin
                  ComponentPointer := ComponentPointer + ComponentSize;
                  Memory[PointerWord] := ComponentPointer;
                  if ComponentPointer = LastWord
                  then begin
                      FillBuffer;
                      if EndOfFile then { buffervar := undefined }
                    end
                end
```

```pascal
              end
      end { getfile };
procedure PutFile;
   var WordAddress, ComponentPointer: WordRange; PutGate: MCWordForm;
   begin
      with PascalFiles[FileIndex] do
         if TextFile
         then begin
                 if BytePointer = LastByte then FlushBuffer;
                 WordAddress := BytePointer div MCBytesPerWord;
                 PutGate.WValue := Memory[WordAddress];
                 MCSetByte
                    (PutGate, BytePointer mod MCBytesPerWord, Memory[BufferWord]);
                 Memory[WordAddress] := PutGate.WValue;
                 BytePointer := BytePointer + 1
              end
         else begin
                 ComponentPointer := Memory[PointerWord];
                 if PackedFile
                 then begin
                         ComponentPointer := ComponentPointer - 1;
                         Memory[PointerWord] := ComponentPointer;
                         if ComponentPointer = LastWord
                         then begin
                                 if WordPointer = LastWord then FlushBuffer;
                                 Packp
                                    (LastWord + 1, ElsPerWord, WordPointer, ElsPerWord);
                                 WordPointer := WordPointer + 1;
                                 Memory[PointerWord] := LastWord + ElsPerWord
                              end
                      end
                 else begin
                         ComponentPointer := ComponentPointer + ComponentSize;
                         Memory[PointerWord] := ComponentPointer;
                         if ComponentPointer = LastWord then FlushBuffer
                      end
              end
      end { putfile };
procedure InitializeFile;
   var Limit: WordRange;
   begin
      with PascalFiles[FileIndex] do
         if TextFile
         then begin
                 LastByte := (FirstWord + BufferSize) * MCBytesPerWord;
                 if Mode = Generation
                 then BytePointer := FirstWord * MCBytesPerWord
                 else begin BytePointer := LastByte; GetFile end
              end
```

```
      else begin
              Limit := FirstWord + BufferSize;
              if PackedFile
              then LastWord := Limit - ElsPerWord - 1 else LastWord := Limit;
              if Mode = Generation
              then begin
                      if PackedFile
                      then begin
                              Memory[LastWord] := 0;
                              Memory[PointerWord] := LastWord + ElsPerWord;
                              WordPointer := FirstWord
                          end
                      else Memory[PointerWord] := FirstWord
                  end
              else begin
                      if PackedFile
                      then begin
                              Memory[LastWord] := LastWord;
                              Memory[PointerWord] := LastWord + 1;
                              WordPointer := LastWord
                          end
                      else Memory[PointerWord] := LastWord - ComponentSize;
                      GetFile
                  end
          end
  end { initializefile };
procedure FinalizeFile;

  var ComponentPointer: WordRange; Padding, FieldWidth: BitRange;

  begin
    with PascalFiles[FileIndex] do
      if TextFile
      then begin
              if BytePointer <> FirstWord * MCBytesPerWord then FlushBuffer
          end
      else begin
              ComponentPointer := Memory[PointerWord];
              if PackedFile
              then begin
                      if WordPointer > FirstWord then FlushBuffer;
                      if ComponentPointer < (LastWord + ElsPerWord)
                      then begin
                              Padding := 0;
                              FieldWidth := MCBitsPerWord div ElsPerWord;
                              while ComponentPointer > LastWord do
                                begin
                                  Memory[ComponentPointer] := 0;
                                  Padding := Padding + FieldWidth;
                                  ComponentPointer := ComponentPointer - 1
                                end;
```

```
                              Memory[LastWord] := Padding;
                              Packp
                                (LastWord + 1, ElsPerWord, WordPointer, ElsPerWord);
                              WordPointer := WordPointer + 1; FlushBuffer
                          end
                end
              else if ComponentPointer > FirstWord then FlushBuffer
            end
    end { finalizefile };
procedure RewriteFile;
  begin
    FileIndex := Memory[Address];
    if FileIndex = UndefinedIndex
    then begin
            NextFileIndex;
            if FileIndex = UndefinedIndex then SystemError(14);
            Memory[Address] := FileIndex; AllocatePascalFile
         end;
    with PascalFiles[FileIndex] do
      begin
        case Mode of
          NotSet : Acquire(BufferSize, FirstWord);
          Generation :
            begin FinalizeFile; Close(Retain) end;
          Inspection : Close(Retain)
        end;
        Open(ForWriting); Mode := Generation; EndOfFile := true; InitializeFile
      end
    end { rewritefile };
procedure ResetFile;
  begin
    FileIndex := Memory[Address];
    with PascalFiles[FileIndex] do
      begin
        case Mode of
          NotSet : Acquire(BufferSize, FirstWord);
          Generation :
            begin FinalizeFile; Close(Retain) end;
          Inspection : Close(Retain)
        end;
        Open(ForReading); Mode := Inspection; InitializeFile
      end
    end { resetfile };
```

{
The Model Compiler generates code to ensure every file is correctly closed. In practice this
need only happen if the file has already been opened. If this is the case, the buffer is flushed
if the file was in generation-mode, prior to releasing the buffer-space. The descriptor is deal-
located by setting the defined field to false, and a call is made to the System File Manager to
close and detach the corresponding physical file.
}

```pascal
procedure CloseFile;
   begin
      FileIndex := Memory[Address];
      if FileIndex <> UndefinedIndex
      then begin
              with PascalFiles[FileIndex] do
                case Mode of
                  NotSet :
                     { external file never used };
                  Generation :
                     begin FinalizeFile; Release(BufferSize, FirstWord) end;
                  Inspection :
                     Release(BufferSize, FirstWord)
                end;
              DeAllocatePascalFile; Close(Detach)
           end
   end { closefile };
```

{
The Pascal I/O Manager also provides higher-level support for the instructions implementing
text I/O. No attempt has been made to provide free-standing binary to decimal conversion,
and thus the formatted input/output of real and integer values is host dependent. With this
proviso, the following procedures provide textual input/output of real, integer, Boolean, and
character data, and the layout functions for writeln, and page.
}

```pascal
procedure DeriveValue(var Digits: TextString; var Result: Number);
   var f: text; i: StringRange;
   begin
      rewrite(f);
      with Digits do
        for i := 1 to Length do begin f^ := String[i]; put(f) end;
      reset(f);
      with Result do
        case Form of
          IntForm : read(f, IntValue);
          RealForm : read(f, RealValue)
        end
   end { derivevalue };
```

```
procedure DeriveDigits(Value: Number; var Digits: TextString);
  var f: text;
  begin
    rewrite(f);
    with Value do
      case Form of
        IntForm : writeln(f, IntValue: 1);
        RealForm :
          case Format of
            Fixed : writeln(f, RealValue: 1: FracDigits);
            Floated : writeln(f, RealValue: TotalWidth)
          end
      end;
    reset(f);
    with Digits do
      begin
        Length := 0;
        while not eoln(f) do
          begin Length := Length + 1; String[Length] := f^; get(f) end;
        while String[Length] = ' ' do Length := Length - 1
      end
  end { derivedigits };
procedure ReadNumber(FormRequired: NumberForms);
  var Digits: TextString; Result: Number;
  procedure BadDigitSequence;
    begin
      case FormRequired of
        IntForm : Error(54);
        RealForm : Error(56)
      end
    end { baddigitsequence };
  procedure CopyBufferWord;
    begin
      with Digits do
        begin
          Length := Length + 1;
          with PascalFiles[FileIndex] do String[Length] := chr(Memory[BufferWord])
        end;
      GetFile
    end { copybufferword };
  procedure DigitSequence;
    begin
      with PascalFiles[FileIndex] do
        if not (chr(Memory[BufferWord]) in ['0'..'9'])
        then BadDigitSequence
        else repeat CopyBufferWord until not (chr(Memory[BufferWord]) in ['0'..'9'])
    end { digitsequence };
```

```
function Signed(cvalue: MCByte): Boolean;
   begin Signed := (cvalue = ord('+')) or (cvalue = ord('-')) end;
begin { readnumber }
   Digits.Length := 0;
   with PascalFiles[FileIndex] do
      begin
         while (Memory[BufferWord] = ord(' ')) and not EndOfFile do GetFile;
         if EndOfFile
         then BadDigitSequence
         else begin
                 if Signed(Memory[BufferWord]) then CopyBufferWord;
                 DigitSequence;
                 if FormRequired = RealForm
                 then begin
                         if Memory[BufferWord] = ord('.')
                         then begin CopyBufferWord; DigitSequence end;
                         if (Memory[BufferWord] = ord('e')) or
                            (Memory[BufferWord] = ord('E'))
                         then begin
                                 CopyBufferWord;
                                 if Signed(Memory[BufferWord]) then CopyBufferWord;
                                 DigitSequence
                              end
                      end;
                 Result.Form := FormRequired; DeriveValue(Digits, Result);
                 case FormRequired of
                    IntForm : Push(Result.IntValue);
                    RealForm : PushReal(Result.RealValue)
                 end
              end
      end
   end { readnumber };
procedure ReadLine;

   begin
      with PascalFiles[FileIndex] do
         begin BytePointer := LastByte; GetFile end
   end { readline };
procedure PutCh(CharByte: MCByte);

   begin
      with PascalFiles[FileIndex] do
         begin Memory[BufferWord] := CharByte; PutFile end
   end { putch };
procedure LeadingBlanks(TotalWidth, FieldWidth: StringRange);

   begin
      while TotalWidth > FieldWidth do
         begin PutCh(ord(' ')); TotalWidth := TotalWidth - 1 end
   end { leadingblanks };
```

```
procedure WriteChar;
   var TotalWidth, CharByte: MCWord;
   begin
     Pop(TotalWidth); Pop(CharByte); LeadingBlanks(TotalWidth, 1); PutCh(CharByte)
   end { writechar };
procedure WriteBoolean;
   var Logical, TotalWidth: MCWord;
   begin
     Pop(TotalWidth); Pop(Logical); LeadingBlanks(TotalWidth, 5);
     case Logical of
       0 :
         begin
           PutCh(ord('f')); PutCh(ord('a')); PutCh(ord('l')); PutCh(ord('s'));
           PutCh(ord('e'))
         end;
       1 :
         begin
           PutCh(ord(' ')); PutCh(ord('t')); PutCh(ord('r')); PutCh(ord('u'));
           PutCh(ord('e'))
         end
     end
   end { writeboolean };
procedure WriteString;
   var TotalWidth, StringLength, Base, Index: MCWord; ByteIndex: MCByteIndex;
       CharByte: MCByte; ByteBuffer: MCWordForm;
   begin
     Pop(TotalWidth); Pop(StringLength);
     if StringLength <= MCBytesPerWord
     then begin Base := StackTop; StackTop := StackTop - 1 end
     else Pop(Base);
     if TotalWidth > StringLength
     then begin
             LeadingBlanks(TotalWidth, StringLength); TotalWidth := StringLength
           end;
     for Index := 0 to TotalWidth - 1 do
       begin
         ByteIndex := Index mod MCBytesPerWord;
         if ByteIndex = 0
         then begin ByteBuffer.WValue := Memory[Base]; Base := Base + 1 end;
         MCGetByte(ByteBuffer, ByteIndex, CharByte); PutCh(CharByte)
       end
   end { writestring };
```

```
procedure WriteInteger;
  var Datum: Number; Digits: TextString; FieldWidth: MCWord; i: StringRange;
  begin
    Pop(FieldWidth);
    with Datum do
      begin Form := IntForm; Pop(IntValue) end;
    DeriveDigits(Datum, Digits);
    with Digits do
      begin
        LeadingBlanks(FieldWidth, Length);
        for i := 1 to Length do PutCh(ord(String[i]))
      end
  end { writeinteger };
procedure WriteReal(FormatRequired: PrintedForms);
  var Datum: Number; Digits: TextString; FieldWidth: MCWord; i: StringRange;
  begin
    with Datum do
      begin
        Form := RealForm; Format := FormatRequired;
        if FormatRequired = Fixed then Pop(FracDigits);
        Pop(FieldWidth);
        if FormatRequired = Floated then TotalWidth := FieldWidth;
        PopReal(RealValue)
      end;
    DeriveDigits(Datum, Digits);
    with Digits do
      begin
        if FormatRequired = Fixed then LeadingBlanks(FieldWidth, Length);
        for i := 1 to Length do PutCh(ord(String[i]))
      end
  end { writereal };
procedure WriteLine;
  begin FlushBuffer end;
procedure PageFile;
  begin
    with PascalFiles[FileIndex] do
      if BytePointer <> FirstWord * MCBytesPerWord then WriteLine;
    PutCh(FormFeed)
  end { pagefile };
```

{

The procedure InitPascIO initialises global variables used by the System File Manager and
the Pascal I/O Manager. The procedure EndPascIO is called prior to P-machine termination to record the state of all currently opened files in word 1 of the file variable block. This
enables subsequent analysis by the Post Mortem Generator to report the file mode and position as well as the value of the buffer-variable.

}

```
procedure InitPascIO;
    var Index: IndexRange;
    begin
      for Index := UndefinedIndex to MaxFileIndex do PascalFiles[Index].Defined := false;
      with NullTransfer do
        begin ByteAmount := 0; BitAmount := 0 end;
      InputId := UndefinedIndex; OutputId := UndefinedIndex
    end { initpascio };

procedure EndPascIO;
    var Index: IndexRange; FileBlock: WordRange; OpBuffer: MCWordForm;
    begin
      for Index := UndefinedIndex to MaxFileIndex do
        with PascalFiles[Index] do
          if Defined
          then begin
                  if TextFile
                  then FileBlock := BufferWord - 2 else FileBlock := PointerWord - 2;
                  Memory[FileBlock + 3] := ord(Mode);
                  OpBuffer.WValue := Memory[FileBlock + 1];
                  if EndOfFile then MCSetBit(OpBuffer, EofBit);
                  if TextFile
                  then if BytePointer = LastByte then MCSetBit(OpBuffer, EolBit);
                  Memory[FileBlock + 1] := OpBuffer.WValue
              end
    end { endpascio };
```

{

CHAPTER 39

Program Execution

The procedure RunProgram performs instruction fetch and execution until the program terminates or halts in error. Every instruction is denoted by a P-code byte-value that additionally serves to identify the number and type of arguments. An instruction may be associated with more than one P-code value if variation in the type of arguments is permitted. The eight distinct instruction formats are:

P-code		
P-code	byte	
P-code	word	
P-code	byte	byte
P-code	word	byte
P-code	byte	bytestring
P-code	byte	wordstring
P-code	word	wordstring

To allow for more than 256 P-code values, instructions are partitioned into two classes. There are seven groups of Class 1 instructions dealing with in-line constants, memory-access, operations, jumps, procedure entry and exit, memory management, and run-time check support. Class 2 instructions deal with the standard procedures and functions, and the mapping of program parameters, and are identified by a prefixed "escape" byte.
}

procedure RunProgram;
  var OpCode: MCByte; Finished: Boolean; Name: Alfa;
    { processor scratchpad }
    Datum: MCWord; Base, Base1, Base2, Start: MCWord;
    Size, Size1, Size2, ReducedSize, CheckSize: MCWord;
    ByteAddress, Offset, FrameOffset, IndexValue: MCWord; CAPBpBlock: MCWord;
    ThisFrame, NextFrame, LabelledFrame, HeapAddress: WordRange;
    LabelEntry: MCWord; Parameters, StackSpace, LockSpace: MCWord;
    RightMost, ElementsPerWord: MCWord; Upper, Lower: MCWord;
    FirstBit, LastBit, EmptyWords: MCWord; Logical1, Logical2: MCWordSet;
    SelectorValue, SelectedValue: MCWord;
    ActiveBits, LockBits, LockWord: MCWordForm; TrapCode: MCWord; i: MCWord;
    OpBuffer, IpBuffer: MCWordForm; Bits: MCWord; Bit: MCBit; Byte: MCByte;

{

The functions NextByte and NextWord fetch the values of byte and word arguments respectively. Word-string arguments are word aligned and are fetched from the next word boundary computed by the function WordBoundary.

}

```
function NextByte: MCByte;
    var CodeWord: MCWordForm;
    begin
        CodeWord.WValue := Memory[ProgramCounter div MCBytesPerWord];
        { recast(codeword,asbytes) }
        NextByte := CodeWord.WBytes[ProgramCounter mod MCBytesPerWord];
        ProgramCounter := ProgramCounter + 1
    end { nextbyte };
function NextWord: MCWord;
    var Buffer: MCWordForm; ByteIndex: MCByteIndex;
    begin
        for ByteIndex := 0 to MCMaxByteNum do Buffer.WBytes[ByteIndex] := NextByte;
        { recast(buffer,asvalue) }
        NextWord := Buffer.WValue
    end { nextword };
function WordBoundary: WordRange;
    var Address: ByteRange;
    begin
        Address := ProgramCounter;
        while (Address mod MCBytesPerWord) <> 0 do Address := Address + 1;
        WordBoundary := Address div MCBytesPerWord
    end { wordboundary };
begin { runprogram }
    { variant activebits := [2,5,8,11,14,17,20,23,26,29] }
    ActiveBits.WValue := 0;
    for i := 0 to MaxVariantLevel do MCSetBit(ActiveBits, 3 * i + 2);
    { variant lockbits := [0,3,6,9,12,15,18,21,24,27] }
    LockBits.WValue := 0;
    for i := 0 to MaxVariantLevel do MCSetBit(LockBits, 3 * i);
```

{

Program execution commences at this point. The following paragraphs contain brief descriptions of each instruction together with argument types and explanatory notes where appropriate. The notation TOS is as shorthand for "top of stack".

}

```
    Finished := false; Overflowed := false;
    repeat
        OpCode := NextByte;
        case OpCode of
```

{

39.1 Constant-Instructions

The following instructions fetch and load in-line constants or their addresses onto the top of the stack.

Instructions	Arguments	Notes
ShortConstant		1
Constant	byte|word	2
ConstMultiple	(byte|word) wordstring	3
ConstRefMultiple	(byte|word) wordstring	4
ConstSet	(byte|word) wordstring	5

(1)   The first 32 P-code values are reserved to denote constants in the range 0..31.

(2)   The argument specifies the constant value to be pushed onto the stack.

(3)   The first argument specifies the length of the multi-word constant to be pushed onto the stack. The second argument is the word-aligned multi-word constant.

(4)   The code address of the multi-word constant is pushed onto the stack.

(5)   The set constant is pushed onto the stack in reduced format.

}

```
cons0, cons1, cons2, cons3, cons4, cons5, cons6, cons7, cons8, cons9, cons10, cons11,
cons12, cons13, cons14, cons15, cons16, cons17, cons18, cons19, cons20, cons21,
cons22, cons23, cons24, cons25, cons26, cons27, cons28, cons29, cons30, cons31 :
  { shortconstant }
  begin Push(OpCode) end;
consb :
  { constant(b) }
  begin Push(NextByte) end;
consw :
  { constant(w) }
  begin Push(NextWord) end;
conmb :
  { constmultiple(b) }
  begin
    Size := NextByte; CodeBase := WordBoundary;
    LoadWords(CodeBase, Size);
    ProgramCounter := (CodeBase + Size) * MCBytesPerWord
  end;
conmw :
  { constmultiple(w) }
  begin
    Size := NextWord; CodeBase := WordBoundary;
    LoadWords(CodeBase, Size);
    ProgramCounter := (CodeBase + Size) * MCBytesPerWord
  end;
```

```
crefb :
  { constrefmultiple(b) }
  begin
    Size := NextByte; CodeBase := WordBoundary; Push(CodeBase);
    ProgramCounter := (CodeBase + Size) * MCBytesPerWord
  end;
crefw :
  { constrefmultiple(w) }
  begin
    Size := NextWord; CodeBase := WordBoundary; Push(CodeBase);
    ProgramCounter := (CodeBase + Size) * MCBytesPerWord
  end;
csetb :
  { constset(b) }
  begin
    Size := NextByte; CodeBase := WordBoundary;
    LoadWords(CodeBase, Size); Push(-Size);
    ProgramCounter := (CodeBase + Size) * MCBytesPerWord;
  end;
csetw :
  { constset(w) }
  begin
    Size := NextWord; CodeBase := WordBoundary;
    LoadWords(CodeBase, Size); Push(-Size);
    ProgramCounter := (CodeBase + Size) * MCBytesPerWord
  end;
{
```

39.2 Memory Access

The following instructions provide access to memory for the loading of operands and storing of results. The group is sub-divided into word access in the local, global, enclosing and intermediate stack-frames, word access by indexing and indirection, partword access, partword indexing, byte access, byte indexing, and multi-word access.

39.2.1 Direct Word Access

Instructions	Arguments	Notes
ShortLoadLocal		1
LoadLocal	byte|word	2
LoadRefLocal	byte|word	3
ShortStoreLocal		1
StoreLocal	byte|word	2
LoadGlobal	byte|word	2
LoadRefGlobal	byte|word	3
StoreGlobal	byte|word	2
LoadEnclosing	byte|word	2
LoadRefEnclosing	byte|word	3

StoreEnclosing   byte|word   2
LoadIntermediate   byte|word   2
LoadRefIntermediate   byte|word   3
StoreIntermediate   byte|word   2

(1)   These instructions perform optimised access to the local stack-frame. The word-offset
      from the stack-frame base is implicit in the P-code value.

(2)   These instructions perform access to the local, enclosing, intermediate, and global stack
      frames. In each case the argument specifies a word offset in the appropriate stack
      frame.

(3)   These instructions push a word address in the appropriate stack-frame onto the stack.
      In each case the argument specifies the word-offset in the frame.

}

```
lodl0, lodl1, lodl2, lodl3, lodl4, lodl5, lodl6, lodl7 :
    { shortloadlocal }
    begin Push(Memory[CurrentFrame + OpCode - lodl0]) end;
lodlb :
    { loadlocal(b) }
    begin Push(Memory[CurrentFrame + NextByte]) end;
lodlw :
    { loadlocal(w) }
    begin Push(Memory[CurrentFrame + NextWord]) end;
lrf0, lrf1, lrf2, lrf3, lrf4, lrf5, lrf6, lrf7 :
    { loadreflocal(0..7) }
    begin Push(CurrentFrame + OpCode - lrf0) end;
lrflb :
    { loadreflocal(b) }
    begin Push(CurrentFrame + NextByte) end;
lrflw :
    { loadreflocal(w) }
    begin Push(CurrentFrame + NextWord) end;
stol0, stol1, stol2, stol3, stol4, stol5, stol6, stol7 :
    { shortstorelocal }
    begin Pop(Memory[CurrentFrame + OpCode - stol0]) end;
stolb :
    { storelocal(b) }
    begin Pop(Memory[CurrentFrame + NextByte]) end;
stolw :
    { storelocal(w) }
    begin Pop(Memory[CurrentFrame + NextWord]) end;
{ global block access }
lodgb :
    { loadglobal(b) }
    begin Push(Memory[GlobalFrame + NextByte]) end;
```

```
lodgw :
  { loadglobal(w) }
  begin Push(Memory[GlobalFrame + NextWord]) end;
lrfgb :
  { loadrefglobal(b) }
  begin Push(GlobalFrame + NextByte) end;
lrfgw :
  { loadrefglobal(w) }
  begin Push(GlobalFrame + NextWord) end;
stogb :
  { storeglobal(b) }
  begin Pop(Memory[GlobalFrame + NextByte]) end;
stogw :
  { storeglobal(w) }
  begin Pop(Memory[GlobalFrame + NextWord]) end;
{ enclosing block access }

lodeb :
  { loadenclosing(b) }
  begin Push(Memory[Memory[CurrentFrame - SLOffset] + NextByte]) end;
lodew :
  { loadenclosing(w) }
  begin Push(Memory[Memory[CurrentFrame - SLOffset] + NextWord]) end;
lrfeb :
  { loadrefenclosing(b) }
  begin Push(Memory[CurrentFrame - SLOffset] + NextByte) end;
lrfew :
  { loadrefenclosing(w) }
  begin Push(Memory[CurrentFrame - SLOffset] + NextWord) end;
stoeb :
  { storeenclosing(b) }
  begin Pop(Memory[Memory[CurrentFrame - SLOffset] + NextByte]) end;
stoew :
  { storeenclosing(w) }
  begin Pop(Memory[Memory[CurrentFrame - SLOffset] + NextWord]) end;
{ intermediate block access }

lodib :
  { loadintermediate(b) }
  begin
    Offset := NextByte; FrameOffset := NextByte;
    Push(Memory[OuterFrame(FrameOffset) + Offset])
  end;
lodiw :
  { loadintermediate(w) }
  begin
    Offset := NextWord; FrameOffset := NextByte;
    Push(Memory[OuterFrame(FrameOffset) + Offset])
  end;
```

```
lrfib :
   { loadrefintermediate(b) }
   begin
     Offset := NextByte; FrameOffset := NextByte;
     Push(OuterFrame(FrameOffset) + Offset)
   end;
lrfiw :
   { loadrefintermediate(w) }
   begin
     Offset := NextWord; FrameOffset := NextByte;
     Push(OuterFrame(FrameOffset) + Offset)
   end;
stoib :
   { storeintermediate(b) }
   begin
     Offset := NextByte; FrameOffset := NextByte;
     Pop(Memory[OuterFrame(FrameOffset) + Offset])
   end;
stoiw :
   { storeintermediate(w) }
   begin
     Offset := NextWord; FrameOffset := NextByte;
     Pop(Memory[OuterFrame(FrameOffset) + Offset])
   end;
{
```

39.2.2 Indirect Word Access

Instructions	Arguments	Notes
LoadIndirect		1
ShortIndex		2
Index	byte|word	3
IndexRef	byte|word	4
IndexCAP		5
StoreIndirect		1
AdjustPlus	byte|word	6
AdjustP1		6
AdjustMinus	byte|word	6
AdjustM1		6
AddAddress		6

(1)   These instructions perform indirect load and store via the word address on the top of the stack.

(2)   These instructions perform indexed load from the base-address on top of the stack. The offset is implicit in the P-code byte value.

(3)   These instructions perform an indexed load from the base-address on top of the stack using the argument as offset.

(4)   These instructions perform indexed load using an index value and base address on top of the stack and the argument as an index scale factor.

(5)   This instruction is used to index-load a conformant array element using the bound pair block to provide scaling information.

(6)   These instructions are used to modify an address value on top of the stack. The adjustment is implicit if it is +1 or -1, and specified by the argument value otherwise.

}

```
    lodin :
      { loadindirect }
      begin Pop(Address); Push(Memory[Address]) end;
    indx1, indx2, indx3, indx4, indx5, indx6, indx7 :
      { shortindex }
      begin Pop(Base); Push(Memory[Base + OpCode - lodin]) end;
    indxb :
      { index(b) }
      begin Pop(Base); Push(Memory[Base + NextByte]) end;
    indxw :
      { index(w) }
      begin Pop(Base); Push(Memory[Base + NextWord]) end;
    ixrfb :
      { indexref(b) }
      begin Pop(IndexValue); Pop(Base); Push(Base + IndexValue * NextByte) end;
    ixrfw :
      { indexref(w) }
      begin Pop(IndexValue); Pop(Base); Push(Base + IndexValue * NextWord) end;
    ixcap :
      { indexcap }
      begin
        Pop(IndexValue); Pop(CAPBpBlock); Pop(Base);
        Push(Base+(IndexValue-Memory[CAPBpBlock])*Memory[CAPBpBlock+2])
      end;
    stoin :
      { storeindirect }
      begin Pop(Address); Pop(Datum); Memory[Address] := Datum end;
    adjpb :
      { adjustplus(b) }
      begin Pop(Address); Push(Address + NextByte) end;
    adjpw :
      { adjustplus(w) }
      begin Pop(Address); Push(Address + NextWord) end;
    adjp1 :
      { adjustp1 }
      begin Pop(Address); Push(Address + 1) end;
```

```
        adjmb :
          { adjustminus(b) }
          begin Pop(Address); Push(Address - NextByte) end;
        adjmw :
          { adjustminus(w) }
          begin Pop(Address); Push(Address - NextWord) end;
        adjm1 :
          { adjustm1 }
          begin Pop(Address); Push(Address - 1) end;
        adadr :
          { addaddress }
          begin Pop(Offset); Pop(Address); Push(Address + Offset) end;
{
```

39.2.3 Part-Word-Access

The following instructions access part-words by means of a stacked part-word address that takes the form:

TOS	:	Right-most bit position of part-word field
TOS-1	:	Width of part-word field
TOS-2	:	Address of word containing the field

Instructions	Arguments	Notes
LoadBit	byte	1
LoadPacked		2
StoreBit		1
StorePacked		2
IndexPackedRef	byte	3
IndexPackedCAP		6
IndexSubWord	byte	4
AdjustPackedRef		5

(1) These instructions access single bits in the word whose address is on top of the stack. The argument is a bit position measured from the least-significant end of the word.

(2) These instructions access part-word fields using the three-word part-word address on top of the stack.

(3) This instruction produces a part-word address corresponding to an indexed element of a packed array. The byte argument specifies the number of elements per word.

(4) This instruction produces a part-word address by indexing from a part-word base address. The byte argument specifies the number of elements per word.

(5) This instruction modifies a part-word address by altering the field width and bit-offset.

(6) This instruction normalises the index value for a packed conformant array.

```
}
        lodbt :
```

```
      { loadbit }
      begin
        Pop(Base); IpBuffer.WValue := Memory[Base];
        MCGetBit(IpBuffer, NextByte, Bit); Push(Bit)
      end;
lodpk :
    { loadpacked }
    begin
      Pop(RightMost); Pop(Size); Pop(Base); IpBuffer.WValue := Memory[Base];
      OpBuffer.WValue := 0;
      for i := 0 to Size - 1 do
        begin
          MCGetBit(IpBuffer, RightMost + i, Bit);
          if Bit <> 0 then MCSetBit(OpBuffer, i)
        end;
      Push(OpBuffer.WValue)
    end;
stobt :
    { storebit }
    begin
      Pop(Base); OpBuffer.WValue := Memory[Base]; Pop(Datum);
      if Datum = 0
      then MCClearBit(OpBuffer, NextByte) else MCSetBit(OpBuffer, NextByte);
      Memory[Base] := OpBuffer.WValue
    end;
stopk :
    { storepacked }
    begin
      Pop(RightMost); Pop(Size); Pop(Base); Pop(IpBuffer.WValue);
      OpBuffer.WValue := Memory[Base];
      for i := 0 to Size - 1 do
        begin
          MCGetBit(IpBuffer, i, Bit);
          if Bit = 0
          then MCClearBit(OpBuffer, RightMost + i)
          else MCSetBit(OpBuffer, RightMost + i)
        end;
      Memory[Base] := OpBuffer.WValue
    end;
ixpkb :
    { indexpackedref }
    begin
      ElementsPerWord := NextByte; Pop(IndexValue); Pop(Base);
      Size := MCBitsPerWord div ElementsPerWord;
      Push(Base + IndexValue div ElementsPerWord); Push(Size);
      Push((IndexValue mod ElementsPerWord) * Size)
    end;
```

```
      ixpcap :
        { indexpackedcap }
        begin
          Pop(IndexValue); Pop(CAPBpBlock);
          Push(IndexValue - Memory[CAPBpBlock])
        end;
      ixswb :
        { indexsubword }
        begin
          ElementsPerWord := NextByte; Pop(IndexValue); Pop(RightMost);
          Pop(Size); Size := MCBitsPerWord div ElementsPerWord; Push(Size);
          Push(RightMost + Size * IndexValue)
        end;
      adjpk :
        { adjustpackedref }
        begin
          Pop(Base1); Pop(Size1); Pop(Base2); Pop(Size2); Push(Size1);
          Push(Base1 + Base2)
        end;
{
```

39.2.4 Byte Access

The following instructions cater for character byte access and indexing.

Instructions	Arguments	Notes
LoadByte		1
StoreByte		1
LoadByteReference		2
IndexByteReference		2

(1)   These instructions perform byte access using the byte address on top of the stack.

(2)   These instructions generate a byte address from the word base address on top of the stack.

}

```
      lodby :
        { loadbyte }
        begin
          Pop(ByteAddress);
          Element.WValue := Memory[ByteAddress div MCBytesPerWord];
          MCGetByte(Element, ByteAddress mod MCBytesPerWord, Byte); Push(Byte)
        end;
      stoby :
        { storebyte }
        begin
          Pop(ByteAddress); Pop(Datum);
          Element.WValue := Memory[ByteAddress div MCBytesPerWord];
```

```
      MCSetByte(Element, ByteAddress mod MCBytesPerWord, Datum);
      Memory[ByteAddress div MCBytesPerWord] := Element.WValue
    end;
lbyrf :
    { loadbytereference }
    begin Pop(Address); Push(Address * MCBytesPerWord) end;
ibyrf :
    { indexbytereference }
    begin
      Pop(IndexValue); Pop(Base); Push(IndexValue + Base * MCBytesPerWord)
    end;
{
```

39.2.5 Multiple Word Access

The following instructions manipulate multi-word fields.

Instructions	Arguments	Notes
LoadMultiple	byte|word	
StoreMultiple	byte|word	
StoreRepeated	byte|word	1
Move	byte|word	
SizeCAP		2
MoveCAP		3
DuplicateCAP		4
ReleaseCAP		5

(1)   This instruction repeatedly stores a value into an array of memory words. The argument determines the size of the array.

(2)   This instruction computes the word size of a conformant array parameter.

(3)   This instruction moves the contents of one conformant array parameter into another.

(4)   This instruction creates a copy of a value conformant array on the heap.

(5)   This instruction releases the copy of the value conformant array from the heap.

}

```
      lodmb :
        { loadmultiple(b) }
        begin Pop(Base); LoadWords(Base, NextByte) end;
      lodmw :
        { loadmultiple(w) }
        begin Pop(Base); LoadWords(Base, NextWord) end;
      stomb :
        { storemultiple(b) }
        begin Pop(Address); StoreWords(Address, NextByte) end;
```

```
stomw :
  { storemultiple(w) }
  begin Pop(Address); StoreWords(Address, NextWord) end;
storb :
  { storerepeated(b) }
  begin Pop(Base); Pop(Datum); Spray(Datum, Base, NextByte) end;
storw :
  { storerepeated(w) }
  begin Pop(Base); Pop(Datum); Spray(Datum, Base, NextWord) end;
moveb :
  { move }
  begin Pop(Base1); Pop(Base2); MoveWords(Base2, Base1, NextByte) end;
movew :
  { move(w) }
  begin Pop(Base1); Pop(Base2); MoveWords(Base2, Base1, NextWord) end;
szcap :
  { sizecap }
  begin
    Pop(CAPBpBlock);
    Push
      ((Memory[CAPBpBlock + 1] - Memory[CAPBpBlock] + 1) *
      Memory[CAPBpBlock + 2])
  end;
mvcap :
  { movecap }
  begin Pop(Base1); Pop(Size); Pop(Base2); MoveWords(Base2, Base1, Size) end;
dpcap :
  { duplicatecap }
  begin
    Pop(Size); Pop(Address); Acquire(Size, HeapAddress);
    MoveWords(Memory[Address], HeapAddress, Size);
    Memory[Address] := HeapAddress
  end;
rlcap :
  { releasecap }
  begin Pop(Size); Pop(Address); Release(Size, Memory[Address]) end;
```

{

39.3 Operations

The instructions in this group perform operations for the manipulation of integer, real, Boolean, pointer, string, and set data. In each case the operand(s) are on top of the stack.

39.3.1 Boolean Operations

}

```
        andop :
          { andoperation }
          begin
            PopLogical(Logical1); PopLogical(Logical2); PushLogical(Logical1 * Logical2)
          end;
        notop :
          { notoperation }
          begin Pop(Datum); if Datum = 0 then Push(1) else Push(0) end;
```

{

39.3.2 Integer Operations

The following instructions perform operations on integer operands at TOS and TOS-1. An integer result is pushed back on the stack.

Instructions	Arguments	Notes
Increment	byte|word	1,2
Incr1		1
Decrement	byte|word	1,2
Dec1		1
AbsInteger		1
NegateInteger		1
SquareInteger		1
AddInteger		1
SubInteger		1
MulInteger		1
DivInteger		1
ModInteger		1

(1)   The operands are checked against the operation requested. If overflow is predicted and run-time checks have been selected, the error is flagged and execution terminates. If overflow is predicted and checks have not been selected, the result is set to the "undefined" word value.

(2)   The argument specifies the increment or decrement.

}

```
incrb :
  { increment(b) }
  begin
    Pop(Operand2); IntArith(Plus, Operand2, NextByte, Result); Push(Result)
  end;
incrw :
  { increment(w) }
  begin
    Pop(Operand2); IntArith(Plus, Operand2, NextWord, Result); Push(Result)
  end;
incr1 :
  { incr1 }
  begin Pop(Operand); IntArith(Plus, Operand, 1, Result); Push(Result) end;
decrb :
  { decrement(b) }
  begin
    Pop(Operand2); IntArith(Minus, Operand2, NextByte, Result); Push(Result)
  end;
decrw :
  { decrement(w) }
  begin
    Pop(Operand2); IntArith(Minus, Operand2, NextWord, Result); Push(Result)
  end;
decr1 :
  { dec1 }
  begin Pop(Operand); IntArith(Minus, Operand, 1, Result); Push(Result) end;
absint :
  { absinteger }
  begin
    Pop(Operand);
    if Operand < 0 then Push(-Operand) else Push(Operand)
  end;
negint :
  { negateinteger }
  begin Pop(Operand); Push(-Operand) end;
sqrint :
  { squareinteger }
  begin
    Pop(Operand); IntArith(Mul, Operand, Operand, Result); Push(Result)
  end;
addint :
  { addinteger }
  begin
    PopOperands; IntArith(Plus, Operand2, Operand1, Result); Push(Result)
  end;
subint :
  { subinteger }
  begin
    PopOperands; IntArith(Minus, Operand2, Operand1, Result); Push(Result)
  end;
```

```
     mulint :
       { mulinteger }
       begin
         PopOperands; IntArith(Mul, Operand2, Operand1, Result); Push(Result)
       end;
     divint :
       { divinteger }
       begin
         PopOperands; IntArith(Idiv, Operand2, Operand1, Result); Push(Result)
       end;
     modint :
       { modinteger }
       begin
         PopOperands; IntArith(Imod, Operand2, Operand1, Result); Push(Result)
       end;
{
```

39.3.3 Integer Comparisons

The following instructions perform comparisons between valid integer values. In each case, the operands are popped off the stack and replaced by a Boolean result value.
}

```
     oddint :
       { oddinteger }
       begin Pop(Operand); Push(abs(Operand) mod 2) end;
     eqint :
       { testiequal }
       begin PopOperands; Push(ord(Operand2 = Operand1)) end;
     neint :
       { testiunequal }
       begin PopOperands; Push(ord(Operand2 <> Operand1)) end;
     ltint :
       { testiless }
       begin PopOperands; Push(ord(Operand2 < Operand1)) end;
     leint :
       { testilessorequal }
       begin PopOperands; Push(ord(Operand2 <= Operand1)) end;
{
```

39.3.4 Scalar Value Checks

The following instructions check if the value on top of the stack is "undefined".

Instruction	Arguments	Notes
CheckTopValue	byte	1,2
CheckTopDefined	byte	1,3
CheckCAP	byte	4

(1)   The byte argument specifies an error code.

(2)   This instruction checks the value at TOS-1 against the check-value at TOS. The instruction is used to perform undefined checking for packed-fields where the check-value is a suitably chosen integer.

(3)   This instruction is used to check TOS against the representation of the machine "undefined" word value.

(4)   The elements of a conformant array whose word address is at TOS-1 are checked against the machine "undefined" value. The size of the array is at TOS.

```
}
        chktv :
          { checktopvalue }
          begin
            Pop(Datum); TrapCode := NextByte;
            if Datum = Memory[StackTop] then Error(TrapCode)
          end;
        chktd :
          { checktopdefined }
          begin
            TrapCode := NextByte;
            if MemoryUndefined(StackTop, 1) then Error(TrapCode)
          end;
        chkcap :
          { checkcap }
          begin
            TrapCode := NextByte;
            if MemoryUndefined(Memory[StackTop - 1], Memory[StackTop])
            then Error(TrapCode)
          end;
{
```

39.3.5 Range-Checks

The following instructions perform range-checking operations. If the range is violated, an error is flagged, otherwise, the checked value is left at TOS.

Instruction	Arguments	Notes
CheckLimits	byte	1
CheckUpper	byte	2
CheckUpper	byte	3
CheckForLower	byte	4
CheckForUpper	byte	4

(1)   The value at TOS-2 is checked against upper and lower limits at TOS and TOS-1.

(2)   The value at TOS-1 is checked against a lower limit at TOS.

(3)   The value at TOS-1 is checked against an upper limit at TOS.

(4)   TOS contains the upper or lower bound of a for-loop control variable, and TOS-1 contains a computed limiting value for this variable. The value is checked against the bound and an appropriate error is flagged if necessary.

```
}
        chklm :
          { checklimits }
          begin
            Pop(Upper); Pop(Lower); Datum := Memory[StackTop];
            TrapCode := NextByte;
            if (Datum < Lower) or (Datum > Upper) then Error(TrapCode)
          end;
        chklw :
          { checklower }
          begin
            Pop(Lower); TrapCode := NextByte;
            if Memory[StackTop] < Lower then Error(TrapCode)
          end;
        chkup :
          { checkupper }
          begin
            Pop(Upper); TrapCode := NextByte;
            if Memory[StackTop] > Upper then Error(TrapCode)
          end;
        chkflw :
          { checkforlow }
          begin
            Pop(Lower); Pop(Datum); TrapCode := NextByte;
            if Datum < Lower then Error(TrapCode)
          end;
        chkfup :
          { checkforhigh }
          begin
            Pop(Upper); Pop(Datum); TrapCode := NextByte;
            if Datum > Upper then Error(TrapCode)
          end;
{
```

39.3.6 Real Operations

Instruction	Arguments	Notes
Float		
AbsReal		
NegateReal		
SquareReal		1

                              AddReal
                              SubtractReal
                              MultiplyReal
                              DivideReal   2
                              TruncateReal   3
                              RoundReal   3

(1)   If checks are requested the operand is checked against the configurable constant
       MCMaxRealRoot, and an error flagged if this value is exceeded. Since the range of
       reals is host-hardware dependent, MCMaxRealRoot is set in this version to the largest
       real whose square exceeds MCMaxint.

(2)   If checks are requested an error is flagged if the divisor is zero.

(3)   If checks are requested an error is flagged if the result is not a valid integer.

}

```
float :
  { floatinteger }
  begin Pop(Operand); PushReal(Operand) end;
absrl :
  { absreal }
  begin
    PopReal(RealOperand);
    if RealOperand < 0
    then PushReal(-RealOperand) else PushReal(RealOperand)
  end;
negrl :
  { negatereal }
  begin PopReal(RealOperand); PushReal(-RealOperand) end;
sqrl :
  { squarereal }
  begin
    PopReal(RealOperand);
    if abs(RealOperand) > MCMaxRealRoot
    then if ChecksOn then Error(32) else RealResult := Undefined
    else RealResult := RealOperand * RealOperand;
    PushReal(RealResult)
  end;
addrl :
  { addreal }
  begin PopRealOperands; PushReal(RealOp2 + RealOp1) end;
subrl :
  { subtractreal }
  begin PopRealOperands; PushReal(RealOp2 - RealOp1) end;
mulrl :
  { multiplyreal }
  begin PopRealOperands; PushReal(RealOp2 * RealOp1) end;
```

```
divrl :
  { dividereal }
  begin
    PopRealOperands;
    if RealOp1 = 0
    then if ChecksOn then Error(44) else RealResult := Undefined
    else RealResult := RealOp2 / RealOp1;
    PushReal(RealResult)
  end;
trurl :
  { truncatereal }
  begin
    PopReal(RealOperand); Fix(RealOperand, Result, Overflowed);
    if Overflowed
    then if ChecksOn then Error(35) else Result := Undefined;
    Push(Result)
  end;
rndrl :
  { roundreal }
  begin
    PopReal(RealOperand);
    if RealOperand >= 0
    then Fix(RealOperand + 0.5, Result, Overflowed)
    else Fix(RealOperand - 0.5, Result, Overflowed);
    if Overflowed
    then if ChecksOn then Error(36) else Result := Undefined;
    Push(Result)
  end;
{
```

39.3.7 Real Comparisons

The following instructions perform comparisons between real operands at TOS and TOS-1.
A Boolean result is pushed back on the stack.
}

```
eqrl :
  { testrequal }
  begin PopRealOperands; Push(ord(RealOp2 = RealOp1)) end;
nerl :
  { testrunequal }
  begin PopRealOperands; Push(ord(RealOp2 <> RealOp1)) end;
ltrl :
  { testrless }
  begin PopRealOperands; Push(ord(RealOp2 < RealOp1)) end;
lerl :
  { testrltorequal }
  begin PopRealOperands; Push(ord(RealOp2 <= RealOp1)) end;
{
```

39.3.8 Pointer Operations

The following instructions perform operations on pointer operands.

Instruction	Arguments	Notes
LoadPointer		1
CheckPointer		3
TestPEqual		2
TestPUnequal		2

(1)   This instruction performs pointer dereference. TOS contains the address of the pointer. If checks are requested errors are flagged if the pointer contents are "undefined" or represent the value "nil", or if key mismatch indicates the pointer is "dangling". The result loaded is pushed back on the stack.

(2)   These instructions perform comparisons of the pointers located at TOS-1 and TOS-3. A Boolean result is pushed back on the stack.

(3)   This instruction checks a pointer value and flags an error if the pointer is found to be undefined or dangling.

```
}
    lodptr :
      { loadpointer }
      begin
        Pop(Address);
        if MemoryUndefined(Address, PointerSize) then Error(4);
        Base := Memory[Address];
        if Base = 0 then Error(3);
        if Memory[Address + 1] <> Memory[Base - 1] then Error(4);
        Push(Base)
      end;
    chkptr :
      { checkpointer }
      begin
        Address := Memory[StackTop];
        if MemoryUndefined(Address, PointerSize) then Error(43);
        Base := Memory[Address];
        if Base <> 0
        then if Memory[Address + 1] <> Memory[Base - 1] then Error(43)
      end;
    eqptr :
      { testpequal }
      begin
        StackTop := StackTop - 2 * PointerSize; Base1 := StackTop + 1;
        Base2 := Base1 + PointerSize;
        Result :=
          ord((Memory[Base1] = Memory[Base2]) and
            (Memory[Base1 + 1] = Memory[Base2 + 1]));
        Push(Result)
      end;
```

```
neptr :
  { testpunequal }
  begin
    StackTop := StackTop - 2 * PointerSize; Base1 := StackTop + 1;
    Base2 := Base1 + PointerSize;
    Result :=
      ord((Memory[Base1] <> Memory[Base2]) or
          (Memory[Base1 + 1] <> Memory[Base2 + 1]));
    Push(Result)
  end;
{
```

39.3.9 String Comparisons

The following instructions perform comparisons between string operands. In each case the byte argument specifies the number of string bytes to be compared. The operands which are loaded at word aligned addresses on the stack, are popped and compared, and a Boolean result pushed back on the stack.
}

```
eqstr :
  { testsequal }
  begin
    Size := NextWord; Result := ord(StringEqual(Size));
    FreeStack(WordsFor(Size) * 2); Push(Result)
  end;
nestr :
  { testsunequal }
  begin
    Size := NextWord; Result := ord(not StringEqual(Size));
    FreeStack(WordsFor(Size) * 2); Push(Result)
  end;
ltstr :
  { testsless }
  begin
    Size := NextWord; Result := ord(StringLess(Size));
    FreeStack(WordsFor(Size) * 2); Push(Result)
  end;
lestr :
  { testsltorequal }
  begin
    Size := NextWord; Result := ord(StringLess(Size) or StringEqual(Size));
    FreeStack(WordsFor(Size) * 2); Push(Result)
  end;
{
```

39.3.10 Set Operations

The following instructions perform operations on set operands.

Instruction	Argument	Notes
LoadSet	byte	1
StoreSet	byte	2
SingletonSet		3
RangeSet		4
SetUnion		5
SetIntersection		5
SetDifference		5
SetExpand	byte	6
TestSetEqual		7
TestSetUnEqual		7
TestSubset		7
Inset		8
CheckSetUpper	byte	9
CheckSetLimits	byte	10

(1) The set whose word address is at TOS is pushed onto the stack in reduced format. The byte argument gives the word-size of the expanded set.

(2) The set value in reduced format at TOS-1 is expanded to a word size specified by the byte argument and stored in the word address at TOS.

(3) The scalar value at TOS is popped and used to construct a singleton set. The set is pushed on the stack in reduced format.

(4) The instruction constructs a range-set of numbers defined by the limiting values at TOS and TOS-1. The constructed set is pushed on the stack in reduced format.

(5) These instructions perform arithmetic on set operands in reduced-format. The result set is pushed on the stack in reduced format.

(6) This instruction expands the reduced-set at TOS to the word-size specified by the byte argument.

(7) These instructions perform comparison between the reduced set operands on the stack. A Boolean result is pushed onto the stack.

(8) This instruction tests membership in a reduced-set on the stack. The set and member values are popped and a Boolean result value is pushed.

(9) This instruction checks that all member values in the reduced-set at TOS-1 are less than or equal to the limit value at TOS. The byte argument identifies the error to be flagged if the condition is not met. The reduced-set is left at TOS.

(10) This instruction performs a set range-check by checking all member values in the reduced-set at TOS-2 lie within the limiting values popped from TOS and TOS-1.

}

```
lodset :
  { loadset }
  begin
    Size := NextByte; Pop(Base); ReducedSize := 0;
    if StackTop + Safety(Size + 1) >= HeapTop then SystemError(11);
    for i := 1 to Size do
      begin
        Operand := Memory[Base + i - 1];
        if Operand <> 0 then ReducedSize := i;
        Memory[StackTop + i] := Operand
      end;
    StackTop := StackTop + ReducedSize; PushSetSize(ReducedSize)
  end;
stoset :
  { storeset }
  begin
    Size := NextByte; Pop(Base); ExpandSet(Size); StoreWords(Base, Size)
  end;
sglset :
  { singletonset }
  begin
    Pop(Datum); Size := (Datum div MCWordSetBits) + 1;
    if StackTop + Safety(Size) >= HeapTop then SystemError(11);
    Start := StackTop + Size - 1;
    while StackTop < Start do Push(0);
    Element.WValue := 0; MCSetBit(Element, Datum mod MCWordSetBits);
    Push(Element.WValue); PushSetSize(Size)
  end;
rngset :
  { rangeset }
  begin
    Pop(Upper); Pop(Lower);
    if Lower > Upper
    then Size := 0
    else begin
        Size := (Upper div MCWordSetBits) + 1;
        if StackTop + Safety(Size) >= HeapTop then SystemError(11);
        Start := StackTop + (Lower div MCWordSetBits);
        while StackTop < Start do Push(0);
        Element.WValue := 0;
        for i := Lower to Upper do
          begin
            if i mod MCWordSetBits = 0
            then begin Push(Element.WValue); Element.WValue := 0 end;
            MCSetBit(Element, i mod MCWordSetBits)
          end;
        Push(Element.WValue)
      end;
    PushSetSize(Size)
  end;
```

```
setuni :
   { setunion }
   begin
      GetSetDetails;
      with SetDetails do
         begin
            for i := 0 to Subset - 1 do
               begin
                  SetElements(Base2 + i, Stride);
                  Element.WSet := Element2.WSet + Element1.WSet;
                  Push(Element.WValue)
               end;
            if Size1 > Size2
            then begin
                    LoadWords(Base1 + Subset, Size1 - Size2); Size := Size1
                 end
            else Size := Size2;
            StackTop := Base2 + Size - 1; PushSetSize(Size)
         end
   end;
setint :
   { setintersection }
   begin
      GetSetDetails;
      with SetDetails do
         begin
            ReducedSize := 0;
            for i := 0 to Subset - 1 do
               begin
                  SetElements(Base2 + i, Stride);
                  Element.WSet := Element2.WSet * Element1.WSet;
                  if Element.WSet <> [] then ReducedSize := i + 1;
                  Push(Element.WValue)
               end;
            StackTop := Base2 + ReducedSize - 1; PushSetSize(ReducedSize)
         end
   end;
setdif :
   { setdifference }
   begin
      GetSetDetails;
      with SetDetails do
         begin
            ReducedSize := 0;
            for i := 0 to Subset - 1 do
               begin
                  SetElements(Base2 + i, Stride);
                  Element.WSet := Element2.WSet - Element1.WSet;
```

```
                    if Element.WSet <> [] then ReducedSize := i + 1;
                    Push(Element.WValue)
                  end;
               if Size2 > Size1 then ReducedSize := Size2;
               StackTop := Base2 + ReducedSize - 1; PushSetSize(ReducedSize)
             end
         end;
setexp :
   { setexpand }
   begin ExpandSet(NextByte) end;
eqset :
   { testsetequal }
   begin
     GetSetDetails;
     with SetDetails do
       if Size1 <> Size2
       then Result := ord(false)
       else begin
               Result := ord(true);
               for i := 0 to Subset - 1 do
                  begin
                    SetElements(Base2 + i, Stride);
                    if Element2.WSet <> Element1.WSet
                    then Result := ord(false)
                  end
             end;
     Push(Result)
   end;
neset :
   { testsetunequal }
   begin
     GetSetDetails;
     with SetDetails do
       if Size1 <> Size2
       then Result := ord(true)
       else begin
               Result := ord(Subset <> 0);
               for i := 0 to Subset - 1 do
                  begin
                    SetElements(Base2 + i, Stride);
                    if Element2.WSet = Element1.WSet then Result := ord(false)
                  end
             end;
     Push(Result)
   end;
```

```
leset :
   { testsubset }
   begin
     GetSetDetails;
     with SetDetails do
        if Size2 > Size1
        then Result := ord(false)
        else begin
                Result := ord(true);
                for i := 0 to Subset - 1 do
                   begin
                     SetElements(Base2 + i, Stride);
                     if Element2.WSet - Element1.WSet <> []
                     then Result := ord(false)
                   end
              end;
        Push(Result)
   end;
inset :
   { inset }
   begin
     Pop(Size);
     if Size < 0
     then Size := -Size
     else if Size > 0 then begin Push(Size); Size := 1 end;
     Base := StackTop - Size; Operand := Memory[Base];
     Offset := Operand div MCWordSetBits;
     Bits := Operand mod MCWordSetBits;
     if (Operand < 0) or (Offset >= Size)
     then Result := ord(false)
     else begin
             Element.WValue := Memory[Base + Offset + 1];
             MCGetBit(Element, Bits, Bit); Result := Bit
          end;
     StackTop := Base - 1; Push(Result)
   end;
chksu :
   { checksetupper }
   begin
     Pop(Upper); TrapCode := NextByte; Size := Memory[StackTop];
     if Size <> 0
     then begin
             if Size < 0 then Size := -Size else Size := 1;
             CheckSize := (Upper div MCWordSetBits) + 1;
             if Size > CheckSize
             then Error(TrapCode)
             else if Size = CheckSize
                  then begin
                          if Size = 1
                          then Base := StackTop else Base := StackTop - Size;
```

```
                              LastBit := Upper mod MCWordSetBits;
                              Element.WValue := Memory[Base + Size - 1];
                              if not MCEmptyField
                                      (Element, LastBit + 1, MCMaxSetBit)
                              then Error(TrapCode)
                           end
            end
      end;
chksl :
   { checksetlimits }
   begin
      Pop(Upper); Pop(Lower); TrapCode := NextByte;
      Size := Memory[StackTop];
      if Size <> 0
      then begin
              if Size < 0 then Size := -Size else Size := 1;
              CheckSize := (Upper div MCWordSetBits) + 1;
              if Size > CheckSize
              then Error(TrapCode)
              else begin
                      EmptyWords := Lower div MCWordSetBits;
                      FirstBit := Lower mod MCWordSetBits;
                      LastBit := Upper mod MCWordSetBits;
                      if Size = 1
                      then Base := StackTop else Base := StackTop - Size;
                      for i := 1 to EmptyWords do
                         if Memory[Base + i - 1] <> 0 then Error(TrapCode);
                      Element.WValue := Memory[Base + EmptyWords];
                      if not MCEmptyField(Element, 0, FirstBit - 1)
                      then Error(TrapCode);
                      if Size = CheckSize
                      then begin
                              Element.WValue := Memory[Base + Size - 1];
                              if not MCEmptyField
                                      (Element, LastBit + 1, MCMaxSetBit)
                              then Error(TrapCode)
                           end
                   end
           end
      end;
{
```

39.4 Jump Instructions

The instructions in this group implement jumps by specifying either a relative byte displacement, or by indirection via an entry in the local jump-table.

Instructions	Arguments	Notes
JumpForward	byte	1
JumpBack	byte	1
JumpVia	byte	2
FJumpForward	byte	3
FJumpBack	byte	3
FJumpVia	byte	3
JumpOut	byte byte	4
FJumpConditional	byte	5
TJumpConditional	byte	5
CaseJump	WordString	6

(1)   The byte argument specifies the destination byte address relative to the current value of the ProgramCounter.

(2)   The argument indexes a jump-table location containing the destination byte address.

(3)   The Boolean value at TOS is popped, and the jump is taken if false. The byte argument specifies a relative byte-offset or an index to a jump-table location.

(4)   This instruction implements non-local jumps. The first byte argument specifies the nesting level displacement between the current and destination stack frames and the second byte argument is an index into the non-local jump-table. To ensure all intervening active blocks are correctly finalised, the return addresses are reset to trigger execution of their respective finalisation code sequences.

(5)   These instructions are used in the short circuit evaluation of Boolean expressions. TOS contains a Boolean value which is popped and compared against the condition implied by the instruction name. If these match, the value is pushed as a result and the jump taken. The byte argument specifies a relative forward displacement.

(6)   This instruction implements a table-driven case jump. The word string comprises a word-aligned jump-table which is indexed by the index value TOS. The first two locations of the table contain upper and lower limits for the index value and an error is flagged if either of these limits is exceeded. The remaining elements of the table contain destination byte addresses as defined by the case-statement labels. An error is flagged if no such address is associated with the index value.

}

```
jmpfw :
  { jumpforward }
  begin Offset := NextByte; ProgramCounter := ProgramCounter + Offset end;
jmpbk :
  { jumpback }
  begin Offset := NextByte; ProgramCounter := ProgramCounter - Offset end;
```

```
jmpvia :
  { jumpvia }
  begin
    CodeBase := Memory[CurrentFrame - CBOffset];
    ProgramCounter := Memory[CodeBase - NextByte]
  end;
fjpfw :
  { fjumpforward }
  begin
    Offset := NextByte; Pop(Result);
    if Result = ord(false) then ProgramCounter := ProgramCounter + Offset
  end;
fjpbk :
  { fjumpback }
  begin
    Offset := NextByte; Pop(Result);
    if Result = ord(false) then ProgramCounter := ProgramCounter - Offset
  end;
fjpvia :
  { fjumpvia }
  begin
    LabelEntry := NextByte; Pop(Result);
    if Result = ord(false)
    then begin
           CodeBase := Memory[CurrentFrame - CBOffset];
           ProgramCounter := Memory[CodeBase - LabelEntry]
         end
  end;
jmpout :
  { jumpout }
  begin
    FrameOffset := NextByte; LabelEntry := NextByte;
    ThisFrame := CurrentFrame; LabelledFrame := OuterFrame(FrameOffset);
    NextFrame := Memory[ThisFrame - DLOffset];
    while NextFrame <> LabelledFrame do
      begin
        Memory[ThisFrame - RAOffset] :=
          Memory[Memory[NextFrame - CBOffset] - FinalsOffset];
        ThisFrame := NextFrame;
        NextFrame := Memory[ThisFrame - DLOffset]
      end;
    Memory[ThisFrame - RAOffset] :=
      Memory[Memory[NextFrame - CBOffset] - LabelEntry];
    ProgramCounter :=
      Memory[Memory[CurrentFrame - CBOffset] - FinalsOffset]
  end;
```

```
fjpcnd :
   { fjumpconditional }
   begin
      Offset := NextByte; Pop(Result);
      if Result = ord(false)
      then begin
               Push(Result); ProgramCounter := ProgramCounter + Offset
           end
   end;
tjpcnd :
   { tjumpconditional }
   begin
      Offset := NextByte; Pop(Result);
      if Result = ord(true)
      then begin
               Push(Result); ProgramCounter := ProgramCounter + Offset
           end
   end;
casejp :
   { casejump }
   begin
      Base := WordBoundary; Pop(IndexValue); Lower := Memory[Base];
      Upper := Memory[Base + 1];
      if (IndexValue < Lower) or (IndexValue > Upper) then Error(51);
      Address := (Base + 2) + (IndexValue - Lower); Offset := Memory[Address];
      if Offset = 0 then Error(51);
      ProgramCounter := Offset + Address * MCBytesPerWord
   end;
{
```

39.5 Procedure Entry and Exit

The following instructions implement procedure and function entry/exit. The entry
sequence consists of the MarkStack instruction to create a hole for the incipient stack frame
header, a series of instructions to evaluate or reference the actual parameters, and a block
call instruction to enter the procedure or function. The block exit sequence consists of a single EndProcedure, EndFunction or EndMultiFunction instruction.

Instructions	Arguments	Notes
MarkStack		1
CallGlobal	byte	2
CallLocal	byte	2
CallLevel	byte	2
CallOuter	byte byte	2
CallFormal		4
EndProcedure		5
EndFunction		6
EndMultiFunction		

(1)   This instruction creates a six-word "hole" on the expression-stack by advancing the
       stack-pointer. The hole is later used to hold header information when the new stack-
       frame is created.

(2)   These instructions call a procedure or function whose nesting level displacement from
       the calling procedure is known. In the case of CallOuter, the displacement is given by
       the first byte argument. The remaining byte argument is an index into the jump-table
       of the block containing the procedure. The jump-table entry holds the code-base of
       the called procedure. The new stack frame is created using information embedded in
       the jump-table header of the called procedure. If checks are requested, that part of the
       new stack frame reserved for local variables is preset to the "undefined" value.

(4)   This instruction is used to call a formal procedure or function. In this case TOS con-
       tains the address of the formal parameter which is a double word field containing the
       address of stack-frame enclosing the actual procedure, and the jump table index for the
       actual procedure.

(5)   This instruction exits from a procedure to the return address in the calling block.

(6)   These instructions exit from a function by popping the function result off the stack,
       popping the current stack-frame, pushing the result back on the stack, and exiting to
       the return address in the calling block. EndMultiFunction is used for multi-word func-
       tion results.

}

```
              mark :
                { markstack }
                begin ClaimStack(FrameSize) end;
              calglo, calloc, callev, calotr, calfml :
                { callglobal
                  calllocal
                  calllevel
                  callouter
                  callformal }
                begin
                  case OpCode of
                    calglo : EnclosingFrame := GlobalFrame;
                    calloc : EnclosingFrame := CurrentFrame;
                    callev : EnclosingFrame := Memory[CurrentFrame - SLOffset];
                    calotr :
                      begin
                        FrameOffset := NextByte;
                        EnclosingFrame := OuterFrame(FrameOffset)
                      end;
                    calfml :
                      begin
                        Pop(Address); EnclosingFrame := Memory[Address];
                        LabelEntry := Memory[Address + 1]
                      end
                  end;
```

```
         if OpCode <> calfml then LabelEntry := NextByte;
         CodeBase := Memory[Memory[EnclosingFrame - CBOffset] - LabelEntry];
         Parameters := Memory[CodeBase - ParamsOffset];
         StackSpace := Memory[CodeBase - LocalsOffset];
         LockSpace := Memory[CodeBase - LocksOffset];
         NewFrame := StackTop - Parameters + 1; ClaimStack(StackSpace);
         SetFrameHeader;
         if ChecksOn and (StackSpace > 0)
         then PresetMemory(NewFrame + Parameters, StackSpace);
         ClaimStack(LockSpace); CurrentFrame := NewFrame;
         ProgramCounter := CodeBase * MCBytesPerWord
      end;
   endp :
      { endprocedure }
      begin
         ProgramCounter := Memory[CurrentFrame - RAOffset];
         StackTop := CurrentFrame - FrameSize - 1;
         CurrentFrame := Memory[CurrentFrame - DLOffset]
      end;
   endf :
      { endfunction }
      begin
         Pop(Result); ProgramCounter := Memory[CurrentFrame - RAOffset];
         StackTop := CurrentFrame - FrameSize - 1;
         CurrentFrame := Memory[CurrentFrame - DLOffset]; Push(Result)
      end;
   endmf :
      { endmultifuunction }
      begin
         Size := NextByte; Base := StackTop - Size + 1;
         ProgramCounter := Memory[CurrentFrame - RAOffset];
         StackTop := CurrentFrame - FrameSize - 1;
         CurrentFrame := Memory[CurrentFrame - DLOffset];
         LoadWords(Base, Size)
      end;
{
```

39.6 Dynamic Variables

The instructions in this group support the implementation of the standard procedures new and dispose.

Instructions	Arguments	Notes
New1	byte|word	1
Dispose1	byte|word	1
CheckNew1		2
CheckDisp1		3
CheckDisp2	byte	3

(1)   These instructions implement calls to new and dispose. TOS contains the address of a
       pointer variable and the argument specifies the number of words of storage required.

(2)   This instruction performs the check for a dereferenced pointer that is used as a factor.
       A non-zero level-byte in the pointer header indicates that the variable was created with
       the extended form of new, and must be flagged in error.

(3)   These instructions perform the run-time checks on dispose. Errors are reported if the
       dynamic variable is locked by an extended reference, or if the first form of dispose is
       used and a previous extended form of new specified a different number of case labels.
       The checks are detected using the lock bit and level byte count embedded in the
       dynamic variable header.

}

```
newp1b :
  { new1 }
  begin Newp(NextByte) end;
newp1w :
  { new1 }
  begin Newp(NextWord) end;
dspp1b :
  { dispose1 }
  begin Disposep(NextByte) end;
dspp1w :
  { dispose1 }
  begin Disposep(NextWord) end;
chkn1 :
  { checknew1 }
  begin
    Pop(Address); IpBuffer.WValue := Memory[Address - HeapLockOffset];
    MCGetByte(IpBuffer, HeapLevelByte, Byte);
    if Byte < > 0 then Error(25)
  end;
chkd1 :
  { checkdsp1 }
  begin
    Pop(Address); IpBuffer.WValue := Memory[Address - HeapLockOffset];
    MCGetBit(IpBuffer, HeapLockBit, Bit);
    if Bit < > 0 then Error(5);
    MCGetByte(IpBuffer, HeapLevelByte, Byte);
    if Byte < > 0 then Error(20)
  end;
```

```
  chkd2 :
    { checkdsp2 }
    begin
      Pop(Address); Datum := NextByte;
      IpBuffer.WValue := Memory[Address - HeapLockOffset];
      MCGetBit(IpBuffer, HeapLockBit, Bit);
      if Bit <> 0 then Error(5);
      MCGetByte(IpBuffer, HeapLevelByte, Byte);
      if (Byte <> 0) and (Byte <> Datum) then Error(21)
    end;
{
```

39.7 Special Instructions

The instructions in this group are largely concerned with implementation of run-time checks.

Instructions	Arguments	Notes
NoOperation		1
Preset		2
PresetRepeated	byte|word	3
LoadStack	byte	4
DuplicateStack		5
PopStack		6
CheckWord	byte	7
CheckRepeated	byte	8
CheckVntField		9
TrapProgramError	byte	10
TrapIfTrue	byte	10
TrapIfFalse	byte	10
SetLock	byte	11
DiscardLocks	byte	12
PurgeLocks		13
SampleAndPurgeLocks		14
HaltProgram		15

(1)   The explicit NoOperation instruction is used as padding to ensure wordstring arguments and jump tables are correctly aligned on word boundaries.

(2)   This instruction is used to preset the memory word whose address is at TOS to the "undefined" value.

(3)   This instruction is used to preset an array of memory words to the undefined value. The base address of the array is at TOS, and the size of the array is given by the byte or word argument.

(4)   This instruction pushes an element on the expression stack onto the top of the expression stack. The byte argument indexes the required stack element.

(5)   This instruction duplicates the top of the stack element.

(6)   This instruction pops the expression stack and discards the element at TOS.

(7)   This instruction flags an error specified by the byte argument if the memory word addressed by the contents of TOS is undefined.

(8)   This instruction flags an error specified by the byte argument if an element of the memory array addressed by the contents of TOS-1 is undefined. The size of the array is given by the contents of TOS.

(9)   This instruction checks accesses to variant record fields. TOS contains the current selector value, TOS-1 contains the selector value required with the access, and TOS-2 contains the record base address. An error is flagged if the selector field is not defined, or the current selector value differs from the required selector value.

(10)   These three instructions are concerned with mandatory and conditional trapping of an error. The error is identified by the byte argument.

(11)   This instruction sets a reference lock by pushing its current-value on the lock-stack before setting it. The byte argument specifies the position of the lock-bit.

(12)   This instruction pops and discards locks from the lock-stack. The byte argument specifies the number of entries to be retained in the lock-stack.

(13)   This instruction purges the lock-bits from the control word of a variant record, when a variant record is passed as a value parameter. TOS contains the address of the control word.

(14)   This instruction is only used in the context of assigning one variant record to another. If the left hand record has references extending to any of its active variants, the assignment is permitted only if the selector values remain unchanged. Such a check would be extremely inefficient and the P-machine employs a simpler but stronger check which prohibits assignment if any selector of the left hand variable is locked. If the assignment is permitted, the lock bits of the source record are purged prior to copying the control word.

(15)   This instruction provides normal program termination.

}

```
      noop :
        { explicit no-operation };
      preset :
        { presetword }
        begin Pop(Base); PresetMemory(Base, 1) end;
      presrb :
        { presetrepeated(b) }
        begin Pop(Base); PresetMemory(Base, NextByte) end;
      presrw :
        { presetrepeated(w) }
        begin Pop(Base); PresetMemory(Base, NextWord) end;
      ldstk :
        { loadstack }
        begin Push(Memory[StackTop - NextByte]) end;
```

```
dpstk :
   { duplicatestack }
   begin Push(Memory[StackTop]) end;
popstk :
   { popstack }
   begin StackTop := StackTop - 1 end;
chkwd :
   { checkword }
   begin
      TrapCode := NextByte; Pop(Base);
      if MemoryUndefined(Base, 1) then Error(TrapCode)
   end;
chkrp :
   { checkrepeated }
   begin
      TrapCode := NextByte; Pop(Size); Pop(Base);
      if MemoryUndefined(Base, Size) then Error(TrapCode)
   end;
chkvf :
   { checkvntfield }
   begin
      Pop(SelectorValue); Pop(SelectedValue);
      LockWord.WValue := Memory[Memory[StackTop]]; Datum := NextByte;
      MCGetBit(LockWord, 3 * Datum + 2, Bit);
      if (Bit = 0) or (SelectorValue <> SelectedValue) then Error(2)
   end;
trapp :
   { trapprogramerror }
   begin Error(NextByte) end;
trapt :
   { trapiftrue }
   begin
      TrapCode := NextByte; Pop(Datum);
      if Datum = ord(true) then Error(TrapCode)
   end;
trapf :
   { trapiffalse }
   begin
      TrapCode := NextByte; Pop(Datum);
      if Datum = ord(false) then Error(TrapCode)
   end;
setlk :
   { setlock }
   begin
      Bits := NextByte; Pop(Base); OpBuffer.WValue := Memory[Base];
      MCGetBit(OpBuffer, Bits, Bit); PushLock(Bit, Base, Bits);
      MCSetBit(OpBuffer, Bits); Memory[Base] := OpBuffer.WValue
   end;
```

```
dislk :
  { discardlocks }
  begin
    Datum := NextByte;
    while Memory[CurrentFrame - LDOffset] > Datum do
      begin
        PopLock(Bit, Base, Bits); OpBuffer.WValue := Memory[Base];
        if Bit = 0
        then MCClearBit(OpBuffer, Bits) else MCSetBit(OpBuffer, Bits);
        Memory[Base] := OpBuffer.WValue
      end
  end;
pglk :
  { purgelocks }
  begin
    Pop(Base); LockWord.WValue := Memory[Base];
    LockWord.WSet := LockWord.WSet - LockBits.WSet;
    Push(LockWord.WValue); Push(Base + 1)
  end;
smpglk :
  { sampleandpurgelocks }
  begin
    Pop(Base1); LockWord.WValue := Memory[Base1];
    LockWord.WSet := LockWord.WSet - ActiveBits.WSet;
    if LockWord.WSet <> [] then Error(2);
    Pop(Base2); LockWord.WValue := Memory[Base2];
    LockWord.WSet := LockWord.WSet - LockBits.WSet;
    Memory[Base1] := LockWord.WValue; Push(Base2 + 1); Push(Base1 + 1)
  end;
haltp :
  { haltprogram }
  begin Finished := true; Termination := Normal end;
{
```

39.8 Class 2 Instructions

The class 2 instructions are distinguished by a preceeding 255 "escape" byte-value. They comprise instructions for I/O, the transfer functions pack and unpack, the arithmetic functions, and program parameter exchange.

```
}
        escape :
          { escape to class 2 }
          begin
            OpCode := NextByte;
            case OpCode of
{
```

39.8.1

The following instructions implement the standard I/O functions.

Instructions	Arguments	Notes
CheckReadMode		1
CheckWriteMode		1
CheckBuffer		10
RewriteFile		2
ResetFile		2
EndofLine		3
EndofFile		3
GetFile		2
ReadInteger		4
ReadReal		4
ReadLine		5
PutFile		2
WriteCharacter		6
WriteBoolean		6
WriteString		6
WriteInteger		6
WriteFloated		7
WriteFixed		7
PageFile		8
CloseFile		9

(1)   These instructions check the mode of the file and flag an error if the actual mode differs from the expected mode.

(2)   These instructions perform the primitive I/O operations of reset, rewrite, put and get. For the first two, TOS contains the address of the file variable. For the second two, TOS contains an index-value identifying the file.

(3) These instructions implement the functions eof and eoln.

(4) These instructions handle real and integer input from text files.

(5) This instruction implements the procedure readln for a text file.

(6) These instructions implement text output for integer, character, Boolean, and string data.

(7) These instructions implement fixed and floating point text output for real data.

(8) This instruction implements the procedure page.

(9) This instruction closes a file, flushes the buffer, and releases the buffer storage and file descriptor.

(10) This instruction performs an existence check on a file buffer and flags an error if any attempt is made to access the buffer-variable of a file prior to an initial rewrite or reset operation.

}

```
                    chkrd :
                      { checkreadmode }
                      begin
                        Pop(FileIndex);
                        with PascalFiles[FileIndex] do
                          if Mode <> Inspection then Error(14)
                      end;
                    chkwr :
                      { checkwritemode }
                      begin
                        Pop(FileIndex);
                        with PascalFiles[FileIndex] do
                          if Mode <> Generation then Error(9)
                      end;
                    chkbuf :
                      { checkbuffer }
                      begin
                        FileIndex := Memory[Memory[StackTop]];
                        if FileIndex = UndefinedIndex then Error(61)
                      end;
                    rewrtf :
                      { rewritefile }
                      begin Pop(Address); RewriteFile end;
                    resetf :
                      { resetfile }
                      begin Pop(Address); ResetFile end;
                    eolnf :
                      { endofline }
                      begin
                        Pop(FileIndex);
                        with PascalFiles[FileIndex] do Push(ord(BytePointer = LastByte))
                      end;
```

```
eoff :
  { endoffile }
  begin
    Pop(FileIndex);
    with PascalFiles[FileIndex] do Push(ord(EndOfFile))
  end;
getf, rdint, rdrl, rdln :
  { getfile
    readinteger
    readreal
    readline }
  begin
    Pop(FileIndex);
    case OpCode of
      getf : GetFile;
      rdint : ReadNumber(IntForm);
      rdrl : ReadNumber(RealForm);
      rdln : ReadLine
    end
  end;
putf, wrchar, wrbool, wrstr, wrint, wrflt, wrfix, wrln, pagef :
  { putfile
    writecharacter
    writeboolean
    writestring
    writeinteger
    writefloated
    writefixed
    writeline
    pagefile }
  begin
    Pop(FileIndex);
    case OpCode of
      putf : PutFile;
      wrchar : WriteChar;
      wrbool : WriteBoolean;
      wrstr : WriteString;
      wrint : WriteInteger;
      wrflt : WriteReal(Floated);
      wrfix : WriteReal(Fixed);
      wrln : WriteLine;
      pagef : PageFile
    end
  end;
closef :
  { closefile }
  begin Pop(Address); CloseFile end;
{
```

39.8.2 Transfer Functions

The following instructions implement pack and unpack.

	Instructions	Arguments	Notes
	Pack	byte	1
	PackC	byte	1
	Unpack	byte	2
	UnpackC	byte	2

(1)   These instructions implement the procedure pack. TOS contains the size of the unpacked array, TOS-1 contains the base address of the packed array, and TOS-2 contains the base-address of the unpacked array. The byte argument specifies the number of bytes per word in the packed array. The instruction PackC is used when runtime checks are requested to check that each unpacked array element is defined.

(2)   These procedures implement the procedure unpack. The stack contains the size of the unpacked array, the packed array base address, and the unpacked array base address. For UnpackC, the stack additionally holds the "undefined" CheckValue for elements of the packed array, and every such element is checked against this value. The byte argument specifies the number of elements per word of the packed array.

```
}
              pckpr :
                { pack }
                begin
                  Pop(Size); Pop(Base1); Pop(Base2);
                  Packp(Base2, Size, Base1, NextByte)
                end;
              pckprc :
                { packc }
                begin
                  Pop(Size); Pop(Base1); Pop(Base2);
                  Packpc(Base2, Size, Base1, NextByte)
                end;
              Upkpr :
                { unpack }
                begin
                  Pop(Size); Pop(Base1); Pop(Base2);
                  Unpackp(Base1, Base2, Size, NextByte)
                end;
              upkprc :
                { unpackc }
                begin
                  Pop(Datum); Pop(Size); Pop(Base1); Pop(Base2);
                  Unpackpc(Base1, Base2, Size, Datum, NextByte)
                end;
{
```

39.8.3 Arithmetic Functions

The following instructions implement the required arithmetic functions. Each instruction pops the real argument off the stack and pushes a real result.

Instructions	Arguments	Notes
Sine		
Cosine		
NaturalExp		
NaturalLog	1	
SquareRoot	2	
ArcTangent		

(1)   If checks have been requested and the operand is $<=0.0$, then an error is flagged.

(2)   If checks have been requested and the operand is negative an error is flagged.

}

```
        sinf :
          { sine }
          begin PopReal(RealOperand); PushReal(sin(RealOperand)) end;
        cosf :
          { cosine }
          begin PopReal(RealOperand); PushReal(cos(RealOperand)) end;
        expf :
          { naturalexp }
          begin PopReal(RealOperand); PushReal(exp(RealOperand)) end;
        logf :
          { naturallog }
          begin
            PopReal(RealOperand);
            if RealOperand <= 0.0
            then begin
                    if ChecksOn then Error(33) else RealResult := Undefined
                 end
            else RealResult := ln(RealOperand);
            PushReal(RealResult)
          end;
        sqrtf :
          { squareroot }
          begin
            PopReal(RealOperand);
            if RealOperand < 0.0
            then begin
                    if ChecksOn then Error(34) else RealResult := Undefined
                 end
            else RealResult := sqrt(RealOperand);
            PushReal(RealResult)
          end;
```

```
                    arctnf :
                      { arctangent }
                      begin PopReal(RealOperand); PushReal(arctan(RealOperand)) end;
{
```

39.8.4 Program Parameter Exchange

The instruction MapProgramParameter provides for the mapping of program parameters to external files. The argument comprises a byte string containing the program parameter name and its position in the program parameter list. The position value is used to set the FileIndex and is used as an identifying value thereafter. This is embedded in the file variable memory block, and a corresponding descriptor is allocated for the file. The variables InputId and OutputId record the index values for the parameters Input and Output.

```
}
                        mapp :
                          { mapprogramparameter }
                          begin
                            Size := NextByte; FileIndex := NextByte; Name := BlankName;
                            for i := 1 to Size - 1 do Name[i] := chr(NextByte);
                            Pop(Address); Memory[Address] := FileIndex; AllocatePascalFile;
                            if Name = 'INPUT          '
                            then InputId := FileIndex
                            else if Name = 'OUTPUT         '
                                 then OutputId := FileIndex else Bind(Name)
                          end
                   end
                 end
             end
          until Finished
       end { runprogram };
```

{

CHAPTER 40

The Driver Program

The P-Machine's main program body initialises chapters as required, loads the object program, and executes it by calling RunProgram. On normal completion of execution, finalisation calls to appropriate chapters are made.

The label 13 is used to finalise any program I/O in progress and output the program corpse if execution is aborted for any reason.

}

```
begin
  InitController;
  SetMCUndefined;
  InitMemory;
  InitSysFiles;
  InitPascIO;

  LoadProgram;

  RunProgram;

13:
  EndPascIO;
  EndController
end.
```

Index of
Major Procedures and Functions
in the P-Machine

The following index lists all major procedures and functions used in the P-machine, together with the page numbers needed to locate their definitions in this version of its text.

{

CHAPTER 41

Postmortem
Generator Overview

This program generates post-mortem information following abnormal program termination on the P-Machine. The program reports the nature of the error and supplements this with a trace-back of all active program blocks together with a symbolic dump of their variables. The interface between the post-mortem generator, the Model Compiler, and the P-Machine is defined by the program heading which is as follows:

}

program PostmortemDump
(CorpseFile, ErrorFile,
CodeMap, DataMap, NameFile, Output);

{

The program parameters have the following nature and purpose:

CorpseFile   is an input file defining the state of the P-Machine and the executing program when the error occurred, and is generated by the P-Machine.

ErrorFile   is an input textfile containing the texts of all error messages issued by the Model Implementation.

CodeMap   is an input file holding the code map generated by the Model Compiler.

DataMap   is an input file holding the data map generated by the Model Compiler.

NameFile   is an input file holding the identifier spellings of all named objects on the data map file, and is generated by the Model Compiler.

Output   is an output textfile on which the post-mortem dump is written.

The principal steps involved in post-mortem analysis are as follows.

(1)   The contents of the corpse, code-map, data-map, and names files are read into appropriate arrays by the procedures in Chapter 42.

(2)   The cause of termination is determined from the corpse, and output as a suitable error message extracted from the error file, by the procedures in Chapter 43.

(3)   If a full postmortem dump has been requested, a trace-back of the procedure calls lead-
       ing to the point of failure, together with a symbolic variable dump for each, is gen-
       erated by the procedures in Chapter 44, which also includes the main program driving
       the postmortem generation process.

As in the Compiler and P-Machine, all global definitions and declarations supporting these
chapters are collected in Chapter 41.

}

CHAPTER 42

Global Definitions
and Declarations

As in the Model Compiler and P-Machine, this chapter contains all of the global definitions and declarations on which the procedures in the subsequent chapters depend. For the most part, these are duplicates of definitions and declarations used in the Compiler and P-Machine to define the diagnostic and corpse file contents which are read by the Generator.

42.1 Another Global Label!

The global label 13 is used to terminate execution in the event of catastrophic failure.

}
label 13;
{

42.2 Global Constants

}
const
{

The following constants describe the model P-machine. Their values are strictly dependent on the host Pascal environment in which the model implementation is to run. An implementor must

1. Investigate how the host Pascal processor implements the packed-variable:

    HostWord : packed array[HostWordSize] of HostBit

    If HostWord[0] is mapped onto the most significant bit position, then set the constant IndexedFromLeft to the value true. Otherwise, set it to false.

2. Set the value of MaxHostChar to the maximum host character value.

3. Redefine the constants prefixed 'MC' for the host machine.

}

IndexedFromLeft = true;	{ for host Pascal compiler }
MaxHostChar = 255;	{ for most character sets }
MCBitsPerWord = 32;	{ bits per memory-word }
MCWordSetBits = 31;	{ bits per set-word }

```
MCBitsPerByte = 8;                                  { bits per memory-byte }
MCBytesPerWord = 4 ;                                { mcbitsperword div mcbitsperbyte }
MCMaxBitnum = 31;                                   { mcbitsperword-1 }
MCMaxSetBit = 30;                                   { mcwordsetbits-1 }
MCMaxByteNum = 3;                                   { mcbytesperword-1 }

MCMaxint = 2147483647;                              { max mc-integer value }
MCRealSize = 2;                                     { real size in words }
MCMaxByte = 255;                                    { max mc-byte value }
MCMaxChar = 255;                                    { max mc-char value }
MCMaxLevel = 32;                                    { max block nesting level }
MCMaxSet = 256;                                     { maximum members per set }

MCMaxMemWord = 16383;                               { max memory-word address }
MCMaxMemByte = 65535;                               { max memory-byte address }

{
```

The following constants define offsets used to access specific locations within the stack-frame headers and code-block headers used by the P-machine.

```
}
SLOffset = 1;                                       { |framebase-1|=staticlink }
CBOffset = 2;                                       { |framebase-2|=codebase    }
DLOffset = 3;                                       { |framebase-3|=dynamiclink }
RAOffset = 4;                                       { |framebase-4|=returnaddress }
LDOffset = 5;                                       { |framebase-5|=lock-stack depth }
LTOffset = 6;                                       { |framebase-6|=lock-stack top    }
FrameSize = 6;

ParamsOffset = 1;                                   { |codebase-1| = parameter size }
LocalsOffset = 2;                                   { |codebase-2| = stack size }
LocksOffset = 3;                                    { |codebase-3| = lock-stack size }
SerialOffset = 4;                                   { |codebase-4| = 0/pmd block serial }

{ file check-bits in file-control block }

FileLockBit = 0;                                    { set when buffer is referenced }
EofBit = 1;                                         { set when eof }
EolBit = 2;                                         { set when eoln for a text-file }

{ constants configuring the generator tables }

NilSerial = 0;                                      { unallocated serial number }
MaxDataSerial = 511;                                { upper bound of data table }
MaxNameIndex = 8191;                                { upper bound of names table }
MaxCodeIndex = 4095;                                { upper bound of code table }

{ constants formatting the generator output }

Leftmost = 2;                                       { left-most print position }
LeftMinus1 = 1;                                     { leftmost - 1 }
RightMost = 80;                                     { right-most print position }
RightPlus1 = 81;                                    { right-most + 1 }
```

MaxField = 78;   { rightmost-leftmost }
Indent = 3;   { record-scope indentation }
RealField = 14;   { print field for reals }

{ configuration constants for the error message file }

StartCode = 0;   { minimum error code }
MaxCode = 499;   { maximum error code }
RuntimeBase = 300;   { runtime errors: 301..400 }
SystemBase = 400;   { system limit errors: 401..420 }
FatalBase = 420;   { fatal errors: 421..450 }
LinesPerText = 2;   { lines per error text }

DispLimit = 20;   { maximum address level }

{

42.3 Global Types

}

type

HostWord = Integer;

{ types describing the model P-machine }

MCBit = 0..1;
MCByte = 0..MCMaxByte;
MCWord = HostWord;
MCScalar = 0..MCMaxint;
MCIntegerForm = HostWord;
MCRealForm = real;
MCCharSet = 0..MCMaxChar;
MCBitRange = 0..MCBitsPerWord;
MCBitIndex = 0..MCMaxBitnum;
MCSetBits = 0..MCMaxSetBit;
MCBitarray = **packed array** [MCBitIndex] **of** MCBit;
MCByteIndex = 0..MCMaxByteNum;
MCByteArray = **packed array** [MCByteIndex] **of** MCByte;
MCWordSet = **set of** MCSetBits;
WordCast = (AsSet, AsBits, AsBytes, AsReal, AsValue);
MCWordForm = **record**
                    case WordCast **of**
                        AsSet: (WSet: MCWordSet);
                        AsBits: (WBits: MCBitarray);
                        AsBytes: (WBytes: MCByteArray);
                        AsReal: (WReal: MCRealForm);
                        AsValue: (WValue: MCWord)
                end;

```
{ compile-time types used to define the data-map file }
Scalar = 0..maxint;
DeclKind = (PreDefined, Declared);
TypeForm = (Scalars, SubRanges, Pointers, Arrays, CAPSchema, Records, Sets, Files,
            VariantPart, Variant);
SetForms = (Unpacked, IsPacked, Constructed);
IdClass = (Domain, Types, Consts, Vars, Bound, Field, Proc, Func, Prog);
WordEntry = ^ListWord;
ListWord = record Word: MCWordForm; Next: WordEntry end;
ByteRange = 0..MCMaxMemByte;
WordRange = 0..MCMaxMemWord;
ValueKind = (Ordvalue, IntValue, BoolValue, CharValue, RealValue, SetValue,
             StringValue, PntrValue);
ObjectValue = record
                 WordSize: WordRange;
                 case Kind: ValueKind of
                   Ordvalue, IntValue, BoolValue, CharValue: (Ival: MCIntegerForm);
                   RealValue: (Rval: MCRealForm);
                   SetValue: (SetVal: WordEntry);
                   StringValue: (Length: MCScalar; StringVal: WordEntry);
                   PntrValue: (Pval: WordEntry)
              end;
FieldLevel = Scalar;
FieldOffset = packed record
                 WordOffset: WordRange; Level: FieldLevel;
                 case PartWord: Boolean of
                   false: (WordSize: WordRange);
                   true: (BitSize: MCBitRange; BitOffset: MCBitIndex)
              end;
AddressLevel = 0..DispLimit;
BlockLabel = packed record BlockLevel: AddressLevel; EntryOffset: MCByte end;
RepKind = (ForScalar, ForSet, ForArray, ForARecord, ForVntRecord, ForFile, ForPnter,
           ForVariant, ForSelector, ForCAP, ForReal, ForString, ForOther);
MachineValue = packed record
                 Multiple: Scalar;
                 case Defined: Boolean of
                   false: ();
                   true: (Magnitude: MCIntegerForm)
              end;
TypeRepresentation = packed record
                        WordSize: WordRange; BitSize: MCBitRange;
                        Kind: RepKind; CheckValue: MachineValue;
                        Min, Max: MCIntegerForm;
                        PresetCode, PostSetCode, CheckCode: BlockLabel;
                        Selector: FieldOffset
                     end;
```

StdTypes = (IntStd, RealStd, CharStd);

SerialRange = Scalar;
DataName = Scalar;
MapIndex = Scalar;

DataObject = **packed record**
                      ObjSerial: SerialRange;
                      case ObjClass: IdClass **of**
                  Domain: ();
                  Types:
                    (ObjRepresentation: TypeRepresentation;
                    case ObjForm: TypeForm **of**
                      Scalars:
                        (**case** ObjScalarKind: DeclKind **of**
                            Declared: (ObjFirstConst: SerialRange);
                            PreDefined: (StdType: StdTypes));
                      SubRanges:
                        (ObjRangeType: SerialRange;
                         ObjMin, ObjMax: ObjectValue);
                      Sets: (SetIsPacked: Boolean; ObjBaseType: SerialRange);
                      Pointers: (ObjDomain: SerialRange);
                      Arrays:
                      (ArrayIsPacked: Boolean;
                       ObjLowBound, ObjHighBound: ObjectValue;
                       ObjAelType, ObjInxType: SerialRange);
                      CAPSchema:
                      (SchemaIsPacked: Boolean;
                       ObjCompType, ObjInxSpec: SerialRange;
                       ObjLowAddr, ObjHighAddr: WordRange);
                      Records:
                      (RecordIsPacked: Boolean;
                       ObjFixedPart, ObjVarPart: SerialRange);
                      Files:
                      (FileIsPacked, FileIsText: Boolean;
                       ObjFelType: SerialRange);
                      VariantPart:
                      (ObjTagField, ObjTagType, ObjFstVariant:
                          SerialRange;
                       ObjSelector: FieldOffset);
                      Variant:
                      (VariantIsDistinct: Boolean;
                       ObjSubFixedPart, ObjSubVarPart, ObjNextVariant:
                          SerialRange;
                       ObjVariantValue: ObjectValue));
                Consts:
                  (ConstName: DataName; ConstValue: ObjectValue;
                   NextConst: SerialRange);
                Vars, Bound:
                  (VarName: DataName; VarType: SerialRange;
                   IsVarParam: Boolean; LocalAddress: WordRange;

```
                    NextLocalVar: SerialRange);
                Field:
                    (FieldName: DataName; FieldType: SerialRange;
                     ObjOffset: FieldOffset; NextField: SerialRange);
                Prog, Proc, Func:
                    (BlockName: DataName; BlockBody: MapIndex;
                     FirstLocalVar: SerialRange)
            end;
```

{ compile-time types used in defining the code-map file }

```
TokenKinds = (StartBody, FlowToken, EndBody);
MapToken = packed record
                case Kind: TokenKinds of
                    StartBody: (BlockSerial: SerialRange; StartLine: Scalar);
                    FlowToken: (CodeOffset, FlowLine: Scalar);
                    EndBody: (JumpTableSize, CodeTableSize: Scalar)
            end;
```

{ generator specific types }

```
CodeRange = 0..MaxCodeIndex;
DataRange = 0..MaxDataSerial;
NameRange = 0..MaxNameIndex;
NameByte = 0..MCMaxChar;
ErrorSpan = StartCode..MaxCode;
ClassOfError = (RuntimeError, SystemError, FatalError, Other);

DataStatus = (Undefined, Unknown, Defined);

FieldWidth = 0..MaxField;
LinePosition = Leftmost..RightMost;

DataField = packed record
                StartWord: WordRange; IsPacked: Boolean;
                StartBit, BitsField: MCBitRange
            end;
{
```

42.4 Global Variables

The global "variable" UndefinedValue holds the representation of an undefined P-machine memory word. This value cannot be represented in Standard Pascal and is therefore constructed on a bit-by-bit basis by the procedure SetMCUndefined when the Postmortem Generator is initialised.

```
}
var
UndefinedValue: MCWord;
```

CorpseFile: **file of** MCWord;
Corpse: **array** [WordRange] **of** MCWord;

ErrorFile: text;
ErrorCode: ErrorSpan;
ErrorClass: ClassOfError;

ProgramCounter: ByteRange;
LocalFrame, GlobalFrame, StackTop, HeapTop: WordRange;
ChecksRequested, PMDRequested: Boolean;

CodeMap: **packed file of** MapToken;
DataMap: **packed file of** DataObject;
NameFile: **packed file of** NameByte;

CodeIndex, CodeLimit: CodeRange;
Code: **packed array** [CodeRange] **of** MapToken;
Data: **packed array** [DataRange] **of** DataObject;
Names: **packed array** [NameRange] **of** NameByte;

{

CHAPTER 43

The Diagnostic Files

This chapter provides procedures which read in the "corpse" file written by the P-machine, and the "code-map", "data-map" and "name" files written by the compiler to enable diagnostic generation.

Throughout post-mortem analysis, the corpse, code map, data map, and name files must be accessed in a non-sequential manner. Since Pascal possesses no indexed-sequential file access method, these files are simply read into tables implemented by the array variables Corpse, Code, Data, and Names. The post-mortem generator will itself terminate via the following procedure if the capacity of these tables is exceeded.

}

```
procedure AbortPMD(AbortCode: Scalar);
  begin
    writeln; writeln(' ': LeftMinus1, '--- PMD error --- '); writeln;
    write(AbortCode: 4, ' :   ');
    case AbortCode of
      1 : writeln('Error file not found. Check call to PMD.');
      2 : writeln('Corpse file not found. Check call to PMD.');
      3 : writeln('Unexpected end of corpse file.');
      4 : writeln('System limit: corpse file too large.');
      5 : writeln('Code map file not found. Check call to PMD.');
      6 : writeln('Name file not found. Check call to PMD.');
      7 : writeln('System limit: program too large. Expand name table.');
      8 : writeln('Data map file not found. Check call to PMD.');
      9 : writeln('System limit: program too large. Expand data table.');
      10 : writeln('System limit: program too large. Expand code table.')
    end;
    goto 13
  end { abortpmd };
{
```

43.1 The Corpse

The procedure ReadCorpse reads the corpse written by the P-machine. The following control information is read from the first eight words of the corpse file.

(1)   A numeric code identifying the reason for program termination.

(2)   The value of the P-machine program counter when the error occurred.

(3)   The stack frame base for the block in which the error occurred.

(4)   The stack frame base for the global program block.

(5)   The top of the P-machine stack when the error occurred.

(6)   The top of the P-machine heap when the error occurred.

(7)   A Boolean value indicating whether runtime checks had been selected.

(8)   A Boolean value indicating whether a post-mortem dump is required.

The remainder of the corpse file contains a dump of the P-machine memory taken when the error occurred, and is read into the array variable Corpse.

The function BlkSerialof uses a stack-frame base within the corpse to extract the serial number of the corresponding block entry within the data map.

```
}
function NextCorpseWord: MCWord;
  begin
    get(CorpseFile);
    if eof(CorpseFile) then AbortPMD(3);
    NextCorpseWord := CorpseFile^
  end { nextcorpseword };

procedure ReadCorpseFile;
  var Index: Scalar;
  begin
    reset(CorpseFile);
    if eof(CorpseFile) then AbortPMD(2);

    { read the 8-word control block }
    ErrorCode := CorpseFile^; ProgramCounter := NextCorpseWord;
    LocalFrame := NextCorpseWord; GlobalFrame := NextCorpseWord;
    StackTop := NextCorpseWord; HeapTop := NextCorpseWord;
    ChecksRequested := (NextCorpseWord = ord(true));
    PMDRequested := (NextCorpseWord = ord(true));

    { now read the remainder of the corpse }
    get(CorpseFile); Index := 0;
    while not eof(CorpseFile) do
      begin
        if Index > MCMaxMemWord
        then AbortPMD(4) else Corpse[Index] := CorpseFile^;
        Index := Index + 1; get(CorpseFile)
      end
  end { readcorpsefile };
```

```
function BlkSerialof(StackFrame: WordRange): SerialRange;
   var CodeBase: WordRange;
   begin
     CodeBase := Corpse[StackFrame - CBOffset];
     BlkSerialof := Corpse[CodeBase - SerialOffset]
   end { blkserialof };
{
```

43.2 The code map

The procedure ReadCodeMap reads the code map written by the compiler into the array Code.

The procedure FindLine translates a code address in the object program into a correpsonding source line number in the source program by searching the code map for the immediately preceding flow-point record. To minimise the search area, the procedure takes a frame-base for the block in which the address is known to lie, determines the corresponding code-base, and hence the serial number of the block entry in the data map, from which the onset of the block within the code map is extracted.

```
}
procedure ReadCodemap;
   var Index: Scalar;
   begin
     if PMDRequested
     then begin
          reset(CodeMap);
          if eof(CodeMap) then AbortPMD(5);
          Index := 0;
          while not eof(CodeMap) do
            begin
              if Index > MaxCodeIndex
              then AbortPMD(10) else Code[Index] := CodeMap^;
              Index := Index + 1; get(CodeMap)
            end;
          CodeIndex := 0; CodeLimit := Index - 1
        end
   end { readcodemap };
procedure FindLine(FrameBase: WordRange; CodeAddress: ByteRange;
                   var SourceLine: Scalar);
   var CodeBase: WordRange; BlockSerial: SerialRange; CodeAdjustment: ByteRange;
       EndOfSearch: Boolean; PreviousToken: MapToken;
   begin
     CodeBase := Corpse[FrameBase - CBOffset];
     CodeAdjustment := CodeBase * MCBytesPerWord;
     BlockSerial := Corpse[CodeBase - SerialOffset];
     CodeIndex := Data[BlockSerial].BlockBody; EndOfSearch := false;
```

```
    repeat
      PreviousToken := Code[CodeIndex]; CodeIndex := CodeIndex + 1;
      with Code[CodeIndex] do
        case Kind of
          FlowToken :
              EndOfSearch := CodeOffset + CodeAdjustment >= CodeAddress;
          EndBody : EndOfSearch := true
        end
    until EndOfSearch;
    with PreviousToken do
      if Kind = StartBody then SourceLine := StartLine else SourceLine := FlowLine
  end { findline };
{
```

43.3 The name file

The procedure ReadNameFile reads the name file written by the Compiler into the array
Names.

The function NameLength and procedure PrintName are then used to incorporate names
indexed within the file into the postmortem output.

}

```
procedure ReadNameFile;
  var Index: Scalar;
  begin
    if PMDRequested
    then begin
          reset(NameFile);
          if eof(NameFile) then AbortPMD(6);
          Index := 0;
          while not eof(NameFile) do
            begin
              if Index > MaxNameIndex
              then AbortPMD(7) else Names[Index] := NameFile^;
              Index := Index + 1; get(NameFile)
            end
        end
  end { readnamefile };
function NameLength(NameIndex: NameRange): Scalar;
  begin NameLength := Names[NameIndex] end;
procedure PrintName(NameIndex: NameRange; PrintField: Scalar);
  var i, Length: Scalar;
  begin
    Length := NameLength(NameIndex);
    for i := NameIndex + 1 to NameIndex + Length do write(chr(Names[i]));
    if PrintField > Length then write(' ': PrintField - Length)
  end { printname };
```

{

43.4 The data map

The procedure ReadDataMap reads the data map written by the Compiler into the array Data, placing each entry at the position dictated by its ObjSerial field.
}

```
procedure ReadDataMap;
  var Index: SerialRange;
  begin
    if PMDRequested
    then begin
            reset(DataMap);
            if eof(DataMap) then AbortPMD(8);
            while not eof(DataMap) do
              begin
                Index := DataMap^.ObjSerial;
                if Index > MaxDataSerial
                then AbortPMD(9) else Data[Index] := DataMap^;
                get(DataMap)
              end
         end
  end { readdatamap };
```

{

CHAPTER 44

Error Message Output

Errors detected by the P-machine are classified as "runtime", "fatal" or "system" according to whether they derive from one of the insecurities in program execution defined in the Pascal Standard, from a catastrophic failure of the P-machine itself, or from a system limitation inherent in the Model Implementation. In each case, the classification of the error is reported together with an explanatory message derived from the error file. Although the Model Implementation is able to detect each of the distinct runtime errors defined in the Standard, it cannot always distinguish the precise context in which they occur. Thus each runtime error message is post-fixed with one or more "D" numbers corresponding to those in Appendix D of the Standard.

The location of the error is deduced by using the code map to locate the sequential program flow-point immediately prior to the point at which the error occurred. Word 4 of the corresponding block jump-table header also holds a block-serial number which is used to locate the corresponding "block-object" descriptor in the data map. This in turn allows the nature and name of the block to be reported. If the program was not compiled with a request for post-mortem information, no attempt is made to locate the error, and the program terminates after printing the error message and the value of the program counter.

The following procedures are executed in sequence to produce the output required.

}

```
procedure SetErrorClass;
  begin
    if ErrorCode > FatalBase
    then ErrorClass := FatalError
    else if ErrorCode > SystemBase
        then ErrorClass := SystemError
        else if ErrorCode > RuntimeBase
            then ErrorClass := RuntimeError else ErrorClass := Other
  end { seterrorclass };
procedure PrintError;
  procedure PrintHeading;
    begin
      writeln;
      case ErrorClass of
        Other : ;
```

```
              RuntimeError : writeln(' ': 8, '--- Runtime Error ---');
              SystemError : writeln(' ': 8, '--- System Error ---');
              FatalError : writeln(' ': 8, '--- Fatal Error ---')
            end;
            writeln
          end { printheading };
        procedure FindText;
          var LineCount: Scalar;
          begin
            for LineCount := 1 to (ErrorCode - 1) * LinesPerText do readln(ErrorFile)
          end { findtext };
        procedure PrintText;
          var LineCount: 1..LinesPerText;
          begin
            for LineCount := 1 to LinesPerText do
              begin
                if not Eoln(ErrorFile)
                then begin
                       repeat write(ErrorFile^); get(ErrorFile) until Eoln(ErrorFile);
                       writeln
                     end;
                readln(ErrorFile)
              end
          end { printtext };
        begin { printerror }
          reset(ErrorFile);
          if eof(ErrorFile) then AbortPMD(1);
          PrintHeading; FindText; PrintText
        end { printerror };
      procedure PrintLocation;
        var BlockSerial: SerialRange; ErrorLine: Scalar;
        begin
          writeln; write(' ': LeftMinus1);
          if PMDRequested
          then begin
                 { return to program-defined block }
                 BlockSerial := BlkSerialof(LocalFrame);
                 while BlockSerial = NilSerial do
                   begin
                     ProgramCounter := Corpse[LocalFrame - RAOffset];
                     StackTop := LocalFrame - FrameSize - 1;
                     LocalFrame := Corpse[LocalFrame - DLOffset];
                     BlockSerial := BlkSerialof(LocalFrame)
                   end;
```

```
                { now locate the error line }
                FindLine(LocalFrame, ProgramCounter, ErrorLine);
                write('at or near line ', ErrorLine: 1, ' of ');
                with Data[BlockSerial] do
                  begin
                    case ObjClass of
                      Prog : write('program ');
                      Proc : write('procedure ');
                      Func : write('function ')
                    end;
                    PrintName(BlockName, 1)
                  end;
                writeln('.')
            end
      else writeln('at address ', ProgramCounter - 1: 1, ' of the program.');
      writeln
    end { printlocation };
procedure PrintComments;
  begin
    write(' ': LeftMinus1); write('The program was compiled with ');
    if ChecksRequested then write('all ') else write('no ');
    writeln('run-time checks requested.');
    if PMDRequested
    then writeln(' ': LeftMinus1, 'Here is your post-mortem trace-back:-')
    else writeln(' ': LeftMinus1, 'No post-mortem information was requested.');
    writeln
  end { printcomments };
```

{

CHAPTER 45

Symbolic Variable Dump

If the option PMDump was selected at compile-time, the post-mortem analysis supplements the error report with a trace-back of active blocks and a symbolic variable dump. The trace-back gives the name and nature of each block, the source-line number of its entry-point, and for procedure and function blocks, the source-line number of the corresponding call statement. For each such block, the variable dump consists of an alphabetically sorted list of local variables and parameter names, together with an analysis of the corresponding variable state. In this version of the Model Implementation, all names are printed in upper case only. Initially the variable state is determined to be ¨undefined¨, ¨unknown¨, or ¨defined¨, with the second value arising only when a program has been compiled without runtime checking code. Those variables classified as undefined are simply reported as such using the notation <<undefined>> to denote this state. The rest are subjected to a further analysis which depends upon the variable's type information recorded in the data file, and which can be summarised as follows.

(1) Scalar variables are described in terms of their values. In each case, the value is represented in a manner consistent with the variable's type-definition. Thus values belonging to an enumerated-type are represented by the appropriate constant identifier, values of the standard type char, are given a graphic representation, and so on.

(2) Pointer variables are described in terms of an address value when the pointer contents are non-zero, or as ¨nil¨. In the first case, the pointer is further qualified as ¨bad¨ if its contents are not located on the heap, or ¨dangling¨ if the dynamic variable has already been disposed.

(3) Set variables are described in terms of their values printed as set constants. Each member is printed in a manner consistent with the base-type of the set.

(4) Array variables, and conformant array parameters are described in terms of their shape and their element types. No attempt is made to print the individual array elements, however the variable state is further analysed as either ¨totally defined¨ or ¨partially undefined¨. The element type is described in source-language terms.

(5) Record variables are described in terms of their individual fields. If the record has a variant part, then each nested variant is analysed in turn. Variant selectors are qualified as ¨locked¨ if a reference has been extended to a component of the active variant, or ¨preselected¨ if the associated variant was specified in a call to the extended form of new.

(6)   A file variable is described in terms of its mode, its position, and its buffer variable. In addition, the file-type as a whole is described in source-language terms.

The source-language description of variable types is complete except for the inclusion of type-identifier names. For example, given the program declarations:

```
type Score = 1..100;
     Colour = (Red,White,Blue);

var  Result: array[Colour] of Score;
```

the state of variable result will be reported as:

```
RESULT = array[RED..BLUE] of 1..100
              and is  ...
```

This version of the post-mortem generator contains no special treatment of errors arising out of infinite or deep recursion, and will generate lengthy trace-backs as a consequence. Additional control can be achieved at no extra cost by simply limiting the number of times a recursive block is dumped as the stack is unwound.

As in the Compiler and P-Machine, the following procedures are needed for manipulation of corpse words:

```
}
procedure MCGetBit(Word: MCWordForm; BitIndex: MCBitIndex;
                   var ResultBit: MCBit);

  begin
    { recast(word,asbits) }
    if IndexedFromLeft
    then ResultBit := Word.WBits[MCMaxBitnum - BitIndex]
    else ResultBit := Word.WBits[BitIndex]
  end { mcgetbit };

procedure MCSetbit(var Word: MCWordForm; BitIndex: MCBitIndex);

  begin
    { recast(word,asbits) }
    if IndexedFromLeft
    then Word.WBits[MCMaxBitnum - BitIndex] := 1 else Word.WBits[BitIndex] := 1
  end { mcsetbit };

procedure SetMCUndefined;

  var MachineWord: MCWordForm;

  begin
    MachineWord.WValue := 0; MCSetbit(MachineWord, MCMaxBitnum);
    UndefinedValue := MachineWord.WValue
  end { setmcundefined };

function MCUndefined(Word: MCWord): Boolean;

  begin MCUndefined := (Word = UndefinedValue) end;
```

```
{
Values of type DataField are used to represent the addresses of data objects within the
corpse.  The following procedures enable their creation and access:
}
procedure InitField(var Field: DataField);
  begin
    with Field do
      begin
        StartWord := 0; IsPacked := false; StartBit := 0; BitsField := MCBitsPerWord
      end
  end { initfield };
procedure AddFields(Base: DataField; Offset: FieldOffset; var Result: DataField);
  begin
    InitField(Result);
    with Result do
      begin
        StartWord := Base.StartWord + Offset.WordOffset;
        if Offset.PartWord
        then begin
               IsPacked := true; StartBit := Base.StartBit + Offset.BitOffset;
               BitsField := Offset.BitSize
             end
      end
  end { addfields };
function DataValue(Field: DataField): MCWord;
  var Word: MCWord; OPBuffer, IPBuffer: MCWordForm; Index: MCBitIndex;
      BitValue: MCBit;
  begin
    with Field do
      begin
        Word := Corpse[StartWord];
        if IsPacked
        then begin
               IPBuffer.WValue := Word; OPBuffer.WValue := 0;
               for Index := 0 to BitsField - 1 do
                 begin
                   MCGetBit(IPBuffer, StartBit + Index, BitValue);
                   if BitValue <> 0 then MCSetbit(OPBuffer, Index)
                 end;
               Word := OPBuffer.WValue
             end;
        DataValue := Word
      end
  end { datavalue };
{
```

The procedure FindStatus determines whether a data object whose corpse address and type are given, is defined or not, by inspection of its corpse representation:

```
}
procedure FindStatus(Field: DataField; TypeSerial: SerialRange; var Status: DataStatus);
  var DefinedFields, UndefinedFields: Scalar;

  procedure InitStatus;
    begin DefinedFields := 0; UndefinedFields := 0;  end;

  procedure RecordStatus(LocalStatus: DataStatus);
    begin
      case LocalStatus of
        Defined : DefinedFields := DefinedFields + 1;
        Undefined : UndefinedFields := UndefinedFields + 1;
        Unknown :
      end
    end { recordstatus };

  procedure TotalStatus(FieldCount: Scalar; var AsAWhole: DataStatus);
    begin
      AsAWhole := Unknown;
      if FieldCount = DefinedFields then AsAWhole := Defined;
      if FieldCount = UndefinedFields then AsAWhole := Undefined
    end { totalstatus };

  procedure LevelStatus(BaseField: DataField;
                        FixedPartSerial, VarPartSerial: SerialRange; Level: Scalar;
                        var Status: DataStatus);
    var FieldCount: Scalar; FieldSerial, NextVariant: SerialRange; Field: DataField;
        FieldStatus, StateNow, VariantStatus: DataStatus; CheckWord: MCWordForm;
        ActiveBit: MCBit; Selector: MCWord; Found: Boolean;
    begin
      InitStatus; FieldSerial := FixedPartSerial; FieldCount := 0;
      while FieldSerial <> NilSerial do
        with Data[FieldSerial] do
          begin
            AddFields(BaseField, ObjOffset, Field);
            FindStatus(Field, FieldType, FieldStatus); RecordStatus(FieldStatus);
            FieldCount := FieldCount + 1; FieldSerial := NextField
          end;
      TotalStatus(FieldCount, StateNow);
      if StateNow <> Unknown
      then if VarPartSerial <> NilSerial
          then begin
                  CheckWord.WValue := Corpse[BaseField.StartWord];
                  MCGetBit(CheckWord, 3 * Level + 2, ActiveBit);
                  case StateNow of
                    Defined : if ActiveBit = 0 then StateNow := Unknown;
                    Undefined : if ActiveBit <> 0 then StateNow := Unknown
                  end;
```

```
            if StateNow = Defined
            then with Data[VarPartSerial] do
                    begin
                        AddFields(BaseField, ObjSelector, Field);
                        Selector := DataValue(Field);
                        NextVariant := ObjFstVariant; Found := false;
                        repeat
                           with Data[NextVariant] do
                             if Selector =
                                   ObjRepresentation.CheckValue.Magnitude
                             then Found := true
                             else NextVariant := ObjNextVariant
                        until Found or (NextVariant = NilSerial);
                        if Found
                        then begin
                                with Data[NextVariant] do
                                LevelStatus
                                   (BaseField, ObjSubFixedPart, ObjSubVarPart,
                                      Level + 1, VariantStatus);
                                if VariantStatus <> Defined
                                then StateNow := Unknown
                             end
                    end
         end;
      Status := StateNow
   end { levelstatus };

procedure ArrayStatus(BaseField: DataField; Elements: Scalar; PackedArray: Boolean;
                AeSerial: SerialRange; var Status: DataStatus);

   var Index: Scalar; Element: DataField; ElsPerWord: 2..MCBitsPerWord;
      ElStatus: DataStatus; CanBePacked: Boolean;

   begin
      with Data[AeSerial] do
        begin
          with ObjRepresentation do
            if WordSize > 1
            then CanBePacked := false
            else CanBePacked :=
                   PackedArray and (BitSize <= MCBitsPerWord div 2);
          Element := BaseField;
          if CanBePacked
          then with Element do
                  begin
                     IsPacked := true;
                     ElsPerWord := MCBitsPerWord div ObjRepresentation.BitSize;
                     BitsField := MCBitsPerWord div ElsPerWord
                  end;
          InitStatus;
```

```
        for Index := 1 to Elements do
          begin
            FindStatus(Element, AeSerial, ElStatus); RecordStatus(ElStatus);
            with Element do
              if IsPacked
              then if (Index mod ElsPerWord) = 0
                    then begin StartWord := StartWord + 1; StartBit := 0 end
                    else StartBit := StartBit + BitsField
              else StartWord := StartWord + ObjRepresentation.WordSize
          end;
        TotalStatus(Elements, Status)
      end
  end { arraystatus };
procedure CAPStatus(BaseField: DataField; BPBlock: WordRange;
                    PackedCAP: Boolean; CompSerial: SerialRange;
                    var Status: DataStatus);

  var Index, Elements: Scalar; Component: DataField; ElsPerWord: 2..MCBitsPerWord;
      CompStatus: DataStatus; CanBePacked: Boolean;

  begin
    with Data[CompSerial] do
      begin
        if PackedCAP
        then CanBePacked := (ObjRepresentation.BitSize <= MCBitsPerWord div 2)
        else CanBePacked := false;
        Component := BaseField;
        if CanBePacked
        then with Component do
                begin
                  IsPacked := true;
                  ElsPerWord := MCBitsPerWord div ObjRepresentation.BitSize;
                  BitsField := MCBitsPerWord div ElsPerWord
                end;
        Elements := Corpse[BPBlock + 1] - Corpse[BPBlock] + 1; InitStatus;
        for Index := 1 to Elements do
          begin
            FindStatus(Component, CompSerial, CompStatus);
            RecordStatus(CompStatus);
            with Component do
              if IsPacked
              then if (Index mod ElsPerWord) = 0
                    then begin StartWord := StartWord + 1; StartBit := 0 end
                    else StartBit := StartBit + BitsField
              else StartWord := StartWord + Corpse[BPBlock + 2]
          end;
        TotalStatus(Elements, Status)
      end
  end { capstatus };
```

```
begin { findstatus }
   Status := Unknown;
   if ChecksRequested
   then with Data[TypeSerial] do
        case ObjForm of
            Scalars, SubRanges :
               begin
                  Status := Defined;
                  if Field.IsPacked
                  then begin
                          if DataValue(Field) =
                                ObjRepresentation.CheckValue.Magnitude
                          then Status := Undefined
                       end
                  else if MCUndefined(Corpse[Field.StartWord])
                          then Status := Undefined
               end;
            Sets, Pointers :
               if MCUndefined(Corpse[Field.StartWord])
               then Status := Undefined else Status := Defined;
            Records : LevelStatus(Field, ObjFixedPart, ObjVarPart, 0, Status);
            Files :
               if Corpse[Field.StartWord] = 0
               then Status := Undefined else Status := Defined;
            Arrays :
               ArrayStatus
                  (Field, ObjHighBound.Ival - ObjLowBound.Ival + 1, ArrayIsPacked,
                     ObjAelType, Status);
            CAPSchema :
               CAPStatus
                  (Field, ObjLowAddr + LocalFrame, SchemaIsPacked, ObjCompType,
                     Status)
        end
   end { findstatus };
{
```

The recursive procedure PrintScope is used to print a linear list of data objects, which may be either the local variables and parameters of a block, or the fields of (the fixed part of) a record or record variant. Its parameters define the list of objects to be printed, the corpse address of the first of these, and the left margin position to be used in their printout.
}

```
procedure PrintScope(FirstItem: SerialRange; ScopeBase: DataField;
                        StartAtPos: LinePosition);
   var Position, StartOfLine: LinePosition; NameField: FieldWidth; ThisItem: SerialRange;
       ItemField: DataField; Indirect: Boolean;
   procedure NewLine;
      begin writeln; Position := StartOfLine end;
   procedure TabTo(NewPosition: LinePosition);
      begin write(' ': NewPosition - 1); Position := NewPosition end;
   procedure NextLine;
      begin writeln; TabTo(StartOfLine) end;
   procedure MakeSpaceFor(PrintField: FieldWidth);
      begin
      if Position + PrintField > RightMost
      then begin
            NewLine;
            if Position + PrintField > RightMost
            then TabTo(RightMost - PrintField) else TabTo(StartOfLine)
         end;
      Position := Position + PrintField
      end { makespacefor };
   procedure Printch(Ch: char);
      begin MakeSpaceFor(1); write(Ch) end;
   procedure PrintString(String : packed array[l..u:Integer] of char);
      var Index, Length: FieldWidth;
      begin
      Length := u - l + 1; MakeSpaceFor(Length);
      for Index := 1 to Length do write(String[Index])
      end { printstring };
   function NextItem(Item: SerialRange): SerialRange;
      begin
      with Data[Item] do
         if ObjClass = Field then NextItem := NextField else NextItem := NextLocalVar
      end { nextitem };
   function ItemName(Item: SerialRange): DataName;
      begin
      with Data[Item] do
         if ObjClass = Field then ItemName := FieldName else ItemName := VarName
      end { itemname };
```

```
procedure SetNameField;
  var Length: Scalar;
  begin
    NameField := 0; ThisItem := FirstItem;
    repeat
      Length := NameLength(ItemName(ThisItem));
      if Length > NameField then NameField := Length;
      ThisItem := NextItem(ThisItem)
    until ThisItem = NilSerial;
    if NameField > MaxField then NameField := MaxField
  end { setnamefield };
procedure PrintValue(Field: DataField; TypeSerial: SerialRange);
  var Status: DataStatus;
  function IntDigits(IntValue: MCIntegerForm): Scalar;
    var Digits: Scalar; SignNeeded: Boolean;
    begin
      SignNeeded := IntValue < 0; Digits := 0;
      repeat IntValue := IntValue div 10; Digits := Digits + 1 until IntValue = 0;
      if SignNeeded then IntDigits := Digits + 1 else IntDigits := Digits
    end { intdigits };
  procedure PrintScalar(ScalarValue: MCWord; TypeSerial: SerialRange);
    procedure PrintConst(Ordinal: MCScalar; FirstConst: SerialRange);
      var ConstSerial: SerialRange; Printed: Boolean; PrintField: FieldWidth;
      begin
        ConstSerial := FirstConst; Printed := false;
        repeat
          with Data[ConstSerial] do
            if Ordinal = ConstValue.Ival
            then begin
                PrintField := NameLength(ConstName);
                MakeSpaceFor(PrintField); PrintName(ConstName, PrintField);
                Printed := true
              end
            else ConstSerial := NextConst
        until Printed or (ConstSerial = NilSerial);
        if not Printed then PrintString('(out of range)')
      end { printconst };
    procedure PrintStd(WordValue: MCWord; WhichType: StdTypes);
      var i: 1..MCRealSize;
          RealMap:
            record
              case Boolean of
                false: (RealValue: MCRealForm);
```

```
                    true: (Words: array [1..MCRealSize] of MCWord)
                end;
            PrintField: FieldWidth;
        begin
          case WhichType of
            IntStd :
              begin
                PrintField := IntDigits(WordValue); MakeSpaceFor(PrintField);
                write(WordValue: PrintField)
              end;
            RealStd :
              begin
                PrintField := RealField; MakeSpaceFor(PrintField);
                with RealMap do
                    begin
                      for i := 1 to MCRealSize do
                          Words[i] := Corpse[Field.StartWord + i - 1];
                      write(RealValue: PrintField)
                    end
              end;
            CharStd :
              begin
                MakeSpaceFor(3); write('''');
                if (WordValue >= 0) and (WordValue <= MaxHostChar)
                then write(chr(WordValue));
                write('''')
              end
          end
      end { printstd };
    begin { printscalar }
      with Data[TypeSerial] do
        case ObjForm of
          Scalars :
              case ObjScalarKind of
                  Declared : PrintConst(ScalarValue, ObjFirstConst);
                  PreDefined : PrintStd(ScalarValue, StdType)
                end;
          SubRanges : PrintScalar(ScalarValue, ObjRangeType)
        end
    end { printscalar };
procedure PrintPointer(Pvalue: MCWord);

  var PrintField: FieldWidth;

  begin
    if Pvalue = 0
    then PrintString('nil')
    else begin
            PrintField := IntDigits(Pvalue); MakeSpaceFor(PrintField);
```

```
            write(Pvalue: PrintField);
            if (Pvalue < StackTop) or (Pvalue > MCMaxMemWord)
            then PrintString(' (bad pointer)')
            else if ChecksRequested
                then if Corpse[Pvalue - 1] <> Corpse[Field.StartWord + 1]
                    then PrintString(' (dangling)')
        end
    end { printpointer };
procedure PrintSet(BaseAddress: WordRange; BaseSerial: SerialRange);
    var First: Boolean; SetWord: MCWordForm; SetBit: MCBit; Index: MCWord;
    begin
        First := true; Printch('[');
        with Data[BaseSerial] do
            for Index := ObjRepresentation.Min to ObjRepresentation.Max do
                begin
                    SetWord.WValue := Corpse[BaseAddress + Index div MCWordSetBits];
                    MCGetBit(SetWord, Index mod MCWordSetBits, SetBit);
                    if SetBit <> 0
                    then begin
                            if not First then Printch(', ');
                            PrintScalar(Index, BaseSerial); First := false
                        end
                end;
        Printch(']')
    end { printset };
procedure PrintRecord;
    procedure PrintLevel(FixedPartSerial, VarPartSerial: SerialRange; Level: Scalar);
        var Locked, Preselected, Active, Found: Boolean; CheckWord: MCWordForm;
            SelectorField: DataField; Selector: MCWord; NextVariant: SerialRange;
        procedure TestBit(BitIndex: MCBitIndex; var Bitset: Boolean);
            var CheckBit: MCBit;
            begin
                MCGetBit(CheckWord, BitIndex, CheckBit); Bitset := CheckBit <> 0
            end { testbit };
        procedure PrintTag(TagSerial: SerialRange);
            var TagField: DataField; PrintField: FieldWidth;
            begin
                with Data[TagSerial] do
                    begin
                        PrintField := NameLength(FieldName); MakeSpaceFor(PrintField);
                        PrintName(FieldName, PrintField); PrintString(' = ');
                        AddFields(Field, ObjOffset, TagField);
                        PrintScalar(DataValue(TagField), FieldType)
                    end
            end { printtag };
```

```
      begin { printlevel }
        StartOfLine := StartOfLine + Indent;
        if FixedPartSerial <> NilSerial
        then PrintScope(FixedPartSerial, Field, StartOfLine);
        if VarPartSerial <> NilSerial
        then with Data[VarPartSerial] do
                begin
                    TabTo(StartOfLine); PrintString('(   ');
                    if ChecksRequested
                    then begin
                            CheckWord.WValue := Corpse[Field.StartWord];
                            TestBit(3 * Level, Locked);
                            TestBit(3 * Level + 1, Preselected);
                            TestBit(3 * Level + 2, Active)
                        end
                    else begin
                            Locked := false; Preselected := false; Active := true
                        end;
                    if Active and (ObjTagField <> NilSerial)
                    then PrintTag(ObjTagField);
                    if Locked then PrintString(' (locked)');
                    if Preselected then PrintString(' (preselected)');
                    NewLine;
                    if Active
                    then begin
                            AddFields(Field, ObjSelector, SelectorField);
                            Selector := DataValue(SelectorField);
                            NextVariant := ObjFstVariant; Found := false;
                            repeat
                                with Data[NextVariant] do
                                if Selector = ObjRepresentation.CheckValue.Magnitude
                                then Found := true
                                else NextVariant := ObjNextVariant
                            until Found or (NextVariant = NilSerial);
                            if Found
                            then with Data[NextVariant] do
                                    PrintLevel
                                        (ObjSubFixedPart, ObjSubVarPart, Level + 1)
                        end;
                    TabTo(StartOfLine); Printch(') '); NewLine
                end;
        StartOfLine := StartOfLine - Indent
      end { printlevel };
  begin { printrecord }
    NewLine; StartOfLine := StartAtPos + Indent; TabTo(StartOfLine);
    PrintString('record'); NewLine;
    with Data[TypeSerial] do PrintLevel(ObjFixedPart, ObjVarPart, 0);
    TabTo(StartOfLine); PrintString('end')
  end { printrecord };
```

```
procedure PrintType(TypeSerial: SerialRange);
  var Bound, LastConst: MCWord; LastSerial, NextSerial: SerialRange;
  function Structured(TypeSerial: SerialRange): Boolean;
    begin
      with Data[TypeSerial] do
        Structured := ObjForm in [Arrays, Records, CAPSchema, Files]
    end { structured };
  procedure PrintParts(FixedPart, VarPart: SerialRange);
    var TagType, FieldSerial: SerialRange;
    procedure PrintField(FieldSerial: SerialRange);
      var NameField: FieldWidth; NextType: SerialRange;
      begin
        with Data[FieldSerial] do
          begin
            NameField := NameLength(FieldName); MakeSpaceFor(NameField);
            PrintName(FieldName, NameField);
            if NextField = NilSerial
            then NextType := NilSerial
            else NextType := Data[NextField].FieldType;
            if FieldType = NextType
            then Printch(' , ')
            else begin PrintString('  :  '); PrintType(FieldType) end
          end
      end { printfield };
    procedure PrintVariant(ThisVariant: SerialRange);
      begin
        if ThisVariant <> NilSerial
        then with Data[ThisVariant] do
                begin
                  PrintVariant(ObjNextVariant); TabTo(StartOfLine);
                  PrintScalar(ObjVariantValue.Ival, TagType);
                  if VariantIsDistinct
                  then begin
                          PrintString('  :  '); NextLine; PrintString('     (');
                          NewLine; PrintParts(ObjSubFixedPart, ObjSubVarPart);
                          TabTo(StartOfLine); PrintString('   )  ; ')
                       end
                  else Printch(' , ');
                  NewLine
                end
      end { printvariant };
    begin { printparts }
      StartOfLine := StartOfLine + Indent; FieldSerial := FixedPart;
      while FieldSerial <> NilSerial do
        with Data[FieldSerial] do
          begin
```

```
                    TabTo(StartOfLine); PrintField(FieldSerial);
                    if (NextField <> NilSerial) or (VarPart <> NilSerial)
                    then PrintString(' ; ');
                    FieldSerial := NextField; NewLine
                  end;
          if VarPart <> NilSerial
          then with Data[VarPart] do
                  begin
                    TabTo(StartOfLine); PrintString('case ');
                    if ObjTagField <> NilSerial
                    then PrintField(ObjTagField) else PrintType(ObjTagType);
                    TagType := ObjTagType; PrintString(' of '); NewLine;
                    StartOfLine := StartOfLine + Indent; PrintVariant(ObjFstVariant);
                    StartOfLine := StartOfLine - Indent
                  end;
          StartOfLine := StartOfLine - Indent
        end { printparts };
  begin { printtype }
    with Data[TypeSerial] do
      case ObjForm of
        Scalars :
          case ObjScalarKind of
            Declared :
              begin
                NextSerial := ObjFirstConst;
                repeat
                  LastSerial := NextSerial;
                  NextSerial := Data[NextSerial].NextConst
                until NextSerial = NilSerial;
                LastConst := Data[LastSerial].ConstValue.Ival;
                PrintScalar(0, TypeSerial); PrintString(', . . . , ');
                PrintScalar(LastConst, TypeSerial)
              end;
            PreDefined :
              case StdType of
                IntStd : PrintString('integer');
                RealStd : PrintString('real');
                CharStd : PrintString('char')
              end
          end;
        SubRanges :
          begin
            PrintScalar(ObjMin.Ival, ObjRangeType); PrintString(' . . ');
            PrintScalar(ObjMax.Ival, ObjRangeType)
          end;
        Pointers :
          begin PrintString('pointer-type') end;
```

```
        Sets :
          begin
            if SetIsPacked then PrintString('packed ');
            PrintString('set of '); PrintType(ObjBaseType)
          end;
        Arrays :
          begin
            if ArrayIsPacked then PrintString('packed ');
            PrintString('array ['); PrintType(ObjInxType); PrintString('] of ');
            if Structured(ObjAelType) then NextLine;
            PrintType(ObjAelType)
          end;
        CAPSchema :
          begin
            if SchemaIsPacked then PrintString('packed ');
            PrintString('conformant array [');
            Bound := Corpse[ScopeBase.StartWord + ObjLowAddr];
            PrintScalar(Bound, ObjInxSpec); PrintString('..');
            Bound := Corpse[ScopeBase.StartWord + ObjHighAddr];
            PrintScalar(Bound, ObjInxSpec); PrintString('] of ');
            if Structured(ObjCompType) then NextLine;
            PrintType(ObjCompType)
          end;
        Records :
          begin
            if RecordIsPacked then PrintString('packed ');
            PrintString('record'); NewLine;
            with Data[TypeSerial] do PrintParts(ObjFixedPart, ObjVarPart);
            TabTo(StartOfLine); PrintString('end ')
          end;
        Files :
          if FileIsText
          then PrintString('text-file')
          else begin
                 if FileIsPacked then PrintString('packed ');
                 PrintString('file of ');
                 if Structured(ObjFelType) then NextLine;
                 PrintType(ObjFelType)
               end
      end
    end { printtype };
procedure PrintArray;
  begin
    PrintType(TypeSerial); NextLine; PrintString('and is ');
    if Status = Defined
    then PrintString('totally defined')
    else PrintString('partially undefined')
  end { printarray };
```

```
procedure PrintFile;
  var CheckWord: MCWordForm; FileBlock: WordRange;
  procedure PrintMode(FileMode: MCWord);
    begin
      case FileMode of
        1 : PrintString('opened for reading by reset');
        2 : PrintString('opened for writing by rewrite');
        0 : PrintString('no previous reset or rewrite')
      end
    end { printmode };
  procedure PrintPosition(Word: MCWordForm);
    var BitValue: MCBit;
    begin
      MCGetBit(Word, FileLockBit, BitValue);
      if BitValue = 1 then PrintString('position is locked ');
      MCGetBit(Word, EofBit, BitValue);
      if BitValue = 1
      then PrintString('eof is true ') else PrintString('eof is false ');
      MCGetBit(Word, EolBit, BitValue);
      if BitValue = 1 then PrintString('eoln is true ');
    end { printposition };
  procedure PrintBuffer(FileName: NameRange; FileType: SerialRange);
    var BufferField: DataField; PrintField: FieldWidth;
    begin
      with Data[FileType] do
        begin
          InitField(BufferField);
          with BufferField do
            if FileIsText
            then StartWord := FileBlock + 2
            else StartWord := Corpse[FileBlock + 2];
          PrintField := NameLength(FileName); MakeSpaceFor(PrintField);
          PrintName(FileName, PrintField); PrintString('^ = ');
          StartOfLine := StartOfLine + Indent;
          PrintValue(BufferField, ObjFelType); StartOfLine := StartOfLine - Indent
        end
    end { printbuffer };
  begin { printfile }
    PrintType(TypeSerial); NextLine; FileBlock := Field.StartWord;
    PrintMode(Corpse[FileBlock + 3]); NextLine;
    CheckWord.WValue := Corpse[FileBlock + 1]; PrintPosition(CheckWord);
    NextLine; PrintBuffer(ItemName(ThisItem), TypeSerial)
  end { printfile };
```

```
   begin { printvalue }
     FindStatus(Field, TypeSerial, Status);
     if Status <> Undefined
     then with Data[TypeSerial] do
            case ObjForm of
               Scalars : PrintScalar(DataValue(Field), TypeSerial);
               SubRanges : PrintScalar(DataValue(Field), ObjRangeType);
               Pointers : PrintPointer(DataValue(Field));
               Sets : PrintSet(Field.StartWord, ObjBaseType);
               Arrays, CAPSchema : PrintArray;
               Records : PrintRecord;
               Files : PrintFile
            end
     else PrintString('<<undefined>>')
   end { printvalue };
begin { printscope }
  SetNameField; ThisItem := FirstItem;
  repeat
    StartOfLine := StartAtPos; TabTo(StartOfLine); MakeSpaceFor(NameField);
    PrintName(ItemName(ThisItem), NameField); PrintString(' = ');
    with Data[ThisItem] do
      begin
        StartOfLine := StartOfLine + NameField + 3;
        case ObjClass of
          Vars, Bound :
            begin
              InitField(ItemField);
              Indirect := IsVarParam or (Data[VarType].ObjForm = CAPSchema);
              with ItemField do
                begin
                  StartWord := ScopeBase.StartWord + LocalAddress;
                  if Indirect then StartWord := Corpse[StartWord]
                end;
              PrintValue(ItemField, VarType)
            end;
          Field :
            begin
              AddFields(ScopeBase, ObjOffset, ItemField);
              PrintValue(ItemField, FieldType)
            end
        end
      end;
    NewLine; ThisItem := NextItem(ThisItem)
  until ThisItem = NilSerial
end { printscope };
{
```

The procedure PrintVariables carries out the generation of the trace-back required, by
unwinding the corpse stack frame by frame, and using the procedure PrintBlock to print the

identity, entry line, locals and calling point for each frame unwound.
}
```
procedure PrintVariables;
  var CallingFrame, FirstFrame: WordRange; StartLine, CallingLine: Scalar;
      BlockSerial: SerialRange; ReturnAddress: ByteRange;
  procedure PrintBlock;
    var FirstField: DataField;
    begin { printblock }
      write(' ': LeftMinus1);
      with Data[BlockSerial] do
        begin
          case ObjClass of
            Prog : write('program ');
            Proc : write('procedure ');
            Func : write('function ')
          end;
          PrintName(BlockName, 1);
          if LocalFrame <> FirstFrame then write(' which');
          writeln(' was entered at line ', StartLine: 1);
          if FirstLocalVar <> NilSerial
          then begin
                  InitField(FirstField); FirstField.StartWord := LocalFrame; writeln;
                  PrintScope(FirstLocalVar, FirstField, Leftmost + Indent); writeln
               end;
          if CallingLine <> 0
          then writeln (' ': LeftMinus1, 'and was called from line ',
                   CallingLine: 1, ' of ...')
        end
    end { printblock };
  begin { printvariables }
    if PMDRequested
    then begin
            FirstFrame := LocalFrame; CallingFrame := LocalFrame;
            repeat
              LocalFrame := CallingFrame; BlockSerial := BlkSerialof(LocalFrame);
              CodeIndex := Data[BlockSerial].BlockBody;
              StartLine := Code[CodeIndex].StartLine;
              if LocalFrame <> GlobalFrame
              then begin
                      CallingFrame := Corpse[LocalFrame - DLOffset];
                      ReturnAddress := Corpse[LocalFrame - RAOffset];
                      FindLine(CallingFrame, ReturnAddress - 1, CallingLine)
                   end
              else CallingLine := 0;
              PrintBlock
            until LocalFrame = GlobalFrame
         end
  end { printvariables };
```

CHAPTER 46

The Driver Program

The overall generation process is driven by the following main program. Label 13 is used for abortion of the generator by the procedure AbortPMD.

```
}
begin
  SetMCUndefined;

  ReadCorpseFile;
  ReadCodemap;
  ReadNameFile;
  ReadDataMap;

  SetErrorClass;
  PrintError;
  PrintLocation;
  PrintComments;

  PrintVariables;
13:
end.
```

Index of
Major Procedures and Functions
in the Postmortem Generator

The following index lists all major procedures and functions used in the Postmortem Generator, together with the page numbers needed to locate their definitions in this version of its text.

Appendix

Error Messages

A complete list of the error codes and messages used by the Model Implementation follows. In the file ErrorFile used by the Compiler and Postmortem Generator these messages are held in fixed format, two lines per potential error code, but for publication purposes they have been reformatted here.

1   A digit-sequence was expected: an unsigned-real is badly formed.

2   A string-quote was expected: a string is not permitted to extend over more than one physical line.

3   One or more characters were expected: an empty string is not permitted.

4   A token-separator (comment, space, or line-separator) is required between numbers and word-symbols.

10   An identifer symbol was expected.

11   An integer-constant was expected.

17   Either a ¨*¨ or a ¨/¨ symbol was expected.

18   Either a ¨+¨ or a ¨-¨ symbol was expected.

19   A ¨<¨, ¨<=¨, ¨=¨, ¨>=¨, or ¨>¨ symbol was expected.

20   A ¨(¨ symbol was expected.

21   A ¨)¨ symbol was expected.

22   A ¨[¨ symbol was expected.

23   A ¨]¨ symbol was expected.

24   A ¨,¨ symbol was expected.

25   A ¨;¨ symbol was expected.

26   A ¨.¨ symbol was expected.

28   A ¨:¨ symbol was expected.

29   A ¨:=¨ symbol was expected.

30   A ¨..¨ symbol was expected.

42   A ¨begin¨ symbol was expected.

50   An "end" symbol was expected.

51   A "then" symbol was expected.

53   An "until" symbol was expected.

54   An "of" symbol was expected.

55   A "do" symbol was expected.

56   A "to" or "downto" symbol was expected.

57   A "program" symbol was expected.

58   Other symbols were expected.

59   Previous symbols were unexpected: input skipped to this symbol.

60   An "=" symbol was expected.

100 The identifier has not been declared as a field identifier for this record-type.

101 The identifier has not been declared.

102 The identifier has already been declared or used in this scope.

103 The identifier is being misused in this context.

104 The identifier does not denote a type in this context.

106 A Boolean-type is required.

107 An integer-type is required.

108 A real-type is required.

109 An integer or a real-type is required.

110 An ordinal-type is required.

112 A pointer-type is required.

113 An array-type is required.

115 A record-type is required.

116 A set-type is required.

117 A file-type is required.

120 Only a constant or constant-identifier that has real or integer type may be signed.

121 An integer or real constant or constant-identifier was expected.

122 The constants defining a subrange-type must have the same ordinal-type.

123 The first value of a subrange-type must be less than or equal to the second value.

124 The case-constant must be type-compatible with the tag type.

125 The value of the case-constant must belong to the set of values defined by the tag-type.

126 An identical case-constant has already occurred in this variant-part.

127 The number of case-labels must be equal to the number of values of the tag-type.

128 The component-type of a file must not be a file-type, or a type containing a component file-type.

130   The label has not been declared.

131   The label was declared local to the block, but never sited within the corresponding statement-part.

132   An identical label has already been declared in this label-declaration-part.

133   A label must be sited in the block which contains its declaration.

134   The label has already been sited in this block.

135   The label is not accessible from a preceding goto statement that references it.

136   The label is not accessible from this goto statement.

137   The value of the label must be greater than or equal to 0, and less than or equal to 9999.

140   The identification of a "forward" procedure or function must not contain a formal parameter list.

141   The identification of a "forward" function must not contain a function result-type.

142   The result-type of a function must have an ordinal, real, or pointer-type.

143   The function result type-identifier was expected.

144   A function or procedure identification was expected: a duplicate "forward" directive is not permitted.

145   A formal value parameter must not have a file-type, or a type that contains a component file-type.

146   A result-value must be assigned to the function identifier.

147   Assignment to the identifier of a standard-function is not permitted.

148   Assignment to a formal function-parameter identifier is not permitted.

149   Use of a function identifier is not permitted in this context.

150   Assignment of a value having a file-type, or a type that contains a component file-type, is not permitted.

151   The identification of a "forward" procedure or function is missing.

152   The expression is not assignment compatible with the destination variable or parameter.

153   The value of the control-variable of a for-statement is "threatened": the statement is not permitted.

154   The directive is not recognized: only "forward" is allowed.

160   The index-expression is not type-compatible with the index-type of the array-variable.

161   A record-variable or file-variable was expected in this context.

162   Only the first parameter of read, readln, write, or writeln, is permitted to be a file-variable.

163   Only integer, real, or character values can be read from a textfile.

164   Only integer, real, Boolean, character, or string-values can be written to a textfile.

165 The expression denoting "totalwidth" of a write or writeln procedure must have integer-type.

166 The expression denoting "fracdigits" in a write or writeln parameter-list must have integer-type.

167 An expression must have real-type if it is to be written using fixed-point format.

168 The parameter to the standard procedure "page" must be a textfile.

169 The array variable must be packed.

170 The array variable must be unpacked.

171 The elements of the packed and unpacked arrays must have the same type.

172 The indexing-expression must be type-compatible with the index-type of the unpacked array variable.

173 The case-constant does not occur in the definition of the corresponding variant-part of the record.

174 The case-constant must be type-compatible with the tag type of the corresponding variant-part.

176 The parameter to the standard function "eoln" must be a textfile.

177 The file parameter in a call to the standard procedure "readln" must be a textfile.

178 The file parameter in a call to the standard procedure "writeln" must be a textfile. A standard procedure is not permitted as an actual procedure parameter.

181 A standard function is not permitted as an actual function parameter.

182 The formal parameter lists of the actual and formal procedures must match.

183 The formal parameter lists and result types of the actual and formal functions must match.

184 An actual variable parameter must not be a component of a packed-variable.

185 An actual variable parameter must not be a tag-field.

186 An actual variable parameter and its corresponding formal parameter must have identical types.

187 The number of actual parameters is not equal to the number of formal parameters.

190 The operator is not compatible with the operand-type.

191 Both operands must have set-types, and both set-types must have compatible base-types.

192 The expression-type is not compatible with the base-type of the set.

193 The operand expressions must both have real-type.

194 The operand expressions must both have integer-type.

195 The operand expressions must both have Boolean-type.

196 Signed operand expressions must have integer or real types.

197 The variable or expression is not type-compatible with the base-type of the set.

198 The operand expressions of a relational expression are not type-compatible.

199 Only "=" and "<>" operators are permitted in a relational expression containing pointer operands.

200 Only "=", "<=", ">=", and "<>" are permitted in a relational expression containing set operands.

201 Only array-variables which have the string-type may appear as operands in a relational expression.

202 The variables are not permitted as operands in a relational expression.

210 A case-constant with an identical value has already been encountered in this case-statement.

211 The case-constant must have the same ordinal-type as the case-index.

220 A non-local variable must not be used as the control variable of a for-statement.

221 A formal variable or value parameter must not be used as the control-variable of a for-statement.

222 The control-variable is "threatened" by assignment in a procedure or function in this block.

223 The initial value of the for-statement is not type compatible with the control-variable.

224 The final value of the for-statement is not type compatible with the control-variable.

225 Nested for-statements must not use the same control variable.

230 An identical identifier has already occurred in the program parameter-list.

231 The program parameter has not been declared in the variable declaration part.

232 The textfile "input" was not included in the program parameter list.

233 The textfile "output" was not included in the program parameter list.

250 Only the innermost dimension of an array schema may be packed.

251 The actual parameter does not conform to the array schema.

252 Actual parameters conforming to the same array schema must have identical types.

253 A conformant array is not permitted as an actual value parameter.

254 Relational operators cannot be applied to conformant array parameters.

301 The index value lies outside the bounds of the array. (D1)

302 The variant field access is inconsistent with the tag-field value, or will destroy an existing reference to the current variant. (D2)

303 A nil pointer cannot be used to reference a variable, or as a parameter to "dispose". (D3,D23)

304 An undefined pointer cannot be used to reference a variable or as a parameter to "dispose". (D4,D24)

305 A dynamic variable cannot be destroyed by "dispose" while a reference to it still exists. (D5)

306 The position of a file cannot be altered while a reference to the buffer variable still exists. (D6)

307 The value of an actual parameter lies outside the interval defined by the type of the formal parameter. (D7)

308 The members of an actual parameter lie outside the interval defined by the base-type of the formal parameter. (D8)

309 A file must be in write-mode immediately prior to any use of "put", "write", "writeln", or "page". (D9)

310 A file variable must be defined immediately prior to any use of "put", "write", or "page". (D10)

311 End-of-file must be true immediately prior to any use of "put", "write", "writeln", or "page". (D11)

312 The file buffer variable must be defined immediately prior to any use of "put". (D12)

313 A file variable must be defined immediately prior to any use of "reset". (D13)

314 A file must be in read-mode immediately prior to any use of "get" or "read". (D14)

315 A file must be defined immediately prior to any use of "get" or "read". (D15)

316 End-of-file must not be true immediately prior to any use of "get" or "read". (D16)

318 For "write", the value of the expression lies outside the range of values defined by the component type of the file. (D18)

319 For a variable created by "new(p,c1,,,cn)", tag-field assignment attempts to select a variant not identified by c1,,,cn. (D19)

320 For "dispose(p)", the dynamic variable was originally created by a call "new(p,c1,,,cn)". (D20)

321 For "dispose(p,k1,,,km)", the dynamic variable was originally created by a call "new(p,c1,,,cn)" where m<>n. (D21)

322 For "dispose(p,k1,,,km)", the variants in the dynamic variable are different from those specified by the case-constants. (D22)

325 A dynamic variable created by "new(p,c1,,,cn)", cannot be accessed or referenced as an entire variable "p^". (D25)

326 In "pack", the index value lies outside the bounds of the unpacked array. (D26)

327 In "pack", a component of the unpacked array is accessed but undefined. (D27)

328 In "pack", the upper bound of the unpacked array will be exceeded. (D28)

329 In "unpack", the index value lies outside the bounds of the unpacked array. (D29)

330 In "unpack", a component of the packed array is both undefined and accessed. (D30)

331 In "unpack" the upper bound of the unpacked array will be exceeded. (D31)

332 For integer or real "x", "sqr(x)" would exceed the maximum integer or real value. (D32)

333 For "ln(x)", "x" is zero or negative. (D33)

334   For "sqrt(x)", "x" is negative. (D34)

335   The magnitude of "x" is too large to allow evaluation of "trunc(x)" as defined by the Pascal Standard. (D35)

336   The magnitude of "x" is too large to allow evaluation of "round(x)" as defined by the Pascal Standard. (D36)

337   For "chr(x)", "x" does not identify a character value. (D37)

338   The value of "succ(x)" exceeds the range of values defined by the type of "x". (D38)

339   The value of "pred(x)" precedes the range of values defined by the type of "x". (D39)

340   For "eof(f)", "f" is undefined. (D40)

341   For "eoln(f)", "f" is undefined. (D41)

342   For "eoln(f)", "eof(f)" is already true. (D42)

343   A variable or buffer variable must be assigned a value prior to its use in an expression or in "put". (D12,D43)

344   In "x/y", "y" is zero. (D44)

345   In "i div j", "j" is zero. (D45)

346   In "i mod j", "j" is zero or negative. (D46)

347   The result of integer addition, subtraction, or multiplication lies outside the interval [-maxint..+maxint]. (D32,D47)

348   The value of the function is undefined. (D48)

349   An expression value or a value read, lies outside the range of values defined by the variable type. (D17,D18,D49,D55)

350   The members of a set-value lie outside the range of values defined by the base-type of the set variable. (D50)

351   None of the case constants is equal to the value of the case index. (D51)

352   The initial value is less than the minimum value of the control variable of the for-statement. (D52)

353   The final value is greater than the maximum value of the control variable of the for-statement. (D53)

354   The sequence of data characters does not form a signed integer number. (D54)

356   The sequence of data characters does not form a signed real number. (D56)

357   The buffer variable is undefined immediately prior to use of "read". (D57)

358   The value of a field-width expression in a write-statement is zero or negative. (D58)

359   The bounds of an actual parameter do not lie within the range defined by the index type of the formal conformant array parameter. (D59)

361   In this implementation, access to the buffer-variable of a file must be preceded by a "reset" or "rewrite" operation on the file.

362   In this implementation, the members of a set must have ordinal values in the range [0..255].

401 System limit on scopes: no more than 19 block or record scopes can be opened simultaneously.

402 System limit on data size: the data cannot be held in P-machine"s 32k-word memory. Reduce or reconfigure.

403 System limit on code size: the program or procedure block is too large to compile. Reduce or reconfigure.

404 System limit on code labels: no more than 251 procedures, functions and statement labels may be defined in one block. Simplify.

405 System limit on "dropout" code: the exit-label cannot be sited within 256 bytes of the dropout branch. Simplify expression.

406 System limit on set-size: sets are limited to a maximum of 256 members. Simplify the base type.

407 System limit on sets: the base type of a set must define values in the range $[0..255]$.

408 System limit on variant records: with checks on, record variants must not be nested deeper than 9 levels.

411 System limit on memory: insufficient memory for P-machine stack.

412 System limit on memory: insufficient memory for P-machine heap.

413 System limit on calls to "new": with checks on, no more than 2*maxint calls may be made to the standard procedure "new".

414 System limit on files: no more than 16 files may be opened simultaneously.

421 Fatal error: unexpected end of program file. Compilation aborted.

422 Fatal error: P-machine stack underflow. P-machine aborted.

423 Fatal error: P-machine heap corrupt. P-machine aborted.

424 Fatal error: empty code file. P-machine aborted.

425 Fatal error: code file too large to load. P-machine aborted.